MW01195474

THE FAILURE OF
POPULAR SOVEREIGNTY

AMERICAN POLITICAL THOUGHT

Wilson Carey McWilliams and Lance Banning
FOUNDING EDITORS

Christopher Childers

The

Failure of Popular Sovereignty

SLAVERY, MANIFEST DESTINY,
AND THE RADICALIZATION
OF SOUTHERN POLITICS

University Press of Kansas

Published by the University Press of Kansas (Lawrence, Kansas 66045), which
was organized by the Kansas Board of Regents and is operated and funded by
Emporia State University, Fort Hays State University, Kansas State University,
Pittsburg State University, the University of Kansas, and Wichita State
University

Library of Congress Cataloging-in-Publication Data

Childers, Christopher.
The failure of popular sovereignty : slavery, manifest destiny, and the
radicalization of southern politics / Christopher Childers.
p. cm.
Includes bibliographical references and index.
ISBN 978-0-7006-1868-2 (cloth : alk. paper)
1. United States—Politics and government—1783–1865. 2. Southern States—
Politics and government—1775–1865. 3. Representative government and
representation—United States—History—19th century. 4. States rights
(American politics)—History—19th century. 5. Slavery—Political aspects—
United States—History—19th century. 6. Slavery—United States—Extension
to the territories. 7. United States—Territorial expansion—Political aspects.
8. Manifest Destiny. 9. Missouri compromise. I. Title.
E302.1.C47 2012
973.3—dc23
                         2012021651

British Library Cataloguing-in-Publication Data is available.

Printed in the United States of America

10 9 8 7 6 5 4 3 2 1

TO LEAH,

who believed even when I did not.

Contents

Illustrations

Maps

Photographs and Drawings

Acknowledgments

Writing history has its moments of solitude, but in truth it is a collaborative effort. Throughout my experience writing this book, I have benefited from the aid and advice of fellow scholars whose help has made my work possible. Numerous archivists aided me in the search for sources. The staff at the Southern Historical Collection at the University of North Carolina at Chapel Hill aided me in the search for the letters and writings of southern leaders and common people alike. The incredibly accommodating staff of the Duke University Libraries provided access to one of the premier collections of southern political papers, while visits to the Historical Society of Pennsylvania, the Newberry Library in Chicago, and the Joseph Regenstein Library at the University of Chicago allowed me to search the papers of northerners involved in the making of popular sovereignty. Finally, I reserve special gratitude for Brian Leigh Dunnigan, Barbara DeWolfe, and the staff at the William L. Clements Library at the University of Michigan. A Jacob M. Price Visiting Research Fellowship from the Clements Library allowed me to read the Lewis Cass Papers as well as other key manuscript collections.

Numerous friends, colleagues, and mentors read and commented on drafts of the manuscript. Gaines M. Foster, Paul Paskoff, Andrew Burstein, and Charles Royster offered numerous suggestions on how to improve my work—and continue to offer encouragement and support. Several friends read various parts of the manuscript. Rachel Shelden read the manuscript and provided a number of insightful comments that challenged me to consider the broader implications of my research. Kris Lawson commented on the chapters concerning the Missouri controversy and offered advice on how to sharpen my analysis. I owe a special debt to Adam Pratt, who reviewed two iterations of the project. Adam and his wife, Jennifer, the closest of friends from our days in graduate school at Louisiana State University, offered encouragement and friendship as I wrote and rewrote chapters. Through his comments and in dozens of conversations, Adam always encouraged me to realize the full potential and consider the full implications of my research. He is the greatest of friends and colleagues.

At the University Press of Kansas, I found a generous supporter of my book in Fred M. Woodward. His guidance through the steps of converting manuscript to book and his patience with a first-time author exemplify the very best qualities of an editor. Just as importantly, Fred selected two outside reviewers who likewise shared their time and advice charitably. Nicole Etcheson's comments on two drafts of the manuscript proved invaluable in my efforts to write a clear, coherent narrative. Most significantly, she challenged me to push the boundaries of traditional political history by exploring the broader meaning of the struggle over slavery in the West. Michael A. Morrison provided extensive comments on the entire manuscript and offered his expert editorial advice. During an unforgettable four-week National Endowment for the Humanities seminar in Philadelphia, Mike shared his thoughts and his wisdom on how to realize the full potential of my research. But his contribution extends beyond the work of an editor; indeed, his guidance taught me much about how to write an effective book. Mike's advice and comments helped this author, who was too close to his subject, to recast the manuscript and make a stronger argument.

I owe my greatest professional debt to my mentor, William J. Cooper, Jr. Truly a scholar and a gentleman, Bill taught me the historian's craft—not only in the classroom but also at the desk as we read through drafts of my dissertation—by the high example he sets as a careful researcher, a thoughtful wordsmith, and an unfailingly decent person. During my years in graduate school, he provided research funds that allowed me to pursue an ambitious research agenda that took me to the numerous archives mentioned above. I came to Baton Rouge seeking an advisor; I left having found a mentor and friend. I only hope I can live up to the impeccable standard he sets.

Family has sustained me in my work. My parents and sister always supported my choice to pursue a career in what really is my hobby, sharing in the highs and lows of my work and unfailingly cheering me onward. My father did not live to see the book in print, but his presence remains in the heart and mind of its author. Finally, the dedication is merely a token of appreciation for a woman who has added an inestimable measure of meaning and happiness to my life.

Though this book has benefited immensely from the aid and assistance of colleagues, friends, and family, this is my work and I accept full responsibility for it.

THE FAILURE OF
POPULAR SOVEREIGNTY

Introduction

In the eighty-five years between 1776 and 1861, the United States of America had grown into a prosperous nation of thirty-four states linked by economic prowess, common heritage, and an abiding, if still developing, sense of nationalism. Yet with growth and prosperity came discontent as the nation's breathless pace of expansion sparked a furious debate over the institution of slavery. Would the slave domain expand with the nation's boundaries or would the institution remain fixed in space? Over the course of the early nineteenth century, slavery indeed became the South's peculiar institution. Slavery, both a labor system and a social system, brought great prosperity to the southern states—and indirectly to the North as well. But a rising tide of moral indignation against American slavery built within the northern states, leading to bitter recriminations between Americans North and South over the future of the institution. Northerners came to demand the prohibition of slavery in the nation's vast territorial domain, while southerners insisted on their right to take slaves into any territory over which flew the Stars and Stripes.

The idea of territorial self-government, or what became known as popular sovereignty, played a critical role in almost every debate over slavery in the territories between the creation of the republic and the onset of the Civil War. From the formation of the Northwest Territory in the 1780s to the admission of Kansas as a free state in 1861, politicians contested whether the power to prohibit slavery rested with Congress or the people residing in the territories. As long as the United States had added territory to its national domain, leaders had discussed whether decisions regarding the expansion of slavery should rest with the federal government, as owner and agent for the territories themselves, or with those who inhabited and who would inhabit them.

Scholars have traditionally dismissed the popular sovereignty doctrine as a supple political contrivance devoid of substantive meaning. My book seeks to restore some of its meaning by analyzing how its definition and application—from the Confederation period to the coming of the Civil War—became enmeshed with the politics of slavery in the South. At its core, the dispute over slavery in the territories paralleled the growing rift in American politics between northern nationalism and southern states' rights advocates. In turn, southern politics became defined by twin commitments to states' rights and slavery. At the same time, my study explains how the slavery debate radicalized southern politics. Popular sovereignty, instead of quieting sectional passions over the extension of slavery, actually gave voice to an increasingly radical, states' rights interpretation of the federal compact that placed slavery front and center in the national political discourse.

Different interpretations of the nature of the Union prevailed between the sections; northerners believed that the people themselves had created the Constitution, while southerners insisted that the states had created the federal government as their common agent, leaving the states with ultimate authority. Yet practically since the founding of the republic, Congress had prohibited slavery in the territories of the North while allowing the southern territories to determine the status of slavery for themselves. Of course, southerners had always established slavery in the founding charters of new states. In other words, territorial self-government had always resulted in the expansion of slave territory. A majority of northerners and southerners alike seemed reasonably content with an arrangement that basically divided the national domain into free and slave territory.

The watershed debate over admitting Missouri into the Union, however, shattered the notion of sectional comity over the slavery question that had prevailed with minimal challenge for some forty years. New York representative James Tallmadge's bid to prohibit slavery in Missouri as a condition of statehood transformed the slavery debate and southern politics by affirming federal power over slavery in the territories. Southerners, fearful of any threat to the institution, joined westerners in vehemently asserting the right of local determination over the issue, while congressmen from the Northeast seemed more reticent to relinquish congressional authority, for they argued that Congress did indeed possess the sovereign right to make the decision.[1] Ultimately Congress reaffirmed the idea of a dividing line between freedom and slavery. Slaves could not pass into the Louisiana Purchase north of 36 degrees, 30 minutes latitude, but to the south of the line citizens could permit or prohibit slavery as they wished. But the Missouri controversy had revealed deep tensions between North and South over the extension of slavery.

In its aftermath, an ever-growing group of southerners resolved to prevent any further interference from northerners with slavery and its extension into the territories. They did so by denying the right of regulation to the federal government. During the 1830s, the slavery debate reappeared with continued territorial expansion and the admission of new states to the Union, which occurred against the backdrop of a growing abolition movement. In the congressional gag rule debates of 1837 and 1838, John C. Calhoun emerged as the proponent of an extreme states' rights doctrine that sought to destroy the rising abolitionist vanguard and secure the future of slavery in the South—and the territories. Once an ardent nationalist, the South Carolinian and his many allies became convinced that federal authority would eventually become a weapon of the antislavery vanguard. With the zeal of a convert, Calhoun maneuvered to repudiate the right of Congress to determine the status of slavery in the territories via a curious mix of states' rights and national power. To the Calhounites, popular sovereignty in the territories permitted local control over the institution while the Constitution trumped localism by dictating that slavery followed the flag into the territories of the West. In the 1830s and 1840s, Calhoun had some difficulty convincing his fellow southerners of his theories; by the late 1850s, they had virtually become political dogma in the South as extension became the manifest destiny of the peculiar institution.

During the 1840s, however, northern Democrats appropriated the popular sovereignty idea for themselves, transforming it into a doctrine that they hoped would appeal to northern and southern Democrats alike, thereby saving their political party and quieting discord over the extension of slavery. Instead, they created a crisis over the meaning of popular sovereignty that further divided North and South. Northerners like Senator Lewis Cass of Michigan and his more prominent colleague, Stephen A. Douglas of Illinois, declared that the people—at any time acting through their territorial legislatures—could permit or prohibit slavery. Southerners insisted that territories became imbued with sovereignty only when drafting a constitution and seeking admission to the Union. In keeping with their states' rights interpretation of the Constitution, southerners believed, according to Don E. Fehrenbacher, "that the most legitimate embodiment of American sovereignty was a state convention drawn from and acting for the people."[2] Did popular sovereignty rest in the masses or in the states, acting on behalf of the people? This was the question that northerners and southerners feuded over, just as they disagreed over states' rights versus nationalism. More than a mere question of constitutional theory, deciding how popular sovereignty would work directly impacted whether the slave domain would expand or not. Almost a decade of persistent discord over the meaning of popular sovereignty destroyed the bisectional Democratic Party, removed the South from the political mainstream of the Jeffersonian and Jacksonian eras, and fostered the growth of a virulently radical form of southern politics designed to uphold states' rights. By 1860, many southerners ironically called for a massive expansion of federal power—via a federal slave code—to protect the right of southern slaveholders to keep slaves in the territories.

My book explores the parallel relationship between the idea of popular sovereignty as applied to the extension of slavery and the nature of southern politics in the early American republic—both of which changed over time and in concert with one another. As northerners grew increasingly hostile toward slavery, southerners became increasingly defensive of the institution, their way of life, and their role within the Union. The debate over what Douglas would come to call popular sovereignty emerged in the earliest discussions of whether to permit or prohibit the expansion of slavery into the national domain. Few historians have recognized the history of popular sovereignty before the 1840s; no scholar has yet portrayed its development as a process beginning with the first territorial acquisitions of the new nation to its establishment as national policy in the 1850s, with passage of the Kansas-Nebraska Act and finally in the Supreme Court's decision in *Dred Scott v. Sandford*, which imbued popular sovereignty with a pro-southern definition that mirrored Calhoun's reasoning.[3] By lending narrative coherence to the story of slavery extension, my book bridges the work of historians who have traditionally examined the doctrine of popular sovereignty as proposed beginning in the late 1840s and the recent writings of scholars who have focused more closely on the struggles over slavery in the early republic.[4] Historians such as Michael A. Morrison have pointed to this approach in their works, suggesting that a "sectionalization of the inherited revolutionary political heritage" transformed American politics in the twenty years preceding the Civil War.[5] According to southerners, northerners saw society in the South as inferior and its peculiar institution as immoral. Just as colonists had chafed at imperial control over local affairs, so slaveholders resented the efforts of antislavery politicians to control the issue of slavery in the territories. Beginning in the late 1840s, Democrats in the North and South "determined to remove this matter of local concern from Congress and eliminate it from national political debate."[6] Their efforts produced precisely the opposite outcome, as slavery subsumed all other issues in national political discourse.

Yet the problem had existed long before the 1840s, and so too had the proposed solution. Recovering the history of popular sovereignty from the nation's founding forward reveals how the expansion of slavery became the most contentious disagreement between North and South, a debate that in no small part led to the coming of the Civil War. Congress implicitly established the principle of popular sovereignty when it created the Southwest Territory in 1790. Slavery was prohibited north of the Ohio River, but the people residing to the south could determine the status of slavery for themselves. Of course, few believed that the settlers would prohibit the institution, but territorial inhabitants desired, and in some cases demanded, a certain degree of political autonomy with respect to the issue of slavery.

My work examines the concept of popular sovereignty by offering a narrative of how it surfaced and evolved during the era of the early American republic and explaining how the debate over its meaning transformed and radicalized southern politics, eventually marking a clear departure in practice and principle from the established norms of American political discourse—which eventually led the South outside the mainstream of Jeffersonian and Jacksonian politics. Because neither North nor South could agree upon the meaning of popular sovereignty, it effectively "constitutionalized" the debate over slavery in the territories by mimicking the debate over the nature of the Union.[7] The issue of when or if a territory could ban slavery became a matter of constitutional interpretation, a process which culminated in the case of *Dred Scott v. Sandford*, when the Supreme Court affirmed the southern interpretation of popular sovereignty. Faced with the solemn vow of antislavery northerners to reject the high court's pronouncement, which they considered immoral and unjust, many southerners began to believe that the federal government—acting as their common agent— would have to take measures to protect slave property in the territories. The idea of popular sovereignty, and indeed southern fealty to the American political system and the Union, crumbled under the ever-increasing weight of cumbersome constitutional rhetoric over the slavery issue. A broader history of the popular sovereignty idea shows how the debate over slavery transformed the South into a rigid sectional bloc dedicated to the protection and perpetuation of slavery, thereby providing essential insight into how and when the Union sundered.

Understanding popular sovereignty requires consulting sources from the North and South, but my focus on southern politics reflects the fact that the South was the fulcrum on which popular sovereignty operated. In almost every context in which it came up, politicians offered the idea of local control over slavery as a way to satisfy the South—or at least to compromise in a way that would not offend the states' rights constitutional scruples of southerners. For almost sixty years, popular sovereignty operated exclusively in the South; the Northwest Ordinance and the Missouri Compromise prohibited the expansion of slavery in the North. After 1847, northern Democrats used the doctrine as a vehicle for compromise, seeking to unify their party across sectional lines by proposing a solution acceptable to southerners. Popular sovereignty usually emerged as a means to assure the people of the South that their voices would be heard, that their concerns would be addressed. Its proponents sought to bridge the Mason-Dixon Line, a division that seemed like a chasm during times like the Missouri controversy, the introduction of the Wilmot Proviso, and the congressional debates of 1849 and 1850. Southern support for popular sovereignty, which had emerged in the Missouri debates, became strongest in the late 1840s and 1850s. Southerners rejected the doctrine, however, when northerners proposed a version of the doctrine that the South believed would halt the expansion of slavery.

In order to chronicle accurately the evolution of the popular sovereignty doctrine and to analyze its significance to the debates over slavery in the antebellum era, my book is organized as a narrative. It begins with an overview of the debate over slavery in the territories from the implementation of the Northwest Ordinance to the time of the Missouri controversy. To understand how the issue became so hotly contested in 1819 and 1820, one must investigate its origins in the first attempts to settle the vast national domain of the Old Northwest and the Southwest regions of the United States. The second chapter addresses southern attitudes toward territorial expansion and their legal formulations regarding the peculiar institution and its expansion, which developed during the Missouri debates. Federal legislation beginning with the Northwest and Southwest Ordinances implicitly created a dividing line between slave and free territory. The Missouri Compromise expanded on this and firmly placed the concept of a division in American legal precedent. The subsequent chapter analyzes this precedent in more detail by studying how specific territories became states and how they exercised local control over the institution of slavery. I also discuss the congressional debate in 1837 and 1838 over the relationship between the federal government and the territories, part of the larger debate over Senator Calhoun's resolutions on the Union. Written in the midst of the well-known "gag rule" debate, Calhoun's resolutions touched on the right of Congress to determine the expansion of slavery in the territories. By addressing these basic legal and political issues, this debate marked another step in the evolution of the southern position on the meaning of popular sovereignty.

The acquisition of more territory from Mexico in 1848 led to the recrudescence of the issue of slavery in the territories in its most disruptive form since the days of the Missouri Compromise. Chapters 4 and 5 analyze the effort to settle this increasingly fractious dispute, as northern Democratic leaders like George M. Dallas of Pennsylvania, Daniel S. Dickinson of New York, and Lewis Cass of Michigan reformulated and articulated the concept of popular sovereignty. The doctrine remained in the national spotlight for the succeeding twelve years; the debate over its application would also continue unabated. The Compromise of 1850 and its settlement for the Utah and New Mexico territories, as explained in chapter 6, put popular sovereignty into practice. But the debate over the compromise measures and the settlement for the territories provoked contention over the idea of popular sovereignty itself. When in 1847 the northern Democrats proposed applying the doctrine to the Mexican Cession, many moderate southerners enthusiastically accepted it as a suitable compromise. Some proponents of the doctrine, most notably Dickinson, explicitly stated that the citizens of a territory had the right to decide on the slavery issue before applying for statehood and crafting a constitution. In his seminal formulation of popular sovereignty, Cass left this question unanswered, most likely in a purposeful effort to appease people on both sides of the Mason-Dixon Line.

Southerners bristled at the idea of allowing the pivotal decision on the future of slavery to be made before the population of a territory had fully developed. Radical southerners who identified with the politics and theories of John C. Calhoun threatened solid southern support for what the Calhounites derisively called "squatter sovereignty." Whigs and Calhounites in the South helped ensure Cass's defeat in 1848 and raised critical questions about just how his version of popular sovereignty would work—questions that Cass himself declined to answer. These issues had particular significance in the case of New Mexico, where southerners accused Mexicans of manipulating the political process in an effort to bar the introduction of slavery. Slave-state leaders argued that this course allowed the conquered to govern the conqueror. The admission of California as a free state and the creation of New Mexico Territory with an openly antislavery government threatened southerners, who withdrew support for popular sovereignty in this form—and for Cass, whom they saw as deceptive.

Sectionalism actually grew before the fiasco in Kansas Territory and the southern rights question became more, not less, salient six years before Lincoln's election. As explained in chapter 7, passage of the Kansas-Nebraska Act in 1854 only widened the sectional chasm by reinforcing southern unity across party lines at a time when the northern Democracy had begun to disintegrate. A pet project of Stephen A. Douglas, Nebraska seemed beyond debate regarding the slavery issue, as it lay north of the compromise line of 1820. Southerners, however, pushed Douglas to divide the vast region into two territories—Kansas and Nebraska—and to include an explicit repeal of the Missouri Compromise line. The Illinoisan obliged, arguing that the Compromise of 1850 had rendered it "inoperative" anyway. Popular sovereignty would replace the line that had become odious to many southerners, a consideration that played no small part in moving many southerners to reconsider the doctrine they jettisoned following the 1850 debate. Chapter 8 explains why popular sovereignty enjoyed greater support from the southern states in 1854 than ever before, but also how that support eroded with the reappearance of the old debate over when a territory's settlers could exercise their popular sovereignty, which would prove its ultimate undoing. The proponents of popular sovereignty looked to the Supreme Court for a final determination on how the doctrine would operate in practice. Southerners rejected Douglas's interpretation of popular sovereignty and heaped scorn upon its chief proponent, who they believed had defined the doctrine against their best interests. When the Supreme Court endorsed the southern version of popular sovereignty in the *Dred Scott* case, many northerners spurned the Court itself and refused to abide by its determination. Faced with the Pyrrhic victory in the Supreme Court, slave-state politicians identified but one remaining course of action: eschew the popular sovereignty doctrine and demand federal protection of slavery in the territories. The epilogue evaluates how popular sovereignty failed and even played a role in the destruction of the Union because neither North nor South could agree on its meaning. The debate between states' rights and nationalism subsumed the popular sovereignty discourse, destroying the series of moderate stances on slavery that politicians had embraced in one form or another for eighty-five years.

A DESIRE FOR SELF-GOVERNMENT

Slavery in the Early American Territories

The luminaries who devised the American constitution and system of government conceived of a Union that would grow over space and through time, allowing for the expansion of population and perpetuation of the republic. Men like Thomas Jefferson and James Madison viewed the lands across the Appalachian fall line as the key to a self-perpetuating agrarian nation. In 1784, the nation's leaders began grappling with the best way to assimilate western lands previously held by individual states into the Union and to prepare them for eventual statehood. Mindful of their former colonial status under the British crown, the founders had no desire to create a system that would create colonies in the West. They recognized, however, the need to impose order on the frontier while acknowledging the people's demand for self-government whereby they could devise their own customs and institutions. But even at the earliest stages of the discussion, the future of slavery in the national domain—and who would decide where it would and would not exist—became a vexing question that remained disputed until the Civil War.

By the end of the new nation's first full decade, America's leaders had settled on a compromise to the slavery issue. By law the Ohio River bifurcated the national domain, where slavery was expressly prohibited on the north bank of the river while settlers to the south could permit or prohibit the institution as they pleased. Convinced that expansion would gravitate toward the vast domain south of the Ohio and that the South would someday hold the majority of the American population, southern slaveholders had readily assented to the Northwest Ordinance of 1787, which allowed for local self-government over the extension of slavery in the Old Southwest.[1] This arrangement worked for several decades, but various developments brought slavery into the center of political discourse. First, the Ohio River hardly proved an impregnable boundary between slavery and freedom, as upland southerners sought to evade the slavery restriction in the Northwest Ordinance. Second, America's insatiable appetite for territorial aggrandizement had exhausted the first national domain and the Louisiana Purchase beckoned a new generation of settlers, reopening the debate over the extension of slavery. Both developments occurred against the backdrop of a slow but steadily growing aversion to slavery among northerners.

IN 1784, the idea of a national domain itself seemed foreign. Several of the original thirteen states, which had held title to vast tracts of lands in the interior of the continent, ceded their claims to the new government created under the newly written Articles of Confederation.[2] Most leaders agreed on the necessity of some sort of uniform code for the orderly settlement of western lands, but in the discussion over how to govern the West, several critical issues emerged. What role would the government have in administering these territories? How could the government ensure a smooth transition from wilderness to settlement—from inchoate territory to organized state? Who possessed the power to impose order on these territories—the federal government, the states, or the people residing therein? These three questions especially troubled national policymakers, for they touched on fundamental principles of the Union itself: the nature of the Union and the power of the federal government vis-à-vis the states. The questions raised seem abstract at first glance, but they held great practical meaning to politicians engaged in the process of securing the new nation and testing the effectiveness of its Articles of Confederation.

Political leaders had difficulty establishing how much self-government a territory should exercise versus how much control the federal government must assume. Many believed that American citizens populating the territories possessed the same rights and privileges as citizens residing in the states. The fragile territorial condition, however, seemed to necessitate a period when the federal government would have to circumscribe the political rights of territorial citizens to ensure the orderly political development of the territory itself. Yet no one seemed to know how to calculate the right blend of territorial self-government and federal control. Furthermore, the issue of federal supremacy over the territories raised questions among the states. Some believed that the territorial laws gave too much power to the federal government at the expense of the states. Questions regarding states' rights would emerge from the territorial debate as well. The lack of consensus on the entire matter proved especially toxic when the question of slavery in the territories arose. Debates ensued, leaders made compromises, the process of creating territories began, but problematic issues lingered.

The first effort at regulating the creation of territories came with the Ordinance of 1784, authored by Thomas Jefferson. His plan's "unhesitating grant of self-governing institutions to inhabitants of new lands from the very beginning" gave citizens great latitude to conduct their own affairs and embodied his vision of a self-perpetuating republic, a blueprint for decentralized territorial administration that southerners would celebrate for years to come.[3] The ordinance prescribed different stages of government, whereby a "state" would progress in development over time until it reached the maturity necessary to become a full member of the Union. The embryo states would initially adopt a constitution of an existing state, operating under that charter until they reached the point where they could apply for statehood. When they reached a population of 20,000, the citizens could organize a constitutional convention to draft their own charter. Finally, when the embryo state reached the population of the least populous of the original states, it automatically could petition for admission to the Union. The people in the territories themselves would possess sovereignty over the issues affecting them.[4]

Jefferson's draft ordinance contained a second provision, however, that restricted territorial sovereignty with regard to slavery, a facet of the Jeffersonian mindset that succeeding generations of southerners strived either to forget or repudiate. The initial draft of March 1, 1784, stated that "after the year 1800 of the Christian era, there shall neither be slavery nor involuntary servitude in any of the said states, otherwise than in punishment of crimes, whereof the party shall have been duly convicted to have been personally guilty."[5] Jefferson's proviso surely reflected his own ambiguity on the institution of slavery by providing for its gradual extinction in the newly created states, yet it also seems incongruous with the ordinance's mandate for broad self-government. If an embryo state could select the constitution of any of the original thirteen states as it saw fit, and then possess the power to enact legislation in conformity with that document, why could it not legislate on the issue of slavery? The records of the Continental Congress give scant detail of the debates, so determining Jefferson's intentions is difficult.

Viewing Jefferson's aim for the clause as a beginning point for the gradual extinction of slavery in the United States does not seem implausible given his feelings toward the institution. The provisions of the Articles of Confederation, however, permitted a southern minority to halt Jefferson's effort to prevent the extension of slavery. On April 19, two delegates representing the southern opposition to a slavery ban, one from North Carolina and the other from South Carolina, moved to strike the proviso from the draft, and a vote to sustain the challenged wording failed. The rules of the Confederation Congress required seven states to vote in favor of retaining the provision. Members of seven state delegations from the North voted unanimously to keep the slavery ban, but New Jersey's delegation had one member absent because of illness. Consequently, its vote did not count and the measure to retain failed. Jefferson resented the outcome, noting that "the voice of a single individual" would have "prevented this abominable crime of spreading itself across the country." His effort to ban slavery in the territories revealed that while some leaders believed that the slavery issue came under the purview of Congress, others saw it as a matter for local jurisdiction. The Ordinance of 1784 mirrored the government at large, with its emphasis on power resting in the constituent states that made up the United States as a nation—essentially the foundation of states' rights theory.[6]

Politicians who led the vanguard for a stronger federal government called for a more nationalistic territorial policy that augmented the power of the center to govern the periphery. Some Federalists, as they came to be known, believed that the national government needed to draw a sharper distinction between embryo states and those extant states on the same footing as the original thirteen. A stronger federal government would have to assume firmer control of its western lands for the safety of the Union. Western separatists, individuals on the frontier who contemplated forming a separate union outside of the United States, saw the Ordinance of 1784 as "an invitation to political action." The expansive degree of self-government granted to settlers in the western lands could play into the hands of western separatists who had little or no allegiance to the young Union. Forthcoming legislation would deal specifically with these issues and implement more rigorous control over what would become known as the territories. Provisions for the orderly settlement of western lands would have to make clear the subordinate nature of unincorporated districts to the federal government. To a considerable extent, the impetus for stronger federal control over the territories necessitated a retreat from the broad assertion of self-government contained in the Ordinance of 1784 and renewed discussion over slavery in the territories.[7]

The efforts at revised legislation to create a territorial system began in September 1786, when the Continental Congress created a committee to draft legislation for governments in the western territories. With "equal (and uncharacteristic) dispatch," Congress unanimously adopted the Northwest Ordinance on July 13, 1787. Particularly with two provisions in the new legislation, Congress sought to assert greater authority in the territories. First, the ordinance carefully delineated the differences between territory and state. The committee dispensed with Jefferson's 1784 ordinance—whereby territories would adopt an existing state constitution—and imposed a plan of governance clearly subordinate to Congress. In the first grade of territorial government, Congress would appoint territorial governors, secretaries, and judges for the newly created territories. Once "five thousand free male inhabitants of full age" came to reside in the territory, it would ascend to the second grade, thereby receiving the power to elect a legislative assembly. The third and final grade came when the territory's population numbered at least 60,000 citizens; at this point, it could apply for statehood. The wording of the ordinance suggested that admittance to the Union did not proceed automatically at some point. Instead, Congress had the discretion to confer statehood "provided the constitution and government so to be formed, shall be republican, and in conformity to the principles" of the ordinance itself.[8]

Second, the most well known feature of the ordinance came at the sixth and final "article of compact":

There shall be neither Slavery nor involuntary Servitude in the said
territory otherwise than in punishment of crimes, whereof the party shall

have been duly convicted; provided always that any person escaping into the same, from whom labor or service is lawfully claimed in any one of the original States, such fugitive may be lawfully reclaimed, and conveyed to the person claiming his or her labor or service as aforesaid.[9]

The article has an unclear provenance, as Congress inserted the clause without debate on the day of the ordinance's passage.[10] Nathan Dane of Massachusetts, a leader in crafting the ordinance itself, most likely appended the article at the last minute. No mention of any intended prohibition of slavery, however, exists in the entire record of the debate over the ordinance until its appearance in the final reading.

Why Congress enacted such a provision in 1787, when three years earlier it had rejected Jefferson's gradual prohibition of slavery, remains unclear. Why slaveholders acquiesced in the prohibition clause proves even more puzzling. Indeed, the ordinance passed by an unanimous vote of the states; only one delegate, a New Yorker, voted nay. Even the purported author of the sixth article professed surprise at its easy passage. "When I drew the ordinance which passed (in a few words excepted) as I originally formed it," Dane wrote to his friend Rufus King, who had attempted to reinstate Jefferson's ban in 1785, "I had no idea the States would agree to the sixth Art. prohibiting Slavery—; as only Massa. of the Eastern States was present . . . but finding the House favourably disposed on this subject, after we had completed the other parts I moved the art—; which was agreed to without opposition."[11] Interestingly, the southern states raised no objections to the sixth article. In a letter to James Monroe, delegate William Grayson of Virginia wrote, "The clause respecting slavery was agreed to by the Southern members for the purpose of preventing Tobacco & Indigo from being made on the N.W. side of the Ohio, as well as for sevl. other political reasons." Identifying those "other political reasons" is difficult, but Grayson suggested that southerners initially did not have a serious interest in settling in the Northwest Territory. Perhaps they believed that slaveholders would not move to the Northwest, but poorer farmers would. Upper South leaders in particular, who held considerable sway in the debate over the ordinance, tended to support securing the expansion of slavery in areas where it already existed or would likely flourish, thereby ignoring areas like the Northwest Territory. Many southerners, James Madison prominently among them, remained convinced that westward expansion would occur chiefly south of the Ohio River rather than in the demographically stagnant Northwest Territory.[12]

Precisely because the territory shared a boundary with southern-dominated lands south of the Ohio River, a few upland southerners believed any states formed out of the Northwest Territory would ally with their section. Of course, northerners believed the exact opposite. In his letter to Rufus King, Dane argued that the territory that would eventually become the state of Ohio would "no doubt be settled chiefly by Eastern people" and would most likely have the same politics.[13] Nevertheless, southerners hoped to influence politics in the Northwest Territory by adding to its population. If southerners would emigrate, they could undoubtedly sway the political attitudes of the three territories that would eventually be created.

Southerners had a second reason for assenting to the ordinance as amended. Some evidence suggests that the North and South had arrived at an implicit compromise on the issue of slavery that would bar its presence from the Northwest Territory while keeping silent on its status south of the Ohio River. In the initial version of a new ordinance for the creation of territorial governments, written in September 1786, the drafting committee made no distinction of what territory fell under its jurisdiction, instead providing for a general form of territorial government that the federal government could apply anywhere and at any time. In July 1787, however, the committee changed the wording to reflect its application to the Northwest Territory, drawing "an explicit East-West line through the Western territories by legislating for the Northwest alone."[14] Limiting the geographic scope of the legislation produced an arrangement by which the Northwest would remain free territory, while the federal government would not intervene on the status of slavery in the territory south of the Ohio River.

Speculation aside, southerners undoubtedly perceived one clear benefit from the 1787 ordinance: it provided security for slavery where it could grow while allowing northerners to phase out the institution in their region as they saw fit. Put in reductive terms, southerners did not manifest the mistrust of the federal government that they would espouse in the next century. No one objected to the slavery prohibition on the grounds that it gave the federal government power over a local matter, an argument that became a staple of the proslavery defense after the 1830s. In 1784, nearly all the southern delegates in the Congress except Thomas Jefferson and one North Carolina delegate voted to strike the slavery prohibition from the Ordinance of 1784. In that case, the interdiction would have applied to all western lands. Furthermore, it provided a specific timetable for the ultimate end of slavery in the future western states. Conversely, the Northwest Ordinance "effectively sectionalized slavery" by making the Ohio River an extension of the Mason-Dixon Line. It banned slavery in a region that did not seem suited to large-scale plantation agriculture but made no judgment on slavery in lands south of the Ohio River, thereby protecting the lands of the Southwest that seemed the most viable outlet for southern expansion.[15]

The fact that the slavery ban in the 1787 ordinance went into effect immediately, however, actually weakened its effect. The ordinance made no statement on the status of the few slaves already in the territory, leaving some ambiguity on their status within the law.[16] The lack of clarity in the ordinance provided an entering wedge, albeit a small one, whereby slavery could possibly exist in the territory. Settlers in the territory would soon exploit the lack of precision in the Northwest Ordinance. Nevertheless, many southerners looked at the Northwest as a secondary concern in western settlement. They fixed their eyes on the rich lands of the Southwest, where plantation agriculture would soon boom. By creating a de facto dividing line between free and slave territory, the future of slavery in the Southwest seemed secure. In later years and with the benefit of hindsight, southerners would regret the decisions they made in the debate on the Northwest Ordinance, but from the vantage point of 1787, it protected their region's interests.

Substantive opposition to federal authority over slavery in the territories appeared initially not among southern slaveholders, but with westerners along the Ohio River border between slavery and freedom. In its final form, the Northwest Ordinance prohibited slavery in the territory, but flaws in the document revealed not only the haste in which the delegates added the slavery prohibition, but also cast doubt on the actual status of slavery in the Northwest Territory. Conflicting language within the ordinance itself muddled the meaning of the slavery prohibition. The delegates left intact language referring to "free male inhabitants" in several parts of the document.[17] The ordinance left considerable room for legal wrangling, if not outright evasion of the intended purpose of the sixth article, to prohibit slavery. Indeed, settlers in the Northwest Territory soon tested the boundaries of the famous sixth article by questioning its true meaning and objecting to its ultimate application. Likewise, they challenged the broad authority of the federal government over the territories—or at the very least its expediency. Specifically, residents in the territory questioned the federal government's power to prohibit slavery in one place and not the other. Some argued that the citizens of the territories themselves—and not Congress—could best regulate their domestic affairs.

The argument over federal versus local authority over the extension of slavery stemmed from the larger issue of constitutional federalism that Americans wrestled with during the 1780s. Indeed, the division of power conceptualized in the Constitution of 1787 was born of political necessity: it "permitted constitutional drafters to avoid very divisive, indeed probably unresolvable, disputes between the states" over a host of issues, including slavery. Nevertheless, differences remained between those who preferred a strong central government with broadly defined powers and those who feared overweening federal control. During the 1790s, the proponents of coordinated federal authority would style themselves Federalists, while the champions of states' rights and localism became the Democratic-Republicans.[18]

Yet when slavery entered the picture, matters became more complicated, for southern Federalists usually sided with their section over their emerging party organization. Northern Federalists firmly believed in federal authority over the territories, which they believed extended to regulating the extension of slavery. Slaveholding Federalists could embrace the former until it adversely affected the latter. Over the course of the 1790s, as Congress organized the territorial domain, they began to recognize that federal power might be used to prevent the extension of slavery. The stakes involved became clear when Congress considered legislation to create the Southwest Territory.

In April 1790, the new federal government created under the Constitution of 1787 accepted North Carolina's cession of the territory that would become the state of Tennessee and one month later completed the bifurcation of slavery with passage of the Southwest Ordinance. The law applied all the terms of the Northwest Ordinance, which the new Congress had itself ratified, to the new territory, "except so far as is otherwise provided in the conditions" of the cession of North Carolina; that is, it excluded the slavery prohibition of the sixth article. North Carolina forced the hand of Congress by stipulating, "That no regulations made or to be made by Congress, shall tend to emancipate slaves." By applying the Northwest Ordinance—save for the sixth article—Congress set a precedent in creating the Southwest Territory, as future territorial legislation usually replicated its terms. Whether as part of an actual compromise, an implicit understanding, or some other unknown arrangement, Congress had implicitly assented to a geographic dividing line for slavery. In this case, Congress undoubtedly believed it was acting in the best interests of settlers in both the Northwest and the Southwest Territories by prohibiting slavery in the former and leaving the question to the people in the latter.[19]

Though Congress quickly dispatched with provisions for territorial government in the Southwest Territory, it did not act with such haste in forming a state from it. Kentucky, which lay along the northern border of the slaveholding region, became a state in 1792, but the Southwest Territory remained just that—a territory. Disgruntled over the lack of local control inherent in federal jurisdiction over territorial government and possessing the requisite number of residents for statehood, the residents of Tennessee petitioned for statehood in early 1796. What might have seemed like a simple legislative process became complicated when some congressmen raised questions about the technical power of admitting a state. In the debate over how a territory gained statehood, two opinions emerged regarding the status of the territory and Congress's role in creating states. On the one hand certain congressmen argued that, in the words of South Carolina Federalist William Loughton Smith, "Congress was alone competent to form the Territory into one or more States"; therefore it possessed the power of *granting* statehood rather than merely certifying that the requirements had been met. Other legislators argued for a more latitudinarian interpretation of the law. Robert Goodloe Harper, another South Carolina Federalist, contended that, "in all questions relative to the formation of Governments, the wish of the people ought to be gratified," that "whenever it should appear to be the wish of the United States, or any considerable portion of them, to be governed in such or such a manner, their inclination should be attended to." Because the Tennesseans desired statehood and had met the requirements as outlined by Congress, their statehood should be granted automatically.[20]

Both interpretations point to the continuing struggle over the meaning of Union. Some politicians sought to put into practice the principles of federalism, with their emphasis on a strong federal government directing territorial policy, while others believed that the states remained the locus of power in the new nation. In the case of Tennessee, Smith and Harper might have disagreed on the power of Congress over slavery in the territories, but most southerners sided with Harper. The debate over the process of statehood might seem esoteric, but the ultimate decision had real implications for the future. Both sides argued from a perspective beyond the immediate concern of Tennessee; they recognized that deciding whether Tennessee would automatically enter the Union or if Congress had to ratify statehood would set precedent for the admission of subsequent states. If the latter interpretation prevailed, Congress could presumably withhold admission to any state that drafted a constitution and laws that Congress found objectionable. Furthermore, the whole issue touched on the delicate situation of territorial government itself. Should Congress actively set policy for the territories or should it grant a broad degree of power to its residents to shape and control their own affairs? The old debates from 1787—where politicians argued over the power of the federal government—had never completely disappeared.

Some members of the Federalist Party—with the exception of Harper—believed that the territories needed a period of gestation in which they could mature into full participation in the political life of the United States. Federalists from New England especially adhered to this view. Their opposition believed that the new system bore more than a faint resemblance to a colonial system of government. Should the nation rule its territories in such an aristocratic manner, they asked, much like the relation of Great Britain to the American colonies? James Madison argued that the "inhabitants of that district of country were at present in a degraded situation," meaning that they had no representation in Congress and a limited power of internal legislation. Madison betrayed his discomfort with the process of creating subordinate territorial governments that limited the sovereignty of Americans who had moved west. Politicians had not yet settled their minds on how much power either the citizens of a territory or Congress should have regarding territorial government or state making, while the issue of slavery in the territories appeared prominently within the discussion. In spite of the fact that the Federalists had expressed opposition to the extension of slavery, the matter remained largely a local matter influenced by regional attitudes and customs rather than party politics. Tennessee gained admission on June 1, 1796, but the issues discussed in the debate over its statehood remained unresolved.[21]

While Congress debated statehood for Tennessee, citizens in the Northwest Territory began raising their own questions about the future of slavery north of the Ohio River. In May 1796, a committee of four citizens in St. Clair and Randolph counties sent a memorial to Congress asking for the suspension of the slavery prohibition. The citizens argued that the sixth article of the Northwest Ordinance constituted an ex post facto law, thereby depriving them of their property "without their consent or concurrence." The political climate in the remainder of the original Northwest Territory after Ohio became a state in 1803 reflected the fact that citizens from both the eastern states as well as the upper South had emigrated to the region, thus fulfilling the predictions of Nathan Dane and many southerners. In 1787, these individuals had claimed that citizens from their respective sections would emigrate and dominate the politics of the territory. As the Northwest Territory grew, settlers in the eastern portion tended to oppose slavery. In the western portion, where upland southerners had settled, politics had a more proslavery bent. A committee appointed by Congress to address the St. Clair and Randolph memorial rejected their request, arguing that "an alteration of the ordinance, in the manner prayed for by the petitioners, would be disagreeable to many of the inhabitants of the said territory." The memorial itself revealed an inescapable fact: slavery existed in the Northwest Territory in spite of the prohibition.[22]

The slavery issue represented two distinct but complementary power struggles ensuing in the Northwest Territory over slavery and the sovereignty of settlers in the territories. First, an internal struggle between Ohio Valley settlers hailing from the South and those who came from the eastern states raised issues of who would control the three districts that would eventually become the states of Illinois, Indiana, and Ohio. Some members of the Federalist Party, most notably the Northwest Territory's governor, Arthur St. Clair, questioned not only the loyalty of the "multitude of indigent and ignorant people" who resided in the territory, but also their ability to govern themselves.[23] On the other side, a cadre of Virginia settlers, many of whom owned slaves, desired the repeal of the sixth article of the Northwest Ordinance and the creation of a slave society, albeit on a drastically smaller scale than that of their home state. In the middle stood a significant group of upland southern yeomen who believed the current territorial status smacked of an aristocracy and arbitrary federal government. They opposed the Federalist leaders, but also resented the introduction of slavery as a hindrance to their prosperity in the new territory. Still, both the Virginians and the southern yeomen believed that they had the upper hand in the struggle and would win if the issue of sustaining or repealing the slavery prohibition came to a plebiscite. This scenario played out in the territory for much of the next ten years. In the process of petitioning Congress for repeal of the slavery prohibition, or in some cases petitioning to sustain it, the settlers of the Northwest Territory showed their desire for self-government—asserting not only that they could best determine their own domestic affairs, but also that it was their right to do so.

Questions concerning who possessed sovereignty over the extension of slavery persisted, as legislators addressed the status of slavery in a vast expanse of land west of the state of Georgia not subject to the provisions of the Southwest Ordinance. That state had claimed rights to the lands making up the present-day states of Alabama and Mississippi for some time. In 1798, the House of Representatives voted against Georgia's claim and immediately set out to organize the large district into the Territory of Mississippi. During the debate, a Federalist congressman from Massachusetts moved to strike out a clause in the bill that exempted the territory from the Northwest Ordinance's ban on slavery. George Thatcher's motion reignited the discussion regarding federal versus local sovereignty over slavery. Southerners vigorously objected to exclusion of slavery in this region. Planters in the Natchez district—the extreme western portion of what would become Mississippi Territory—already held slaves. Furthermore, southerners saw the vast territory as a natural place to escape the depleted soils of the Atlantic states and to extend their agricultural pursuits. Any effort to prohibit slavery in Mississippi Territory constituted an attack on southern economic expansion, a group of Natchez planters argued in a 1797 petition to Congress. In September of that year, surveyor Andrew Ellicott had noted opposition to a slavery ban in the Natchez district to Secretary of State Timothy Pickering. Ellicott, a Pennsylvania Quaker opposed to slavery, had worked with the Spanish authorities in the district to implement the boundaries defined in Pinckney's Treaty of 1796 and possessed an intimate knowledge of the political situation in the region. Though Ellicott described slavery as "disagreeable to us northern people," he recommended that the federal government permit it "upon the same footing it is at present in the southern States." The people of the Natchez district, he noted, objected to the Northwest Ordinance precisely because of its ban on slavery.[24]

So, too, did other southerners. Slave state legislators in Congress likewise raised two points: slavery remained a matter under local jurisdiction and the sectional division of slavery settlements rendered congressional intervention unnecessary and impolitic. "In the Northwestern Territory the regulation forbidding slavery was a very proper one," Robert Goodloe Harper argued, "as the people inhabiting that part of the country were from parts where slavery did not prevail" whereas in Mississippi Territory, "that species of property already exists, and persons emigrating there from the Southern States would carry with them property of this kind." Other southerners—and at least one New England Federalist—concurred. Harrison Gray Otis of Massachusetts argued that southerners would settle the Mississippi Territory; therefore, Congress should assent to the wishes of the people who would live there. Furthermore, he predicted a slave insurrection among slaves in the Natchez district if Congress passed the amendment of his Massachusetts colleague. A Virginia congressman articulated a theory that would become a staple of the slavery-in-the-territories argument. Barring slavery at this point made no sense, John Nicholas of Virginia argued, as the territory could make that determination for itself at the time it applied for statehood.[25]

Nicholas and other southern leaders had other reasons for defending self-government over slavery in Mississippi. Numerous Upper South slaveholders and leaders had come to embrace the idea of diffusion—that spreading slavery over space would actually weaken the institution over time. Even as the nineteenth century approached, many southerners still saw slavery as an evil, albeit a necessary one. Diffusion, they argued, would ameliorate the poor living and working conditions of slaves by reducing their concentration in the old states. Slave revolts in Virginia and the Upper South left many whites fearful and eager to decrease the slave population density in their region. The opening of territories suited to staple agriculture gave them a market for their surplus slaves and therefore another reason to embrace the diffusion principle. Diffusionists rested their principle on both benevolent and practical reasons.[26] The idea, however, was premised on the opening of new territories suited to staple agriculture. Northern opposition to the expansion of slavery threatened the plans of diffusionists and the economic hopes of slaveholders.

The brief debate over slavery in the Mississippi Territory revealed lines of division that would intensify in the future. Thatcher rejected the diffusionists' position, stating that they simply wanted to "plague others" with their surplus slaves. Thoughtful leaders, he provocatively argued, could find no way to sanction the expansion of slavery in a nation "founded on the rights of man." The Constitution had tolerated slavery owing to the necessity for compromise; now Congress wanted to sanction the institution by law, a proposition that Thatcher could not tolerate. Not only did slavery degrade the Africans in bondage, but it also reduced whites to a status where they relied on the labor of others for their subsistence. Many of his northern colleagues agreed, though using milder language. Southerners like Harper and Nicholas did not address the moral argument itself, except in asserting that the diffusion of slavery would actually prove a boon to the slaves. Instead, they assumed a position that the prohibition against slavery would hinder emigration and prevent free white property holders in exercising their right to own slaves. Southerners believed that the debate had portrayed their section, according to John Rutledge, Jr., of South Carolina, "in an odious light." Rarely in these years did congressmen engage in such heated criticism aimed at one section from another. In the case of Mississippi, though, a northerner argued to prohibit slavery in a region understood as within the orbit of the South, and in unusually harsh terms. Rutledge responded in kind, chastising Thatcher for "uttering philippics against a practice with which his and their philosophy is at war." Though many southerners embraced the diffusion argument and spoke of an eventual end of slavery in America, they resented the northern offensive against their peculiar institution.[27]

Southerners insisted that Congress should not interfere with slavery in Mississippi Territory, but that the decision should rightfully be left to those who settled in the region. Their argument did not necessarily deny Congress of the legal *right* to bar slavery from the territories, but it certainly questioned the *expediency* of congressional action. In an uncharacteristically bitter debate, the members of the Fifth Congress went a long way to define the boundaries of the argument concerning slavery in the territories. The effort to prohibit slavery in a territory south of the Ohio River—the first instance of its kind—failed when the act creating the Mississippi Territory became law on April 7, 1798. Just days before, Timothy Pickering penned a letter to Andrew Ellicott notifying him that the bill had passed in the Senate and would almost certainly become law. Mississippi Territory had become the first territory created beyond the aegis of the Northwest and Southwest ordinances, but the dividing line between free and slave territories explicitly created by those acts now seemed reified. Southerners had made their case that only the residents of the territory could make the final decision on whether to permit or prohibit slavery south of the Ohio River. They had not yet articulated the theory that Congress could not legislate against slavery in the territories.[28]

Leaders from the Upper South contented themselves with securing the expansion of slavery in the southwestern regions of the nation. Indeed, Congress had established a pattern by which territories north of the Ohio River would remain free, while those south of the river would remain open to the institution— the latter an implicit endorsement of the principle of territorial self-government. At the federal level, few antislavery politicians held office and few proslavery leaders perceived a tangible threat to the expansion of slavery in places where it would likely flourish. On the local level, however, the boundary between slavery and freedom—the Ohio River—did not prove as impregnable or satisfying. Settlers living in the Northwest Territory continued to argue about slavery within their region, with some calling for repeal of the slavery prohibition. Congress's rejection of the 1796 memorial asking for suspension of the sixth article had not laid to rest to the desire of some settlers to introduce slavery in some form within that territory.

The territory of Indiana became another flash point in the dispute over the Northwest Ordinance, testing the boundaries of slavery and sectional comity. Created in 1800 as preparation for the entry of Ohio into the Union, Indiana Ter-

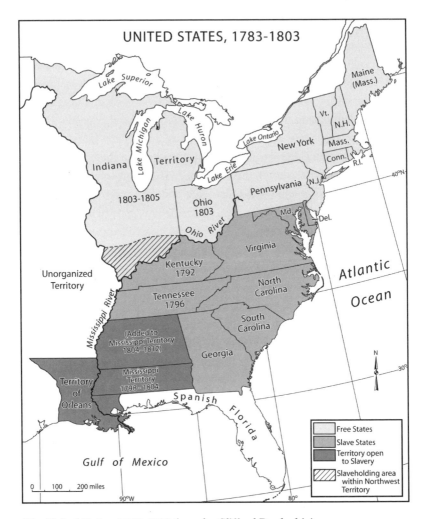

The United States, 1783–1803 (map by Clifford Duplechin)

ritory encompassed a long and wide swath of land bounded on the south by the Ohio River and on the west by the Mississippi. The settlers in the Ohio portion of the Northwest Territory never seriously countenanced slavery, but frontiersmen to the west held different opinions.[29] Numerous Virginians and poorer farmers from the Upper South, in addition to settlers from the eastern states, had moved into what became Indiana Territory. Upland southern migrants did not agree with their former neighbors who espoused the diffusion principle, which was premised on the weakening of slavery. Instead, they saw a chance for upward economic mobility by engaging in a small-scale, slave-based agriculture in the southernmost portions of the Northwest Territory.

The mix of southerners and easterners made for occasionally fractious politics in the region. In February 1803, William Henry Harrison, governor of Indiana Territory and the president of a proslavery convention called to explore the option of suspending the slavery prohibition, sent a memorial to Congress "declaring the consent of the people of Indiana" to remove the ban on slavery for a period of ten years.[30] After the ten-year period had ended, the prohibition of slavery would resume, but any slaves in the territory and their issue would remain enslaved. The Vincennes petition would ensure a small but perpetual slave community in Indiana, and quite possibly provoke an eventual repeal of the sixth article.

Harrison most likely had called for a proslavery convention in December 1802 because he believed that slavery would fuel economic growth in the territory. Proslavery citizens believed the admission of slavery would encourage emigration to the territory and provide a ready labor source for agriculture there.[31] The way in which Harrison and his allies went about seeking their goals, however, proved most interesting. The governor and the delegates to the Vincennes Convention recognized that Congress had continually wrestled with the competing ideas of federal control over territorial affairs versus local self-government. By arguing that suspension of the sixth article had "the consent of the people of Indiana," Harrison and his allies appealed to those legislators who endorsed greater authority for settlers over their own internal affairs. Yet Harrison could hardly prove that the Vincennes Convention represented the will of a majority of the territory's citizens.

The committee appointed by the House of Representatives to examine the Vincennes memorial recommended that the full chamber deny the request, as "the labor of slaves is not necessary to promote the growth and settlement of colonies in that region." The northern makeup of the committee likely influenced this argument; only its chairman, John Randolph of Virginia, lived in a slaveholding state. Indiana's proximity to Canada, too, may have provoked fear that the British would resort to their old tactics of offering freedom to American slaves in the case of a war. The committee may also have recognized that Harrison could hardly lay claim to represent the true will of the majority. For reasons unclear, Congress deferred action on the petition and the Randolph committee's report. In the next session, another committee composed solely of southern congressmen drafted a far more favorable report, recommending that Congress suspend the sixth article as requested. However, the committee called for gradual emancipation of the descendants of any slaves brought to Indiana. For a short time, the proslavery faction in Vincennes held out hope based on the committee's report. One Indianan wrote to a friend that "the prospect of establishing Slavery among us brightens daily," and alleged that "the president is decidedly in favor of th[e ar]ticle in our ordinance [against] Slavery being repealed." In spite of the report and the high hopes of the proponents of slavery, Congress took no action on the Vincennes memorial.[32]

Undeterred, the proslavery faction persisted in its efforts. A steady stream of petitions made their way to Washington over the next few years as proslaveryites in Indiana sought to get their way, while antislavery settlers aimed to prevent the repeal of the sixth article. Both sides used the rhetoric of local government and popular will to get their way. The proslavery faction followed up their initial efforts with a subsequent series of petitions asking for suspension of the sixth article for ten years. Again the petitioners asserted, though hardly proved, that the petition represented the popular will. And again in 1805 a committee in Congress endorsed a new set of proslavery memorials, noting, "The suspension of this article is an object almost universally desired in that Territory," a point the antislavery faction would certainly debate.[33] Regardless of whether a majority of the territory's citizens preferred suspension, Congress again followed the now-familiar pattern of calling a committee to address the Indiana memorials and then taking no action on the committee report.

Undeterred, the proslavery settlers in Indiana Territory sought to assert local control over the slavery issue by circumventing the prohibition. They created a system of "indentured servitude," by which slave owners held their slaves to a term of service rather than in perpetuity. This extralegal method of permitting de facto slavery outraged the antislavery faction in the territory, which petitioned Congress on its own behalf in 1807. Once again undeterred, the proslavery settlers controlled the territorial legislature, which had recently passed another set of resolutions calling for the repeal of the sixth article, this time accusing the federal government of depriving the residents of Indiana their equal rights. The memorialists asserted that the territory's citizens "decidedly approve of the toleration of slavery" and that allowing it to exist there would provide a safety valve for the southern states—a nod to the supporters of diffusion. But this time they went a step further, posing a question to Congress: "Slavery is tolerated in the Territories of Orleans, Mississippi, and Louisiana: why should this Territory be excepted?" The petitioners asserted that the Northwest Ordinance deprived them of rights equal to those of settlers in the other territories. Once again, Indiana's proslavery leaders appealed to the spirit of local government and congressional nonintervention by arguing that Congress had wrongly imposed conditions on matters of local concern.[34]

Disgusted equally with the action of the territory's legislative council and the indecisiveness of the House of Representatives, antislavery forces called for their own convention to demonstrate that the proslavery faction did not represent the will of the majority in Indiana Territory. Clark County antislavery petitioners called for Congress to "suspend any legislative act on this subject until we shall, by the constitution, be admitted into the Union, and have a right to adopt such a constitution, in this respect, as may comport with the wishes of a majority of the citizens." The antislavery coalition used the strategy of their proslavery adversaries and appealed to Congress to let the territory decide the issue for itself when drafting a state constitution. One student of Indiana history has remarked that this appeal represented the doctrine of popular sovereignty, "antedat[ing] by forty years the letter of General [Lewis] Cass in which the doctrine is commonly supposed to have been first enunciated."[35]

By now, Congress had wearied of the infighting in Indiana and the steady stream of petitions sent from that territory. The House committee that received the memorial of the Indiana territorial legislature had recommended suspending the sixth article on the terms asked for, noting that many of the emigrants to that territory came from southern states and citing a need for increased emigration.[36] Nine months later the Senate endorsed the antislavery resolutions from Clark County, declaring its support for the ordinance's slavery prohibition. The political seesaw that the slavery issue had become began to slow after this last report. The flow of petitions slowed, too, as proslavery settlers found it easier to evade the law than to change it, and as antislavery settlers mobilized and began to assume more control of territorial affairs.[37]

In a pattern that would repeat itself in later territorial contests, proslavery and antislavery forces resolved the issue at the local level—sometimes through extralegal means. Leaders in Washington could set policy, but usually could not control the actions of settlers on the frontier. Evasion of the law became particularly egregious in Illinois Territory (which was carved out of the original Indiana Territory), where settlers actively practiced the "indentured servitude" ploy first devised in Indiana Territory. Fractious politics there had provoked settlers in what became Illinois to seek a second division of the remaining Northwest

Territory in 1809, which "virtually killed proslavery hopes in what was to become Indiana itself."[38] In Illinois, however, history seemed to repeat itself as proslavery and antislavery forces repeated the battles fought to the east. Proslavery partisans controlled the legislature and passed a series of laws designed to circumvent Article Six. Leaders devised a strategy similar to that of Indiana's proslavery faction, but it was also informed by Hoosiers' ultimate failure to change policy. Proslavery Illinoisans resolved to maintain their indentured servant laws until the territory achieved statehood. After becoming a state, the proslavery party believed it could move for a constitutional amendment to permit slavery. Of course, any such amendment would imply that the Northwest Ordinance had no bearing on the region once the separate territories became states, an argument that some northerners considered dubious and certainly in bad faith. In the meantime, indentured servitude would suffice. Though the outright ban on slavery in the ordinance prevailed in much of the Northwest Territory, opposition to the slavery ban had surely emerged in the southernmost region—and would continue for some time.

Just as issues concerning territorial self-government and slavery had held a significant place in the discussion over American territorial expansion into the lands east of the Mississippi River, so, too, did the same concerns appear during the settlement of the nation's grandest territorial acquisition—the Louisiana Purchase. The acquisition of the vast region from France seemed to defy comprehension; indeed, neither seller nor buyer knew its exact boundaries. The mammoth territory promised to be a tremendous space for national expansion, even as it presented numerous challenges to the federal government, which would have to organize and secure the land as well as try to assimilate its residents—once foreign subjects but now American citizens.[39]

Slavery had existed in Louisiana practically since the colony's founding. Settlers of French and Spanish descent held human chattel in a system that at one time had been far more permissive than its Anglo-American counterpart. By the 1790s, though, slavery in Louisiana had become rigid.[40] In its treaty negotiations with the United States, France ensured that any residents of Louisiana would not only gain citizenship, but also all of the rights of property and religion—both delicate issues—that Americans had by their constitution. Consequently, the federal government would have to contend with the treaty's stipulation whenever it began the process of creating territories in the purchase.

Congressional leaders initiated the process of organization promptly, desiring to establish control quickly over the territory and its citizens and begin the process of assimilation. Regarding the citizens and their interests, a judge from Indiana Territory expressed his hope that Congress would "promote their future prosperity by Granting them a Territorial Government in their own Country And Organize Such a System of Policy as may be Consonant with their wishes And Congenial to the American Character." According to an inhabitant of Louisiana, encouraging southern emigration required that the government make clear that slave property would have legal protection. The citizens of Louisiana, he wrote a Kentucky congressman, "are very much Interested in Obtaining a Ulimited [*sic*] Slavery Many of them hold a considerable part of their Estate in that Species of property." Most settlers strongly desired a broad degree of self-government and the right to determine their own local customs.[41]

Congress addressed the issue of territorial self-government in the early months of 1804 when it debated the organization of territories in the Louisiana Purchase. Louisiana presented Congress with a problem that it had not encountered in any previous effort to organize a territory: its citizens (at least those at the time of the purchase) would be naturalized Americans. They had lived as colonial subjects under a monarchy; they would now be citizens in a federal republic. In December 1803, a Senate committee began drafting legislation to create territorial governments for the southernmost portion of the purchase. Some three weeks later, the full Senate received the committee's work and began deliberations on the bill. The fourth section of the Senate's initial legislation stipulated that the president would select "thirteen of the most fit and discreet persons of the Territory" to serve as a legislative council, which would advise the territorial governor on internal matters. Some senators feared that the naturalized citizens of Louisiana could not govern themselves effectively or that they might govern against the interests of the United States. Neither Congress nor the residents of Louisiana initially linked the principle of self-government to slavery because no threat against the institution had yet emerged.[42]

Senators approved legislation that allowed the president to create the territory's legislative branch, but the bill faced considerable opposition in the House of Representatives. In February 1804, that body began a lengthy debate over the ability of the Louisianans to govern themselves in the American mold.[43] House members quickly began deliberations on an act to create two territories out of the vast purchase, but found it difficult to agree on how to structure the legislative branch of the territorial governments. The clause in the Senate's bill differed from recent practice. As many congressmen noted, the legislation for Mississippi Territory provided for popular election of a legislative council. Some individuals, including members of Congress, questioned why this sufficed for Mississippi Territory and not the territories of the Louisiana Purchase.

The representatives quickly fell into two camps, neither of which neatly coincided with party lines. One side demanded the striking of the original fourth section and its replacement with a clause permitting popular election of a council. The other side argued for the wisdom of the section as drafted, as it would allow the naturalized citizens of the territories to mature and learn the way of American republican institutions. As William Eustis of Massachusetts argued, "The principles of civil liberty cannot be suddenly ingrafted upon a people accustomed to a regimen of a distinctly opposite hue." The people of Louisiana, according to Eustis and his like-minded colleagues, could not yet be trusted with self-government because they had never done so before. Giving them such a broad franchise could allow unscrupulous men to seize control of the territorial government. Furthermore, such action could allow those not professing loyalty to the American government to attempt some sort of coup against American authority. A Pennsylvania congressman cited reports that when American authorities in New Orleans lowered the French flag and raised the Stars and Stripes, the people present wept, proving that the cession "had not been received with approbation by them." Other congressmen suggested that Congress had a duty to provide for Louisiana's government, as the territory stood "in nearly the same relation to us as if they were a conquered territory." "The object of this bill," James Holland of North Carolina noted, "is to extend the laws of the United States over Louisiana, not to enable the people of Louisiana to make laws." To his mind, Congress needed to provide a system of government specifically suited to the unique conditions under which Louisiana became American property. Only after American rule had been established and the allegiance of the territories' citizens secured could Congress consider granting self-government.[44]

The opposition, primarily from the western states, met these arguments with considerable vigor. First, several legislators posited that Congress had little choice but to grant the Louisiana territories self-government, as the treaty between the United States and France had provided. Representing the opinion of many of his western colleagues, a Tennessee congressman argued that the majority of Louisianans "conceive themselves entitled" to the right of self-government by the terms of the treaty. Second, several members of the House noted that the federal government had granted Mississippi Territory self-government on local affairs. Congress owed it to the residents of Louisiana to integrate them fully within the American political system—specifically by granting them self-government as would normally proceed from any other act of territorial organization. After all, might not Louisiana's citizens resent not having the same powers as their neighbor to the east? "I cannot conceive," remarked George Washington Campbell of Tennessee, "what can have rendered them so different from those people of the Mississippi Territory; they were once the same people and under the same Government, and they could not have then become unfit for self-government." Nathaniel Macon of North Carolina concurred, asking, "will they not expect the same grade of government with the inhabitants of the Mississippi Territory, with whom they will have a constant intercourse?"[45]

Many of the congressmen who rejected the proposed restrictions added a new dimension to the argument for self-government in Louisiana by attacking the notion of a pervasive federal presence and interference in territorial affairs. Such misuse of federal authority compromised the freedom of American citizens, regardless of how they gained their citizenship or for how long they had held it. They cast the debate in the terms of liberty versus slavery, an argument that southerners in later years would use to defend the expansion of slavery in the territories. Matthew Lyon of Kentucky castigated the opposition, stating that "the most ludicrous idea I have heard expressed on the subject is, that these people must be kept in slavery until they can be learned to think and behave like freemen." Another congressman asked, "Are they blind to the difference between liberty and slavery? Are they insensible to the difference of laws made by themselves, and of laws made by others?" These congressmen rejected outright the notion of territorial tutelage, instead arguing that Congress had the obligation to let Louisianans govern themselves. They did not conceive of the American territorial system as one of quasi-colonial control over unincorporated lands, but as a system that granted as broad a degree of self-government as possible while providing for the orderly transition from territory to state.[46]

The House of Representatives voted by a sizeable majority to strike the original fourth section of the bill and replace it with a provision for popular election of the legislative branch. The bill faced considerable opposition in conference negotiations with the Senate, which preferred its original wording. Ultimately, the bill passed with the original section left intact, ostensibly because a popular election of council members could result in legislators of different nationalities who spoke different languages serving together, thereby confounding their work. Congress exhibited considerable unease with the prospect of assimilating once-foreign subjects into the Union. Macon stated it best when he said, "It is extremely difficult to legislate for a people with whose habits and customs we are unacquainted."[47]

Nevertheless, the debate had proven provocative to those who still wrestled with notions of how the American territorial system should operate. Widely differing opinions still existed on how much self-government a territory could or should exercise. For some time, settlers had chafed under the rigid system by which Congress had provided for territorial government, particularly the fact that politicians in Washington—and not settlers in the West—initially selected individuals to serve as a legislative council. Congress, however, feared that unscrupulous men could manipulate the process of self-government and jeopardize American sovereignty over its territories. The federal government, therefore, faced the difficult task of balancing demands for self-government in the territories with the need to ensure that the far-flung territories would maintain allegiance to the United States. Establishing a clear sense of who supported broad self-government and who endorsed strict federal control of the territories proves difficult, yet certain general patterns appear. For the most part, congressmen from the newer western states supported granting self-government to the territories of Louisiana. Many, but not all, southerners joined them. The key support for the fourth section as originally proposed came from the northeastern congressmen. Although roll call votes exhibit these general patterns, however, they also reveal that the stark sectional divisions on the question of slavery and self-government had not yet appeared. For its part, the Senate overwhelmingly supported presidential appointment of the council; only nine senators voted to concur with the House and revise the legislation.[48]

The 1804 debate over the Louisiana territorial legislation had steered clear of the slavery issue, which also helps to explain why rigid sectional lines had not formed. Most leaders understood, however, that the issues Congress addressed in the Louisiana deliberations would have the potential to impact the institution at some point. At this moment, both houses of Congress seemed convinced that the widespread presence of slavery in the territory and the treaty's provisions concerning property rights militated against any effort to prohibit the institution. Slavery had a strong presence in the southern portion that became known as the Territory of Orleans, though settlers in the northern portion of the purchase—the Louisiana Territory—exhibited wariness about the federal government's intentions. The Territory of Orleans had a far greater population and, therefore, the means to organize a government quickly. Conditions in the more sparsely settled Louisiana Territory presented challenges for creating a viable territorial government, which might prompt Congress to debate whether to annex temporarily the northern territory to Indiana Territory for executive and judicial purposes.

Linking the governments of the Louisiana and Indiana territories posed a threat to the future of slavery in the remainder of the Louisiana Purchase. Once again, slavery and self-government would become twin concerns as proslavery settlers sought to protect the peculiar institution and their property. Exhibiting a keen awareness of the conflicted affairs in the Northwest Territory, William C. Carr, a St. Louis lawyer, expressed concern with placing Louisiana under the executive and judicial authority of Indiana Territory. "Many were apprehensive that slavery would not only be prohibited," he wrote to Kentucky resident John Breckinridge, "but the more ignorant were fearful lest those already in their possession would also be manumitted. I discern from the Law, or that part of it which relates to this district that Congress has been silent on the subject altho' it has been permitted in the territory of Orleans under certain restrictions."[49] Actually, the issue of slavery would soon enter the discussion in both the Territory of Orleans and the Louisiana Territory.

Congress created the Territory of Orleans effective October 1, 1804, dividing the Louisiana Purchase at the thirty-third parallel. The land south of this line became the Territory of Orleans and that north became the District (later Territory) of Louisiana. Immediately upon becoming a territory, the citizens of Orleans examined the enabling legislation and found it wanting, concurring with their allies in Congress that the law deprived them of self-government guaranteed by the treaty of cession and the American Constitution. They quickly submitted a memorial to Congress, objecting to the enabling legislation and arguing that it had "no one principle of republicanism in its composition." Its authors, Pierre Sauve, Pierre Derbigny, and Jean Noel Destrehan, sharply criticized the actions of Congress and challenged its authority to enact such restrictive legislation. They evinced a clear knowledge of the principles written in the Declaration of Independence and the Constitution and accused Congress of not living up to these high standards in creating territorial governments for the Louisiana Purchase. According to the petitioners, the law placed Louisiana in a seemingly perpetual state of subordination, claiming that "no manifestation of what awaits us at the expiration of the law is yet made." Accordingly, the people of Orleans would remain inferior to other American citizens until, *"in the school of slavery, we have learned how to be free, our rights shall be restored."*[50]

In addition to demanding the right of local self-governance, the petitioners raised a most delicate subject—the foreign slave trade. The territorial legislation strictly forbade the importation of slaves from Africa, a trade that the Constitution forbade after 1808 anyway. The slave trade clause had provoked a debate separate from that of self-governance, particularly in the Senate, where members argued over whether to accept the amendment by James Hillhouse of Connecticut banning the foreign slave trade in Louisiana, or, in the words of a Georgia senator, to "Let those people judge it for themselves—the treaty is obligatory upon us." The law as passed imposed stiff penalties for engaging in the foreign slave trade. Under colonial rule, however, Louisiana's citizens had engaged heavily in the African slave trade. The Territory of Orleans, too, found itself caught in the delicate American politics over the issue; South Carolina had recently decided to reopen the African slave trade—in no small part to corner the market on supplying slaves to the Louisiana Purchase. Territorial leaders objected to its ban as unfair and an inconvenience to agriculture in the territory. They almost assuredly saw economic benefits in renewing their own African slave trade. Echoing the words of the Georgia senator, Sauve, Derbigny, and Destrehan wrote, "We only ask the right of deciding it for ourselves, and of being placed in this respect on an equal footing with other States."[51]

The House of Representatives received the memorial of the citizens of Orleans and referred it to a special committee chaired by John Randolph of Virginia. The committee was balanced along sectional lines, but five of its seven members belonged to the Republican Party, which proved far more sympathetic to territorial expansion and self-government than the Federalists. Jefferson's Louisiana Purchase had alarmed his opponents, especially those from the Northeast. Betraying the same fears that southerners would begin to voice some forty years later, New England Federalists feared that westward expansion would weaken their political power and augment southern control of the federal government. Slavery provided an additional boon to southern designs, as the three-fifths compromise enhanced southern political clout. The Federalist Party, already beset by internal dissension, had reason to fear westward expansion inasmuch as the residents of the territories overwhelmingly supported the Jeffersonian Republicans. With Republicans in control of the Randolph committee, and with a southerner in the chair, the Louisianans' request had fallen into sympathetic hands.[52]

Some in Washington questioned the loyalty of the three petitioners, given their French ancestry and their chastisement of the federal government and its approach toward territorial government in Louisiana. The Randolph committee quickly answered the petition, stating that though "the memorialists may have appreciated too highly the rights which have been secured to them by the treaty of cession," Congress should not disregard their grievances. Randolph, who during the first session of the Eighth Congress had voted in favor of expanding territorial self-government, argued that revising the existing law would quiet discord in the territory and draw the citizens closer to the Union. As long as Louisianans obeyed federal law, he wrote, "your committee are at a loss to conceive how the United States are more interested in the internal government of the Territory than of any other State in the Confederacy." However, the committee rejected outright the memorialists' objections to prohibiting the foreign slave trade. With a considerable number of southerners, especially those from the Upper South, and almost all northerners regardless of party against the foreign slave trade, leaders in Washington opposed calls for its revival. The report nevertheless showed that certain members of Congress still supported granting the territories broader power to legislate on their own affairs.[53]

The Randolph committee evidently discussed their report with Sauve, Derbigny, and Destrehan—who had presented their memorial to Congress in person—before submitting it to the full chamber. At its invitation, the three delegates from the Territory of Orleans penned a rejoinder to the committee's report. Not content with letting Randolph have the last word on the subject, they further questioned the power of Congress to impose such strict control on the territories, raising an argument that would become a central component of future territorial debates. Noting that some politicians had cited Article Four, Section Three of the Constitution (that Congress "shall have Power to make all needful Rules and Regulations respecting the Territory or other property belonging to the United States") as the basis for the territorial law, the Louisianans retorted that this clause "has no relation whatever with the situation of the inhabitants of Louisiana, and is evidently relative only to the disposal and management of the property of the United States." And in an apparent effort to head off any future attack on slavery within the territory, the writers rejected any notion that the Northwest Ordinance applied to Louisiana. Here the petitioners were on solid ground, especially since the Ohio River boundary between slave and free territories—if extended west—bisected the Louisiana Purchase. They noted that the citizens had received guarantees concerning their property in the treaty of cession—a circumstance not addressed by the ordinance. The treaty did not provide for admittance to the Union in accordance with the Northwest Ordinance, but "according to the principles (the elemental laws) of the constitution." Accordingly, the terms of cession demanded that the property and rights of Louisiana's residents receive full protection.[54]

The committee of three sent by the people of the Territory of Orleans had stated their case in stark terms, perhaps too bold in the opinion of some Washington leaders. Yet their arguments outlined and encompassed the same fundamental disputes and complexities regarding the territorial system that had existed for some time. As the United States continued to add territory to its domain, questions of self-government would continue to arise, particularly in relation to the institution of slavery. The often disparate arguments over territorial policy and the expansion of slavery slowly coalesced into a question of whether the citizens of a territory could legislate on slavery for themselves.

Although Sauve, Derbigny, and Destrehan spoke primarily for the citizens of the Territory of Orleans, they also echoed the concerns of citizens north of the thirty-third parallel in the newly created Louisiana Territory. Its settlers, too, feared "the fetters of an endless territorial infancy." Citizens from the northern territory submitted their own petitions to Congress, asking for changes in the territorial system and for guarantees that their property in slaves would receive protection under the law. In September 1804, the Louisiana territorial legislature drafted a statement strongly opposing the annexation of Louisiana Territory to Indiana Territory for executive and judicial affairs, an arrangement that it feared would threaten their title to slave property. "Is not the silence of Congress with respect to slavery in this district of Louisiana," they wrote, "and the placing of this district under the Governor of a Territory where slavery is proscribed, calculated to alarm the people with respect to that kind of property, and to create the presumption of a disposition in congress to abolish at a further date slavery altogether in the district of Louisiana?" The citizens asked for an explicit guarantee that the federal government would not disturb their right to hold slave property and that they would allow for the importation of slaves, "under such restrictions as to Congress in their wisdom will appear necessary." The settlers in Louisiana Territory presented an artfully balanced case, asking for local control over slavery while explicitly recognizing congressional authority over the slave trade.[55]

Congress received the protests of citizens in both territories favorably and sought to allay their fears and act on their grievances. They refused to countenance, however, the petition to allow importation of slaves. Indeed, the government would seek to strengthen the ban in the Ninth Congress. Congress quickly passed legislation granting the Orleans Territory the second grade of territorial government, allowing for broader local control of internal affairs. It also sought to assuage any fears of an eventual ban on slavery by excluding the sixth article of the Northwest Ordinance from operation in Orleans. The act for the government of Louisiana Territory gave the territory its own governor and judicial system, essentially imposing the first grade of territorial government to Louisiana. Though the law remained silent on slavery in the territory, most people assumed that the treaty of cession guaranteed and protected slave property. And because Louisiana would not be under the control of Indiana Territory, most settlers were relieved and reassured. Louisianans remained persistent, however, in seeking stronger assurances that the federal government would not legislate against slavery in their territory. In 1810, Congress responded to a petition by drafting legislation that would grant the settlers' requests, including a provision that exempted the territory from the Northwest Ordinance's ban on slavery. Congress repeatedly delayed the legislation until finally passing an amended version in May 1812, which inexplicably omitted the exemption clause. Nevertheless, the law granting Louisiana Territory—now known as Missouri Territory to avoid confusion with the new state of Louisiana—did not explicitly address the slavery issue, as many settlers in the territory had desired. The language of the legislation, however, implicitly sanctioned slavery and admitted its presence.[56]

The residents of the Louisiana Purchase had repeatedly asserted their right to control the institution of slavery, while Congress continued to betray a lack of clarity on the expansion of the institution and territorial policy in general. Some politicians insisted on strict control of territorial affairs by contending that the Constitution authorized Congress to govern the territories, while others believed that the territories possessed the right to govern themselves concerning matters of local concern. Opponents of the former view argued that placing the territories under strict federal control reduced their citizens to vassals and deprived them of their constitutional rights. Many leaders who endorsed the latter view had begun to see federal control over the territories as a threat to the institution of slavery. The Louisiana Purchase had complicated the issue by introducing naturalized citizens into the debate. Some in Congress questioned whether these former French and Spanish subjects deserved the trust of the American government to exercise self-government and exhibit loyalty to the Union, yet many American citizens from the east would emigrate to the new western lands. They questioned how the federal government could rightly treat them as subordinates. Congress debated these questions and imposed regulations designed to accommodate both views.

As for the slavery question, Congress essentially let the principle of self-government hold sway by its inability to decide conclusively how to address the issue. Louisiana entered the Union as a slave state in 1812, but Congress would not address statehood for the more sparsely populated Territory of Missouri for seven more years. During that time, Congress's silence on the slavery issue essentially allowed the territory to exercise self-government concerning slavery issues. The institution came to prosper in Missouri, though not on the scale of the states and territories farther south.

With territorial affairs largely settled in the Louisiana Purchase, the federal government's attention once again turned to the Northwest, where Indiana and Illinois prepared for statehood. In both territories, the issue of slavery remained unsolved. In January 1816, Indiana's territorial legislature sought admission to the Union, which Congress granted just three months later. Indiana became the nineteenth state on December 11, 1816, after drafting a constitution that confirmed the antislavery party's victory in the debates over Article Six. Although it "temporized" on the matter of indentured servants, the new state's constitution stipulated that no amendment could ever allow slavery. After almost a decade of debate, self-government in Indiana resulted in an antislavery constitution.[57]

Two years later Illinois applied for statehood, but the issue of slavery did not pass quietly there as it had in Indiana. Proslavery leaders planned to achieve statehood and then after entering the Union in full standing, amend their constitution to permit slavery. Recognizing the states' rights strategy of the Illinoisans, one New York congressman objected to the territorial resolution appealing for statehood. James Tallmadge argued that the framers of the draft constitution had not "sufficiently prohibited" slavery, a clear violation of the sixth article of the Northwest Ordinance. The Illinois constitution "contravened this stipulation, either in the letter or the spirit." Once again, the Northwest Ordinance and its slavery prohibition entered the debate, with congressmen arguing over its true meaning and application. One Kentucky congressman retorted, "Still less were the people of the Northwestern Territory a party to the compact, as the gentleman supposed it, not being represented at all, nor consulted on it." A prominent Ohio congressman echoed his Kentucky colleague. Even though he personally opposed slavery, William Henry Harrison—the former governor of Indiana Territory and president of the Vincennes convention of 1803— "wished to see that State, and all that Territory, disenthralled from the effects of articles to which they never gave their assent, and to which they were not prop-erly subject." The congressmen who spoke against Tallmadge's objection each raised the same critical point: they believed that the Northwest Ordinance had impaired the ability of the territory's citizens to determine their own local af-fairs. The debate over slavery in Illinois after statehood was granted persisted into the 1820s and 1830s as the state continued to face questions over legal title to slaves held in Illinois.[58]

Over thirty years had passed since the Northwest Ordinance had asserted federal authority over both the territories and the expansion of slavery. Con-gress had implicitly partitioned slavery in the West, expressly prohibiting it north of the Ohio River and allowing for local determination to the south. North-erners and southerners in Congress and the states had generally agreed to the arrangement, but recalcitrant westerners residing along the border between slavery and freedom continually tested the boundary, causing much dispute in the southernmost portions of the Old Northwest. Further territorial expansion, however, had also tested the limits of the sectional compact. The proposed ex-tension of slavery in the Louisiana Purchase had provoked resistance from northerners who opposed the institution. They recognized that national policy could end slavery in the western lands, whereas it could not in the existing states. James Tallmadge's objection to the 1818 Illinois constitution illustrated the thought of those opposed to the extension of slavery. Just months later he would again raise an objection to slavery in the Territory of Missouri, one that would prove far more notable.

"SHALL THE CREATURE GOVERN

THE CREATOR?"

Self-Government and
the Missouri Compromise

When James Tallmadge rose in the House of Representatives to introduce an amendment to the Missouri statehood bill prohibiting "the further introduction of slavery or involuntary servitude" and providing for the eventual manumission of slaves within its borders, he set into motion a furious debate that threatened the stability of the Union.[1] In the immediate moment of that February day in 1819, many of Tallmadge's colleagues may have wondered why the New York representative proposed an amendment to end slavery in a place where it had existed since its inception as a territory seven years earlier. After the initial shock and the opening volley in the war of words that would span two congresses, it became clear that the debate over statehood for Missouri had inaugurated a new phase in the discussion over the extension of slavery, its effect on American politics, and the idea of slavery itself. The greatest change, however, occurred within southern politics, as the Missouri debates revealed the possibility that antislavery Americans could use the politics of territory making and statehood formation as a means of confining the boundaries of slavery—or eventually eliminating it. Southerners responded with fury that led to the refinement of a states' rights theory of politics driven by the desire to protect the South and slavery from outside interference.

Thomas Jefferson remarked that the Missouri question "like a fire bell in the night, awakened and filled me with terror."[2] His statement—so frequently quoted by historians to illustrate the gravity of the Missouri crisis—lent drama to the Missouri controversy; but it stretched the truth. For over thirty-five years, Americans had debated the effect of extending slavery into the territories. The Missouri controversy, however, presented an altogether different set of circumstances than previous debates on the expansion of slavery. In the past, Congress had wrestled with permitting or prohibiting slavery in the territories well before any discussion of statehood. Some northerners had shown a desire to limit or even halt its extension, while some southerners exhibited the willingness to defend the expansion of a system of labor increasingly becoming *their* peculiar institution. Congress had traced a dividing line between slavery and freedom down the Ohio River, a decision that both North and South viewed as appropriate and equitable, if not perfect. Missouri Territory lay west of the river, but north of the artificial line established by Congress. Nevertheless, after settlers in the territory had petitioned the government to let the people and geography decide whether slavery could exist there, Congress permitted slavery within Missouri.

Thus Tallmadge proposed a startling volte-face when he advocated an end to slavery in Missouri as a condition for statehood. His move awakened and alarmed slaveholders to the possibility that the federal government could use its power to end slavery where it already existed. For Jefferson, who had worked harder than any other political leader to ensure that new states could enter the Union on equal grounds with the older states in perpetuity, the cause for anxiety came not in the threat to slavery itself, but in the fact that the Tallmadge amendment violated the principle of state equality and blurred the lines of power between the states and the federal government. For southerners who believed in the ideals of Jeffersonian republicanism, the New Yorker's preemptive strike against slavery destroyed state equality and impaired states' rights, thereby threatening slavery in the present and future. It breathed new life into the demon of overweening federal power that slaveholders had feared before.[3]

Tallmadge's amendment forced the issue by affirming the power of the center to control the periphery. The congressman and his allies asserted federal authority to prohibit slavery in the West. Southerners who had once acquiesced, if not endorsed, federal authority over the extension of slavery now vehemently disagreed, arguing that only the people within the territories had the right to determine the status of slavery. In this respect, southerners made an equally astounding volte-face by invoking a states' rights doctrine to deny congressional authority over the statehood process. Something remarkable was about to occur, as the South would embrace a revised interpretation of federal authority with impressive but alarming unanimity. Faced with opposition to slavery in a territory where it already existed from an unexpectedly strong northern phalanx, southerners took a defensive posture by denying the right of Congress to affix conditions to statehood. In the end, the South accepted compromise by agreeing to a partition of the national domain into free and slave territory, for which they received Missouri as a slave state. Portraying the compromise as a cold political bargain, however, only captures part of the story. From the Missouri controversy emerged a more ardent proslavery defense that embraced two notions. Both during and after the Missouri controversy, slaveholders would defend their right to hold slaves, assert their rights to carry them into the territories, and demand that northerners respect their equality within the Union.

SOME 10,000 slaves resided in Missouri Territory during the late 1810s, approximately 15 percent of the total population. Although the territory seemed unlikely to become a major producer of the traditional southern agricultural staple—cotton—planters did employ slave labor in a significant hemp-growing market. Regardless of the nature of agriculture in the region, the Missourians expressed a desire to maintain slavery as a labor force.[4] Many had emigrated to the territory from the southern states, bringing with them the political and cultural ideals of a slave society. Indeed, a strong pro-southern and proslavery sentiment existed throughout the territory. Missouri also counted the slave states of Kentucky and Tennessee as its neighbors. Each of these states would try to exert influence in the territory's political formation. Yet geographically the territory itself rested at the outer limits of the traditional slave domain. And because most of Missouri lay north of the Ohio River, some anti-slavery Americans believed that the territory should become a free state. It shared the Mississippi River border with the free state of Illinois, itself an anomaly with its free-soil northern contingent and a population in the southern part of the state sympathetic to slavery and southern interests. Therefore, any debate over the future of slavery in Missouri would test the future northern boundary of the slaveholding section of the Union.

Not long after gaining territorial status, Missourians began clamoring for statehood. Four new states had joined the Union in this decade. Indiana gained statehood in 1816 after definitively settling its own long dispute over slavery within its borders. Congress admitted Illinois two years later under similar circumstances. Two slave states entered the Union immediately following Indiana and Illinois. Mississippi became a state in December 1817, while Alabama, carved out of the eastern portion of the old Mississippi Territory, followed almost exactly two years later. Because Congress had defeated a motion to prohibit slavery in the Mississippi Territory in 1798, no one challenged its existence in the incoming states twenty years later. Thus and not surprisingly, on November 21, 1818, the Missouri territorial legislature applied for admission to the Union, citing a grossly inflated population of 100,000.[5]

Missouri's proposed and contested boundaries necessitated creation of a new territory to the south, Arkansas, which greatly complicated the Missouri issue. Now Congress would have to debate the slavery question both in Missouri, a territory about to become a state, and its nascent southern neighbor. Prominent New York representative John W. Taylor, like Tallmadge an antislavery Republican, moved to insert a clause in the legislation prohibiting slavery in the new territory. While the Missouri issue addressed the right of Congress to legislate on slavery for an established territory seeking admission to the Union, the creation of Arkansas tested whether Congress could or should prohibit slavery in a territory from the outset. With Missouri and Arkansas both on the agenda, the second session of the Fifteenth Congress would address the whole gamut of issues concerning states' rights, self-government, and federal jurisdiction over slavery in the territories.[6]

Contemporaries puzzled at the freshman congressman's motives, and historians since have added little to their conjectures. Thomas Jefferson surmised that New York governor DeWitt Clinton had pushed Tallmadge to propose the amendment as part of a Federalist plot to agitate the slavery issue and thus resuscitate the party, a conjecture that historians have discredited. Tallmadge himself provided a more plausible explanation: he introduced the amendment in an effort simply to halt the spread of slavery.[7] Regardless of his intentions, why so many northern politicians "rallied to Tallmadge's side" intrigues even more. Northern political leaders seemingly desired to make a stand on the slavery extension issue at this time. Tallmadge's objections to Illinois's proposed constitution of 1818 presaged the Missouri controversy, as he represented the wishes of certain northerners who desired to limit the expansion of slavery. A New Hampshire congressman proposed what became the "first intimation of a Northern attempt to restrict slavery in Missouri," but while his attempt at restriction, in the form of a constitutional amendment, failed to gain support, Tallmadge's strategy succeeded.[8]

Over the course of the Missouri controversy, southerners resisted the efforts of northerners to restrict the expansion of slavery into the territories by articulating the doctrines of state sovereignty and self-government, which had been two distinct ideas that now became linked during and after the crisis. Southerners accused Tallmadge and his northern allies of legislating against the wishes of Missourians—and overruling the action of a previous Congress—by violating state sovereignty. In effect, the restrictionists sought to rescind the latitude of self-government over the slavery issue that had been given to the inhabitants' representatives in the territorial act. The Tallmadge amendment, according to its opponents, not only ignored the fact that slavery already existed in Missouri, but it also interfered with the right of Missourians to draft a constitution according to their own wishes. The issues raised in previous discussions over the expansion of slavery and territorial policy—whether Congress or the people within the territories themselves had the right to permit or prohibit slavery—coalesced dangerously in the Missouri debate and produced a true crisis of the Union. Northern restrictionists like Tallmadge sought to assert federal authority over the expansion of slavery; their opponents argued that Congress was limited to ensuring that an incoming state's constitution provided a republican form of government. Southerners, along with their northern allies who composed the antirestrictionist faction, used the concepts of states' rights and self-government to refute congressional intervention on the slavery issue.[9]

Congress had equivocated on the issue of federal power over slavery in the territories in the past, leaving considerable room for debate on how far federal authority extended. The Tallmadge amendment imposed conditions on Missouri as a territory *and* as a state because it effectively rescinded the right to hold slaves in Missouri and imposed conditions on which it could enter the

Union. Tallmadge's amendment assumed federal control over the territories as a routine matter of course by not only placing the question squarely in the domain of Congress, but also by asserting that it could impose conditions on a territory seeking admission into the Union. Southerners found both points unacceptable. Why had the opponents of slavery not raised their objections when Congress created the Territory of Missouri in 1812, they asked? Proslavery individuals doubted the constitutionality of a ban on the institution and the right of Congress to impose it, and they feared the reason why people in the North supported it. Heretofore, southerners only weakly resisted congressional authority over slavery in the territories, but now that an emerging northern antislavery bloc resolved to use congressional authority to prohibit slavery in a territory where it had existed, proslavery leaders would not stand idly by. Southerners began to question the wisdom of federal authority over the territories once it became clear that northern congressmen—both Federalists and some Republicans—could and would act to restrict slavery.

Politics in this so-called Era of Good Feelings played a crucial role in the Missouri controversy, as the crisis shifted already decaying political allegiances and revealed strong proslavery and antislavery voting blocs. The Missouri crisis shattered sectional comity and dissolved existing political affiliations. Missouri's bid for statehood and the ensuing struggle over the slavery question came at a most inopportune time for political parties given their fragile status following the War of 1812. The Federalist Party had become a casualty of the war, suffering a mortal wound dealt by its own members who had considered secession at the ill-fated Hartford Convention. Federalists harbored a long-standing antipathy toward westward expansion, which they believed enhanced the power of the South at the expense of New England. The Hartford Convention, however, had permanently damaged the party's image and power, leaving it impotent to resist the expansion of slavery into the Louisiana Purchase. Federalists remaining in Congress hesitated to take the lead in advocating the restriction of slavery in Missouri, lest the restriction movement ironically become branded with the secessionist label that foes used so successfully against the dying party. Federalists sensed that the Missouri issue could perhaps revitalize their party and create a North-West political alliance against the South, but they also recognized that their involvement could taint the restriction agenda.[10]

The antislavery impetus came from an unexpected corner as the Mid-Atlantic states, especially New York and Pennsylvania, emerged as stalwart restrictionists. Most restrictionists belonged to the Federalist Party, but some northern Republicans joined in opposition to the extension of slavery, having grown resentful in a Jeffersonian political coalition increasingly dominated by southerners. Not only did they fear that the extension of slavery would further augment southern political power, but the northerners also had grown to believe in the immorality of slavery itself. For years the South had espoused the idea of slavery as a necessary evil, advocating diffusion across space as a means of improving the conditions of slaves and perhaps providing the first necessary step for its eventual demise. Thoughtful northerners questioned the actual effects of diffusion and the true intentions of southern slaveholders. A significant number of Republicans from the Mid-Atlantic and Northwest states, men who had previously allied with the South, emerged as proponents of restriction because they believed that their best self-interests required greater public distance from the institution and perhaps even necessitated the demise of slavery itself. Missouri had therefore awakened southerners to the possibility that "in the absence of partisan conflict, where northern politicians had need of southern support, the South had no real allies in its defense of slavery."[11] Tallmadge, a New York Republican, had confirmed their fears.

Southerners reacted strongly because they believed that the restrictionist cause threatened the future of slavery not only in the territories, but perhaps even in the states. After all, the Tallmadge amendment proposed an end—albeit gradual—to slavery in a place where it already existed. For some time, northern and southern Republicans had worked together as allies in Congress. Southerners had come to expect some antislavery agitation from northern Federalists, but the Republican movement to restrict slavery in Missouri caught slaveholders off guard. The southern reaction materialized quickly and with a ferocity not before seen in previous disputes over the expansion of slavery. Slave state representatives responded to the threat as a united sectional bloc, regardless of party affiliation.[12]

In "probably the most candid discussion of slavery ever held in Congress," northerners rallied behind the Tallmadge effort, while southerners battled against what they saw as a bold usurpation of local power and states' rights. The opponents of restriction "contended that Congress had no right to prescribe to any State the details of its government, any further than that it should be republican in its form." Besides, any territory once admitted to statehood possessed the "unquestioned right" to amend its constitution, therefore rendering the whole debate moot. Restrictionists refuted this claim by arguing that "Congress had the right to annex conditions to the admission of any new State" and that slavery "was incompatible with our Republican institutions." Put simply, Congress had a duty to impose the ban on slavery in Missouri.[13]

Key northern congressmen allied with Tallmadge to assert federal authority over slavery in Missouri. John Taylor helped frame the agenda for the antislavery effort by placing two questions before his colleagues: did Congress have the authority to demand that Missouri's constitution prohibit slavery as a condition of statehood? And if so, should Congress do it?[14] He answered both in the affirmative, interpreting Article Four, Section Three of the Constitution, the territorial clause, as granting "unlimited" authority to Congress in the matter. "It would be difficult," Taylor argued, "to devise a more comprehensive grant of power." Politicians had debated the true meaning of the "needful rules and regulations" clause before; but from the Missouri debates to secession in 1860–1861, the provision would attract the attention of almost every individual considering the limits of congressional power over slavery in the territories. Taylor had articulated the argument that northern Republicans would use over the course of the Missouri controversy: Congress could and must prohibit slavery in Missouri. Concern for morality or rather the immorality of the institution and securing true republican government ostensibly motivated the northern faction. "At the heart of the Republicans' reasoning," argues historian Sean Wilentz, "was their claim that the preservation of individual rights, and strict construction of the Constitution, demanded slavery's restriction."[15] Without irony southerners had already resorted to Federalist attacks that states' rights, preservation of individual rights, and strict construction demanded that Congress not interfere with slavery.

The Missouri controversy caused a schism within the Jeffersonian Republican party as northerners took up the antislavery cause and the South united (regardless of political affiliation) to resist congressional power over slavery in the territories and those states seeking admission to the Union. In the middle stood a small but influential group of northern and southern nationalists committed to preserving the Union by quieting the rhetoric on both sides of the issue. Speaker of the House Henry Clay of Kentucky led the moderate nationalists, even as he initially refuted key points of the northern argument. Congress had "no right to prescribe any condition whatever to the newly organized States," Clay argued, "but must admit them by a simple act, leaving their sovereignty unrestricted."[16] The Speaker went further, challenging the northerners who criticized the South's peculiar institution. "What comparison did he make between the 'black slaves' of Kentucky and the 'white slaves' of the north," the *Washing-*

Speaker of the House Henry Clay, a Kentucky slaveholder who
nevertheless expressed a desire to gradually end the institution,
shepherded the Missouri Compromise through a contentious debate
over federal power in the nation's periphery. (Library of Congress)

ton Daily Intelligencer commented, "and how instantly did he strike a balance in
favor of the condition of the former."[17] Clay's efforts notwithstanding, northern
Republicans had touched a raw nerve in the South, which intensified the tenor
of the debate on Missouri. Federalists joined their erstwhile opponents, seeking
to earn much-needed political capital and perhaps reinvigorate their party by
forming a sectional bloc opposed to the power of the South in the form of the
Missouri statehood bill. A Massachusetts Federalist challenged the Clay rejoin-

der, stating, "The attempt to extend slavery to the new States is in direct violation of the clause which guaranties a republican form of government to all the
States."[18] Interestingly if erroneously, many southerners "insisted at every turn
that Federalists were the principal *provocateurs*."[19] Federalists certainly saw the
debates as a golden opportunity to exploit the slavery issue in an effort to regain
lost political power, yet northern Republicans led the restriction vanguard.
More ominously, the Missouri controversy ushered in more of a sectional than
party division. Although the Era of Good Feelings marked the end of interparty
conflict on key economic issues that had animated Jeffersonians and Federalists, the Missouri crisis revealed that the politics of slavery could fill the void,
thereby dividing the nation along sectional lines over the extension of slavery.

The key to understanding the southern response to restriction lay in how
they interpreted the Constitution. They quickly countered that the document
forbade infringing on the rights of a people to draft a state constitution. Put in
reductive terms, southerners now argued that the sanctity of state sovereignty
extended to the people of a territory when drafting a constitution and seeking
admission to the Union.[20] Heretofore few southerners had objected in the past
to federal control over the territories because Congress always had protected
the interests of slavery where it would most likely flourish. The South began to
reconsider its position on federal authority, however, when northern congressmen sought to restrict the institution. Philip P. Barbour of Virginia, for one, suggested that if Congress had wished to ban slavery in Missouri, it should have
done so through territorial legislation. The Old Republican asserted, however,
that Congress should consult the people of Missouri to discern their opinions
on the issue, "because [otherwise] we should be legislating directly against the
wishes of a people who were competent to legislate for themselves."[21]

Barbour made clear the southern stance: Congress could not abrogate the
people's right to draft their own state constitution as they saw fit, save that it embody republican principles. Missourians themselves joined in chorus, revealing
their bitter resentment of restriction. Territorial delegate John Scott thundered
against the Tallmadge amendment, accusing restrictionists of reducing Missouri to a lesser among equals. The proposed amendment created a "discrimi-
nation not warranted by the Constitution."[22] Congress had no right to prescribe
conditions to admission into the Union, even according to James Madison, who
argued that Congress must only ascertain that the incoming state guaranteed a
republican form of government. Beyond that, all decisions were reserved to the
local authorities. As Scott explained: "In no part of the Constitution was the

power proposed to be exercised, of imposing conditions on a new State . . . nor in any portion of the Constitution was the right prohibited to the respective States, to regulate their own internal police, of admitting such citizens as they pleased, or of introducing any description of property, that they should consider as essential or necessary to their prosperity."[23] The restrictionists had proposed exactly what Madison had pronounced unconstitutional. Missourians could not abide this infringement on their rights. Antirestrictionists, however, failed to persuade a sufficient number of their colleagues that Congress could not impose the Tallmadge amendment on the Missouri statehood bill. After a closing statement by its author, the amendment passed in the House of Representatives on a strictly sectional vote.[24]

With the Missouri bill dispatched to the upper chamber, the House commenced deliberations on the territorial bill for Arkansas. Almost immediately, John Taylor moved to insert a clause in the legislation prohibiting slavery in the new territory.[25] Although the Missouri debate addressed the right of Congress to legislate on slavery for a prospective state, the creation of Arkansas would test whether Congress could or should prohibit slavery in a territory from the outset.

Slave-state congressmen rallied in opposition to Taylor's effort to prohibit slavery in Arkansas, arguing that the people who actually lived there should make the decision for themselves. For forty years after the debates of 1820, southerners would maintain that the purest form of popular sovereignty lay in the unfettered right of a people to draft a state constitution free from congressional interference and thereby decide on the future of slavery for themselves. In the Arkansas debate, however, one sees a tentative but unmistakable step of extending popular sovereignty to a territorial government. Felix Walker of North Carolina contended that Congress had "no legitimate power to legislate on the property of the citizens." The northern effort to restrict slavery in Arkansas Territory encroached on the rights of slaveholders who might wish to settle there. More important, according to Walker, it deprived "the people of this territory the natural and Constitutional right of legislating for themselves, and impos[ed] on them a condition which they may not willingly accept." His argument drew from the reasoning of Thomas Jefferson, who since drafting the Ordinance of 1784 had contended that a future state could enter the Union on the basis of equality with the existing states only "if it constituted itself, without outside interference, and if it was received into the union 'on an equal footing.'" The Jeffersonian interpretation of territories, statehood, and Union served as the bedrock of southern opposition to restriction and southerners' endorsement

of congressional nonintervention. Walker articulated and built on the Jeffersonian view more clearly than any of his colleagues. "In organizing a territorial government, and forming a constitution," he contended, "they and they alone, have
the right, and are the proper judges of that policy best adapted to their genius
and interest, and it ought to be exclusively left to them."[26]

In deeming the people of Arkansas and the western territories "competent
judges of their Constitutional rights" and therefore able to settle the slavery
question for themselves, Walker had given form to the doctrine of popular sovereignty as no one else had done before.[27] His formula for territorial self-
government seemed to suggest that the settlers of Arkansas could legislate on
the slavery issue in the earliest stages of territorial development. Walker, however, never seemed to consider that self-government could produce any other
outcome than securing slavery in Arkansas or any other territory. Most likely
he concerned himself with present circumstances alone, believing that southerners would migrate to Arkansas and secure its status as a future slave state.
Southerners of the next generation, however, would learn that territorial self-
government could work against slaveholding interests.

Walker's colleagues expressed some trepidation at his call for self-
government on the frontier. Refusing to concede constitutional ground to the antirestrictionists, but in "an effort to do justice to our Southern brethren," a Massachusetts Federalist suggested that Congress permit slavery in Arkansas
Territory to balance the effect of restriction in Missouri and thus avoid the issue
of territorial sovereignty. Several congressmen, in fact, began suggesting some
form of compromise to settle the dispute over restriction. Louis McLane, a freshman representative from Delaware, attempted to steer clear of Walker's proposal
for territorial sovereignty while "fixing of a line west of the Mississippi, north of
which slavery should not be tolerated"—in other words, extending the Ohio
River precedent. Indeed, a number of congressmen had begun considering compromise proposals that extended the dividing line between slavery and freedom.
After the House rejected John Taylor's amendment to prohibit slavery in the
Arkansas Territory, he offered a second amendment that would ban slavery
north of the line of north latitude 36 degrees, 30 minutes. His second effort failed
as well, drawing criticism from Virginians who feared compromising on the
question of state sovereignty. The most strident southerners argued that the proposal created inequality in the territories "by applying a rule to one portion and a
different rule to another portion of citizens having equal rights and placed under
similar circumstances"—something that had not troubled their predecessors

who had endorsed the Northwest and Southwest Ordinances. Politicians quickly passed the bill creating the territory, effective July 4, 1819, realizing that they still had to settle the Missouri issue. The territorial legislation contained no mention of slavery, implicitly leaving the matter to the people.[28]

Restrictionists scored a victory when they passed the Missouri bill with the Tallmadge amendment, but the Senate, after "a long and animated debate," refused to concur. Thomas Ritchie, editor of the *Richmond Enquirer* and a devoted Old Republican, held out hope that the Senate would "strike out this obnoxious feature. It is a struggle of Eastern prejudice against southern principles." He had good reason to express optimism. The northern states held a majority of seats in the Senate, but southerners believed they could count on the support of Illinois's senators. The Senate divided the question of restriction and considered the two stipulations of the Tallmadge amendment separately. Senators voted against the latter part, which provided for the gradual emancipation of slaves in Missouri, by seven to thirty-one. A more closely divided Senate also voted down the motion to prohibit slavery in the state of Missouri. The Illinois delegation, a Vermont senator, and the enigmatic Federalist Harrison Gray Otis of Massachusetts voted with the entire southern contingent to strike down this part of the Tallmadge amendment. Absent a consensus between the two houses of Congress on the slavery issue, Missouri remained a territory at the end of the second session of the Fifteenth Congress.[29]

People across the country took up the Missouri debate where their representatives had left off. Newspapers published a voluminous correspondence that revealed just how significant the slavery issue had become outside of Washington. Missourians in particular argued their case with great force. Nathaniel Beverley Tucker, writing under the pseudonym "Hampden," considered the restriction an insult to the citizens of Missouri Territory who had proved their loyalty in the War of 1812. Tucker, a Virginian who had emigrated to Missouri in 1816 and had been appointed as a judge in St. Louis, emerged as a leading voice against restriction. He reminded his audience that as Americans, the citizens of Missouri deserved the right to legislate their own local affairs. He took particular aim at those who misinterpreted the needful rules and regulations clause of the Constitution to sanction restriction. Offering an opinion that would become a staple of the southern movement against congressional interference with slavery, Hampden argued that the clause had nothing to do with congressional authority over local law; instead, it addressed federal property in the territories.[30]

Linking notions of territorial authority with the Tenth Amendment to the Constitution—the bulwark of states' rights ideology—Hampden argued that self-government "is inherent in, and is moreover expressly 'reserved to the states respectively, or to the people.' The state of Missouri then, can derive none of its *powers* from Congress; all it needs from that quarter is the *means of organization*." Northerners who supported restriction earned the enmity of many southerners who now asserted that state sovereignty made that encroachment on states' rights unconstitutional. "Is it not insulting to our common sense, to be told that a constitution not only permitting, but partly based on domestic slavery" would allow for federal interdiction of the institution, Hampden asked. "But it is just such a doctrine as I should expect to hear" from those who believed that *"congress have power to make laws to bind the territory in all cases whatsoever."* Local committees also met and passed resolutions denouncing the Tallmadge amendment. A citizens' meeting in Montgomery County, Missouri, attacked the hypocrisy of Congress in admitting Alabama Territory without restriction, "while the people of this territory have been refused, unless they would stoop to a condition, which degrades them below the rank of free men, and lays the foundation of a slavery more abject than that which congress pretends to be so zealous to reform."[31]

Proslavery Missourians portrayed restrictionists' efforts as an attack on the freedom of American citizens residing in the territory to govern themselves. "If congress can with impunity enforce a single restriction in direct opposition to the will of the people of this territory," argued one correspondent, "they may go on to what lengths they please, fearless of our being able to compete with them." When someone did speak out in favor of restriction as a way to protect the idea of free labor in the territory, fellow citizens responded with more attacks on the actions of Congress. "Are the only legitimate sovereigns on earth to be told that they hold their liberties at the will of 'seventy-eight' of their servants" who voted for the Tallmadge amendment, a proslavery Missourian asked. "Shall the *creature* be permitted to assume an absolute sovereignty over his *creator*, and to stifle even an inquiry into his powers?"[32]

To the minds of southerners, restrictionists asserted that living in a territory necessitated surrender of certain rights enjoyed by Americans living in the states and that Congress could dictate the terms on which a territory could then become a state. In sum, restrictionists intended to strike a blow indirectly at states' rights and local government by restricting the authority of an incoming state. Imposing conditions on territories seemed to contradict the idea that people could govern themselves. Why could not Americans living in a territory govern their affairs with as much competence as those residing in a state? Both restrictionists and their opponents had stumbled over a series of legal questions that had confounded politicians since Thomas Jefferson had drafted the Ordinance of 1784. By its own uncertainty, the federal government had created a sort of liminal state where a territory became imbued with the power to draft a constitution and apply for statehood. No one disputed that a territory had to seek permission to draft a constitution and seek entry to the Union; but could Congress dictate what provisions its constitution must or must not contain? Southerners contended that congressional oversight only extended to ensuring that a new state's constitution was republican in character. All other power ended with the conferral of the power to draft a constitution.

Forced to respond to rising antislavery sentiment during the Missouri crisis, southern politicians insisted that states' rights began with the power to craft organic law. Each territory seeking admission had a right to create its own organic law, a constitutional theory of popular sovereignty steeped in Jeffersonian republican ideology that "became the centerpiece of the southern stand against restriction." Voicing a concern of many southerners, Beverley Tucker claimed that restriction would "establish a precedent that will sap the foundation of state authority and make this federal government a consolidated nation." Ignoring the Northwest Ordinance, he argued that Congress could not restrict the right of a citizen to move to any territory with his personal property. The fact that a person held slaves as property did not allow for an exception to the rule. When a territory prepared for statehood, its inhabitants could decide in convention whether to permit or prohibit the institution of slavery within its bounds. This authority, according to a Kentucky writer who appealed to the logic of the Tenth Amendment, "is unquestionably one of those rights which the citizens did not surrender by the federal constitution."[33] According to southerners, the restrictionists proposed to take away the sovereign right of the people of Missouri and subject them to the will of Congress merely because they resided in a territory rather than a state.

Restriction also drew criticism from individuals who noted that the third article of the treaty of cession between France and the United States—the Missourians' "Magna Carta," in the words of one historian—had guaranteed the property rights of the residents of the Louisiana Purchase. Ignoring the treaty's stipulation "divested [Missourians] of the only right which gives value to citizenship—the right of governing themselves."[34] Because the federal government had made no effort to prohibit slavery in Missouri at the outset of its territorial period, settlers in the region considered the restriction movement in the Fifteenth Congress doubly impolitic. In the period between sessions of Congress, antirestrictionist writers reminded the public of the treaty as yet another reason to challenge the authority that the restrictionists claimed for the federal government.

The South viewed restriction as the first step in circumscribing the boundaries of slavery, the expansion, and ultimately the safety of the South. Accordingly, southern politicians used the rhetoric of states' rights and popular sovereignty to resist the restrictionist movement in the North. Free white men, according to the southern argument, had the right to emigrate with their property wherever they desired. Furthermore, they possessed the power to form their own government and domestic institutions when crafting a sovereign state out of a territory. Restriction jeopardized southern interests by threatening the right of Americans in the territories to choose between permitting or prohibiting slavery.

Opponents of restriction in the South and West seized these issues to use as ammunition against the antislavery northerners, charging them with trying to upset the sectional balance of power and even questioning their loyalty. Some labeled opponents of self-government in Missouri as supporters of the secessionist Hartford Convention or members of the Essex Junto, an alleged cadre of New England sectionalists. By linking the restrictionists with the idea of secession, southerners hoped to completely discredit their movement. They believed that northerners ignorantly impugned the character and honor and allegiance of western settlers. But these so-called "enlightened men" of the North would find themselves "wofully [sic] disappointed if they expect that the people here have degenerated, have forgotten the rights which they will never alienate because they inhabit a territory, or have not had the good luck to come from the Land of Steady Habits."[35]

In between congressional sessions, southerners and Missourians laid out a comprehensive rebuttal of the argument for the restriction of slavery. Though many politicians conceded that the federal government had a role to play in organizing territories, southerners insisted that slavery remained beyond the jurisdiction of Congress. Northerners, however, rejected the notion that Congress did not possess the discretionary power to impose conditions upon a territory asking for admission to the Union. Congress could and should use its power to admit new states as it deemed fit, and to stipulate conditions for the admittance of a new state. Although the Constitution "admits all the *original* states to hold slaves as they please," an observer wrote, the *"discretionary* power granted to admit new states into the union, by simply saying, 'new states may be admitted,' necessarily supposes a right in congress to designate the conditions of admission." As an Illinois correspondent noted, if Congress could not impose conditions on admission, then the federal government had robbed Illinois of the right to establish slavery within its bounds.[36]

Using the Tenth Amendment and the concept of states' rights, southerners accused antislavery leaders of endorsing federal consolidation. In rebuttal, northerners criticized southern leaders for their disingenuous defense of self-government. "In an extent of country capable of supporting six millions of our inhabitants," an Illinois editor asked, "shall it be considered a reasonable demand for the nation to allow a few thousand the right of deciding a question of such vital importance, merely because the few, from pecuniary interest, wish for the future toleration of slavery?"[37] The writer did not necessarily oppose submitting the decision to the will of the people, but he contended that all of the people and not just those in Missouri had a right to decide the issue. Both sides argued that all of the United States had purchased the territories with common treasure. Both sides used theories of constitutional law to support their respective arguments that slavery should or should not pass into the territories of the Louisiana Purchase. And both sides attempted to galvanize popular majorities to support their reasoning.

As the days of late autumn passed and the country prepared for the opening of the Sixteenth Congress, the Missouri issue increasingly became a struggle over constitutional interpretation. Americans frequently met in committee to discuss political issues and issue resolutions expressing their views to their elected representatives. At numerous meetings in the northeastern states, restrictionists claimed that Congress could deny admission to statehood if it considered slavery "to be inconsistent or inimical to republican institutions."[38] Recriminations flew back and forth in the war of words over the extension of slavery as both sides used republican rhetoric to gain political advantage ahead of the upcoming session. Southerners, too, sought to fuse the link between their section and the West by appealing to the democratic spirit of settlers on the frontier.

Numerous conventions met in the largest northern states to express their support for the restriction of slavery in Missouri, a development that Thomas Ritchie considered a "source of regret to the southern and western states." In the autumn of 1820, citizens held a final set of meetings at Trenton, New Jersey, New York City, Philadelphia, Boston, and other northern cities. On the whole, they added little to the debate that had raged all summer and fall, but their proceedings suggest a further hardening of the sectional lines that divided the nation on Missouri's admission. Each committee passed resolutions stating that Congress did have the power and the obligation "to prohibit the admission of slavery into any state or territory hereafter to be formed and admitted into the union." Indeed, the "honor and interests of the country" demanded congressional action. Of course, southerners and the Missourians responded in kind, arguing that the "solemn faith" of the nation demanded Missouri's admission "on an equal footing with the other states." They also exhibited considerable resentment that Missouri's proposed admission to statehood had become entwined with the larger issue of slavery. "Nothing has been done to promote our local interests," argued a Kentucky correspondent, "and every scheme to give us a fair participation in the benefits of the union, has been thwarted or defeated."[39]

Southerners and proslavery westerners resented northerners' attempts to thwart admission for Missouri because they increasingly viewed the restriction movement as part of a broader movement to end slavery. Sensing the gravity of the issue, state legislatures throughout the Union passed resolutions addressing the crisis. Nine northern states passed resolutions instructing senators to vote for restriction in Missouri, a stance that southerners decried as an attack on their section. A series of resolutions from Pennsylvania particularly offended antirestrictionists. Ritchie stated, "It is contrary to the whole genius of our constitution to colonize the regions to the West of the Mississippi."[40] The northern scheme promised to deny western settlers their rights by transforming their choice of residence into a colony. Southerners found this unacceptable.

As legislatures in state capitals and citizens in public meetings weighed in on the right of Congress to restrict the expansion of slavery, James Monroe monitored the debate from Washington. The president had remained silent on the matter in his State of the Union message to Congress in December 1819, but he expressed privately his opinions to advisors. To his son-in-law and political confidant George Hay, he wrote, "I indulge a strong hope that the restriction will not pass." The Virginian Monroe, who had disputed the constitutionality of the Northwest Ordinance's prohibition of slavery, sided with the South on the Missouri issue by arguing that Congress could not admit a new state on conditions different from the old states and that it could not prohibit slavery in the territories. In questioning the force of the Northwest Ordinance, Monroe represented the prevailing opinion of his home state—and indeed the South at large. Ignoring southern support for the Northwest Ordinance some forty years earlier, Ritchie had cited the 1787 act as a "usurpation" of power and believed that the ordinance had gained passage "without adequate discussion and deliberation."[41]

Unlike Ritchie and many of his Old Republican colleagues from Virginia, the president did appear amenable to some sort of compromise to end the increasingly dangerous dispute, although he could not say so publicly. Indeed, the Old Republicans' strong opposition to any compromise on the matter left Monroe in a politically precarious situation. If Monroe and his advisors openly endorsed a compromise, "they were vulnerable to attack from the South because of their broadly national stance; they could hardly allow themselves to appear flexible in the defense of slavery." The president faced reelection in 1820; if he wanted a second term, he had to pay heed to the opinions of his southern power base—particularly Virginia—by resisting the northern encroachment on the South's peculiar institution. He also had to keep the nation from falling apart over slavery in the territories.[42]

When the members of a new Congress arrived in Washington, returning to the Capitol for the first time since the British had burned the structure in 1814, they faced the grim task of resolving the crisis over Missouri and restoring sectional comity. One absence from the House of Representatives gained notice; an ailing James Tallmadge had declined to run for a seat in the new Congress. The end of his short tenure, however, certainly did not mark the death of his amendment. Three weeks later, the House of Representatives resumed debate on the Missouri statehood bill. Speaker of the House Henry Clay left the Speaker's chair to deliver a speech from the floor, in which he recapitulated the debate that had consumed the second session of the last Congress. The Speaker took the position of his fellow southerners and westerners by arguing that his northern colleagues attempted to treat the territory like "she is our vassal, and we have the right to affix to her conditions not applicable to the States on this side of the Mississippi." Clay rejected such expansive congressional authority, arguing, "When the population and extent of a territory had been such as to entitle a territory to the privilege of self-government, and the rank of a State, the single question had presented itself to admit or reject it, without qualification."[43]

The Speaker's opening remarks on the Missouri bill left little doubt that the affair had become a great debate over constitutional interpretation as it pertained to slavery, states' rights, and self-government. Northerners had committed a grievous error, southerners estimated, by seizing on the Missouri bill as an opening to attack the institution of slavery. As the debate in Congress proceeded, legislators from North and South lined up to offer their interpretation of the Constitution's impact on the issue of slavery in the territories. Again, southerners argued that the federal government had no power to restrict Missouri's sovereign right to permit or prohibit slavery within its bounds. In the previous session of Congress, the Senate had remained largely silent on the matter, leaving members of the House of Representatives to conduct a vigorous debate. In this session, however, senators eagerly engaged the issues first raised in the House. Both of Georgia's senators rose in defense of slavery in Missouri. In addition to the now-familiar arguments of congressional authority over slavery in the territories and the terms of the treaty of cession and its impact on the rights of slave owners, the concept of self-government emerged in the Senate debate. Georgia's Freeman Walker argued that the citizens of Missouri, "who certainly ought to be esteemed at least as capable of judging of this matter as those so far removed," opposed congressional interference, instead "wishing to have the privilege of regulating their internal police as in their judgment shall best promote their happiness and welfare." His argument resonated in the minds of those who objected to congressional interference with Missouri's right to draft a constitution of its own choosing. "Let us grant to them the boon of self-government without alloy," Walker declared.[44]

Just as southern members of Congress took the lead in assaulting the northern restriction effort to "alloy" the right of self-government and restrict the expansion of slavery in Missouri, so, too, did the southern press coordinate resistance outside of Washington. In particular, Ritchie's *Richmond Enquirer* became a leading voice against restriction. One regular correspondent took great care in analyzing the nature of territorial government itself, citing the "temporary" character of a territory. Restricting slavery hardly represented a needful rule or regulation as envisioned by the framers of the Constitution; indeed, it embodied an abuse of power. Northerners proposed a massive expansion of federal power over territorial organization and state making. They resolved to force policies on the people of Missouri that they did not want. "And if we can make their constitution, and render it perpetual," argued a Virginian, "what will the people of that territory be but *slaves*?"[45]

Southerners insisted that northern restrictionists desired to force their beliefs on the people of Missouri against their will, an unacceptable infringement on their personal liberty. In speech after speech, southern congressmen attacked the northern antislavery vanguard and its cavalier attitude toward the sovereignty of the people. "A wise Legislature," noted Senator Nathaniel Macon of North Carolina, "will always consider the character, condition, and feeling, of those to be legislated for." He charged that Senator Rufus King, recognized as the Senate's leader on restriction, and his antislavery colleagues meant to run roughshod over the rights of settlers in Missouri, instead of leaving them "free to do as they pleased." Northerners had made an issue of the expansion of slavery, and in their zeal they threatened the Missourians' right to choose whether to become a free or slave state.[46]

To southerners who believed in the virtues of states' rights and self-government, the northern restriction movement proved that the specter of consolidation loomed larger than ever before. Across the Capitol rotunda in the House of Representatives, southerners gained a northern ally who spoke in uncommonly prescient terms about the danger of the Missouri debates. Henry Meigs, a lawyer and first-term Republican congressman from New York, lamented the "increasing spirit of local and sectional envy and dislike between the North and South." He gave a wide-ranging defense of the principles of self-government, noting that Congress could not and should not meddle in Missouri's sovereign right to govern its own local affairs. "We are attempting here to legislate for Missouri, without a due attention to the situation, the genius of the people, soil, climate, and all the matters which ought to constitute good law." In a thinly veiled attack on the New England Federalists, Meigs chastised the efforts of those who held "in doubt and apparent dread the extension of Republican Government." Why did they fear the will of the people?[47]

Southerners cried that the restrictionists' argument treated the Missourians as children and viewed them as inferior to the men of the East, which betrayed a northeastern elitism that incensed southerners. But Meigs advanced the antirestriction argument further by articulating a theory that would become famous some thirty-five years later. He argued that Congress had no power to enact laws "contrary to the genius and will of a people. . . . Such attempts will be mere absurdities—violence will be committed upon the fundamental principles of all law, and can never be executed."[48] Meigs likely drew from knowledge of northwesterners' evasion of the slavery prohibition in the Northwest Territory as he made a crucial point that became a foundation of the argument for self-government: settlers would only stand for so much federal interference before they started evading the law. Consequently, it behooved Congress to practice a policy of nonintervention not only as a matter of *right*, but of *expediency*.

In other words, Meigs argued, Congress did not possess the power to prohibit slavery in Missouri, nor did it really want that authority lest it offend the settlers and provoke resistance to the rule of law. His speech garnered praise from his southern colleagues and enmity from those of the North, especially New England Federalists, whom he attacked most strongly. Certainly southerners agreed with his characterization of the Federalists, particularly King, who had become a favorite target of the southern press. "With this evidence of feeling and of fact before his eyes," the *Richmond Enquirer* asked, "will Mr. King contend that it is expedient to go on?—What! are the opinions of the people of Missouri, having the deepest interest in the question, nothing?"[49]

Jeffersonian Republicans from both the North and South, who espoused the principles of limited national government, strict construction, and states' rights, had united in opposition to restriction. Their ideological affinity on the issue of governance transcended differences over the institution of slavery, thereby providing a united phalanx against restriction in the short term and the groundwork for the Democratic Party organization that would emerge in the 1820s. Other northern Republicans joined Meigs in his criticism of the restrictionists' efforts, noting that discussing the slavery question in national councils threatened the safety of the Union. Mathew Carey, a Philadelphia printer and political practitioner of the Jeffersonian Republican persuasion, rejected the efforts to prohibit slavery in Missouri and warned of dire consequences if "we are to persist in shackling her with restrictions." Carey opposed slavery; indeed, he argued that had southerners looked to the future, they would themselves have approved a restriction similar to the Northwest Ordinance. But many southerners did not believe restriction constitutionally possible. Carey assessed the southern argument, especially the notion that restriction would deprive southerners of equal rights within the Union, and deemed it "sufficiently plausible." Northerners erred in using Missouri as a convenient means of attacking the institution of slavery, according to Carey and Meigs, and in the process they endangered the Union. Though Carey expressed his belief in the evil of slavery, his constitutional arguments could not have pleased southerners more. Men like Carey and Meigs proved that the South still had allies in the northern states; their pronouncements bade well for compromise and for making slavery a completely local matter.[50]

At the same time that southerners chided northern restrictionists for interfering in the purely local matter of slavery in the territories and newly created states, they also struck back at the northern attack on the institution of slavery itself. For generations before the Missouri crisis, southern politicians characterized slavery as an evil foisted upon them by their ancestors. Leaders expressed hope that someday the institution would pass away through means most often left unclear. Some politicians, like Henry Clay, argued that African colonization provided the best solution for the problem. Contemporaries and historians alike have questioned the sincerity of these pronouncements in favor of a gradual end to the peculiar institution. The Missouri crisis, however, changed the southern position on slavery. When northerners attacked slavery in the debates over Missouri, "southern congressmen had no choice but to defend it." Senator Macon of North Carolina, an early leader in the southern defense of slavery, challenged northerners' arguments. "The Constitution tolerates [slavery]; and that was not adopted from necessity, but through choice. If the necessity ever ceases, who is to decide when? Congress did not decide for Pennsylvania, or any other State; she decided for herself. Let Missouri do the same." Some writers went a step further, offering a biblical and historical defense of slavery designed to refute the institution's critics and discredit their efforts to cast the South in an unfavorable light over the issue. As the Missouri debate continued and ideological lines hardened, "leading white southerners accepted their section's identification with slavery and fought for its interests and reputation with increasing vigor," a development that marked a significant change in the southern stance on slavery.[51]

Even as the debates exhibited the increasing intransigence of both sides on the issue of slavery's expansion into the territories and new states, congressional leaders explored compromise. Samuel Foot of Connecticut suggested that Congress should leave the question "to the good sense of the people of the States to be formed out of that Territory," but if anyone questioned the right of slavery to exist in any such state, "it might be left for the proper tribunal, the Supreme Court, to determine it." Foot's proposal sounded much like popular sovereignty, or permitting the people to make their own decision, but it actually discouraged such a popular referendum on the issue of slavery by placing the issue under the jurisdiction of the federal judiciary. Given the makeup of the Supreme Court in 1820, with the nationalist John Marshall as its chief justice, the tribunal would almost undoubtedly have sided with the restrictionists. Indeed, southerners feared the nationalist impulse of the Supreme Court as well, viewing the recent decision in *McCulloch v. Maryland* as a harbinger of federal consolidation that might not bode well for the future of slavery. Foot's suggestion went nowhere, but some twenty-eight years later John Clayton, a Delaware

Whig congressman, would revive the notion when Congress became mired in a debate over slavery in the Mexican Cession.[52]

Northern Republicans composed the vanguard for compromise. The first overtures toward a mutual concession on the slavery issue had emerged in the previous Congress, when Louis McLane of Delaware, a congressman from a state evenly divided over the slavery issue, proposed to draw a dividing line between free and slave territory. The plan died in that session, but by January 1820 it had gained momentum. Another proposal would have banned slavery in any territory north of the thirty-eighth parallel, a compromise that the House rejected for the moment. But on February 3, Illinois Senator Jesse Thomas made a similar proposal in the upper chamber, suggesting that Congress prohibit slavery in the Louisiana Purchase—excepting Missouri—north of the line thirty-six degrees, thirty minutes. Because the southerners in the Senate had successfully maneuvered to combine the admission of Maine with that of Missouri, Thomas's proposal seemed an appropriate compromise. Maine would enter the Union as a free state, Missouri would become a slave state, and slavery would be prohibited in the remainder of the Louisiana Purchase, save the newly created Arkansas Territory.[53]

The Thomas plan seemed to offer a way out of the congressional impasse. Yet the southern maneuver to link Maine and Missouri's statehood had "deeply alienated the North and stiffened the South." The ensuing debates in the House and Senate reflected animosity on both sides, even as certain individuals moved toward compromise. Circumstances in his home state forced McLane to approach the debate warily. Though he argued "that Congress does not possess the power to impose the contemplated restriction," McLane shied away from the states' rights pronouncements of his southern colleagues. Instead he asserted that Congress had vacated its power to impose conditions on Missouri when it permitted slavery in the territorial enabling bill. He faltered on the question of congressional jurisdiction over slavery in the territories. In some parts of his speech, he maintained that only the people themselves could make their own municipal regulations, while in other instances he noted that Congress "can give laws to a Territory." His lack of consistency revealed that most politicians concerned themselves more with the sovereign right of a territorial convention to draft a constitution than the policy of congressional oversight during the territorial phase.[54]

The Old Republicans of Virginia emerged as the most ardent defenders of southern interests and slavery in the territories, advancing arguments against restriction that threatened the initiative for compromise. "Can we compromise with the constitution of our country?" Ritchie asked. The Thomas compromise proposal did just that, according to Ritchie. Another Virginian noted that the "publick mind is all in a ferment about this compromise spoke of in Washington." The writer concurred with Ritchie's condemnation of compromise. "If the Southern people yield —the consequences will be serious—and unless the Northern people retrace their steps, the result will be equally so—the naked question will then be presented—war or disunion." Congress could not legally restrict even a territory, according to some of the southern conservatives. After a speech by an Illinois congressman, who mockingly accused southern supporters of Thomas's compromise overtures "as conceding the point, that Congress has the power to make the restriction or territorial prohibition perpetual and binding on the States hereafter," the ardent states' rights members of Congress stood firm in their convictions.[55]

Philip Barbour of Virginia advanced one of the most sophisticated arguments about congressional power and territorial sovereignty in the course of the debate. For the sake of argument, he demurred on the original question of territorial sovereignty—though he suggested that the people of a territory had the right to determine their own local institutions—and assumed a position similar to that of Louis McLane. Even conceding that point (for the sake of argument only), Barbour posited, Congress had delegated the power of local legislation by statute. In the case of Missouri, he noted, "we have, by one of our own regulations, given it a legislative body; that we have extended to that body the whole power of legislation, subject only to the limitation that their laws shall not be inconsistent with the Constitution and laws of the United States." Because "the question of slavery is one of a legislative character; it, therefore, already belongs to them to decide it by our own grant." John Scott of Missouri quickly adopted the argument of Barbour and the Old Republicans, noting that when Congress promoted Missouri to the second grade of territorial government, it ended congressional "superintendence over the laws of the territory" and gave the territorial legislature "all legislative power without reserve."[56]

The reasoning of the Old Republicans and their zealous western allies established their definition of popular sovereignty as the right of a prospective state to draft its constitution without interference, thereby placing the issue of slavery extension outside of congressional jurisdiction. They had not yet advanced the notion of territorial sovereignty, but had laid the groundwork for it in the future. Southerners contended that Congress had "already spoken on the slavery issue" when it established territorial governments for Louisiana, Missouri, and Arkansas, without legislating on the issue of slavery, but northerners persisted in bending the "needful rules and regulations" clause of the Constitution to re-assert authority over the issue. A South Carolinian argued that "in making such regulations for the government of the territory, [Congress is] no more author-ized to inhibit slavery in the territory, than they are in the State—for, if they should have the power, it would indirectly effect the same thing." Southern politicians and their constituents continued to ascribe the actions of northern-ers to a concerted effort at augmenting federal authority and assaulting the in-stitution of slavery by advancing a dubious interpretation of the Constitution.[57]

Northern restrictionists had willfully misinterpreted the Constitution to ad-vance their antislavery program and to change the nation's political calculus by creating more free states and striking a blow at the heart of self-government, ac-cording to southerners. Their efforts, the antirestrictionists argued, threatened the liberty of Americans residing in the territories. As Thomas Ritchie noted, "What is a territorial restriction to-day becomes a state restriction to-morrow." Congress could not interfere with the rights of a citizen just because that person resided in a territory. "By whom has that Territory been settled?" asked a Vir-ginia representative. "Are the inhabitants strangers, foreigners, aliens to our Government, manners, religion? Or are they native citizens of the United States? They are native citizens; many of them have fought and bled in defence of the principles of which we all here so proudly boast."[58]

Congress threatened to commit a grievous injustice, they argued, by depriv-ing American citizens of the right to self-government. John Tyler, a Virginia con-gressman and future president, disputed the right of Congress to intervene in the slavery issue at any stage within the territorial period or at the point of state-hood, accusing the northerners of wanting the government to act as a colonial power. "England denied to us the right to legislate, except by her special au-thority; nay, she proclaimed the very principle which you now proclaim as appli-cable to Missouri—the right to bind you by her own system of legislation."[59] By invoking the memory of the American Revolution, Tyler appropriated the ideals of the founders to stop the northern advance against slavery.

For all their powerful oratory, southern legislators failed to persuade their northern Federalist colleagues. Restrictionists rejected outright the southern interpretation of the needful rules clause in the Constitution. They specifically attacked any notion of territorial sovereignty as expressed by many antirestric-tionists and maintained that Congress could attach conditions to the admission of a state. The "passing of one act prescribing the manner in which laws for the Territory shall be made," a northern restrictionist argued, "does not commit Congress; they can change the mode at their pleasure." Northerners attempted to exploit a lack of unity among their opposition, many of whom preferred to remain silent on the question of territorial sovereignty, instead focusing on the rights of a territory preparing for statehood. "Even gentlemen on the opposite side of the question admit we may" legislate for the territories, noted one congressman.[60] Restrictionists, however, failed to recognize that a small but growing number of southerners at this time did not believe that Congress could legislate on slavery at any stage in the territorial existence.

Additionally, some northern congressmen raised questions about the nature of popular sovereignty in the territories itself that revealed strong ideological differences on the nature of local government. According to a Massachusetts representative, "absolute sovereignty resides, not in minute portions or States, but in the whole people, whose will, expressed by their Constitutional organs, is the law, and must be obeyed."[61] Popular sovereignty could not rest in an inchoate community such as a territory, and respecting the governance of the territories themselves, it could not rest in the individual states of the Union. The federal government possessed exclusive power over territories from their infancy to the moment Congress granted them statehood. Few other members of Congress advocated such a nationalist agenda in such stark terms.

Restrictionists argued that Congress possessed the *discretionary* power to admit states. If the national legislature did not believe admitting a territory to statehood represented the best interests of the nation at large, it could deny admission. In the case of Missouri and any other territory seeking admission as a slave state, members of Congress had a right and a duty to "judge for themselves, whether it will be for the good of the Union to admit new members who hold mankind as slaves."[62] No territory could demand admission to the Union from Congress; no treaty could trump the right of Congress to grant admission as it saw fit. Any contrary argument denied the sovereign power delegated to Congress by the people.

In spite of the rigid rhetorical positions taken by members of both sides of the Missouri debate, Congress appeared poised to enact a compromise by the middle of February. Moderates indicated their willingness to negotiate on the terms of the Thomas amendment. Mathew Carey had hinted at drawing a compromise line in his pamphlet on the Missouri controversy, written in early 1820. He cited an "understanding" between the free and slave states, "that slavery should be tolerated within a certain line, and excluded beyond it." Carey almost certainly referred to the use of the Ohio River as a dividing line between free and slave territory. The Thomas proposal, it seemed, merely extended the precedent. The House of Representatives held out for some time, refusing to concur in the Senate's Thomas amendment to the Missouri bill. But by March, a final settlement seemed imminent. Outside of Washington, however, considerable resistance to compromise developed. Some northerners looked at the Thomas amendment with alarm, as drawing a line between slave and free territory "would seem to establish different interests, and create the worst sort of parties that we can possible have."[63]

To the minds of southern conservatives, the compromise yielded on the issue of congressional authority over slavery in the territories, a constitutional point that they believed their section could not afford to concede. Congress had "no right to restrict even the territorial government," nor did it have the right to "shackle future sovereign states" on the issue of slavery. Yet the Thomas amendment did both by yielding on the issue of territorial sovereignty north of the 36 degree, 30 minutes line and by making the prohibition perpetually binding. "Why use this very expression which seems copied from the ordinance of '87," the *Richmond Enquirer* asked, "if it be not intended to pursue the precedent set in the N.W. territory?" President Monroe, who quietly observed the proceedings in Congress and the public debate from the White House, concurred. The Thomas amendment implied "that the restraint should apply to territories, after they become states as well as before. This will increase the difficulty incident to an arrangement of this subject, otherwise sufficiently great, in any form, in which it can be presented."[64]

An uncertain Monroe consulted with several colleagues on the legality of the compromise emerging from Congress. James Madison provided the president with a carefully reasoned treatise on the subject. Madison recognized that the Constitution left much pertaining to the territories open to interpretation. The "ductile nature" of the needful rules and regulations clause left "much to legislative discretion." The territories needed some manner of oversight in their infancy, but the "suspension of the great principle of self-government, ought not to be extended farther nor continued longer than the occasion might fairly require." In the specific case of Missouri, Madison deemed the restriction unconstitutional.[65]

In addition to contacting the fourth president and framer of the Constitution for his interpretation of the issues of states' rights and self-government, Monroe summoned the members of his cabinet to the White House for a meeting on March 3. The president asked his advisors to submit written opinions on two questions: whether Congress had the right to prohibit slavery in the territories and whether the Missouri bill, which interdicted slavery forever north of the compromise line proposed by Thomas, applied only to territories or to states after their admission to the Union. The cabinet members discussed their opinions in person in addition to submitting written opinions. Secretary of the Treasury William H. Crawford, Attorney General William Wirt, and Secretary of War John C. Calhoun—all slaveholders—responded that the federal government did indeed possess the power to prohibit slavery in the territories. Secretary of State John Quincy Adams noted the aberration immediately. "The progress of this discussion has so totally merged in passion all the reasoning faculties of the slave-holders," Adams wrote in his diary, "that these gentlemen, in the simplicity of their hearts, had come to a conclusion in direct opposition to their premises, without being aware of or conscious of inconsistency." The three men, however, believed that the slavery prohibition in the bill applied only to the territories. Adams concurred on the first point with his southern colleagues, but argued that the slavery prohibition would apply even in statehood, because "by its interdiction in the territory, the people, when they come to form a Constitution, would have no right to sanction slavery." Having consulted with his advisors and received their sanction for the proposed compromise plan, Monroe resolved to sign the bill as received from Congress.[66]

The president certainly helped shape the bill that he signed into law on March 6, 1820. Historians have reexamined the record in recent years and argued that Monroe worked behind the scenes to craft a moderate coalition between the sections that would vote for compromise. To achieve a workable adjustment, Monroe and the compromise-minded in Congress, led by Speaker Clay, had to secure enough northern votes to gain passage. Fourteen northerners voted with the southern delegation for the compromise bill, including Henry Meigs, who had so eloquently articulated the antirestrictionist argument in Congress. These "doughfaces," a pejorative term coined by the eccentric John Randolph of Virginia, gave Clay and the administration enough support in the House of Representatives to pass the compromise bill. Randolph mocked these northern men with southern principles, saying that he knew that these men who "*were scared at their own dough faces*" would cave in to southern demands. Nevertheless, the "seventeen or eighteen doughfaces whom Randolph belittled made sectional peace possible in 1820."[67]

Those doughfaces would have to explain their actions to their constituents after the close of the congressional session. Admitting Missouri assuaged the South, explained a congressman from the District of Maine, while the Thomas proviso inhibited "slavery from a territory larger than all of the original thirteen United States, in exact conformity to the ordinance of 1787." A second representative from Maine, John Holmes, added that the Constitution represented a "compromise of conflicting rights and interests" that necessitated accommodation of diverse opinions. Of course, the linking of Maine's admission as a state with that of Missouri might have motivated both of these congressmen as well. Holmes played an instrumental role in gaining statehood for Maine by working on the Arkansas and Missouri bills. Although his constituents gratefully acknowledged his efforts, Holmes never escaped the brand of being a doughface. He resigned after the end of the session and never returned to Congress.[68]

To strict constructionists, the southerners in Congress had compromised on the issue of congressional nonintervention; endorsing the Thomas amendment conceded that Congress could determine the status of slavery in the territories, at least north of 36 degrees, 30 minutes. Yet most southerners saw the compromise as an extension of a precedent endorsed by the previous generation of southern leaders. They saw a good deal and accepted the terms, believing that the compromise conceded far less than it seemed. Some southerners "doubted that Congress would actually impose the restriction when the region was organized into territories."[69] In Illinois and Indiana, for example, Congress had largely ignored the efforts of slaveholders to bypass the Northwest Ordinance, leaving the battle over slavery to local citizens. Furthermore, they interpreted the clause that "forever prohibited" slavery in the territory north of the compromise line as applying only to the territorial phase. Once a territory in the region gained statehood, it could amend its constitution to permit slavery if it wished. Regardless of what applied during the territorial phase, no law of Congress could overrule the sovereign right of a state to create and alter its own organic law. For a time, it had seemed that the Old Republicans would insist on congressional sanction of the right of settlers in the territories to determine the legality of slavery. The moderates prevailed, choosing instead to focus on strengthening slavery via their states' rights doctrine rather than seeking to bar the federal government from exercising control over local issues in the territories. In the future, however, they would come to regret their decision and insist that the maintenance of states' rights and the institution of slavery also required an end to congressional interference with slavery in the territories.

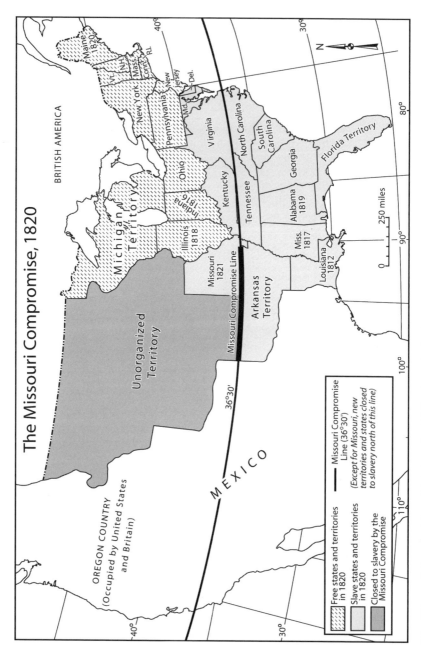

The Missouri Compromise, 1820 (map by Clifford Duplechin)

Finally, the legislation left a considerable portion of territory south of the compromise line open to slavery if settlers in those areas desired to permit the institution. Southerners could feel secure in their rights to hold slaves and to hold a commensurate power in the halls of government given the political calculus that emerged from the Missouri debates. The arrangement provided for a balance between free and slave states that would keep southern interests safe. Speaker Clay, who played an instrumental role in shepherding the bill through a hostile House of Representatives, expressed his relief at the denouement of the crisis. "I gave my consent to and employed my best exertions to produce this settlement of the question," he wrote to a political friend, "and I shall be rejoiced if the community will sanction it."[70]

Over the course of the Missouri controversy, northerners had equated self-government in Missouri and the western territories as de facto establishment of slavery in the region. The cases of Illinois and Indiana ten years earlier seemed to bolster their claims. In both territories, even the Northwest Ordinance's provision against slavery did not settle the issue. A long battle over slavery ensued in both territories, indeed in Illinois it had not yet ended. Northern restrictionists could not allow the territories to decide the issue, for if the federal government affirmed self-government "alone to decide the institution's fate, human nature and the demands of western settlement dictated that western territories would choose slavery over freedom." Thirty years later, southerners would utilize the same argument to dismiss popular sovereignty as an antislavery tool to make the western territories free states.[71]

Southerners responded to the passage of the compromise with mixed reviews. Some castigated those who voted for the bill and lamented that their fellow southerners had compromised on self-government in the territories. "A constitution warped from its legitimate bearings, and an immense region of territory closed for ever against the Southern and Western people—such is the 'sorry sight' which rises to *our* view," Thomas Ritchie wrote. Alternatively, a Georgia correspondent reflected the attitudes of the moderate camp by encouraging a novel application of popular sovereignty. "Now, I think if we go to the people we shall find a decided majority in favor of the proposed restriction, at least such appears to be the fact from the votes of their more immediate organ, the House of Representatives." His readers could debate the existence of a "decided" majority—southerners in the House had voted 39–37 in favor of the Thomas proviso. In Washington, John C. Calhoun confided to Andrew Jackson that the Missouri controversy may have "contributed to weaken in some degree the attachment of our Southern and Western people to the Union; but the agitators of that question have, in my opinion, not only completely failed; but have destroyed to a great extent their future capacity for future mischief." The North-South Republican alliance had crushed the Federalist call for restriction in Missouri but had also neutralized the threat that the moribund party might renew its assault at a later date. Regardless of the vote tally or the objections of strict constructionists, the larger point remained intact: many southerners saw the compromise bill as acceptable.[72]

Southern press coverage made another point clear in the days after President Monroe signed the Missouri Compromise: many southerners still believed that Congress did not possess the power to prohibit slavery in the territories. Now Missouri had a solemn duty to conduct. "Never has a Territory so young been called upon to act so great a part; for now is thrown into its hands the decision of a question upon which depends not only the liberties of the Missouri people and of their unborn posterity, but also the safety of the Republic and the preservation of the Union."[73] The Missourians now had to frame a constitution and defend its rights and those of the South.

When the Missourians did submit their constitution to the second session of the Sixteenth Congress, it provoked another firestorm that threatened the initial compromise and renewed the rancorous debate. The draft constitution forbade passage of any law that emancipated slaves without the consent of their owners and directed the legislature to pass legislation that would prohibit free blacks and mulattoes from living in the state. In their efforts to strike back at Congress for attempting to legislate their affairs, many legislators believed that the Missouri constitution's framers had overstepped their bounds and violated the U.S. Constitution. Baltimore editor Hezekiah Niles argued, "It can hardly be believed that congress will sanction either of these provisions: the first, in the present state of the public feeling, is inexpedient . . . and the second is unconstitutional."[74] The first provision did not violate the constitution, but it offended many northerners who already viewed the compromise with contempt. The second clause clearly violated Article Four, Section Two of the Constitution, which states, "The Citizens of each State shall be entitled to all Privileges and Immunities of citizens in the several States." Because free blacks and mulattoes held citizenship in some northern states, Missouri could not constitutionally enforce the offending clause.

Restrictionists fully intended to do battle again with the proslavery forces in Congress. Even many southerners realized that the clause violated the U.S.

Constitution. It would take all the skill of Henry Clay to broker another compromise that would appease the restrictionists while keeping intact the original compromise. Clay and a joint congressional committee drafted a resolution that gave tacit approval to the Missouri constitution, but declared that the free blacks clause "shall never be construed to authorize the passage of any law" that would exclude any American citizen "from the enjoyment of any of the privileges and immunities" of the United States Constitution.[75] Clay averted another crisis that could have threatened the stability of the Union. With the terms of the first Missouri Compromise secure, the nation hoped to put the divisive issue of slavery extension to a rest. Moderates who merely wanted the slavery issue to disappear would see their hopes dashed, however, as antislavery and proslavery forces would continue the battle over slavery and its extension into the ever expanding West.

"FORGOTTEN PRINCIPLES OF

THEIR FOREFATHERS"

Retreat from the Missouri
Compromise

Following passage of the Missouri Compromise many Americans breathed a collective sigh of relief, believing that Congress had averted a crisis through compromise. Questions regarding the expansion of slavery might reappear, they reasoned, but the Missouri Compromise formula would provide a lasting means of settlement. As Hezekiah Niles wrote in his newspaper just five days after President James Monroe signed the first Missouri Compromise into law, "In the acquisition of *new* territories (say of Florida, the only new territory that we ever wish to see added, taking the line as fixed by the late treaty with Spain for our boundary west), the question may be partially revived, but sufficient for the day is the evil thereof."[1] Yet that day would come sooner rather than later as the nation extended its boundaries and organized territories and states throughout the 1830s and into the 1840s. Northern antislavery forces became emboldened by a slow, measured, but unmistakable change in public opinion over the morality of slavery. In turn, the South rose in defense of its peculiar institution, accusing the antislavery vanguard of depriving southerners of their equal status within the nation even after they had conceded to the terms of the Missouri Compromise. A persistent sectional division over slavery remained despite the creation of a new party system designed to squelch the vexing issue and train America's focus on social and economic issues. Southerners actively participated in the new politics of economic development, but the Missouri Compromise and the steady development of antislavery sentiment in the North steeled their resistance against outside interference against slavery and its extension. In turn, they moved toward creating a unique political system designed to ensure that southerners governed slavery and to protect slaveholders' rights to hold slaves in the territories.

Not all Americans expressed such a sanguine attitude toward the compromise that their leaders in Washington had brokered. In the twenty-five-year interval between the Missouri controversy and the annexation of Texas, many southerners became convinced that moderates from their section had acquiesced in a compromise that infringed on the people's sovereignty north of an artificial line of latitude. Another fact provoked even greater concern: the South had conceded the cornerstone of their argument in the Missouri debates. "Thoughtful southern leaders recognized that they had suffered at least a partial defeat in the Missouri controversy" by acquiescing in congressional power to legislate on the issue of slavery in the territories. Likewise they believed that their representatives had conceded a legal point crucial to the defense of the South and her institutions: Congress had no right to interfere with the people's sovereign right to draft a state constitution. In the aftermath of the Missouri controversy, southern sectionalists predicted that the compromise would not satisfy the restrictionists' "insatiable appetite" for the eventual extinction of slavery. And over the course of the 1820s and 1830s, they crafted a defense of slavery and sought to reclaim the doctrine that the federal government could not force territories to prohibit slavery as a condition of statehood.[2]

The debates over territorial organization and statehood during the 1830s only confirmed southern suspicions. Furthermore, the rise of antislavery sentiment in the North, expressed through sheaves of petitions to Congress, provided additional evidence that within only a decade the restrictionists of 1820 had become ardent antislavery partisans. Southern leaders responded with a two-front attack against the antislavery vanguard. They sought to silence the antislavery campaign, with its congressional petitions and rhetorical attacks, while expressing themselves a revised version of constitutional interpretation that made slavery—whether in the states or within territories—sacrosanct. The debates over slavery in Arkansas and Florida revealed the persistence of the slavery issue, especially with respect to its extension into the territories, exposing sectional fissures within the American political establishment, as northerners fought more boldly to circumscribe the limits of slavery within the Union and southerners fought to protect the existence and extension of their peculiar institution. Swayed by antislavery and abolitionist rhetoric, northerners challenged the morality of slavery and sought to limit its existence to the states of the South.

THE SOUTHERN POLITICIANS who labeled themselves Old Republicans—champions of Jeffersonian republicanism and the "principles of '98"—feared that the South had abandoned strict construction and states' rights by accepting the Missouri Compromise. The *Richmond Enquirer*'s Thomas Ritchie, a putative leader of the Old Republican faction, pounced on the twin concessions of the Missouri Compromise. He criticized the compromisers who ceded so much territory to the antislavery interests and conceded the right of Congress to legislate for the territories on the slavery issue. The compromise had blocked the northward migration of slaveholders based on an artificial and arbitrary line. "If we are cooped up on the north, we must have elbow room to the west," Ritchie noted. The Adams-Onís Treaty, however, had blocked the westward migration of slavery as well by setting the southwestern boundary of the nation at the Sabine River. Southern expansionists had alleged that the Louisiana Purchase included much of eastern Texas, a claim the Spanish dismissed as absurd. The South did gain the Territory of Florida, but the further westward expansion of slavery after 1821 seemed unlikely given the realities of the Missouri Compromise and the treaty with Spain. Domestic and foreign events had hemmed in the South, leaving no room for westward expansion after the states of the Old Southwest became populated. No slaveholder would move into a territory where his slaves could not follow. Southerners believed that they possessed the constitutional right to emigrate to the federal domain with their property—slaves included. More pragmatically, the older portions of the South relied on the continued westward migration of slaveholders and potential slave-holders to provide a market for surplus slaves in states like Virginia.[3]

The outcome of the Missouri debates led many southerners to believe that westward expansion provided the only way to safeguard slavery and southern interests in the future. They began to reiterate the belief, too, that the sanctity of states' rights and the rights of slaveholders to move west with their human chattel precluded federal restriction of slavery in the territories. In the same issue of the *Enquirer* in which he expressed the need for southerners to look westward toward expansion, Ritchie chastised northerners for assaulting the right of territorial sovereignty north of the Missouri Compromise line. That "Congress should forever take from [the settlers of the territories] the privilege of self-government, under the pretence that it is a 'needful regulation,'" smacked of arbitrary government. Southerners could not afford to permit what he perceived as an unconstitutional assumption of power. In his remonstrances against congressional intervention with slavery in the territories, Ritchie represented a set of principles commonly identified with southern conservatives. The Missouri controversy revitalized the notion of states' rights and strict construction embodied in the Virginia and Kentucky Resolutions of 1798, the twin documents that the Old Republicans saw as bulwarks of self-government and states' rights, as well as a defense against centralized power. Yet their conservative vision looked not backwards but toward the future. Only by defending their interpretation of the nation's founding principles could the South protect its strength and its future in the republic. Ritchie and other southern conservatives cloaked themselves in the mantle of strict construction to decry the expansion of federal authority over domestic institutions in the territories. Nathaniel Beverley Tucker, who during the Missouri controversy had defended the principle of self-government in his Hampden letters, believed that southerners had to "stand in the breach between our native states and their assailants—and to call back our countrymen to the forgotten principles of their forefathers."[4]

Perhaps the strongest critique of the Missouri Compromise from a southern conservative came from the pen of John Taylor. A brilliant political theorist from Caroline County, Virginia, Taylor had long supported libertarian views on federal authority and a states' rights interpretation of the constitution.[5] In his book *Construction Construed, and Constitutions Vindicated*, the Virginian deprecated the Missouri crisis as an "absurd controversy," yet he took great pains to evaluate the implications of the compromise on southerners and their institutions. Chastising those who thought that a dividing line could settle the slavery exten-

sion issue once and for all, Taylor argued in characteristically prolix language
that the Missouri Compromise's "balance of power contemplates two spacious
territories, with the population of each separately integral, as conglomerated by
an adverse interest, and though substantially federal in themselves, substantially anti-federal with respect to each other." In other words, Congress had divided the national domain over the issue of slavery's expansion into two antagonistic sections. Taylor may have ignored the precedent of dividing free and
slave territory, but he identified its most dangerous consequence, which highlighted the growing division between North and South over slavery.[6]

Repeating the argument expressed by many southerners during the Missouri debates, Taylor asserted that Congress had no right to *make* a state, but
only to *admit* it once the people of a territory had written a constitution and petitioned for admission to the Union. "Do congress participate of this sovereignty
with the people of Missouri," Taylor asked, or is the sovereignty of the people
subservient to that of the federal government? The antirestrictionists had maintained that only the people of the territory themselves could draft a constitution,
and Taylor concurred. "It must be the work of the sovereignty of the people,
associating by their title to self-government," he concluded. Although self-
government had prevailed in Missouri and Arkansas, Congress had established
a different set of rules for the remainder of the Louisiana Purchase, a point that
Taylor and his fellow southern conservatives considered unconscionable. In attempting to force conditions upon Missouri's admission, Congress assumed
power over local legislation, a move that Taylor considered "evidently inconsistent with reason, with the essential character of representation." Southern conservatives had resisted, only to see the Missouri Compromise give legal sanction
to the practice north of an arbitrary line. In ratifying the Constitution, according
to Taylor, no state had conceived of conveying the power to Congress—or to a
majority of states—the right to enact local legislation for another state. Yet northerners had precisely this aim; they sought to exercise "feudal power" over the
territories in order to check the expansion of slavery. Southerners would rue
passage of such an odious measure, Taylor insisted, for it allowed antislavery
leaders to attack the institution of slavery and the equal rights of the South.[7]

Southern conservatives hearkened back to the principles of 1798—as embodied in the writings of Thomas Jefferson and James Madison—by insisting on
states' rights and strict construction. But they also began advancing their corre-
late—the doctrine of territorial self-government—as another means of defense
against rising antislavery sentiment. From the carefully drawn arguments found

in the writings of John Taylor to the essays found in daily newspapers such as Ritchie's *Enquirer*, southerners asserted the primacy of self-government, a principle that had served as "the keystone of the South's entire constitutional defense system in 1819–1821." Asserting the right of territorial self-government in Missouri and Arkansas seemed to vindicate southerners' claims, but they again insisted that the positive exclusion of slavery north of the compromise line had contravened that principle. Why did Congress deem it safe to only allow self-government south of 36 degrees, 30 minutes? Few Americans lived in the northern portion of the Louisiana Purchase in 1821, the area Zebulon Pike had described as uninhabitable and that two years later, in 1823, Stephen Long would label the "Great American Desert." Certainly some southerners, too, considered the land uninhabitable. Conversely, slaveholders could and did settle in Arkansas and Missouri.[8] For these reasons, southern moderates likely saw benefit in accepting the Missouri Compromise and partially conceding the point of territorial self-government for the sake of sectional harmony and Union. Conservatives, however, continued to chafe at any retreat on the principle of the matter.

Southern moderates had prevailed in the effort to carry the Missouri Compromise, but they paid a price for their conciliatory politics. When southern moderates and conservatives battled over the merits of compromise in the early 1820s, the conservatives won the rhetorical advantage and then the battle at the polls. The Thomas proviso had divided the South "between those who were more sensitive to the relationship of slavery to politics and those who were less so." Southern conservatives solidified their power by persuading the electorate that northerners threatened to imperil the federal Union as conceived by men like Jefferson. The Missouri crisis revealed that opposition to southern power via the three-fifths clause had become "entwined with the humanitarian movement against slavery" and that the South had lost some of its northern Republican allies. Faced with a changing political atmosphere, southern leaders sought to achieve sectional solidarity in defense of states' rights and nonintervention with slavery. Indeed, after 1820 "it became increasingly difficult for a defender of slavery to support the expansion of federal power." In 1822, the southern electorate sided with the conservatives by reelecting 70 percent of the congressman who had voted against compromise. Conversely, only 39 percent of the congressmen who supported the Thomas proviso gained reelection, a clear "measure of the resurgence of Old Republicanism." Many southerners believed that their section would have to guard assiduously its rights in the future against further antislavery activism.[9]

For southerners, the fear of northern encroachment on slavery and its expansion became a reality as traces of a more aggressive antislavery movement began to take shape. The argument over slavery in the territories quieted after 1821 only because the Union had organized the preponderance of the national domain. By the end of the decade, however, the appearance of abolitionism portended a renewal of the slavery debate. Southerners had voiced warnings in the early 1820s that their section must remain vigilant against interference with the extension of slavery. Northerners responded in kind, expressing their own concerns about slavery and sectional power. By 1831, abolitionists had started to form a movement in the North to advocate the end of slavery. Though slavery in the existing states may have seemed secure to all but the most fearful southerners, the abolition movement represented a direct and immediate threat to the future of slavery.[10]

Abolitionism and abolitionist rhetoric of the Garrisonian stripe infuriated southerners, who continued to insist that decisions on the slavery issue were reserved to the states, or to the people, as the Tenth Amendment to the Constitution provided. Abolitionists, southerners argued, used incendiary techniques that could potentially stoke resistance among slaves and provoke fear among slaveholders. Perhaps no event so vividly illustrates the motives of abolitionists as their efforts to flood Congress with antislavery petitions. Likewise, few other episodes in antebellum history reveal southerners' resistance to abolitionism as the effort to impose a "gag rule" on Congress by refusing to receive the antislavery petitions. The gag rule controversy of the mid-1830s heightened tensions in Congress over the slavery issue, further hardening the lines between North and South. And in the midst of the debate over antislavery petitions, Arkansas Territory asked for admission to the Union. Once again, territorial politics and slavery became linked in contentious congressional deliberations over the issue of slavery.[11]

The slavery debates of the 1830s differed in one key respect from the Missouri controversy fifteen years earlier. A new party system—in some ways constituted from the remnants of the Jeffersonian era parties—had emerged as an alternative to the dangerous one-party politics that had engendered sectional discord and threatened the Union in 1820 and 1821. Men like Martin Van Buren of New York, Thomas Ritchie of Virginia, and numerous other devotees of the Jeffersonian Republican alliance of old sought moderation and conciliation by devising a new alliance of the "planters of the South and the plain Republicans of the north" to allay sectional tensions over the divisive slavery issue by channeling political energy to party concerns. The charismatic westerner Andrew Jackson led the Democracy to victory in 1828. Southern moderates and conservatives alike became drawn to the new party because it rested on the premise that slavery fell entirely under southern purview, a belief that had already become dogma in the South. This premise may have cemented the bond between southerners and northerners, but at the same time it also represented a significant weakness for the party. Northern and southern Democrats could agree on a plethora of political issues, but by recognizing southern supremacy over slavery they implicitly conceded that slavery remained a divisive and perhaps insoluble issue. For a time, however, the sectional alliance within the party successfully bridged the Mason-Dixon line as southern Jacksonians allied with mid-Atlantic northerners to champion the principles of Jeffersonian republicanism in a new age. For southerners, the new party system seemingly portended an end to the nationalist politics of the Era of Good Feelings that had strengthened the federal government and threatened the institution of slavery.[12]

The debates over antislavery petitions and the discussion over slavery in the territories that emerged from Arkansas's application for statehood tested the Jackson party's commitment to southern rights by renewing the public and congressional discussions over slavery, state sovereignty, and the scope of federal power. The citizens of Arkansas had carefully watched national political developments for much of the year 1835. Fearing a further intensification of antislavery fervor among northern opponents of slavery, the Jacksonian pro-statehood element in Arkansas Territory advocated the immediate drafting of a constitution and petitioning Congress for statehood in the first session of the Twenty-Fourth Congress. They had several reasons for settling on this course of action. Michigan Territory seemed poised to become a state at the same time, and it would enter the Union as a free state. To keep the sectional balance of power in the Senate, statehood for Arkansas, which would certainly permit slavery within its bounds, would most likely gain broad support in Congress.[13]

Without contradiction proponents of statehood for Arkansas also predicted Missouri redux, citing the recent flurry of petitions entering Congress advocating the prohibition of slavery in the District of Columbia and the territories. Arkansans also recognized that if they sought statehood at some later time, without a free-state complement to preserve the balance of power, northerners would almost certainly object to their entry into the Union. One correspondent from the territorial capital of Little Rock summed up the dilemma that the territory faced if it delayed the push for statehood to a later date: "We apprehend that strong opposition will be made to our admission, unless trammeled with restrictions which the people of Arkansas will never submit to." Pro-statehood citizens within the territory contended that northerners almost certainly would try to block Arkansas's entry as a slave state. "That an *attempt* of the kind will be made, whenever we do apply," one resident wrote, "by some of the miserable fanatics of the northern and middle States, we have pretty good reason to believe." Moreover, if Michigan entered the Union alone, without a slave state counterpart, northern legislators would have added leverage to impose conditions on the admission of Arkansas to the Union.[14]

In order to avoid this dangerous possible turn of events, pro-statehood leaders argued, the citizens of Arkansas needed to move forward rapidly with plans to draft a constitution and apply for statehood. Congress had already failed to pass an enabling act to permit the residents of Arkansas to form a constitutional convention. Arkansas's territorial delegate to Congress, Ambrose H. Sevier, noted that Michigan had organized a constitutional convention without congressional sanction and declared that his territory should do the same. The Jacksonian Sevier emerged as a leader in the statehood movement, mobilizing political operatives in the territory to expedite the process of applying for statehood. In an appeal to the citizens of the territory written in March 1835, he portrayed the statehood movement as a safeguard against congressional interference with the status of slavery. Sevier unmistakably implied that delaying admission to the Union and failing to assert the right of self-government could jeopardize the future of slavery in Arkansas.[15]

Slavery had not exactly flourished in the territory during its fifteen years of existence, but slaveholders remained determined to maintain their society free from congressional interference. In 1830, slaves composed only 15 percent of the territory's population, a figure similar to that of Arkansas's northern neighbor, Missouri. Though certainly not on the scale of America's other southern territory, Florida, in which slaves were 54 percent of the total population, slavery played an important role in the agricultural economy of Arkansas Territory.[16] The supporters of immediate statehood increased the intensity of their pleas to support statehood and to avoid the potential disaster of repeating the history of the Missouri crisis. Although not all citizens of the territory considered the statehood movement wise policy, those who did ceaselessly cited the efforts of northerners to reignite the inflammatory issue of slavery in the territories in order to end the policy of congressional nonintervention. The ardently pro-southern editor Duff Green wrote in his Washington, D.C., newspaper that the abolitionists intended to "direct their missiles against the institutions of the south" by moving against slavery in the nation's capital and then in the territories. Green predicted that "Arkansas and Florida are next to be reformed" as the supporters of abolition sought with increasing vigor to make inroads against slavery.[17]

Arkansas residents replied by vigorously objecting to any possible interference with the territory's sovereign right to draft its own constitution, with or without slavery. "Florida and Arkansas are to be stopped at the door, and stripped of their property, before they are admitted into the Union," cried one writer, a move that would "operate destructively upon our interests" as well as violate the rights of Arkansas's citizens. Although northerners made "a doleful howling about humanity" in their condemnation of slavery, they covertly sought to end the institution by abridging the rights of their fellow Americans. "When we ask for admission into the Union, we ask for a Constitutional right, but when Congress stops us at the door, until we consent to abandon our property, she acts the part of a tyrant." Northerners sought the establishment of rights for slaves at the expense of the rights of freemen, an Arkansas writer observed, a proposition that Arkansans and southerners alike could not countenance in any way. The crisis assumed immediacy with Arkansas preparing for statehood, leading some observers to predict that the territory could "prevent a renewal of the alarming difficulties of 'The Missouri Question'" only by seeking prompt admission concurrently with Michigan.[18]

In the months immediately before Congress prepared to go into session, the territorial government of Arkansas officially endorsed immediate admission. Echoing the sentiments of Sevier and others who feared delaying statehood, territorial governor William S. Fulton convened the Arkansas legislature in October by warning the solons of the peril of delay. Fulton expressed dismay at the efforts of abolitionists, who sought to prohibit slavery in a territory surrounded by slaveholding states. He surmised that the "momentous question of the right of restriction, which once threatened the integrity of the Union, will again be agitated with reference to this Territory" and that "the rights of the citizens in any portion of the Union will again be disturbed by it."[19] By recalling the memory of the Missouri controversy and predicting a similar calamity if northerners should have their way with the debate in Congress over statehood for Arkansas, the governor astutely appealed to southerners who believed that northerners could not even abide by the Missouri Compromise—a pact that had given so much to their section at the expense of the South. Fulton's call for immediate statehood resonated with Arkansans and southerners alike, but he badly miscalculated by making the radical claim that Congress most likely did not possess the power to require submission of the constitution for approval, an argument that clearly violated the federal Constitution's provision that Congress had the duty to ensure a republican form of government for territories seeking admission to the Union as states. Northerners who remained zealous in exercising control over the territories pounced on the incendiary statement as evidence that southerners would use extreme means to ensure the future of slavery in the territories, even flouting the authority of the constitution. Sevier worked assiduously in Washington to undo any harm caused by Fulton's gaffe, assuring the president and members of Congress that the proponents of statehood had no intention of forming a state government and dissolving the territorial government *"without the approbation of Congress."* Sevier and his allies had good reason to assuage politicians in Washington, for Arkansas had elected delegates to a constitutional convention that would soon draft a charter for the territory. No one wanted to cloud the legitimacy of its work and risk delaying statehood.[20]

The convention convened at Little Rock on January 4, 1836, and promptly began the process of writing a constitution that expressly protected slavery. The committee assigned to address slavery recommended passage of a clause prohibiting the General Assembly from emancipating slaves without the owners' consent and without compensation. Furthermore, the constitution guaranteed the right of emigrants to bring their slaves into the state. The committee borrowed the substance of both provisions from the constitutions of Alabama, Mississippi, and Missouri, all three of which established explicit protections for slavery and slaveholders' rights to their property. The convention delegates approved the committee's draft of the slavery provisions without discussion. Within the month, the convention had completed and ratified their work and sent it to Congress for approval. Because similar provisions for slavery had garnered criticism in the past, southern congressmen expected that their northern counterparts would revisit the issue of slavery and constitutional law. The day after Congress received the constitution, Sevier wrote to his associate William E. Woodruff, the pro-statehood editor of the *Arkansas Gazette*, "Don't be astonished if we should have another *Missouri discussion upon the subject of slavery.*"[21]

Thomas Hart Benton, the Democratic senator from Missouri, also feared the potential for a fight over the slavery provisions. When the Senate opened debate on April 4, 1836, he "alluded to the great agitation on the subject of slavery" and sought to calm the atmosphere by dismissing the significance of the issue. Hoping symbolism would assuage sectional insecurity, the senator noted that

Arkansas's application had been referred to a senator from a free state, James Buchanan of Pennsylvania, while the Senate had placed Michigan's constitution in his hands—a senator from a slave state—illustrating the "total impotence of all attempts to agitate and ulcerate the public mind on the worn-out subject of slavery." Benton's effort proved ineffective; a Vermont Whig senator rose immediately to object to the slavery clause in the Arkansas constitution.[22]

Arkansas's bid for statehood soon became enmeshed in a web of national politics, which had changed considerably since the Missouri controversy. Opposition in Congress came chiefly from the anti-Jackson political party that would become known as the Whigs. Established by members of Congress who opposed Andrew Jackson and his use of executive power, the Whig party continued to take shape and solidify as an organization during the election year of 1836. The anti-Jackson forces knew that Arkansas would enter the Union as a staunchly Democratic state, leading many Whigs to oppose statehood at least until the fall election had passed.[23] More significantly and most ominously, the northern Whigs followed in the steps of the old Federalists in opposition to the expansion of slavery. Northern Whigs opposed the states' rights, strict construction platform of the Democrats, and in the process established themselves as the opponents of the expansion of slavery.

In the South, the rise of an opposition party followed a completely different trajectory. Though the South was not a political monolith, a clear majority of southerners endorsed a circumscribed federal government. When Whigs did appear in the South, they chiefly rallied against two of Jackson's policies: his expansive use of federal power to coerce the Nullifiers of South Carolina and his removal of deposits from the Bank of the United States. In order to have any chance of gaining office, however, southern Whigs had to endorse the "southern determination to maintain slavery as a southern question," a stance that put them at odds with their northern brethren. For a generation, southern Whigs would battle with the Democrats over which party would best protect slavery and southern interests, keeping the institution at the forefront of slave-state politics. Thus although southern party divisions animated the section's politics, those partisan divisions never jeopardized the South's united commitment to keeping issues related to the institution of slavery a matter of self-government and local governance. The only disagreement there lay in which party could best do the job. Yet in spite of the effort to keep the slavery debate a matter of local purview, southern stridency on the slavery issue often played out on the national level. Accordingly, southern Whigs rallied in opposition to federal inter-

vention against slavery in the territories and the effort to delay statehood for
Arkansas while the northern Whigs established themselves as the opponents of
slavery's expansion. True to Van Buren's design, the Jacksonian party had neutralized the slavery issue within its ranks, but the opposition had already divided over the issue.[24]

The Senate dispatched the Arkansas issue within a relatively short period of
time, passing the statehood bill on April 6 by a vote of 31–6. In spite of objections from northern Whigs that the Arkansans had drafted their constitution
without congressional sanction and that the slavery clause "made slavery perpetual," few senators believed that they could in good conscience block admission. Doing so would violate the principle of self-government and render Congress as a colonial administrator. An Ohio Democrat asserted that Congress
had no reason not to believe that the proposed constitution expressed "the opinions and wishes" of the people of Arkansas. Furthermore, congressional leaders
had paired the admission of Michigan with Arkansas in order to allay fears that
one section would gain power over the other. Citing the support of the president
and several southern senators as critical to the swift passage of the bill with minimal debate on the slavery issue, Arkansans demanded immediate statehood.[25]

The Arkansas debate briefly resumed a week later when Henry Clay introduced a set of petitions from antislavery citizens of Philadelphia opposing the
territory's constitution. Apparently Clay knew some of the petitioners as casual
acquaintances, which most likely explains why he felt compelled to submit the
documents to the Senate. The Great Compromiser, however, made clear that he
did not support the petitioners' aims since his compact had settled the issue.
Clay argued that "all the new States admitted into the Union were bound by the
terms of the Missouri compromise; that all those north of the line described in
the bill were prohibited from holding slaves, and that all those south of the line
were permitted to hold them."[26] In the Kentucky senator's mind, the Compromise of 1820 offered a permanent and inviolate adjustment for the issue of slavery in the territories.

Southern conservatives who opposed the Missouri Compromise argued to
the contrary that the old specter of restriction and the new petition drive threatened the South and slavery, especially with the rise of the antislavery movement. William King, an Alabama Jacksonian, bitterly resented the introduction
of the antislavery petitions, especially when the Senate had already voted on the
Arkansas bill—a point Clay himself had conceded. King expressed regret at his
role in the passage of the Missouri Compromise, stating that "he had yielded

too much in a spirit of conciliation and harmony; and that, under like circumstances, he never would consent to yield so much again." To his mind, the South had conceded a great deal in the compromise negotiations only to find that northerners wished to renege on the agreement. Territories seeking admission to the Union should possess the freedom to "make what regulations they pleased on the subject of slavery, or any other subject relating to their internal concerns," according to King. An abolitionist phalanx sought to abridge this right, which in the case of Arkansas directly violated the Missouri Compromise. What assurances, then, did Clay's grand compromise offer to the South? None, according to King and other southerners who likewise regretted their support of the Missouri Compromise.[27]

The House of Representatives greeted the Arkansas bill with a sheaf of petitions from northerners who opposed the slavery clauses in the proposed constitution. Southern members rallied to meet the challenge posed by their northern counterparts who, as one North Carolina representative argued, sought to advance the designs of "a miserable degraded faction" of abolitionists.[28] With passions running high in the lower chamber of Congress, the Arkansas statehood bill became entwined with the long-running debate over slavery petitions and the rising abolition movement. Meanwhile, supporters of statehood for Arkansas sought to renew support for their cause, lest the slavery petition controversy eclipse and then frustrate their efforts. Exasperated with the plodding pace of the House debate on the Arkansas bill, the indefatigable Sevier moved to end the waiting and secure passage of the statehood bills for Arkansas and Michigan. On June 13, the House finally addressed the Arkansas bill, but not before the former president and current Massachusetts representative John Quincy Adams made one final attempt to block passage by introducing a resolution condemning the proposed state constitution for its stance on slavery. His three-hour effort to introduce the amendment went for naught, as the House moved to pass the bill and admit Arkansas to the Union by a vote of 143–50. Those who voted against the admission of Arkansas overwhelmingly came from the New England and mid-Atlantic states and belonged to the nascent Whig Party.[29]

Party politics did successfully contain the slavery issue for some time, as politicians raised and debated other salient issues that the nation faced. The slavery issue, however, always tended to transcend party lines and take on distinctly sectional overtones. Especially in the South, the slavery issue never strayed far from the political scene. First and foremost, southerners demanded protection for their peculiar institution from outside encroachment. Southern

Democrats believed that territorial sovereignty, which they still defined as the right to draft a constitution free from congressional interference, provided the safest means of securing slavery's future. Partisan leaders from both the Whig and Democratic parties knew this and sought to portray their respective parties as the more trustworthy protectors of slavery and southern rights.[30] Though southern Democrats could usually count on substantive support from the northern wing of their party, the Whigs remained hopelessly divided on the slavery issue throughout their history. Consequently, and as seen in the Arkansas debate, the Whig Party divided on statehood while Democrats North and South tended to support the bill for admission.

The rise of abolitionism in the North and the efforts of some northern politicians to block the expansion of slavery threatened slaveholders, who looked to their representatives in both parties for answers on how to check the advance of antislavery sentiment and abolitionist agitation. According to many southerners, northern antislavery partisans not only sought to promote the abolitionist agenda at the expense of the South, but they did so by reneging on the Missouri Compromise. Southern congressmen had thwarted the attempts of abolitionists to delay statehood for Arkansas, but many slaveholders worried that the situation would merely repeat itself the next time a southern territory, namely Florida, applied for statehood. Furthermore, the Arkansas debate had given conservative southerners the opportunity to vocalize their disdain for the Missouri Compromise. At the same time, the injection of abolitionism into political discourse led some southerners to devise more radical solutions for securing the future of slavery extension. As the Arkansas debate closed, one prominent southerner, a former nationalist who had come to regret the expansion of federal power because of its potential to threaten slavery, began preparing a comprehensive plan to assert southern rights and the sanctity of slavery.

In the winter of 1837 and 1838, the nation had entered a sharp economic downturn that had become greatly politicized because of Andrew Jackson's epic—and ultimately successful—war against the Bank of the United States. Old Hickory left his handpicked successor Martin Van Buren an economy in a precarious position, which only grew worse as the Panic of 1837 began and recriminations flew in the halls of Congress. More significantly for the slavery issue, the continuing discord over petitions to abolish slavery had not abated. Indeed, the abolitionists had only strengthened in their resolve by sending more petitions to the legislators in Washington; in 1836 alone, some 100,000 petitions arrived at the capitol. The petition movement alarmed South Carolina Senator

Though an ardent nationalist during the 1810s and 1820s who had approved of the Missouri Compromise's restriction principle, John C. Calhoun had transformed into a states' rights defender of slavery by the 1830s. His political theories provided the intellectual background for a more radical form of southern politics. (Library of Congress)

John C. Calhoun, who held the abolitionist movement in great contempt as he carefully watched its movements.[31]

Petitions from abolitionist organizations always angered southerners, who detested the members of such organizations and viewed their work as incendiary, but one petition from the Vermont legislature particularly infuriated southern senators. In November 1837, that state's legislature passed a series of resolutions affirming the right of the federal government "to abolish" slavery and the slave trade "in the several Territories of the Union where they exist" and arguing that Congress "ought immediately to exercise that power." After Benjamin Swift of Vermont introduced the petition to the Senate on December 19, 1837, southern senators and their constituents immediately protested. "The intermeddling of any of the States, or their representatives in Congress" to abolish slavery in the states or the territories, a Georgia editor wrote, "is an assault on the Southern States, and should be considered by their citizens as a direct attack upon the institutions of the slave holding States." Abolitionists in Vermont advocated what southern conservatives had feared for years—using federal power to prohibit slavery in the territories from their inception. As early as the 1820s, Old Republicans had predicted just such an attack; now it had become a reality.[32]

An apoplectic Senator Calhoun could hardly believe that a state legislature had taken up the abolitionist mantle. "You have seen the Vermont resolutions," he wrote to Nathaniel Beverley Tucker. "They go far beyond the wildest fanaticks."[33] Calhoun vigorously objected to one sovereign state attempting to impair the sovereignty of others, or of the territories and the District of Columbia. He believed the actions of the Vermont legislature marked a radical departure from precedent and intended to take action to prevent other states from taking similar action. Calhoun determined to meet this latest abolitionist assault with his own defense of slavery and pronouncement on the nature of the federal government, one designed to ensure the safety of slavery where it currently existed and to ensure its potential expansion in the territories. In doing so, he would explicitly assert an idea that southerners had begun to develop over fifteen years: the federal government had no right to prohibit slavery in the territories at any point.

Calhoun's attempt to unite the South behind a series of resolutions designed to assert southern rights and protect the South and slavery from future attacks marked a new phase in the debate over slavery and its extension to the West. In the years after the Missouri controversy, a rift between nationalists and Radicals who imbibed Old Republicanism had beset South Carolina politics. Calhoun had slowly gravitated away from the orbit of the nationalist faction for the sake of political survival, but he also perceived that an ardent nationalism might empower the federal government and could come to threaten the extension of slavery and its future in the states. Launching his attack against the abolitionist cadre on December 27, 1837, Calhoun introduced in the Senate a series of six resolutions concerning slavery and the Union. "My object," he wrote to a northern associate, "is to rally all States rights men of any creed on the old States rights principles of '98, against the dangerous sperit [*sic*] of fanaticism now abroad." Abolitionist fervor threatened the safety of the Union, Calhoun would claim repeatedly. In his resolutions, the South Carolinian essentially distilled the complex theory of the nature of American government that he had formulated over the course of the previous decade. Two of the resolves specifically addressed the issue of slavery in the states and the territories, respectively. In the fourth resolution, Calhoun contended that "domestic slavery, as it exists in the Southern and Western States," composed an integral part of their society that neither Congress nor any other state of the Union could abridge. Calhoun almost certainly made the conscious link between the southern and western states to isolate the North as a section bent on imposing arbitrary authority on sovereign states. Southerners had long sought to ally themselves with the people of the West as fellow slaveholders and defenders of local self-government.[34]

Calhoun's fifth resolve addressed the issue of slavery in the territories by attacking outside interference with the institution, whether by Congress or by the petition of citizens from any portion of the Union. He wrote "That the intermeddling of any State or States, or their citizens, to abolish slavery in this District, or any of the Territories, on the ground, or under the pretext, that it is immoral or sinful; or the passage of any act or measure of Congress, with that view, would be a direct and dangerous attack on the institutions of all the slaveholding States."[35] Clearly aimed at contemporary abolitionist petitioners of the North, Calhoun's logic bore many hallmarks of arguments past, from the implicit assumption that northerners meant to abridge the rights of southerners to the explicit assertion that neither Congress nor the people of other states could legislate for the domestic affairs of a territory or state.

Calhoun implied that the abolitionists had forced southerners to stand for their rights and demand that Congress and northern citizens alike leave southerners and their peculiar institution alone. Indeed, Calhoun insisted that the concern for southern safety and slavery transcended party lines and political considerations; the South had to unite as a *section* to counteract the abolitionist assault. Moreover the senator had altered his opinions on federal jurisdiction over slavery in the territories. During the Missouri controversy, Calhoun, then a nationalist, had confirmed the federal government's power to prohibit slavery in the national domain. Responding to the changed political climate of the 1830s, especially the rise of the abolition movement in the North, the South Carolinian saw congressional intervention as a back door movement "to usurp the power to suppress slavery in the Southern States."[36]

The Calhoun resolves provoked considerable debate in the Senate, especially among moderate Democrats who saw the southern rights platform as a direct threat to intersectional party harmony. Northern Democrats could not simply dismiss Calhoun's missive, but neither could they sanction his platform.
James Buchanan, a Pennsylvania Democrat, expressed dissatisfaction with Calhoun's tactics. "I therefore deprecate a protracted discussion of the question
here," Buchanan stated, after explaining how his colleague had acted rashly. "It
can do no good, but may do much harm, both in the North and in the South."
Ever the careful politician, he recommended forming a select committee to discuss Calhoun's grievances and report its own set of resolutions, which surely
would prove less offensive. Other northern senators stood with their antislavery
constituents in attacking Calhoun's handiwork as extremist. A Massachusetts
Whig dismissed as absurd Calhoun's implication that northerners meant to attack slavery in the states. Defending the petitioners, the senator noted that
"they repudiate, and very properly, all right to interfere with the States, and confine themselves to the Territories and the District of Columbia." Anyone who argued that northerners meant to tamper with slavery in existing states merely
sought to fan the flames of sectional discord, he argued. The Massachusetts
senator sought to refute claims that the North aimed to end slavery throughout
the Union. To the minds of southerners like Calhoun, however, he defeated his
own argument by advocating the right of congressional intervention in the territories.[37]

Calhoun unflinchingly asserted that Congress had no power to prohibit slavery in the territories. But who did possess the power to legislate on the issue? In
answering this question, the South Carolina senator broke new ground by arguing that Congress could not grant to a territory a power that it did not itself possess, an interpretation that the Supreme Court would affirm twenty years later
in *Dred Scott v. Sandford*. In his memoirs, Thomas Hart Benton summarized
Calhoun's position brilliantly. "Congress had no power to legislate upon slavery
in a territory, so as to prevent the citizens of slaveholding States from removing
into it with their slave property," Benton recalled. This part of Calhoun's statement merely reiterated the southern argument as it had stood since the Missouri Compromise. He moved beyond this point, however, by affirming that
"Congress had no power to delegate such authority to a territory," nor did the
territory possess the power itself. Benton acidly wrote that Calhoun's logic left
"the subject of slavery in a territory without any legislative power over it at all."
Actually, Calhoun raised a critical point in the interpretation of territorial sover-

eignty. Southerners had never before objected to allowing the people of a territory to legislate for themselves on the slavery issue because, in the past, such
action had always provided for the expansion of slavery. In fact, scattered voices
in the South had actually advocated the idea during the Missouri controversy,
but to no avail. The concept of territorial self-government implied that the citizens of a territory had a choice in the matter.[38]

Historians have often misunderstood Calhoun's reasoning on the territorial
question. His logic anticipated the possibility that the antislavery movement
could use some version of territorial sovereignty to advance their interests, just
as the South had used it to secure the extension of slavery. Indeed, he suggested that a territory's citizens could potentially move to bar slavery within its
borders even before applying for statehood, a prediction that would later come
true in Kansas. In his formulation, because the states held the territories in
common trust, the Constitution dictated that slavery could go into any territory
over which the American flag flew. Almost every other southern senator, and
some northerners, agreed with Calhoun's initial supposition that the government "had no right to interfere, either to protect or to invade any institution."
Any semblance of accord ended there, however. Calhoun, it seemed, wanted
congressional nonintervention in one instance, and congressional intervention
in another. The resolutions assumed, an Indiana senator argued, "that it may
become necessary for this nation to attach territory (*Texas*) to the Union, for the
purpose of *protecting* and *extending* the domestic institutions (*slavery*) of the
South." By no means would northerners sustain such a policy, he concluded.[39]

Even some southerners found Calhoun's opinions unpalatable. When on
January 9, the Senate commenced debate on the fifth resolution, John J. Crittenden of Kentucky delivered a stinging rebuke to the resolutions. Calhoun "reiter-
ates, over and over again, the trite theme and cry of 'danger to the Union,'" Crittenden argued, and if the Senate did not pay heed to his words, Calhoun "urges
the inevitable consequence of the 'destruction of the Union.'"[40] In other words,
Calhoun went too far in his efforts to defend southern institutions; by going on
the offensive his resolutions offended allies North and South. Many senators
questioned the wisdom of his methods, even as they objected to the movement
of abolitionists against slavery in the territories.

Henry Clay had listened quietly to the debate as it developed in the Senate,
growing especially concerned at the remarks of some ardent northerners and
southerners who sought to bring the issue of Texas annexation into the debate.
In August 1837, officials from the Republic of Texas had presented a plan to the

Van Buren administration for the annexation of Texas to the United States. Believing that annexation would provoke war with Mexico, Van Buren declined the offer, to the chagrin of American expansionists. For their part, northerners feared that admitting Texas to the Union would provide a vast new domain from which numerous slave states could grow. Southerners, on the other hand, hailed the prospect of annexation for precisely the reason that they could expand the slave society west. The injection of Texas into the discussion alarmed the Kentuckian and prompted him to speak. Clay worried that the deliberations over the resolutions could quickly spiral out of control if someone did not restore some sense of order to the proceedings. Like his junior colleague Crittenden, Clay opposed Calhoun's definition of the power of Congress over slavery in the territories. Accordingly, Clay submitted to the Senate his own substitutes for Calhoun's resolutions, and "a battle of the Titans began." Whereas Calhoun had spoken in "strong language, menacing tones, and irritating measures," Clay sought "conciliation" through "firm, but temperate language."[41]

In his alternative for Calhoun's fifth resolution, Clay wrote that "it would be highly inexpedient to abolish slavery in Florida, the only Territory of the United States in which it now exists, because of the serious alarm and just apprehensions" such action would surely provoke. Clay consciously made a point of limiting the discussion to Florida and not allowing it to enter into the Texas debate. In the second part of his resolution, Clay reaffirmed the standard southern interpretation of congressional nonintervention—one that he had offered during the Missouri crisis—by advocating the principle of territorial self-government. Congress should refrain from abolishing slavery in Florida "because the people of that Territory have not asked it to be done, and, when admitted as a State into the Union, will be exclusively entitled to answer that question for themselves." Furthermore, any intervention by Congress would violate the "solemn compromise" of 1820. In his efforts to craft a more moderate version of the Calhoun resolves, Clay advocated, in the words of one constitutional historian, an "early version of the doctrine later popularized by Lewis Cass and Stephen A. Douglas known as popular or squatter sovereignty." However that may be, Clay actually upheld an established interpretation of territorial self-government that he had articulated in 1820 and that southerners had endorsed as sound constitutional law for much of the early nineteenth century.[42]

Clay espoused established southern doctrine on the issue of slavery in the territories, but some of his southern colleagues objected to the conciliatory wording of his resolution on the issue. Some wondered if the Kentuckian had diluted Calhoun's sentiments too much. Clay's suggestion that Congress should *refrain* from abolishing slavery in Florida obfuscated the true constitutional interpretation that Congress *could not* abolish slavery there. Put in different terms, suggesting that Congress refrain from abolishing slavery in the territory implied that it had the power to do so. William Cabell Rives of Virginia raised this issue, noting that the "rights and interests of the inhabitants" in any of the territories precluded congressional intervention. Even though Clay's colleagues certainly understood—and in most cases endorsed—his efforts to quiet agitation on the Texas issue, they believed that any satisfactory resolution must include a statement on the territories in general and not just Florida. An Alabama senator suggested inclusion of all the territories in the resolution, to which Clay agreed.[43]

Undeterred by the proponents of moderation, Calhoun persistently entreated the Senate to adopt his resolution on slavery in the territories and to reject a more conciliatory version. The South could no longer afford to compromise on equal rights in the territories, he maintained. Clay's proposal "would be an utter abandonment of the entire ground assumed in the resolutions already adopted." Calhoun proposed a new, permanent constitutional interpretation that would affect all future territorial acquisitions. The Senate had passed four of the six resolutions initially proposed by Calhoun. And now Clay's compromise version of the fifth threatened the meaning of Calhoun's entire platform. The South Carolinian "regarded slavery, wherever it exists throughout the whole Southern section, as one common question, and is as much under the protection of the Constitution here, and in the Territories, as in the States themselves; and herein lies our only safety." He intoned a final warning, "Abandon this, and all is abandoned." Calhoun would not retreat from his effort to refine and redefine the southern doctrine on congressional nonintervention.[44]

Calhoun's proslavery clarion call provoked a northern backlash, as senators from the North renewed long-running protests against congressional nonintervention with the slavery in the territories. Daniel Webster emphatically stated that the Constitution left the issue "entirely to the discretion and wisdom of Congress," but his characteristically impressive efforts to defend the right of Congress to legislate on slavery in the territories failed to persuade. Most senators focused on endorsing either Clay's interpretation of congressional nonintervention or Calhoun's expanded doctrine on the issue. Even the South Carolinian began to recognize that he did not possess the support necessary to gain passage of his resolution on slavery in the territories. A majority of senators clearly favored Clay's version, amended to include all of the territories within its scope and not merely Florida. Southerners wanted assurances that Congress would not interfere with slavery in any of the territories currently held or subsequently acquired. In vain, Calhoun fired one last broadside against Clay's resolution by attacking the Missouri Compromise itself. The South, according to Calhoun, had committed a grievous error by acquiescing in the Compromise of 1820, which in no small part led to the circumstances the nation found itself in in 1838. Calhoun conceded that he had favored the compromise in 1820 and as a member of the Monroe cabinet had pronounced it constitutional. He "now believed that it was a dangerous measure, and that it had done much to rouse into action the present spirit" of abolitionism and antislavery politics. The South had practically invited antislavery agitation by conceding its true constitutional rights in an effort to achieve sectional concord.[45]

Not all southerners saw the slavery struggle in such stark terms as Calhoun. They still believed that territorial sovereignty provided sufficient protection for the expansion of slavery. The South Carolinian lost his battle on the fifth resolution, as the Senate overwhelmingly passed Clay's less incendiary version. Eight New England Whigs and one Pennsylvania Democrat voted against the Clay substitute, exhibiting again that the locus of antislavery sentiment came from the New England states. "Calhoun, in fact, had nothing approaching united southern support for his extremist position," a preeminent historian of the slavery issue has noted. Continuing the division between Calhounites and moderate southerners—both Whig and Democrat—that had existed since the beginning of the petition controversy, moderates determined that they simply could not accept the redefinition of the southern position on slavery in the territories as Calhoun proposed. They accepted the Clay substitute as sufficient protection, provoking even Calhoun to concede defeat and voted in its favor.[46]

Calhoun foresaw the slavery issue as a coming hurricane; many of his fellow southerners only saw a storm that the South could weather. And yet the South Carolinian had inaugurated a transformation of southern politics that would mature in the following two decades, as slavery extension would eclipse all other political issues, overshadow public political discourse, and obscure the economic issues that led to the formation of the Jacksonian political system. The debate over the Calhoun resolutions had no practical effect in squelching abolitionist fervor, but it did help to define where northern and southern politicians stood on the issue of slavery in the territories. Clearly, northern Whigs stood most strongly against the expansion of slavery. Calhoun knew precisely that the issue of congressional power over slavery in the territories remained ambiguous, ironically and in part because the South had unwisely compromised on the issue in the past. He also knew that his fellow southerners considered the ongoing abolitionist petition drives menacing. Moreover, they believed the Vermont legislature's resolutions had, in the words of one Virginia writer, "given to this matter a new and more serious aspect than it has yet assumed." A state government had endorsed the tactics of the abolitionists that southerners considered fanatical by calling for a federally imposed ban on slavery in the territories. The South would have to wait and see what northerners would next do regarding this matter when the last slaveholding territory—Florida—asked for admission to the Union.[47]

When Congress had established Florida Territory in March 1822, it implicitly recognized the role that slavery played in the region's society and economy by making no attempt to intervene against the institution.[48] Furthermore, few congressmen considered debating the merits of slavery in the southernmost territory of the United States, especially after passage of the Missouri Compromise. If Henry Clay's masterstroke of sectional conciliation did represent a compact between North and South, no one could consider prohibiting slavery in Florida. Over the course of fifteen years, however, the political calculus of the slavery issue had changed drastically. As the debate over statehood for Arkansas in 1836 and the Calhoun resolutions the following year on the nature of the Union amply exhibited, so southerners believed, antislavery northerners would not limit their actions against slavery based on geographic lines or sectional compacts. Southerners anticipated that Florida's petition for statehood would provoke a struggle similar to the experience of the Arkansas debate.

Plagued with internal dissension over the potential of dividing the territory into its two historical segments—West and East Florida—versus asking for immediate statehood for the entire territory, Florida took a long and circuitous route to statehood. In 1838, the territory finally elected a convention to draft a constitution and to seek admission to the Union. The St. Joseph convention took almost exactly the same approach with regard to slavery as did the Arkansas constitutional convention of 1835–1836. The Committee on the Subject of Domestic Slavery proposed that the state legislature would have "no power to pass laws of the emancipation of slaves" and that emigrants to the state possessed the right to bring slaves with them. The committee also recommended banning free blacks from settling in the state. The convention accepted the recommendation without debate and included the article regarding slavery into their final product.[49]

Abolitionist newspapers in the North immediately raised objections to the proslavery clauses in Florida's proposed constitution, especially that which prohibited the state legislature from abolishing slavery. Abolitionists may have lost their battle to block admission of Arkansas based on its proslavery constitution, but they intended to renew the attack again with Florida. Abetting the abolitionists' offensive, Florida's own citizens would delay their efforts and thus prolong the debate. During the first half of 1839, it seemed that ratification of the constitution might fail in the territorial referendum because of the ongoing battle over immediate statehood versus division of the territory. Finally, in August, the constitutional convention announced that voters had accepted the document by a majority of just ninety-five votes. Internal dissension persisted, and Florida would wait six years for statehood. Congress received conflicting petitions asking both for immediate statehood and division of the territory, leaving legislators in Washington perplexed. Finally, Florida presented a united front in 1844 and 1845 and asked for immediate statehood based on the St. Joseph Constitution of 1838. Congress paired Florida with Iowa in the long-standing practice of admitting one free state and one slave state to maintain sectional balance in the Senate.[50]

Predictably, northern members of Congress raised objections to the admission of Florida with its ardently proslavery constitution. A Maine representative moved to force an amendment of Florida's constitution as a condition of admission to the Union, predictably prompting a debate over the right of the citizens of Florida to determine their own form of government. Southerners objected to any interference with Florida's right to draft its own constitution. "But here came a proposition from the extreme northern portion of this Union," a Virginian objected, "to remodel the form of government which the people of Florida had adopted for themselves—a proposition which, on its very face, assumed that the people of Florida were not able to judge what form of constitution was best adapted for them." The citizens of Florida possessed the express right to install whatever provisions they deemed necessary to protect slavery. After all, northern abolitionists had driven the South to take such precautions in order to protect their rights.[51]

The deliberations over Florida statehood became especially bitter because of the concurrent debate in Congress over the annexation of Texas. The Texas issue took center stage in the congressional session of 1844–1845 as legislators debated the merits of annexation and the effect that incorporating Texas into the Union would have on the welfare of the nation itself. Northern antislavery partisans viewed the situation with concern, because Texas annexation would give the South a sectional advantage in the Senate. Furthermore, many Americans from North and South believed that Texas would eventually be divided into several smaller states, promising more sectional imbalance in the Senate and protracted political conflict in the future as the South gained more slave states. A New York journal linked the Florida and Texas issues by accusing the South of engaging in aggressive efforts to expand the slave domain. "While the South was content with so much slavery as the constitution tolerates she was safe, but the attempt to enlarge its boundaries and increase its power, will surely be resisted."[52] Texas annexation occupied far more attention than did the petition of Florida for statehood because of the higher stakes involved in bringing the Lone Star Republic into the Union as a state and because most in and out of Congress anticipated Florida's admission with slavery. Nevertheless, Florida represented the latest battleground over the interpretation of congressional authority over slavery in the territories, a point not lost on northern and southern members of Congress.

Northern and southern lawmakers seemed never to grow weary of debating who possessed the power to legislate on slavery—Congress or the people of the territories themselves. A young Democratic representative from Illinois sought to bridge the gap between the sections by occupying a middle position on the matter. Stephen A. Douglas made clear that he did not support all of the provisions of the constitutions of either Florida or Iowa. Determining the prudence of individual clauses within a prospective state's constitution, however, did not fall within the purview of Congress, arguing, "it could never have entered the minds of the framers of the constitution that Congress was to pass on the propriety and expediency of each clause of the constitution of the new States." Congress could not and should not exercise control over "regulations and institutions, local and domestic in their character."[53]

Douglas framed the congressional authority over state making in a way that few, if any, southerners would have found objectionable. He repeated an argument standard to the defense of self-government: that the "people of each State are to form their constitution in their own way and in accordance with their own views, subject to one restriction only; and that was, it should be republican in its character." The Illinoisan made clear that the privilege of self-government applied only at the moment that a territory sought statehood and not a moment before. Noting that "the father may bind the son during his minority," he argued that Congress possessed jurisdiction over the territories until they reached the point where they could safely and responsibly assume statehood, a time he left undefined. Douglas, however, "was not yet prepared to concede the same freedom to the people of a territory."[54]

In essence, Douglas assumed the traditional southern position on slavery in the territories, but his reference to *when* a territory's people became sovereign or could exercise that sovereignty presaged arguments that would later alter the definition of territorial self-governance. By advocating congressional authority during the territorial phase, Douglas assumed ground more akin to the northern argument on federal power in the national domain. Florida had matured to the point where it could assume its place as a state and therefore, Douglas argued, members of Congress should drop their objections to the prospective state's constitution and approve its admission to the Union.

Just as had transpired in the Arkansas statehood debate nine years before, northern Whigs voted en masse against the Florida bill. Nevertheless, on February 13, the House of Representatives passed the bill by a vote of 145–46.[55] Thirty-eight Whigs from across the North voted against the bill, while only one Maryland Whig joined his northern colleagues in opposition. Even though the Whigs had to know that opposition would prove futile, they still objected to Florida and its proslavery constitution. With passage secured, the House sent the bill to the upper chamber, where an abbreviated debate soon ensued over the slavery issues the representatives had debated.

On March 1, the same day that President John Tyler signed the joint resolution of Congress annexing Texas, the Senate began debate on Florida statehood. The senators merely reiterated the arguments made in the House. Northern antislavery senators announced their intentions to vote against the bill because of the slavery provisions in the constitution. Southerners and some westerners refuted the northern argument by insisting that Congress had only to ensure that Florida would have a republican form of government. Late in the evening of March 1, the Senate—now far more concerned with the issues surrounding Texas—voted to admit Florida to the Union by a vote of 36–9. In the Senate, only the New England Whigs maintained opposition to the admission of Florida.[56]

The debates in the 1830s and 1840s over admitting Arkansas and Florida to statehood revealed that the Missouri Compromise had not settled the issue of slavery extension or territorial self-government. In one respect the sectional accord did work, as both North and South acquiesced in the parameters set by the compromise line. But it only masked the underlying issues of constitutional interpretation; it did not settle them. Southerners still claimed the constitutional right to carry slaves into any territory, even though they had seemingly ceded that right north of 36 degrees, 30 minutes. Northerners claimed that Congress possessed the indisputable right to prohibit slavery in any territory as it saw fit. And both sides held to their views with increasing tenacity. With both Arkansas and Florida, the South claimed that antislavery northerners sought to break the Missouri compact by attempting to deny statehood based on the slavery issue. The South, many of its residents believed, could not trust the North to let territorial self-government prevail.

The debate over the resolutions of John C. Calhoun exhibited all too clearly for southerners, however, that their section hardly presented a united front on the issue of slavery in the territories. Some southerners promoted sectional unity as the only means of defending slavery. During the debate on Calhoun's resolutions, a Georgia editor wrote, "So long as we are divided, feverish and powerless, we cannot expect the northern fanatics to cease their mischievous endeavors to wound our feelings."[57] Yet a significant number of southerners could not accept Calhoun's original resolution on slavery in the territories. Calhoun had advocated a bold new stance on the issue; the right to hold slaves in the territories transcended territorial law or congressional intervention. Supposedly the Constitution protected the sanctity of slave property across state and territorial boundaries, but many southerners did not support Calhoun's doctrine. They adhered to the long-standing rule of territorial self-government as sufficient protection for slavery. The admission of Texas into the Union in 1845 promised further debate on the subject as northern Whigs—and an increasing number of northern Democrats—accused the federal government of currying slaveholder favor through the dubious annexation resolution. Sectional lines had undoubtedly hardened over the course of the past twenty years, and if the United States ever did gain additional territory, no one knew how Americans would respond in the changed atmosphere.

"A FIT OF CONVULSIONS"

The Wilmot Proviso and
Slavery in the West

"The bill was debated both before and after recess on Saturday, and all was going merrily as wedding bells towards its consummation," a correspondent to the *National Intelligencer* reported, "when the apple of discord was thrown into the midst of the majority by a motion of Mr. Wilmot of Pennsylvania."[1] The Two Million Bill, granting President James K. Polk funds to conclude a peace treaty with Mexico and obtain a cession of territory, begat the Wilmot Proviso, an amendment to prohibit slavery in any territory gained at the war's conclusion that would shape much of the trajectory of American politics in the succeeding fifteen years. Yet all was not going merrily, and sectional and intraparty discord had loomed long before Democratic representative David Wilmot made his motion on August 8, 1846. For much of the previous two years, northern and southern Democrats had differed on the issue of extending slavery to the western territories. The annexation of Texas in 1845 and the ratification of the Oregon Treaty, in which Polk conceded a northern boundary at the forty-ninth parallel, in June 1846, had given rise to diverging opinions within the Democracy on the limits of slavery. The president had enthusiastically pursued the settlement of the Texas boundary issue, to the point of declaring war with Mexico, while delaying action on Oregon and ultimately settling for less generous terms. Some northern Democrats, who had grown resentful of southern domination within the party, declared that their wing of the party had acceded to slave-state interests sufficiently. When in 1846 the United States declared war on Mexico, the smoldering fight came into the open as northern Democrats accused their southern colleagues of supporting a war of conquest to extend the slave domain, a claim that southerners rejected. Wilmot and his allies sought to call the southern bluff by seeing if they would support a war for conquest without expanding the borders of slavery.

The Wilmot Proviso, however, brought a new dimension to the long-standing dispute over the extension of slavery. Previous attempts to prohibit slavery had focused almost exclusively on states entering the Union, not territorial acquisitions. Slaveholders had opposed previous efforts to proscribe slavery from incoming states as an infringement on the right of a territory to draft its constitution and establish local institutions free from congressional intervention. The Wilmot Proviso not only renewed that conflict, but also extended it to the contested terrain of the territories. In response, southerners retorted that neither the federal government nor a territorial legislature could prohibit its expansion into the territories. There stood the antislavery and proslavery positions, which would become more extreme and would eventually threaten the system of party politics that had coalesced in the 1830s. The heady period of westward expansion in the 1840s and the concomitant reappearance of the slavery issue in its most virulent form led southern Democrats and Whigs to reconsider their beliefs and search for new ways to secure the future of slavery in the West.

TEXAS ANNEXATION revivified the debate over territorial expansion, not only pitting Whigs against Democrats along familiar political lines, but also engendering discord within the parties themselves. Indeed, "Texas struck a popular chord in the South unmatched by any political issue since the initial outburst of abolition activity back in 1835 and 1836." When the Texans proffered annexation in 1837, both Andrew Jackson and his successor, Martin Van Buren, the architect of the intersectional Democratic party, proved reticent to accept. Van Buren in particular feared that annexation would engender discord within the Democracy and upset sectional harmony. But by 1841, circumstances had changed dramatically, as John Tyler, the nominal Whig and ardent expansionist, assumed the presidency. The president staked his political future on Texas annexation. Northern supporters of annexation steeped in the Jeffersonian agrarian tradition looked to the economic and social benefits of westward expansion. Southerners saw the issue in similar terms, but Tyler and John C. Calhoun, in their efforts to unite their section behind their cause, added a new dimension: Texas annexation protected the future of slavery from British encroachment and secured new territory for southerners to inhabit. Southerners, especially pro-expansion Democrats, viewed annexation as essential to the stability of their section, to the continued prosperity of their agricultural economy, and for the future of slavery. Southern Democrats gleefully followed the lead of a Virginia president who had literally been read out of the Whig Party. Tyler's allegiances lay first and foremost with the South and its interests.[2]

The Texas issue dominated the 1844 presidential election contest, as Democrats sought to exploit the popularity of westward expansion and Whigs sounded alarm about unbounded territorial aggrandizement. Democrats intended to capitalize on the popularity of annexation and expansion, but rifts within the party surfaced when frontrunner Martin Van Buren, bowing to pressure from fellow northerners, came out in opposition. Some northern Democrats objected to territorial expansion that amounted to extension of the slave domain. Southern Democrats fumed at the Little Magician's apostasy, repudiating his candidacy and his control of their party. Southern leaders whipped their section's voters into a proslavery frenzy by issuing stark predictions of a bleak future if the nation did not annex Texas. The party had to find a new candidate who would rally the ranks of annexationists. They found their quarry in James K. Polk, a slaveholding Tennessee Democrat who rivaled Tyler and Calhoun in his zeal for acquiring Texas.

As politicos debated the implications of Texas annexation during the election season, a second front emerged in the nation's territorial situation. The sizeable influx of American citizens settling in the Willamette River valley since 1842 had finally forced the issue of defining the boundaries of the Oregon country. Pro-expansion Democrats of all stripes eagerly embraced the Oregon issue as a natural complement to Texas annexation and the natural progression of westward expansion that defined Jacksonian politics and Jeffersonian agrarianism. Yet voices of discord among the party faithful revealed a subtle but telling difference of opinion that bode ill for Democratic unity: northerners evinced far more zeal for Oregon, while southerners focused much more on Texas. Hints of a sectional divide appeared during the election year, most tellingly when the Senate defeated a treaty of annexation on June 8, 1844, in a 16–35 vote that illustrated the opposition to expansion not only from Whigs, but also northern Democrats. It did not disappear thereafter.

Meanwhile, Kentucky senator Henry Clay—that perennial presidential contender and Whig standard-bearer of 1844—feared the deleterious consequences of rapid and rampant expansionism. Better to refine, develop, and secure the Union as it existed rather than add additional territory and fuel the growing discord over the extension of slavery. Clay entered the 1844 campaign seeking to cool the annexation fever. Texas placed southern Whigs in a precarious position, however. Whigs recognized that the Democrats had successfully built support for annexation, which might encourage party defections among expansionist colleagues. Like their northern counterparts, southern Whigs feared the sectional agitation that the Texas issue would surely provoke. Yet opposing a move that would secure the expansion of slavery over a vast domain would also endanger their strength in the South. Fearing the wrath of proslavery expansionists and seeking to bolster party unity, most southern Whigs opposed annexation quietly lest they offend the increasing number of southerners who supported territorial expansion.[3]

Texas annexation came in the form of a joint resolution of Congress on March 1, 1845, just three days before James K. Polk assumed the presidency. The United States had assumed a slaveholding republic into its national union as a state. Additionally, the joint resolution for annexation provided for the formation of four additional states should Texas consent. The resolution extended the Missouri Compromise line through Texas; any additional states formed to the south of 36 degrees, 30 minutes could seek admission with or without slavery, while the institution was prohibited in the small and irregular portion north of the line. It seemed unlikely that Texas would someday consent to a division of its domain into smaller states unless their residents preserved slavery. Perhaps most importantly, the furor over annexation greatly intensified both antislavery and proslavery machinations. The potential that five new states, including Texas, could enter the Union almost certainly as slave states alarmed the opponents of slavery. Likewise, Texas galvanized the southern resolve to counteract antislavery forces and secure the future of slavery. Their efforts would only gain urgency as the nation went to war against Mexico in May 1846 and discussion of a "territorial indemnity," or the assumption of Mexican lands into the territorial domain of the United States gained traction.[4]

Northern Democrats accused President Polk of delaying action on the Oregon issue, which lingered long after the consummation of Texas annexation. Once the United States declared war against Mexico on May 13, 1846, the president showed little desire to provoke a second fight with Great Britain over American claims in the Oregon country. After years of tedious, and occasionally bellicose, debate between the United States and Great Britain, the two nations signed the Oregon Treaty on June 15, 1846, setting the northern boundary of the territory at the forty-ninth parallel. Ratification sorely disappointed those who cried fifty-four forty or fight, but in negotiating the treaty, Secretary of State James Buchanan had averted war with the British. The treaty could not, however, avert a battle within the Democratic Party. Northern Democrats expected that a free territory of Oregon would offset the recent acquisition of slave Texas; indeed, the Democratic platform of 1844 had implied as much. Soon, however, Texas annexation overshadowed events concerning Oregon. When Congress took up discussion of the Oregon treaty, "the pent-up resentments of the northern Democrats burst out in a flood of bitter incrimination." Angered by the actions of President James K. Polk's administration, with their proslavery implications, the Democratic Party for the first time split on sectional lines over the Oregon treaty. Indeed, northern Democrats nearly derailed the president's plans. The bitter feelings created by ardent support for Texas annexation and tepid endorsement of incorporating a smaller Oregon into the territorial domain wounded the Democratic Party, prompting its leaders to search for ways to compromise on the expansion of slavery.[5]

Northern Democrats committed to antislavery policy resolved to stand firm against the doughfaces, especially their expansionist president. A wellspring of antislavery sentiment in parts of New England and the Old Northwest had grown in the aftermath of Texas annexation, leading other northern Democrats who once evinced less interest in the politics of slavery to reconsider their stance—if only to preserve their chances at election time. Accordingly, some northern Democrats distanced themselves from the southern wing of the party.[6] Their efforts to resist the expansion of slavery culminated in the discussion over assuming Mexican territory into the United States.

On August 10, 1846, President Polk reported in his diary, "Late in the evening of Saturday, the 8th, I learned that after an excited debate in the House

a bill passed that body, but with a mischievous & foolish amendment to the effect that no territory which might be acquired by treaty with Mexico should
ever be a slave-holding country." Assuming that congressional Whigs would attempt to derail the legislation, Polk arranged to have the Two Million Bill introduced at the end of the congressional session in order to minimize, if not stifle,
debate. Though the president certainly did not know it, and the members of the
House on the floor that Saturday night could hardly have predicted what would
happen, a Pennsylvania Democrat, not an anti-expansion Whig, had started the
trouble. The "mischievous & foolish amendment" proposed by David Wilmot, a
young and relatively unknown first-term representative, injected the issue of
slavery expansion into the debate over the Two Million Bill. Perhaps most
alarming, the vote on the bill produced a sectional cleavage as nearly the entire
southern bloc voted against the bill with Wilmot's amendment attached while
the northern representatives voted in the affirmative. After the House passed
the bill on the last day of the session the Senate let the session expire without
taking a vote. Though the Wilmot Proviso had failed to pass Congress amid the
bustle of the ending session, it had transformed the debate over slavery in the
territories. "Grave topics to be decided during a fit of convulsions!" the editor of
Niles' National Register remarked.[7]

The Wilmot Proviso would provoke fits of convulsions for the next fourteen
years, because it fused westward expansion with the slavery extension issue
stronger than ever before while linking the debates of 1846 with past discussions and conflicts over restriction. Wilmot borrowed the language of his proviso from the Northwest Ordinance—that "neither slavery nor involuntary
servitude shall ever exist in any part of said territory, except for crime, whereof
the party shall first be duly convicted."[8] The proviso also bore striking resemblance to the amendment of James Tallmadge in the Missouri debates twenty-
seven years earlier. Tallmadge's amendment sought to check the westward expansion of slavery just as did the Wilmot Proviso. Of course, Tallmadge sought
to legislate for territory within the Union, whereas Wilmot sought to check slavery expansion in a territory not yet possessed by the United States; nevertheless, both borrowed from an antislavery heritage that could be traced back to
the Northwest Ordinance.

Antebellum party politics, however, added a new dimension to the debate
over the extension of slavery. For a generation, the Jacksonian Democrats had
marched in lockstep against agitation over the slavery issue. Yet Wilmot's proviso exposed growing resentment among northern Democrats who believed

that the South used the party as cover for proslavery expansionism. The "friends of the administration led off the opposition to their southern brethren," according to a Baltimore editor, because of "the 'bad faith' of the south, as they called it." To their minds, the southern members of Congress and the president had pushed zealously for Texas annexation and proslavery interests while practically abandoning the northerners' pet project of Oregon. These sentiments held true to a degree, but many northern Democrats did not intend to take a "gratuitous slap at the South." They initially sought to maintain the support of their constituents who were similarly uneasy about a Democratic administration with a southern tilt. But it soon became clear that antislavery Democrats had united with their erstwhile opponents, known as the Conscience Whigs, in opposing the expansion of slavery on constitutional grounds. In sum, antislavery politicians had taken a first, major step toward dissolving party lines that had held reasonably firm since the 1830s. In the past Americans had witnessed the sectionalization of politics when Congress deliberated the extension or restriction of slavery. The introduction of the Wilmot Proviso reinvigorated and intensified those same old debates. Many northerners had committed themselves to the antislavery agenda, while southerners increasingly sought to defend their interests. Alarmed Democrats from both sections sought a compromise solution to heal their fractured party. The massive expansion of territory that seemed all but imminent with victory in the war against Mexico gave the utmost urgency to the issue.[9]

Expansionists eager to gain a "territorial indemnity" from Mexico had looked to California with covetous eyes even before war commenced. But would slavery follow the flag west? Virginia Democrat Henry Bedinger received a letter from a northern friend arguing that slavery would never enter California because it could not take root and prosper there. "I think the southern members [of Congress] manifest too much feeling," he wrote. "You admit slavery to be an evil, but a necessary one, why then impose it on a country in which it is not necessary[?]"[10] Many northerners, especially those Democrats who sought to bridge the divide in their party that the Wilmot Proviso had created, maintained that slavery could never exist in California and thus any discussion of the issue inflamed sectional tensions for the sake of a mere abstraction. Southerners naturally countered that they sought to defend their constitutional rights and their equality within the Union, which to their minds, was hardly an abstraction.

Even if climate and soil did preclude the successful introduction of slavery in California, a point that many southerners disputed with good reason, the fact that Mexican law prohibited slavery further complicated the question. South-erners feared that the antislavery native Mexican population would work against the extension of slavery. Indeed, Bedinger's friend proved remarkably prescient when he predicted that the people in the territories would chiefly de-termine whether slavery could or would exist there via some form of popular sovereignty. "It will be said that Congress has no right to interfere with this question in her territories; so I think, but she has done it, and if the people of the territories do not concur, it has no effect." In the case of California, "Anti slavery has the start there and will preclude the introduction of slaves."[11] Just as Calhoun had predicted nine years earlier, popular sovereignty in the territories could produce an antislavery outcome, too. Issues of territorial self-government vis-à-vis the ability of the federal government to impose its will on its territories would become vital to the debate over the expansion of slavery.

Politicians interested in maintaining party lines feverishly sought ways to navigate the slavery debate. In particular, Democrats seeking to maintain party unity revisited the concepts of self-government and territorial sovereignty that had appeared years before. Prominent leaders in the North and South began to suggest that endorsing the principle of self-government could alleviate sectional tension by removing the question from Congress and leaving the slavery issue to the people of the territories. Southerners would hail the triumph of local gov-ernment and states' rights, northerners could hope that the people would choose freedom over slavery, and Congress could bask in the quietude of re-moving themselves from the acrimonious debate.

During the debate over Texas annexation in January 1845, the Missouri General Assembly had sent a series of resolutions to Congress addressing the slavery issue and advocating territorial self-government. According to the legis-lators, Missouri's citizens overwhelmingly endorsed annexation, but they pre-ferred "that Texas should be annexed to the United States without dividing her territory into slaveholding and non-slaveholding States," instead "leaving that question to be settled by the people who now, or may hereafter, occupy the ter-ritory that may be annexed." Texas would not prove the most direct instance in which to apply popular sovereignty, but the Missouri resolutions show that westerners endorsed it as a logical way to settle the debate over slavery and ter-ritorial expansion. They clearly endorsed a form of popular sovereignty, though the document's authors did not consider the implications of Texas entering the Union as a state. Could Texas itself impose conditions on the division of its do-main into several smaller states? In one sense, the question would prove moot;

no one doubted that Texas and any states carved from its vast domain would enter the Union as slave states. For this very reason, since the late 1830s a significant number of northern Democrats and Whigs alike had criticized Texas annexation as a blatant proslavery expansion project.[12]

Northern Democrats who feared for their party's future explored the idea of territorial sovereignty as a compromise that could heal the party's sectional breach by satisfying southern states' rights advocates and northern moderates alike. The need to find a middle ground between restriction and unbridled slavery expansion gained far greater urgency as moderate northern Democrats groped their way toward a compromise to bury the Wilmot Proviso, safely dispense with the slavery issue, and thereby assuage their southern brethren. The rebellion against the Polk administration had emerged most virulently in Pennsylvania, Ohio, and New York, so conciliation would have to come from elsewhere. In June 1846, moderate Democrats in New Hampshire endorsed territorial expansion in the broadest terms. At their annual convention, Franklin Pierce, an affable former Senator and future president, reported a series of resolutions that carefully addressed the Texas and Oregon issues, hailing both acquisitions as equally important to the future of the Union. More interestingly, the resolutions committee endorsed self-government as a compromise for addressing slavery in the territories, stating, "That the policy to be pursued in reference to slavery, rests with the States and Territories within which it exists— that whatever parties may *profess*, it is only as citizens of such States and Territories that the members of those parties can efficiently influence that policy."[13] Though few historians have recognized it, the Pierce committee had outlined the basic tenets of territorial self-government, or what would become known as popular sovereignty.

Allowing the people of the territories to decide the issue capitalized on the democratic spirit of American politics, present since the Revolution itself, by affirming the sovereignty of the people in their local concerns. It neutralized the Wilmot Proviso by denying the expediency, if not the right, of Congress to legislate on the local institution of slavery. It showed, in sum, significant promise as a policy that could heal the broken Democratic Party. Yet the New Hampshire resolution also and without contradiction promised a reprise of the debate over slavery and self-government that had emerged in the Missouri controversy. Pierce and the New Hampshire Democrats, however, had subtly altered the idea of territorial self-government by stating that the citizens of territories could pass laws concerning slavery, a sleight of hand designed to appease antislavery northerners that the Mexican Cession would remain free territory while presumably honoring the South's constitutional scruples. The New Hampshire Democrats, along with many of their northern brethren, predicted that a combination of native Mexicans opposed to slavery and American settlers from the North would never permit slavery in the cession.

Some Democrats, however, had no intention of compromising if it meant papering over their antislavery beliefs. New York Representative Preston King dealt a significant blow to party reconciliation when the Twenty-Ninth Congress convened for its short session in December 1846 by reintroducing the Wilmot Proviso in a fiery speech that gave no ground to the southern Democracy. He noted that the North had yielded on the issue of slavery in Texas. As for the Mexican Cession, King intended to yield no further. He specifically rebuked those who preferred to let the slavery matter alone by deferring to the people. "If left alone, slaves, more or less, will be carried to the new territory; and if the country, while it remains a territory should be settled by a population holding slaves, the new and additional question of abolition is presented, and in order to get a free state, slavery must first be abolished." Whether ignoring Pierce's new version of territorial sovereignty or being unaware of it, King assumed that the concept would operate as it had in the past; the territories would make their decision to permit or prohibit slavery in constitutional convention preparatory to statehood. If Congress truly wished to respect the voice of the people on slavery in the cession, he observed, it would prohibit the institution during the territorial phase. "In order, then, to secure this freedom of choice to the state and to the people, slavery must be excluded from the country while it shall be a territory, and until it shall become a state."[14] The New Yorker, of course, firmly believed that slavery could exist in the cession only if Congress afforded it express protection.

King's speech and his renewal of the Wilmot Proviso dismayed the president. Polk called his efforts "a fire-brand in the body" and criticized the effort to renew an "abstract question." Indeed, only the most ultra southerners endorsed federal protection of slavery in the territories. The president knew that the Wilmot Proviso threatened his efforts to acquire territory by uniting northern free-soil Democrats and Whigs against the expansion of slavery. It threatened, too, the stability of his party by alienating southerners. Nevertheless, King's speech galvanized the free soil element in the northern Democracy. It, too, would be a summons to the South to action. Polk surely recognized the implications of the King speech when he convened his cabinet to discuss the issue, but they gave little comfort to their worried executive. "All deprecated the discussion now going on in Congress," Polk wrote laconically, "but all feared it would be impossible now to arrest it." Prescient observers of the debate in Congress concurred. "Old party distinctions—war measures and peace measures—president making and tariff making," the editor of *Niles' National Register* wrote, "are all influenced by the new line of parties which this question chalks out."[15]

The abstract nature of the slavery debate, to the minds of Polk and many pro-expansion Democrats, rendered the remarks of King and his colleagues as needless as they were inflammatory. Polk flatly denied that slavery could ever exist in the Mexican territory, an argument that many in his cabinet—most notably Secretary of State Buchanan—would endorse. "There is no probability that any territory will ever be acquired from Mexico in which slavery could ever exist," the president argued. But southerners vigorously disagreed with those who portrayed the debate as an abstraction. Just before Congress convened, Polk had met with John C. Calhoun to discuss possible treaty issues with Mexico and reiterated his belief that slavery would never thrive in a Mexican Cession. Calhoun "readily assented," but noted, "if the slavery restriction was put into a Treaty, it would involve a principle, and that whatever the other provisions of the Treaty were, he would vote against it."[16]

Calhoun spoke with some authority when he informed Polk that neither he nor his fellow southerners in either party would stand for the Wilmot Proviso in any form, proving that the slavery debate continued to transcend established partisan divisions in the South. Virginia Democrat James Seddon defended the rights of the South and reaffirmed southern support for territorial sovereignty. "On what ground," he cried, should the North "arrogate superiority, and claim exclusive appropriation" of all the territories? Northerners, Seddon argued, had abandoned any semblance of compromise or sectional comity to promote their antislavery agenda—all at the expense of southern rights. "Let the white men of the north and of the south, each with privilege," emigrate to the territories with their property as they saw fit. "Let them determine for themselves according to their circumstances and necessities whether they will be free or slave states. As they determine, in such character admit them to full communion in the Union, composed alike of slaveholding and free states." The southern press echoed Seddon's protest against the free soil movement. The *Richmond Enquirer* took a cautious approach in venting anger towards the antislavery bloc. "All patriots will deeply regret to see the question of slavery introduced into the discussions in Congress," its editor wrote. "It is premature and mischievous." In a more comprehensive examination of the Wilmot Proviso and slavery in the Mexican Cession, the *Charleston Mercury* directly accused the proviso's supporters of misinterpreting the constitutional relationship between the federal government and the "embryo States." The territories, according to the *Mercury's* editor, were "raw material for States, to be finally admitted into the Union upon the same terms as the Old Thirteen." Congress had no right to prohibit slavery in the territories; only the people of the territories themselves, in constitutional convention, could legislate on slavery.[17]

In denying the constitutionality of the proviso, the *Mercury* left little, if any, room for sectional conciliation on the issue, referring to the Missouri Compromise itself as "mere shallow clamor." A significant number of Democrats, especially in the North, however, believed that extension of the compromise line of 1820 might avert the present sectional crisis. The veteran politician James Buchanan emerged as the leading proponent of extending the Missouri line to the Pacific Ocean, having introduced the idea in a cabinet meeting and receiving the approbation of his colleagues. Polk himself assented to the idea, but resolved to wait until the terms of a potential territorial cession became clearer to "recommend it to the Congress as the policy of administration."[18]

The proposed extension of the Missouri Compromise line had already surfaced in a curious congressional debate over creating a territorial government for Oregon. An enabling bill had emerged from the Committee on Territories that extended the Northwest Ordinance to Oregon Territory. Few believed that slavery would ever exist in Oregon, but southern congressmen promptly objected to the slavery provision because it set a precedent for congressional intervention over slavery in the territories. Of course, the precedent had already been set—in 1787 and again in 1820. They intended to use the Oregon bill as a test case for extension of the Missouri line. Oregon, consequently, "assumed strategic importance as a bargaining point" in the ongoing debate over the Wilmot Proviso. A Virginia representative argued that applying the sixth article of the Northwest Ordinance stemmed from a "predetermined purpose here to apply that article to all the territory of the United States no matter how acquired, or where situated or in what manner it may be affected by past compromises of legislation." Other southerners agreed that it served no other purpose than to inflame slaveholders. South Carolina Representative Armistead Burt, a Calhoun disciple, introduced an amendment to the bill that provided that Oregon would remain free territory because it lay north of the Missouri Compromise line, but conversely permitted slavery in any cession from Mexico because it would lay south of the line. Burt lamely refused to concede the constitutionality of the Missouri Compromise but proposed his solution as a compromise to escape the current crisis.[19]

Though many southern leaders found Burt's terms amenable, others maintained pressure on the antislavery phalanx. Democrats in South Carolina and Mississippi insisted on vigorous resistance, Georgians espoused conciliation, and Virginians stood divided among themselves. Above them all stood John C. Calhoun, who supported Burt's amendment while urging southern unity regardless of party label. A considerable number of southerners supported the extension of the Missouri line, even if they debated or doubted its constitutionality, in order to secure the right to carry slaves into at least part of the potential cession. More inflexible southerners, however, opposed the maneuver. Virginia Representative Shelton F. Leake declared his opposition by pronouncing himself "heartily sick of 'compromises'" and maintaining that the South had compromised too often, only to see the North breach its part of the compact. He saw the extension of the Missouri line as cover for a movement among northerners to deny the South equal privilege in the common territories. Speaking for the South, the irascible southern rights Democrat stated, "We maintain that it is a matter of municipal regulation, with which this Government cannot, rightfully, interfere; but which ought to be left to the people of the States and Territories to arrange for themselves." Instead of extending the Missouri Compromise line, Leake advocated territorial sovereignty regarding slavery.[20]

Other southern Democrats joined Leake in opposition to compromise. South Carolina Representative Robert Barnwell Rhett recapitulated the old southern argument that the "needful rules and regulations" clause of the Constitution did not allow Congress to legislate for the territories. Sovereignty rested in the people, not the government, lest the people become ruled, "and do not rule themselves." But in what way and at what time could the citizens of the territories exercise sovereignty over the slavery issue? Like Leake, Rhett believed that the territories could prohibit slavery only in constitutional convention. Rhett essentially staked out a position similar to that of his fellow South Carolinian John C. Calhoun, as had Leake, though their statements largely fell on deaf ears. On January 15, 1847, the Burt amendment failed in the House of Representatives by a vote of 82–113, yet 76 southerners had voted in the affirmative and all opposition had come from the free states. Southern support of the compromise line would not die with the failure of Burt's amendment. The South, according to a Georgia writer, would abide by an extension of the Missouri Compromise line but would go no further in compromise. Over the course of 1847 as the debate over the Wilmot Proviso continued, northern and southern Democrats would revisit the extension issue in their efforts to unite on a compromise program.[21]

The failure of the Burt amendment, however, gave the Calhounites ammunition to attack the premise of compromise itself. Its defeat merely confirmed to them that northerners would not abide by compromises in any event. "Let us be done with compromises," John C. Calhoun cried in the Senate. "Let us go back and stand upon the Constitution!"[22] Echoing the earlier statements of his southern colleagues that the time for compromise had passed, he introduced resolutions affirming southern rights in the territories. Calhoun stated "that it is a fundamental principle in our political creed, that a people in forming a constitution have the unconditional right to form and adopt the Government which they may think best calculated to secure their liberty, prosperity, and happiness."[23] Congress could not abridge the right of a territory in its constitutional convention to draft its own organic law provided that it embodied republican principles. Calhoun's resolutions stated explicitly what Leake's speech on territorial self-government had implied: that southerners believed that a territory could act on the slavery issue only at the moment of the formation of its state constitution.

John C. Calhoun made a percipient observation regarding popular sovereignty that would haunt its southern supporters until the coming of the Civil War: the doctrine may have virtually guaranteed the expansion of slavery in the past, but it likely would result in the creation of free states in the future. The senator knew that northerners could use the doctrine as an antislavery weapon if they could emigrate to the West in sufficient numbers. Furthermore, he predicted that if the emerging northern interpretation of popular sovereignty that permitted territorial legislatures to permit or prohibit slavery prevailed, antislavery Americans could take control of territorial governments and ban slavery before southerners could populate the territories. Accordingly, to Calhoun's dark view of the southern position in the Union, the South had to hew to a less flexible and accommodating position that would secure slavery and southern interests in the face of a strengthening—and perhaps more determined—antislavery vanguard.

In developing a southern "counterpoise" to the Wilmot Proviso, Calhoun advanced a subtly different version of self-government that advanced what has become known as the common-property doctrine on the territories.[24] Indeed, Calhoun's statement regarding slavery in the territories built on the political theories that he had developed over his long political career. Two of his points reiterated established southern policy. First, Calhoun asserted that neither Congress nor a territorial legislature could prohibit slavery in the territories. Most southerners had agreed for at least the past forty years that Congress had no right to legislate for the territories on domestic institutions, a point that Calhoun himself had declared in his 1837 resolutions on slavery in the territories. The right of a territorial legislature to pass laws restricting slavery remained in doubt, largely because it had never been tested. The Missouri Compromise had basically settled the issue by dividing the territorial domain. Second, Calhoun believed that a territory could legislate on slavery only when drafting a constitution, an assertion likewise rooted in traditional southern political doctrine on the issue of slavery and territorial expansion. Southerners had amply explained and defended the people's sovereignty to craft their own organic law regarding slavery during the Missouri controversy and in subsequent debates on statehood for Arkansas and Florida.

Calhoun added a new element to the debate over slavery in the territories, arguing that slavery indeed followed the flag; it existed in territories purchased or conquered by the United States and remained a legal institution unless a territory prohibited it as part of their constitution. Then, and only then, could slavery be prohibited. Calhoun himself did not assert that the federal government must protect slavery, but within a decade radical southerners would extend his theories to call for a federal slave code. The senator also launched a preemptive attack against any legislator who would argue that territorial legislatures could prohibit slavery if they so desired, anticipating future trouble over the implementation of territorial sovereignty. In sum, Calhoun's doctrine represented the extreme southern position, just as the Wilmot Proviso was the extreme northern position. More conciliatory politicians would have to stake out a position somewhere in between.

In spite of the continued enthusiasm for the Wilmot Proviso in the North and the emergence of Calhoun's proslavery doctrine as the ultra southern stance, extension of the Missouri Compromise line remained the leading solution to compromise into the summer of 1847. Indeed, no other resolution seemed more likely to gain sufficient support from the public and in Congress. Leading southern journals approved of extension as a way of securing southern rights in at least a portion of any potential cession from Mexico. The *Milledgeville Federal Union*, for example, reaffirmed the support of the South for extension of the 36 degrees, 30 minutes line: "Thus far she will go, but not an inch beyond." Other writers echoed the sentiment. "We go for the compromises of the constitution," one Louisiana editor wrote, "as continued and carried out by the Missouri compromise." The *Richmond Enquirer* maintained its pressure on supporters of the Wilmot Proviso, insisting that Congress had no right to "fetter" the territories by imposing conditions on their admission into the Union. The South could not afford to "trust the whole matter to the justice and good sense of Congress—which would make us admit that Congress has the *power* to abolish slavery in our territories, and to *impose* conditions on new States coming into the Union." Herein lay the problem with extending the Missouri Compromise line. When moderate southerners endorsed extension, they risked tacitly admitting that Congress possessed the power to legislate over the territories. Thomas Ritchie himself, who had edited the *Enquirer* until 1845, had lamented passage of the Compromise of 1820 precisely on the grounds that it surrendered the South's constitutional rights north of 36 degrees, 30 minutes.[25]

Twenty-five years earlier, southerners chose to ignore the reality that the Missouri Compromise implicitly granted Congress power over slavery in the West. In the charged political climate of the 1840s, however, the South could not and would not concede that authority to a Congress increasingly populated by those hostile to the extension of slavery. Calhoun had illustrated the inherent flaw in the Missouri Compromise when he advocated his own theory on slavery in the territories. The South Carolina senator, however, conveniently neglected to mention that he had supported the compromise as a member of President James Monroe's cabinet. Nevertheless, Calhoun raised an important caveat that southerners—regardless of party affiliation—had to heed. Could the South afford to surrender constitutional ground—even in the spirit of compromise—at a time when it had less influence in national councils than ever before? Ironically, northern free-soil Democrats feared that the South exercised overweening power in the federal government. Moderate southern Democrats still saw their national party as an appropriate safeguard for southern interests, but Calhounites expressed doubts that anything less than a united South—regardless of party distinctions—could protect the expansion of slavery in the territories and the continued existence of slavery in the states. Calhoun gave a rousing speech in Charleston, South Carolina, upon his return home from the late congressional session, stating: "As constituent members of the Union, all the Territories and other property of the Union belong to them, as joint owners or partners, and not to the Government, as is er[r]oneously supposed by some." Calhoun excoriated the abolitionist minority that used its power to sway elections in several key northern states where Whigs and Democrats consistently ran even in balloting, charging they used party politics to advance their anti-southern agenda. Calhoun also claimed that abolitionists exhibited no reverence for the Constitution in attempting to deny southern slaveholders equal participation in westward expansion.[26]

Most southerners still believed that the American political system provided safety and security for southern interests, but Calhoun saw party politics as corrosive to southern unity because it forced southerners to compromise with northerners. Because slavery seemed poised to eclipse all other political questions, he believed, southerners could no longer place their trust in Whigs and Democrats; they must eschew party affiliations and unite under the banner of the South alone. In Alabama, Calhoun found a close ally in his efforts to galvanize southern resistance to the Wilmot Proviso and to advocate his doctrine on slavery in the territories. In May 1847, William Lowndes Yancey, a former representative and ardent advocate of southern rights, advanced a series of resolutions that resembled the Calhoun doctrine at a state Democratic meeting. Rejecting the call for compromise, Yancey "demonstrated that northern Democrats, who claimed to be strict constructionists, were in fact willing to compromise true constitutional principles in order to win elections." His words resonated among many southerners, as Democratic Party conventions in Virginia, Georgia, and Alabama drafted resolutions affirming the right of any citizen to enter the territories with his property and vowing to oppose any presidential candidate who did not state his opposition to the Wilmot Proviso. Whereas many Democratic regulars throughout the South wished to restore party unity and cooperation with the northern Democrats, Yancey sided with Calhoun in considering southern rights paramount to intersectional political collaboration. Yancey's resolutions at the May 1847 Democratic meeting in Montgomery stated the familiar refrain that Congress had no power to interfere with slavery in the territories. At another Alabama Democratic meeting, party regulars vowed to oppose any presidential candidate who did not explicitly refuse to interfere with slavery in the territories. In time, Yancey would link the two ideas in a formidable defense of southern rights squarely in the Calhoun tradition and a call for an exclusively southern political organization.[27]

Despite Calhoun's warnings and the movement of his allies in other southern states, most Democrats pressed on with their efforts to achieve compromise and mollify Americans on both sides of the slavery issue. The senator may have found "perfect unanimity" in Charleston regarding his recent pronouncements on slavery and the territories, but some southerners as well as many northern Democrats continued to look for common ground. The efforts at sectional conciliation within the Democratic Party came almost solely from the North. James Buchanan took the lead by offering the most reasoned rationale for extending the Missouri Compromise line. In a practice common in nineteenth-century politics, presidential aspirants announced their candidacy by drafting a letter to a friend, who in actuality was a campaign supporter. Buchanan announced his candidacy in a letter to the Democrats of Berks County, Pennsylvania, by reiterating his position that the "harmony of the States & even the security of the Union itself require that the line of the Missouri Compromise should be extended to any new territory which we may acquire from Mexico." In what became known as the Old Berks letter, the presidential hopeful asserted that designing politicians advocated the Wilmot Proviso for no practical reason. Slavery could never exist in any territory acquired from Mexico. "Neither the soil, the climate, nor the productions of that portion of California south of 36° 30 , nor indeed of any portion of it North or South, is adapted to slave labor." Buchanan's assessment of whether slavery could thrive in the Mexican territory most likely came from reports from the West. Numerous commentators considered the land unsuitable for slavery and plantation agriculture. One observer wrote that Americans had overestimated "to an absurdity the arable surface of California"; he believed that only 4 percent of the land would prove suitable for "the purposes of civilized life."[28]

By endorsing extension of the Missouri Compromise line, Buchanan became the first presidential contender to clarify his position on the Wilmot Proviso. Other politicians soon followed. "Parties are beginning to define their position with somewhat more clearness on this vexed question" of the Wilmot Proviso, *Niles' National Register* editor Jeremiah Hughes noted, "and we find considerable diversity of opinion prevailing in the same party in different sections of the country, in regard to it." In the southern press, Democratic journals maintained pressure on Whigs and the northern Democracy to reject the idea of congressional power over slavery in the territories. The *Richmond Enquirer* endorsed the Buchanan plan, citing the Old Berks letter as "evidence that our friends at the North do not mean to desert us at this crisis." Democratic moderates throughout the South looked to extension as a viable compromise and a hopeful sign that abolitionism had not co-opted the northern wing of their party.[29]

At the same time, however, wary southerners maintained a steady drum beat against the restriction issue by affirming its unconstitutionality. The *Rich-*

mond Enquirer chastised its Whig counterpart for the "insidious" contention "that because the old Federal Congress of 1787 thought itself empowered to prohibit slavery in the territory ceded by Virginia, the present establishment . . . must have greater, or at least equal, power over slavery."[30] Debate over the proviso had risen to the level of a constitutional discourse, as did so many issues in mid-nineteenth-century politics. This had the ironic and contradictory effect of providing greater impetus to reach a compromise on the vexed slavery issue, but simultaneously making compromise more difficult.

Many Democrats received Buchanan's compromise proposal favorably precisely because of the need to restore intersectional party unity for the upcoming election. Thomas Ritchie, now the editor of the Democratic Party's national organ, the *Washington Union*, endorsed the Old Berks letter as sound policy, noting that the Polk administration "oppose[s] all restrictions upon the South, and all efforts to restrict slavery south of the 36° 30 north latitude." Ritchie signaled that the extension of the Missouri Compromise line, which the Polk administration had endorsed privately since January 1847, had become the president's favored policy. Moderate northern journals also exhibited willingness to embrace compromise. In New York, a state riven with political discord over the slavery issue, moderate Democrats acknowledged the futility of imposing the Wilmot Proviso on the South. Like Buchanan, a number of northern editors considered slavery in the Mexican territories an abstraction. Several New York editors noted that "the moment state governments are formed, the power of Congress ceases—and the people, acting in their sovereign capacities, can establish slavery at any moment."[31] Why, then, jeopardize the harmony of the Union and the successful negotiation of a territorial indemnity over the issue of slavery?

A number of southern politicians also began to express their views on slavery in the territories as presidential politics intensified in late 1847. Mississippi Senator Jefferson Davis recognized the need for party unity, but demanded that prior to nomination of a presidential candidate northern Democratic delegates profess "a disavowal of the principles of the Wilmot Proviso; an admission of the equal right of the south with the north, to the territory held as the common property of the United States; and a declaration in favor of extending the Missouri compromise to all States to be hereafter admitted into our confederacy." In other words, Davis insisted that the party endorse congressional noninterference with slavery in the territories. Even southern Whigs insisted on gaining equal rights in the territories, though many endorsed the no-territory position as the safest means of maintaining the Union. Georgia Senator John M. Berrien, one of the architects of the concept, asked his constituents "if they would consent to acquire this territory by our common sufferings, blood and treasure, and have it, except upon terms of perfect equality with our northern territory and exclude slavery from it?" No southerner, of course, could accept such unequal terms. "Far better go with our whig brethren at the north, leave our weak and distracted sister republic to the possession of her territory, and save the constitution and the country." In the South, the no-territory formula suffered from one weakness: by avoiding territorial acquisition, and thereby avoiding conflict over the slavery question, Whigs seemed insistent on avoiding a fight over southern rights. Most Americans embraced the idea of a Mexican cession; most southerners demanded the right to possess slaves in the territories. The Union would simply have to find a way to compromise on the slavery issue.[32]

The machinations behind presidential politics produced a second compromise formula that would compete with the Missouri formula for Democratic fealty. Vice President George M. Dallas held hopes of becoming president after serving a long and distinguished career in a variety of public offices. The Pennsylvanian, however, had never exhibited any outstanding qualities for the highest office; indeed, he gained the vice-presidential nomination in 1844 only after New York senator Silas Wright declined the offer. Dallas wanted to seek the Democratic presidential nomination in 1848, but he had to find a way to distinguish himself from his bitter rival and fellow Pennsylvanian James Buchanan, by most accounts the leading contender in late 1847. He did so by rejecting extension of the Missouri Compromise line and espousing the doctrine of popular sovereignty.[33]

Dallas launched his presidential campaign in a speech given at Pittsburgh in September 1847. Though the vice president discussed other issues such as the conduct of the Mexican war and the tariff, he directed most of his remarks to the Wilmot Proviso and the slavery issue. Acknowledging the antislavery faction of the Democratic Party, Dallas recognized their objection to the extension of slavery on moral grounds. He claimed, however, that the Constitution prevented the federal government from interfering with the institution of slavery where it existed. If they wanted to end slavery, they would have to do so through amending the Constitution, a prospect that Dallas certainly knew would prove impossible.

After chastising free soilers for their misinterpretation of the Constitution, Dallas turned to the issue of compromise. "But we hear, in some quarters, much talk of what is called *compromise*," Dallas stated. Portraying himself as a legitimate heir to Jeffersonian republicanism, and thereby proclaiming his fealty to the strictures of states' rights and local self-government, Dallas declared, "I am of that old school of Democrats who will never compromise the Constitution of my country."[34] Appealing to the heirs of Jefferson and Jackson, Dallas sought to identify himself and his proposal for settling the slavery issue with democracy—the right of the people to govern themselves. Dallas charged that Whigs, on the other hand, either assumed expansive federal power over the territories or ducked the question altogether by espousing the no-territory platform. Either way, according to the vice president, they thwarted the will of the people. Democrats, on the other hand, believed that territorial sovereignty honored the principle of states' rights and local self-government. More pragmatically, a growing number of northern Democrats believed they could construct a formula for territorial sovereignty that would satisfy northerners and southerners by virtue of its ambiguity. The Janus-faced version of territorial sovereignty advocated by Dallas had antislavery and proslavery visages.

Dallas sought to establish himself as a Democrat who would strive to maintain intersectional party unity, unlike a growing number of northern Democrats who seemingly wished to declare independence from the party's connections to southern slaveholders. He followed with a stinging criticism of the Missouri Compromise designed to appeal to southern Democrats who shunned the mantle of conciliation. In 1820, Dallas argued, "men got together and talked of compromises, and made compromises, and one-half insisted on what they had no right to ask, and the other half submitted to that which they never should have submitted to."[35] Such compromises actually undermined, rather than preserved, constitutional government and sectional comity. By perpetuating an already flawed compromise formula, Buchanan's proposal to extend the Missouri Compromise line would only exacerbate sectional tensions.

Dallas proposed an appealing way to settle the dispute over the expansion of slavery and bury the dreaded Wilmot Proviso. "The very best thing which can be done," he argued, "will be to let it alone entirely—leaving to the people of the territory to be acquired, the business of settling the matter for themselves." Dallas asserted that the people of the territories would achieve their desires regardless of congressional mandate, "for where slavery has no existence, all the legislation of Congress would be powerless to give it existence; and where we find it to exist the people of the country have themselves adopted the institution; they have the right, alone, to determine their own institutions."[36] The vice president ended his remarks on slavery in the territories by appealing to both sides of the issue not to condemn the other for their respective opinions on the slavery issue.

Dallas's speech marked the first occasion that a prominent northern Democrat had seized upon the traditionally southern formula of territorial sovereignty. Dallas had essentially called his party to maintain the North-South alliance devised by Martin Van Buren and the Old Republicans three decades before. Territorial sovereignty, he believed, would remove the slavery issue from national councils and allow the Democrats to concentrate on other issues in order to gain votes and maintain power. In the course of his short speech, Dallas had proposed a thoughtful application of territorial self-government that would captivate the attention of the Democrats, especially from the North, as a promising means of bypassing the Wilmot Proviso and assuaging the party rank and file in the North and South. Dallas had carefully articulated his proposal in a way that conceded specific points to each section. He would surely have objected to calling his plan a compromise, but in fact the vice president had developed just that—a proposal that balanced northern and southern concerns regarding the expansion of slavery. Dallas personally disliked slavery, but he condemned the abolitionists' rhetoric. He rejected their efforts to interfere with slavery in the South, but in doing so he clothed himself with the armor of the Constitution. "If you can accomplish the abolition of slavery in the Southern States through its instrumentality," Dallas advised abolitionists and free-soilers, "why do so. . . . The only true test, however, to which we can submit this question, or any other that may arise, is the Constitution."[37] He implicitly reminded southerners, however, that territorial sovereignty allowed the people in the territories to choose between slavery and freedom; neither southerners nor northerners had a right to decide for them. In donning the constitutional mantle, Dallas appealed to moderate northerners and the southern wing of the Democracy by implicitly accusing abolitionists of operating against the Constitution.

Dallas's condemnation of the Missouri Compromise served a twofold purpose: it immediately distinguished him from his archrival James Buchanan and it appealed to southerners who viewed any compromise with skepticism. Calhoun and his followers had raised concerns about extending the compromise line that resonated with southerners. The Dallas plan merely dispensed with extension altogether by assuming the old southern argument that the Compromise of 1820 was at least extra-constitutional, if not unconstitutional. Again, Dallas appealed to the higher authority of the Constitution as the final arbiter of the slavery issue. Upholding the tenets of the founding charter, however, required some plan of action because the Constitution clearly dictated that the people themselves would have to decide whether to permit or prohibit slavery within their bounds. The Tenth Amendment, in the vice president's somewhat stretched reasoning, represented not only fundamental law, but also an axiom of political behavior. The Constitution affirmed that powers not delegated to the federal government resided with the states, or the people. Therefore, the states possessed sovereignty over slavery within their bounds. Though the Tenth Amendment did not explicitly apply to the territories, Dallas advocated granting them the power to determine their own domestic institutions. Regardless of what Congress dictated, the people would decide the issue for themselves. Constitutional law and human nature suggested no other way.

The Dallas plan, however, raised several significant questions that the vice president himself did not answer. No one disputed the power of the states to determine their own domestic institutions, but could a territory—as an inchoate political community—possess such power? From the organization of the Louisiana Purchase onward, all southerners, and many northerners, had affirmed that the territories could permit or prohibit slavery when drafting a constitution. More recently, Calhoun had taken this opinion in articulating his theory on slavery in the territories. But if read another way, Dallas's speech seemed to suggest that the people of the territories, during the *territorial phase*, could legislate on the matter for themselves. Might territorial legislatures, then, have the power to permit or prohibit slavery? Again, Calhoun had anticipated this possibility. The Dallas speech left unanswered the questions of how to apply the doctrine of territorial sovereignty in order to maintain its inherent ambiguity and appeal to Democrats in both sections.[38] Without further clarification, northerners could view the Dallas plan as essentially antislavery. Northern Democrats knew that Mexican law prohibited slavery. If settlers could legislate on the institution during the territorial phase, the Mexican inhabitants could reaffirm their prohibition of slavery before slaveholders had a chance to emigrate to the territory. Conversely, southerners could argue that Dallas had merely reaffirmed the longstanding policy of the Democratic Party and Calhoun's formulation.

Southerners hailed the Dallas speech as a bold defense of their rights in the territories. "Could the most ultra opponent of the Wilmot Proviso—the most rigid stickler for the rights of the South," the *Richmond Enquirer* asked, "take stronger ground?" A Louisiana journal stated that Dallas's pronouncement essentially endorsed the Calhoun theory on slavery in the territories. Some southerners expressed their satisfaction with the speech to the vice president himself. One Mississippi citizen applauded Dallas's rejection of the Missouri Compromise. "Had you supported the principles of the Missouri compromise as being the true standard, & set it up before the Union as a reason why the line should not be continued upon the present compromise parallel to the Pacific, we could not have reposed our confidence in you to the same broad extent which we do now." A Pennsylvania jurist, though openly professing his antislavery beliefs, felt reassured that Dallas's "long tried democratic principles have not been extinguished by the centralism which has long been at war with the rights of the states." Praise from the North and South showed that Dallas's malleable statement for self-government seemed to have potential as a compromise.[39]

Prospects of harmony proved more elusive for the southern Whigs, who found themselves at odds with the northern wing of their party over westward expansion and the slavery issue. Whigs in the North naturally opposed the extension of slavery, but they also perceived great danger in obtaining territory from Mexico. They wanted to follow the advice of Daniel Webster, who during the Texas annexation debate, "cited the admonition of an ancient Spartan to his countrymen: 'You have a Sparta, embellish it!'"[40] Northern Whigs saw little need for expansion and indeed believed that it could harm the Union by reigniting the slavery issue. Southern Whigs, however, represented a very different constituency. They sought to discredit the new popular sovereignty formula and to portray themselves as the true defenders of slavery and southern rights.

Southern Whigs viewed Dallas's proposal for territorial sovereignty as a potentially dangerous stance for southerners to endorse. The prosperous planters who composed much of southern Whiggery had scant interest in westward expansion, but they did have great interest in protecting the sanctity of slavery in the states. To them it seemed that talk of slavery's expansion only galvanized antislavery sentiment, which bade ill for the South. The *Richmond Times*, a Whig journal, argued that "Southern interests would be far more certainly secured by the adoption of Mr. Buchanan's proposition, than by leaving the question open, as Mr. Dallas advises, to the bone of future contentions." Criticism of Dallas stemmed from the Whigs' fear of territorial expansion. The Democrats, in the words of a Maryland Whig, "blindly pursue a war of conquest having in view the acquisition of more territory without considering the effect such a course may have upon our domestic institutions." Even southern Whigs who took the no-territory stance, though, had to defend the institution of slavery in the states and territories in order earn the trust of southern voters. The same

Marylander who objected to the Mexican war also emphatically stated that the expansion of slavery "should be a discretionary matter with the State or States that may be carved out of Territory. It is a matter with which the general government has no concern, the constitution having invested them with no despotic power." In this one sense, southern Whigs had to pay respect to the doctrine of self-government.[41]

Dallas's plan for territorial sovereignty had the potential to overshadow Buchanan's call for extension of the Missouri Compromise line because of its unmistakable link to democracy and popular government. Furthermore, it hewed to the Democratic Party's position on limited government and states' rights and to its commitment to democracy itself. A South Carolina Whig best explained the difference between Buchanan and Dallas on the slavery issue, at least according to southerners. In a speech at Greenville, South Carolina, Waddy Thompson offered resolutions "complimentary to two distinguished citizens of Pennsylvania, who have the boldness and virtue (rare in these times) to take high ground in favor of the south, and one of them (Mr. DALLAS) in support of our constitutional rights." Even Thompson, a no-territory Whig, perceived the difference between Buchanan and Dallas. Buchanan's proposal merely extended a compromise that many southerners found imperfect at best, while Dallas advocated a plan that seemed congruent with the statements of the most ardent southern rights men. Men of the South, even some Whigs, found great appeal in the Dallas plan and the "noble stand" the candidate had taken "in defence of her institutions."[42]

The Polk administration remained aloof from the debate between the competing plans of how to dispose of the Wilmot Proviso. The president himself seemed reluctant to choose sides, for fellow Democrats might construe an endorsement of either the Buchanan or Dallas plan as backing the candidate himself. The administration's official newspaper made note of the Dallas speech and his denunciation of the Missouri Compromise, but made no further comment on the matter.[43] The vice president remained an outside contender; in the fall of 1847, Buchanan seemed a stronger choice. But a number of southern Democrats had shifted their support from the Missouri Compromise solution to Dallas's proposal. Given the delicacy of the situation and the fact that the presidential election season had only recently begun in earnest, the administration chose to remain silent awaiting further developments.

To some degree Polk's reticence may have stemmed from the lingering questions regarding how Dallas's version of self-government would work in practice. The vice president had imbued his plan with great ambiguity; to northerners it seemed that territorial legislatures could use the doctrine to prohibit slavery, while southerners tended to view the pronouncement as a defense of their belief that the territories could rule on the issue when drafting a constitution. A New York editor perhaps unwittingly illustrated the confusion inherent in the Dallas statement when he endorsed the vice president's speech. "Let [the Democrats] leave the embarrassing question of slavery where the framers of the constitution left it; let them leave to the future what belongs to the future, and await the influence of time and the dispensations of Providence, and all will be well."[44] More perceptive political observers knew that the future would eventually arrive, with all its questions about how to apply territorial sovereignty.

Abolitionists from the North took quick aim at the doctrine, arguing that territorial legislatures did not constitutionally possess the power to pass laws concerning slavery. Former Liberty Party presidential candidate James G. Birney asked rhetorically, "Is it not true, that if Congress choose for any reason to give its legislative authority to a Territorial legislature, it cannot give a power which it did not itself possess[?] Congress, being responsible, too, the Territorial legislature cannot exercise a power that it did not receive."[45] Birney clearly based his argument on the fact that slavery did not exist in Mexican territory, and to his mind could not unless Congress or territorial legislatures passed enabling legislation. Indeed, neither legislative body had the power to *permit* slavery. Interestingly, John C. Calhoun and his followers attacked the doctrine of territorial self-government by raising almost the same questions, but asserting conversely that the U.S. Constitution would supersede existing Mexican law, dictating that slavery would follow the flag. Calhoun insisted, too, that neither Congress nor territorial legislatures had the power to *prohibit* slavery.

Although abolitionists became the major critics of territorial self-government in the North, Whigs in the South pointed out the danger in adopting the Dallas principle, especially if the implication that territorial legislatures could decide the slavery issue prevailed. A Virginia Whig editor posed the pivotal question: who were "the people" of the territories? Using explicitly racialized language designed to inflame southern opinion, the editor wrote, "Interpreting Mr. Dallas' obscurity with the aid of the light imparted by his official rival, we must believe that the people in question are, *'in large proportion, a colored population,'* among whom *'the negro does not socially belong to a degraded race.'* Must the South return thanks for the boon which Mr. Dallas proffers it, through the hands of such delectable governors?"[46] By asking the question "Who governs?" southern

Whigs had raised an issue that would plague Dallas and any other proponent of territorial sovereignty. They sought to show that the Dallas plan could potentially grant the power to determine slavery's future to a nonwhite population. Could the people of any territory gained from Mexico prohibit slavery before southern slaveholders, in theory, had the chance to emigrate to the West?

James Buchanan, who had an equally low estimation of the Mexican people, used the politics of race to advance his own plan to extend the Missouri Compromise line, questioning their ability to adapt to American government and institutions. "How should we govern the mongrel race which inhabits" the territory, Buchanan asked General James Shields. "Could we admit them to seats in our Senate & House of Representatives? Are they capable of Self Government as States of this Confederacy?"[47] Other politicians such as Senator Lewis Cass of Michigan had questioned territorial acquisition because they believed the inhabitants could not govern themselves effectively, according to Buchanan. Many Americans viewed the Mexican republic as a farce and the people of Mexico as unable to contribute to Anglo-American society—in no small part because of their racial heritage. They presumably would need a period of tutelage where they could learn the ways of American society and political institutions.

Buchanan argued that Mexicans once incorporated into the republic through territorial acquisition would never consent to establish slavery. They had ended the institution of slavery within a decade of gaining their independence. Buchanan argued that the United States could never establish slavery there not only because of the climate, but also because of the people themselves. Should the United States gain a territorial indemnity, he wrote, "it is still more improbable that a majority of the people of that region would consent to re-establish slavery."[48] Buchanan basically admitted that the inhabitants of any territory gained from Mexico would have, by virtue of their very presence, some role in deciding whether slavery would or would not exist within the territory— a prospect that many Americans in 1847 would find troubling. The racialized anti-Mexican rhetoric only intensified as politicians continued to debate self-government and the expansion of slavery into the future Mexican Cession.

Even as critics assailed the Dallas plan for its potential to exacerbate rather than ameliorate sectional tensions over the extension of slavery, the candidate did little to clarify his position on slavery in the territories or address the concerns of his critics. Indeed, clarifying his position would remove its bisectional appeal. As long as northern Democrats believed that territorial sovereignty could produce an antislavery outcome and southerners believed it would operate as it had in the past, both sides would remain content. In a speech given at Hollidaysburg, Pennsylvania, just over a month after his Pittsburgh address, Dallas merely reiterated his interpretation of the Constitution that Congress had no right to "extinguish the privilege of self-government, and to do precisely with the local communities what it pleased."[49] The vice president once again neglected to state *when* a territory could legislate on slavery, an omission that many southern Democrats ignored. For the sake of party unity they embraced the Dallas formula in spite of the questions concerning its application.

The commingling of the politics of slavery with partisan presidential competition actually exacerbated tensions over the extension of slavery and hastened the disruption of traditional party conflict between Whigs and Democrats. Southern Whigs who sought to strengthen their own party's record on slavery immediately pounced on the inconsistencies of the Pennsylvanian's plan for territorial self-government. "So long as the Democracy of the South, can find such men at the North to sustain their principles," a Georgia editor declared, "they will not despair of the republic." Yet the lack of clarity in Dallas's position ultimately put southern Democrats on the defensive, as their Whig opponents and ultra southern rights men would question what the doctrine of self-government as articulated by northern Democrats would actually mean in practice. Opponents of the Dallas doctrine, however, could not overcome the popularity of the idea of self-government as defined by the vice president. Although the introduction of the doctrine raised serious questions regarding when people in the territories could permit or prohibit slavery, a significant number of southern Democrats embraced the concept while dismissing or ignoring the caveats raised by their opponents. The power of Congress over the territories, a Virginia correspondent wrote, "must be determined by the Constitution also and the reserved rights of the community. Where a doubt rises in the construction of the former, it may often be solved by reference to the latter." Moderate northern Democrats largely agreed. If new states carved from the western territories desired to permit slavery, the *New York Herald* asked, "what right would the people of Massachusetts or Connecticut have to interfere with their regulations?"[50]

By the time that the Thirtieth Congress convened in the first week of December 1847, territorial sovereignty had surpassed extension of the Missouri Compromise as the preferred Democratic stance on the slavery expansion issue. Several Democratic senators from the North had decided to test congressional support for self-government by refining Dallas's iteration of the doctrine. After consulting with several Senate colleagues, including presidential con-

Three northern Jacksonians who fit the description of "doughface"—John Taylor's famous pejorative—Vice President George M. Dallas (upper left), New York Senator Daniel S. Dickinson (upper right), and Michigan Senator Lewis Cass all embraced different versions of the popular sovereignty doctrine after the Wilmot Proviso had reignited the debate over the extension of slavery. (Library of Congress)

tender Lewis Cass of Michigan, Daniel S. Dickinson of New York introduced resolutions endorsing territorial sovereignty. The senator argued that the federal government could impose no conditions on states or territories that placed them in an inferior status to the original thirteen states. More importantly, he specifically sanctioned the practice of self-government by the territories themselves. "That in organizing a territorial government for territory belonging to the United States," Dickinson wrote, "the principles of self-government, upon which our federative system rests, will be best promoted, the true spirit and meaning of the Constitution be observed, and the confederacy strengthened, by leaving all questions concerning the domestic policy therein to the legislatures chosen by the people thereof."[51]

Dickinson's interpretation of territorial sovereignty removed any inherent uncertainty from the version presented by Vice President Dallas three months earlier. Territorial legislatures would have the express right to legislate on slavery within their boundaries, a stipulation that fixed precisely when territorial self-government went into effect. As soon as Congress enabled a territory to elect a legislature, commonly known as the second grade of territorial government, it could permit or prohibit slavery as it wished. In sum, Dickinson had taken sides on the issue of how to apply the practice of self-government by rejecting the notion that a territory could legislate on slavery only when drafting its constitution and seeking statehood.[52]

The full Senate delayed consideration of Dickinson's resolutions for several weeks, but that did not stop senators and the public alike from commenting on their merits. As many politicians might have expected, John C. Calhoun emerged as the fiercest critic of Dickinson's version of territorial self-government. By resolving the ambiguity of the Dallas proposal and asserting the power of territorial legislatures to pass laws concerning slavery, the Dickinson resolutions repudiated the Calhoun doctrine on slavery in the territories and offended the South. The South Carolinian immediately attacked the resolutions as a free soil maneuver, though he ascribed them to the Polk administration. Calhoun believed that the president had sanctioned their introduction as a compromise measure designed to unite moderates on both sides of the slavery issue. He wrote, "Much circumlocution is used, in order to disguise their real meaning, but their real object is to affirm, that the territorial Legislatures may exclude the introduction of slaves, while they deny that Congress can."[53]

Calhoun had also absorbed the racial rhetoric that southern Whigs had leveled against the territorial sovereignty proposal. He vehemently objected to the notion that the Mexicans residing within the territory the United States stood to gain in the war with Mexico could have a hand in determining the future of slavery in the southwest. "Now, when we reflect that the Mexicans are all abolitionists," he wrote to a close associate, "it is easy to see that the scheme will, as effectually exclude slavery, as would the Wilmot Proviso itself." Calhoun stated that he would rather let Congress decide the matter "than to leave it to the Mexicans to decide." To Calhoun's mind, the Dickinson resolutions effectively barred the South from expanding into the Mexican territories regardless of whether the land could sustain slavery. The venerable South Carolinian, however, doubted that a majority of southerners would see the resolutions as he did. "There are Southern men, who I fear will be either too blind to see the truth, or too much devoted to party & President making" to oppose the Dickinson resolutions and endorse his stronger line.[54]

Calhoun assumed correctly that his opposition to the Dickinson resolutions lacked unified support in the South. One of Georgia's leading Democratic journals immediately endorsed the Dickinson resolutions as constitutionally sound and "acceptable to the South." Indeed, a state Democratic convention in Milledgeville, Georgia, sanctioned territorial sovereignty. The convention's resolutions affirmed that the South did not ask Congress for positive establishment of slavery in the territories—a request that the federal government could not grant constitutionally. The states of the South "simply require that the inhabitants of each territory shall be left free to determine for themselves, whether the institution of slavery shall or shall not form a part of their social system." Georgia Democrats emerged first as the proponents of the Dickinson resolutions, but their effusions of praise are significant as much for what they did not say as what they did. They praised the principle of self-government, but made no comment on Dickinson's assertion that territorial legislatures could pass laws concerning slavery. In other words, a number of southern Democrats desperate to preserve their party professed support for the Dickinson resolutions, but in reality they maintained the ambiguous interpretation of George Dallas. Most committed Democrats in the South either ignored the implications of Dickinson's resolutions for the sake of party unity, or simply maintained the traditional southern interpretation of territorial self-government in spite of what their northern brethren said.[55]

Support for popular sovereignty among moderate southern Democrats revealed the impetus for compromise and party harmony. Hopkins Holsey, an Athens, Georgia, editor and political operative, expressed his support for the

Dickinson resolutions, which, he stated, "assumed the same ground taken by Mr. Dallas of Pennsylvania last summer." Like a number of southern Democrats, though, Holsey questioned whether the northern wing of the party would support the doctrine of territorial self-government. "Satisfactory as this position must be to us in all respects (leaving out the absolute monomania of the Calhoun faction) it becomes us to ascertain, before we adopt it as the basis of our action in the next campaign, whether the Northern Democracy will rally to its support?" While self-government seemed the preferred choice over extension of the Missouri Compromise line, southerners recognized the necessity of finding a position that Democrats from the North and South could agree upon.[56]

Holsey declared that he expressed the fears of other southern Democrats that party unity would fail over the slavery issue, surmising that extension might prevail over self-government in the North because it enabled northerners to "retain their constitutional prepossessions."[57] But southern Democrats who professed this belief underestimated the extent to which the Calhoun faction had discredited the Missouri Compromise in the South. Even though the Calhounites did not enjoy sufficient support to advance their position on slavery in the territories—at least in late 1847, they did in part succeed by appealing to the South's own constitutional prepossessions. Those who endorsed self-government over extension did so in no small part because it allowed them to steer clear of widespread southern opinion that the Missouri Compromise was unconstitutional.

By the end of 1847, the slavery debate had advanced to a point where a compromise seemed within grasp. Yet the party system remained imperiled as the extension of slavery subsumed all other political issues. The coming of a presidential election season linked the issue of slavery in the territories with the politics of president making. Already two Democratic contenders for president had advanced competing plans for disposing of the Wilmot Proviso. Extension of the Missouri Compromise line seemed a straightforward policy, but tepid support from southern Democrats and the Polk administration had compromised support for the plan. The ambiguous version of territorial self-government proposed by Vice President Dallas had received warm approval from southern Democrats and even some Whigs. Abolitionists from the North had attacked the Dallas plan as a proslavery subterfuge, while Calhounites in the South characterized it an antislavery policy clothed in the rhetoric of moderation. Southern Whigs had taken the lead in illustrating the dangers inherent in the nebulous compromise plan, arguing that it merely deferred the serious questions surrounding slavery and westward expansion to a later date. The efforts of Daniel Dickinson to clarify the doctrine and assert the right of territorial legislatures to pass laws concerning slavery only made matters worse among skeptical southerners.

As northern Democrats had debated the merits of one compromise plan over the other, a third Democratic presidential hopeful had observed developments and quietly waited to make his own statement launching his presidential campaign. Senator Lewis Cass of Michigan, an experienced politician who had served in government for over thirty years, understood the calculus of the political situation in 1847. No Democratic presidential candidate could seriously contend for the office without advancing a plan to eliminate the threat of the Wilmot Proviso and reunite the fractured party. While Dallas and Buchanan had sparred over their competing proposals and the Democratic Party remained split in factions, Cass worked behind the scenes to enhance his chances while maintaining silence in public. The Michigan senator's prospects for gaining the nomination looked promising. In late September 1847, Cass had written a political confidant, "I am however very quiet, and am determined to remain so. I shall write no letters for publication, author no inquiries, give no pledges."[58] In the interim, though, Cass had circulated a major policy announcement concerning slavery in the territories among his Democratic allies, including Dickinson, who supported Cass's bid for the presidency. By late December, Cass decided to break his silence and enter the presidential field with his own pronouncement on the slavery issue. As a formidable competitor against Buchanan and Dallas for the Democratic nomination, political observers eagerly awaited his solution to the crisis over slavery in the territories.

5

"INTENDED TO DELUDE

THE SOUTH"

Northern Democrats Redefine
Popular Sovereignty

On Christmas Eve, 1847, Lewis Cass finally broke his silence on the territorial issue with a public letter designed to appeal to northerners' antislavery proclivities as well as southerners' constitutional scruples. Following the lead of George Dallas and James Buchanan, Cass announced his presidential campaign in the letter to Tennessee political operative Alfred O. P. Nicholson. Like his rivals for the nomination, Cass rejected the Wilmot Proviso and sought to offer an alternative to settle the question over slavery in the territories that would heal the rift within the Democratic Party. Out of political necessity, slavery ranked first and foremost on his political agenda. The Michigan senator had bided his time, waiting until the right moment to enter the political fray with a bold statement of his principles on that vexing question. At last, the time seemed appropriate for Cass to enter the presidential race and to make a significant statement on the slavery issue that would propel him to the top of the list of presidential contenders. Popular sovereignty would become Cass's vehicle to the presidency.[1]

Once again, territorial expansion and slavery extension would play a critical role in a presidential election. Texas had dominated the canvass of 1844; four years later the presidential aspirants would have to address the issue of slavery in the Mexican Cession. The Whigs tried their best to evade the question by nominating a war hero, Zachary Taylor, to lead their party to victory. The Democrats, however, faced the daunting task of reuniting their sectionally fractured party. Northern party leaders like Cass believed that the ambiguous doctrine of popular sovereignty would appease their southern colleagues. But slave-state radicals striving to convince their constituents that untrustworthy antislavery northerners had imperiled the future of slavery raised questions about the meaning of the popular sovereignty doctrine. Southern Democrats demanded that their party's candidate uphold the right of slaveholders to equal participation in the Mexican Cession—by which they meant the right to carry slaves into the West. And in the end, southerners would not place their trust in an all-too-malleable doctrine defined by a senator from Michigan. Lewis Cass's version of popular sovereignty, designed to placate northerners and southerners alike, ended up proving a liability—a doctrine that inflamed antislavery and proslavery partisans while failing to rally a sufficient number of moderates on the slavery question.

THE AVID EXPANSIONIST Cass had hoped to secure the Democratic presidential nomination in 1844 but saw his slim hopes dashed by a younger Tennessean in the mold of Andrew Jackson—James K. Polk. Cass still yearned for the presidency, and in a political system designed to reward fealty to party, he felt certain that his fellow Democrats would reward him for his years of service. Dallas and Buchanan had launched their candidacies some three months earlier, engaging in a contest that meant nearly as much about who would control Pennsylvania state politics as it did about winning the upcoming presidential contest. Other contenders such as Levi Woodbury of New Hampshire and former New York governor Silas Wright had expressed interest in securing the nomination. The sixty-five-year-old Cass hoped to gain the nomination—and the presidency—in 1848, when a mentally and physically exhausted Polk declined to seek a second term in office, but he had to find the right platform to outmaneuver his competition.[2]

Any presidential contender—Democrat or Whig—had to contend with the dangerous slavery question and how it affected party affiliations in the South. Southerners would abandon any political organization that made the Wilmot Proviso part of its platform. In the new political atmosphere where slavery had begun to subsume all other issues, southern party leaders actively sought to portray their opponents at home as weak on the slavery question in order to gain political advantage. The politics of slavery, however, also affected northern politics as party stalwarts and presidential candidates from the free states sought solutions to the issue of slavery in the territories. Democrats like Lewis Cass sought "temporary refuge" in popular sovereignty, while Whigs "as a party looked traditionally to the federal government to shape and direct the nation's growth." Both parties in both sections would face substantial challenges to their plans and would have to change plans in order to remain viable in the rapidly changing political atmosphere.[3]

Cass used the issue of slavery in the territories to advance his candidacy for president by promising to dispose of the Wilmot Proviso and the principle of congressional intervention in territorial affairs with one sweeping plan. During the silent phase of his presidential campaign in the latter months of 1847, Cass had circulated a draft of the Nicholson letter among thirty to fifty members of Congress and almost certainly communicated with other political operatives in an effort to draft an alternative policy to the Wilmot Proviso. He also had a strong association with New York Senator Daniel S. Dickinson, who had very likely introduced his resolutions advocating territorial self-government with Cass's blessing. Ten days after the Senate received the Dickinson resolutions, Cass endorsed popular sovereignty in his letter to Nicholson.[4]

Cass recognized, however, that the Dickinson version of popular sovereignty had offended the southern Democratic establishment. Unlike Dickinson's resolutions, which unequivocally affirmed that territorial legislatures could permit or prohibit slavery, Cass's letter restored the ambiguity that gave popular sovereignty intersectional appeal by evading the question of when a territory could exercise its sovereignty. Like many doughface Democrats, Cass recognized that his constituents had grown increasingly hostile toward the expansion of slavery while southern party regulars demanded its protection. By advocating popular sovereignty without defining when it went into effect, Cass hoped to appease antislavery and proslavery Democrats alike. In the Nicholson letter, Cass advanced a carefully wrought and artfully vague argument that not only confused his contemporaries, but has puzzled historians ever since. The Wilmot Proviso had disrupted national politics by forcing Congress to resolve the slavery issue, a duty it had heretofore proved unable to discharge. Cass endorsed the Jacksonian doctrine that southerners had advanced for almost thirty years—the slavery issue "should be kept out of the national legislature, and left to the people of the confederacy in their respective local governments." After penning a statement that would surely please southern Democrats, the senator aimed to satisfy his fellow northerners. Cass maintained that like many northerners, he disliked the institution of slavery. Regardless of the morality of the institution, however, Congress did not have the power to interfere with the institution where it currently existed. Matters concerning slavery rested solely with the local governments in places where it existed. "Local institutions," Cass declared, "whether they have reference to slavery, or to any other relations, domestic or public, are left to local authority; either original or derivative."[5]

But what about slavery in the territories, namely in any territory gained from Mexico, where slavery did not exist by virtue of local law? Heretofore, Cass had made no original statement; he had merely affirmed the established Democratic orthodoxy by taking great pains to portray himself as a northern man attuned to southern interests—a doughface. Yet he had also stated his own distaste for slavery, a clear gesture toward northern Democrats hostile to conciliation with the South. After avowing that slavery was a local institution, Cass now turned to the situation in the territories. He noted that territories, as inchoate political communities distinct from states, did not have the same political standing within the Union. The only explicit passage regarding the territories—the "needful rules and regulations" clause—had provoked considerable debate since the earliest days of the republic. After briefly citing the history of the debate over the territories clause, Cass sided with those who believed the clause referred solely to the territories as tangible property. To his mind, it did not "extend to the unlimited power of legislation" over them.[6]

In order to uphold the principles of the Constitution and preserve the safety of the Union, Cass argued, the nation had to reject the Wilmot Proviso and its assumption of federal control over local institutions. Here the senator summed up his stance on the slavery issue: "I am opposed to the exercise of any jurisdiction by Congress over this matter; and I am in favor of leaving to the people of any territory, which may be hereafter acquired, the right to regulate it for themselves, under the general principles of the constitution." Cass claimed the right of the territories to determine the status of slavery for five reasons. First, whether or not the Constitution gave Congress jurisdiction over slavery in the territories—and here Cass was maddeningly vague—he argued that it should not interfere with the institution and instead leave it to the people of the territories. Second, Cass believed that implementing the Wilmot Proviso would "sow the seeds of future discord, which would grow up and ripen into an abundant harvest of calamity"—an overt reference to the possibility of civil war. Southerners, he implied, would not stand for the passage of the Wilmot Proviso. Third, implementation of the Wilmot Proviso would handicap the efforts to conclude successfully the Mexican War. If Congress did not remove the offending proviso from efforts to fund the war effort, it might never pass a bill to fund the army. Likewise, Cass argued that if the Wilmot Proviso became law, southerners in Congress would withhold support for any peace treaty with Mexico providing for a territorial indemnity.[7]

Finally, Cass returned to the heart of his argument by addressing the issue of state versus territorial sovereignty. Even if the Wilmot Proviso became law and barred slavery from the proposed Mexican Cession, it would only carry force during the territorial phase—a point that southern Democrats had insisted upon for decades. Once settlers carved states from the cession and gained admission to the Union, the right of Congress to impose a ban on slavery would unquestionably disappear. State sovereignty would prevail, leaving the people to determine the status of slavery for themselves. Here Cass broached the nettlesome issue of when a political community gained sovereignty. For many, if not most Americans, a territory gained sovereignty only when an elected convention drafted a constitution and sought admission to the Union. Cass responded to the question of state sovereignty and constitutional law with a pragmatic question: why should Congress assume jurisdiction over the status of slavery during the presumably brief territorial phase when its authority would cease with the territory's admission to the Union? "Is the object, then, of temporary exclusion for so short a period as the duration of the Territorial governments," Cass asked, "worth the price at which it would be purchased?" Most of Cass's statements up to this point had merely reiterated the developing Democratic interpretation of popular sovereignty. Many Democratic politicians had simply insisted that Congress had no power to address the issue of slavery in the territories, without addressing the locus of jurisdiction. At this critical point of his argument, however, Cass vacillated by shrouding in mystery the precise point at which the territories could exercise authority over slavery. Indeed, throughout the entire Nicholson letter, Cass sought to obfuscate the doctrine's application by alternately giving credence to both the northern and southern interpretations of local and congressional authority over the extension of slavery. In sum, the veteran politician had written a document that readers could interpret in multiple ways—depending on which side of the Mason-Dixon line they resided.[8]

To a considerable degree, Cass's popular sovereignty formula presupposed an almost idyllic, Jacksonian view of the American republic—that the principles of strong local government remained paramount. In reality, the "new, pernicious political division founded on sectional distinctions" had nationalized the slavery issue, meaning that neither northerners nor southerners could resist meddling with the extension of slavery.[9] Too much was at stake on either side for nonintervention to prevail.

On one level, Cass had advanced a thoughtful appeal for political pragmatism, urging northerners to disavow congressional intervention and calling on southerners to set aside their ultra states' rights scruples and allow territorial legislatures some degree of sovereignty over slavery. Both sides had to leave the extension of slavery to those whom it impacted—the people of the territories themselves. Portraying the Wilmot Proviso as an absurd attempt by Congress to legislate on the slavery question for a brief period of time and in a place where it did not currently—and most likely, never would—exist, gave the Nicholson letter a tone of sensible statesmanship.

But what did the Cass doctrine, as many would come to call it, really mean? Though many Democratic partisans wanted to believe that "Gen. Cass's letter contains its own best interpretation," the document actually left supporters and opponents alike befuddled. Like many of his predecessors during the earlier debates over the expansion of slavery, Cass did not take an explicit stand on the right of Congress to legislate on slavery in the territories. He merely considered congressional intervention ill advised and a departure from the first principles of the government and his own party. More interestingly, many of Cass's contemporaries as well as historians up to the present have advanced competing theories on the true meaning of Cass's version of territorial self-government. As one scholar has colorfully written, the senator "was as silent as the dumbest oracle on the precise stage of territorial development at which inhabitants were to regulate slavery."[10]

Paeans to the revolutionary doctrine of popular sovereignty and self-government did not settle the question of when the settlers of a territory could exercise their presumptive right to permit or prohibit slavery within the bounds of their territory. In spite of the Nicholson letter's intentional lack of precision, Cass left conflicting clues as to when he believed settlers of a territory could decide the slavery issue. Whereas southern Democrats believed that self-government came in the phase immediately preceding statehood, when a territorial convention met to draft a constitution, Cass implied that Congress should let settlers decide the question at some point earlier. He had asked his readers whether a "temporary exclusion" of slavery from the territories was worth the inevitable struggle that would result, clearly implying that Congress should let territorial governments decide the slavery issue rather than risk a firestorm of sectional discord over the Wilmot Proviso and congressional intervention for or against slavery in the territories. Conversely, Cass made clear that any territorial action regarding slavery must comport with the principles of the Constitution, an argument designed to pacify southerners who believed that constitutional law forbade any territorial interference with slavery until a convention drafted a state constitution.[11]

Cass did little to clarify his position on when a territory could legislate on slavery, almost certainly because of the sharp criticism leveled against the Dickinson resolutions in the Senate. Some two weeks after the Nicholson letter appeared in the press, the New York senator rose to defend his resolutions calling for territorial self-government. In part, Dickinson basically echoed the reasoning of the Nicholson letter. Why risk sectional discord in Congress for a prohibition that would carry no force once a territory became a state, Dickinson asked. His resolutions promised to "leave, under the Constitution, all questions concerning the admission or prohibition of this institution in the territories, to the inhabitants thereof, that its intrusion may not hereafter arrest the policy, defeat the measures, or disturb the councils of the nation." Dickinson took a position stronger than any other legislator, including Cass, on the right of self-government in the territories. He argued that the territories should possess the same sovereignty as other "political communities," a point that considerably blurred the difference between territory and state. Dickinson maintained that Congress could not abridge the rights of an American citizen because he resided in a territory rather than a state. Certainly the framers of the Constitution did not intend to impose a colonial status on the territories and their inhabitants, he reasoned. The New York senator's position went too far, however, in the opinion of a number of his colleagues. Immediately following Dickinson's speech in the Senate, David Yulee of Florida introduced a resolution of his own, stating that "the federal government has no delegated authority, nor the territorial community any inherent right, to exercise any legislative power" that might prohibit slavery.[12]

Yulee's resolution embodied the Calhounite position that neither settlers in the territories nor Congress could interfere with the right of an American citizen to emigrate to a territory with his slave property. The Calhounites left open the absurdly inconsistent possibility that a territorial legislature could enact slave codes to regulate the institution, but they explicitly denied the right of anyone to prohibit slavery in a territory. Yet by omitting the possibility that a territory might not pass a slave code, Yulee's resolution pointed toward Calhoun's own emerging belief that slavery in the territories needed positive federal protection. All ultra southerners agreed that Dickinson's resolutions potentially usurped the right of slaveholders to enjoy the common property of the territories, which Congress merely administered as an agent for the states. Seeing no lack of clarity in the pronouncements of the northern Democrats and ignoring the differences between their various popular sovereignty proposals, the Calhounites believed that Cass and Dickinson's version of territorial self-government unquestionably gave settlers the right to prohibit slavery during the territorial phase. Calhoun remarked to an associate that the speeches of Dallas and the letters of Buchanan and Cass "are intended to delude the South."[13] Throughout the election year of 1848, politicians and interested observers attempted to give precision to the Cass doctrine. As individuals lined up for and against the principles embodied in the Nicholson letter, the doctrine of territorial self-government itself assumed different meanings. Cass's initial statement may have lacked clarity, but proslavery and antislavery partisans would further muddle its meaning in order to gain political advantage at home.

Northern Democrats who saw abolitionists as radicals bent on destroying the Union and who consequently sought to steer a more conciliatory course welcomed the impetus for popular sovereignty. "The Wilmot Proviso as it is termed or whoever may be its putative Father," a New York Democrat wrote to Dickinson, "I have always considered Abolitionism in disguise."[14] But Cass and Dickinson provided a compromise that seemed able to reunite the fractured Democratic Party. Sensing Cass's astute political calculations, James Gordon Bennett, editor of the *New York Herald*, called the letter "one of the most important moves on the political chess-board." Echoing the sentiments of individuals from both sections, the *Herald* posited that Cass "goes farther than Mr. Calhoun himself."[15]

Antislavery Democrats heartily agreed, lamenting that Cass had conceded

In this editorial cartoon from the 1848 presidential campaign, Richmond newspaper editor Thomas Ritchie, a southern moderate, serves Lewis Cass to the body politic. Radical southerners did not trust the veteran Michigan Democrat or his popular sovereignty formula and they lambasted moderates for supporting the northern candidate. (Library of Congress)

much to proslavery interests. In an effort to "make the amplest reparation for his former support of the Wilmot proviso," a Washington correspondent noted, the senator had given the South "not only all it requires, but what it never dreamed of asking."[16] Recognizing that many northerners abhorred the institution of slavery and did not entirely trust southern politicians to promote national interests, some northern Democrats expressed their fears of ceding too much power to slaveholder interests. They extended only a tepid endorsement of the Nicholson letter by affirming the ages-old doctrine that Congress could not interfere with slavery in the states, but ignored Cass's implication that territorial legislatures could pass laws permitting or prohibiting slavery.

Moderate southern Democrats hailed the Nicholson letter as an important defense of southern rights in the territories in which southerners could find safety. The senator had developed a strong argument based on principles of the past, a doctrine most Democrats believed "destined to become the platform" of the party. "Gen. Cass has taken his place side by side with Buchanan and Dallas upon this great question," a Georgia editor effused. "What a brilliant trio! And they all are Democrats!" Southern Democrats noted that their section still had friends in the North who would stand for the constitutional rights of slaveholders and non-slaveholders alike. The Cass doctrine promised to heal the division caused by the Missouri Compromise over twenty-five years before. Democrats in the South insisted that territorial self-government would give southerners equal rights in the territories, which the Compromise of 1820 had denied—at least north of the 36 degrees, 30 minutes line.[17]

Nevertheless, considerable differences existed within the South over the interpretation of the Nicholson letter, its definition of territorial self-government, and the application of self-government itself, which subtly changed over the course of the election year. In the first half of 1848, Georgia Democrats emerged as stalwart supporters of the Cass doctrine. Congress had no right "to interfere either one way or the other in a question of slavery in the territories," a Milledgeville Democrat opined, because the Constitution "looks with equal regard upon the respective social organization of the different states. The whole disposition of the matter must then be with the Territorial Legislature." Moderate Georgia Democrats saw danger in the Calhounite position, which they believed would effectively force slavery upon the territorial legislatures by denying their right to prohibit the institution, but allowing them to pass slave codes. If Congress possessed the power to force slavery upon a people, could it not conversely force abolition?[18]

Still other Democrats exhibited a curious understanding of what their northern brethren meant in proposing territorial self-government, either not fully understanding or choosing to ignore the implications of Dickinson's resolutions and Cass's Nicholson letter. More likely they advocated the traditional southern interpretation of popular sovereignty to suit their own political purposes. Georgia politician Henry L. Benning wrote to his close friend Senator Howell Cobb, "The resolutions do not declare what principle ought to govern in *the interval* between the time of acquiring the territory and the time at which the people thereof may choose to settle those 'questions of domestic policy', which it is left to them to settle."[19] Benning took a unique stance that straddled the line between the position of northern Democrats that territorial legislatures had the unquestioned power to legislate on slavery and the Calhounites, who insisted that neither Congress nor territorial legislatures could exercise such power. He did not object to allowing territorial legislatures, once created, to decide the slavery question. Benning did propose adding a clause to the resolution on terri-

torial self-government, however, that would permit slaveholders to enter the territory until a territorial legislature passed laws to the contrary.

A significant number of southern Democrats committed themselves to territorial self-government, but they did so with certain reservations and on their
own terms. Many never entirely trusted the Michigan senator, making Cass's
version of popular sovereignty a hard sell in many southern states. In Alabama,
for example, moderate Democrats who supported the doctrine faced stiff opposition from the allies of William Lowndes Yancey, who had endorsed the Calhounite position. At a state Democratic convention, the moderates resolved to
combat the rhetoric of the Yancey faction by expressing their satisfaction with
"the Democracy of the North for their conduct on the Slavery question." Yancey
and his followers, however, would stiffen in their opposition to the Cass doctrine over the course of the election year. And in Georgia, where significant support among moderates emerged for territorial self-government, moderate Democrats feared that the northern wing of the party would withhold support for the
Cass doctrine because of their objections to the institution of slavery. "Why,
then, will not our Northern brethren," a Milledgeville editor asked, "consent for
this doctrine to apply to territory which may be hereafter acquired?"[20]

More conservative southerners indicated that they could not accept the
Cass compromise and its blithe dismissal of their constitutional rights, focusing
on his reasoning concerning the viability of slavery in the Mexican territory as
fodder for their opposition. The senator essentially adopted the stances taken
by Secretary of the Treasury Robert J. Walker and James Buchanan on slavery;
the institution could never exist in the cession because of the race of the indige-
nous population and because the laws of nature precluded the development of
plantation agriculture. In 1844, Walker, then a senator from Mississippi, had asserted that slavery would never exist in California and New Mexico "not only
because it is forbidden by law, but because the colored race there preponder-
ates in the ratio of ten to one over the whites; and holding, as they do, the government and most of the offices in their possession, they will not permit the en-
slavement of any portion of the colored race, which makes and executes the
laws of the country."[21]

Walker's pronouncement had offended southerners—and their hostility to
his argument had not abated in the intervening years. Southern Democrats especially rejected the notion that the Mexican laws prohibiting slavery would
have force under American control. Furthermore, many considered the
prospect that Mexicans would control territorial governments in the cession

outrageous. Allowing Mexicans to govern the cession amounted to the conquered governing the conqueror. And to the minds of many southerners, both points seemed to deprive Americans of their sovereignty in the Mexican Cession, an assertion that one could argue directly controverted Cass's aim in the Nicholson letter—to affirm popular sovereignty. During the election year, southern Whigs and Calhounites alike exploited the fact that the Nicholson letter implicitly endorsed the statements of Walker.

Cass, however, faced an even greater obstacle than any offending remarks found within the Nicholson letter. In the waning days of the Twenty-Ninth Congress when the Senate deliberated over the Two Million Bill, Cass had tacitly agreed to vote for passage with the Wilmot Proviso. Of course, the Senate did not vote on the bill—the House had adjourned before Senate managers could take a vote—but Cass had made his position clear. Even after the session's end, the senator remarked to a New York congressman that the northern Democrats had agreed to vote for the amended bill and that "'he regretted very much' not receiving the opportunity to vote on it." Cass had almost assuredly made his statements with his Michigan constituency in mind, without considering the extent of southern feeling against the proviso. He instead opted to support prosecution of the war, even if it meant accepting the amendment. His opinion had changed by the time he penned the Nicholson letter. Indeed, when Cass wrote of a "great change" in the public mind, as well as his own, he may have intended an oblique reference to his actions in August 1846.[22] When news surfaced of Cass's conversation with the New York congressman, though, a number of southerners fumed at the presidential candidate's one-time support of the hated Wilmot Proviso.

Democrats faced a daunting task in 1848: "to gain South and not lose North," in the words of Henry L. Benning. Democrats had to convince southerners that their party would best protect slavery and southern interests in the territories, but at the same time keep northerners who objected to slavery and addressing southern demands in the party fold. They faced considerable opposition in both sections. As early as March, some southern Democrats doubted if Cass could garner sufficient votes from either northerners or southerners. Growing northern hostility to the institution of slavery had forced some Democratic politicians to reckon with the Wilmot Proviso and to abandon efforts to build intersectional ties with southern leaders. In the South, moderate Democrats had to contend with the Calhounites, who doubted the efforts of Cass and the northern wing of the party. Calhoun's followers insisted on a platform that would give positive protection to southern rights in the territories.[23]

Democrats from the North and South never expected to convert either abolitionists or antislavery zealots to their cause. According to a southern observer who believed that "Politics & Fanaticism are confederated for our destruction," antislavery northerners viewed slavery "as sinful—and they think that if they suffer new[,] free territory to be occupied by Slaves[,] the sin will be upon them." In opposition, party regulars portrayed themselves as moderate patriots who sought to save the bonds of Union from the machinations of antislavery fanatics. Antislavery northerners criticized Cass for his stance on the slavery issue. "Mr. Cass does not mean to be behind Messrs. Woodbury, Buchanan or Dallas, who are each anxious to receive the reward of their subservience to slavery," a New Hampshire editor wrote. Cass merely presented another example of a doughface doing the bidding of the South. The efforts of moderate Democrats to unite the party fell flat with the increasingly strident opponents of slavery in the North.[24]

Antislavery leaders responded to the Nicholson letter as expected; so too did the Calhounites, who had objected vociferously to the proposals of northern Democrats. Recognizing the devious allure of Cass's duplicitous position on the slavery question and seeking to solidify his ranks in support of the common property doctrine, Calhoun highlighted the hypocrisy of a Democratic Party determined to bend the meaning of popular sovereignty to suit both North and South. Dallas, Buchanan, and Cass certainly opposed the Wilmot Proviso, "but not the end at which it aims; to exclude the South from whatever Territory may be acquired from Mexico."[25] The Nicholson letter offended Calhoun by quoting the remarks of Buchanan, who had insisted that slavery would never thrive in the Mexican Cession. To Calhoun, the viability of slavery in the West did not matter; the right of a slaveholder to carry his property into the territories was paramount.

Northern Democrats had drafted grand proposals to replace the Wilmot Proviso with an affirmation of the people's right to determine their own institutions. But what people—American citizens or Mexican inhabitants? And for what purpose? Buchanan and Cass had both suggested that slavery would never exist in the Mexican Cession. Calhoun pounced on these issues and directed his associates to do the same in an effort to rally the South behind his banner. His supporters soon followed suit. Cass and Dickinson had maintained that their proposal preserved southern rights in the territories, according to a Charleston editor, but they "had also said, in the way of a confidential whisper to the north, 'the inhabitants of the territory that may be acquired will have the right to decide whether slavery shall have entrance upon the soil or not; and as the institution has now no existence there, and is regarded with great aversion by the people, there is no danger whatever that slavery will ever be permitted to advance beyond its present limits.'" The northern Democrats, according to Calhoun and his allies, wanted to gain votes in the South by proposing the right of the people, rather than Congress, to determine the status of slavery in the West. They also wanted to keep wary northerners in the Democratic fold by suggesting that slavery would never take root in the Mexican Cession. Calhoun sought to prove his earlier predictions true—northern Democrats now saw self-government in the territories as an essentially antislavery doctrine.[26]

Calhoun's indictment of the Cass doctrine resonated with those southerners who trusted neither the northern Democrats nor the current residents of any Mexican cession to uphold southern rights. Though most southerners endorsed the principle of self-government in its broadest definition, more doctrinaire citizens of the section disagreed with the application of popular sovereignty as proposed by Cass and other northerners. Because Mexican law prohibited slavery, it seemed highly unlikely that the current residents of any ceded territory would consent to introducing the institution. Only if Americans emigrated to the cession and took control of the institutions of territorial government could slavery have a chance to flourish. This necessitated two preconditions. First, slaveholders needed time to emigrate to the West. Southerners—indeed all Americans—could not allow the Mexican citizens to shape American law. Second, and particularly in the minds of the Calhounites, the federal government had to affirm and defend the right of slaveholders to carry their property into the cession.[27] Calhoun believed that slavery in the territories merited federal protection, but a majority of southerners in 1848 did not yet concur. Instead, moderate southerners had looked to extension of the Missouri Compromise line as a viable compromise solution because it would have prevented antislavery politicians from interfering with slavery in the cession.

At this point, however, the South Carolinian deviated from ideological consistency, perhaps because of the role he played almost thirty years earlier in creating the Missouri Compromise. In one respect, Calhoun's own strict construction of the Constitution contributed to the rejection of extending the Missouri Compromise line, since he had vigorously attacked the old compact as an infringement on the South's constitutional rights. In July 1848, Calhoun gave a speech in the Senate opposing the extension of the Missouri Compromise line to the Pacific Ocean.[28] Yet the compromise, to which he had affixed his constitutional imprimatur in 1820, offered perhaps the best alternative by which Congress could dispose of the Wilmot Proviso and restore sectional harmony. It would have essentially permitted slavery in a significant portion of the Mexican Cession and, by past convention, would presumably have delayed the decision of whether to permit or prohibit slavery to the moment when the territories drafted their respective constitutions and applied for statehood, an argument to which the Calhounites held fast.

In the waning days of the congressional session, the Senate—Calhoun included—voted for a measure that would have extended the Missouri Compromise line to the Pacific Ocean, but the bill died in the House of Representatives. Calhoun supported extension only as a temporary measure and denied that it would set any constitutional precedent for congressional restriction of slavery. Nonetheless his support for extension, however tepid, must have puzzled those who heard his effusions against the Missouri Compromise in the past. President Polk's timidity to endorse extension of the compromise line—he did not express support for the proposal until June 1848—and radical southern hostility toward a division of the cession encouraged politicians to find an alternate solution.[29]

The Nicholson letter and its endorsement of territorial self-government seemed to fill the void between restriction and the extension of the Missouri Compromise line. Nevertheless, the Calhounites could not and would not endorse Cass's version (or his vision) of popular sovereignty with its implication that territorial legislatures could potentially prohibit slavery. The venerable South Carolina senator had devoted allies in Congress and in key southern states who raised objections to the efforts of moderate Democrats to settle the slavery question. Just weeks after Yulee denounced Dickinson's resolutions, Alabama Senator Arthur P. Bagby introduced a resolution that supported Yulee's position, asserting that Congress could not confer a power on a territorial legislature that it did not itself possess. Neither Congress nor territorial legislatures, Bagby claimed, could prohibit slavery in the territories.[30]

Aside from the pronouncements of Calhoun himself, the most sustained objections to popular sovereignty came from William Lowndes Yancey. Brilliant in oratory yet a dour, insecure man with a violent temper, Yancey moved in lockstep with John C. Calhoun in an effort to unite southerners in a "bipartisan southern political bloc."[31] Whereas Calhoun operated outside the orbit of the party system in his quest for a southern political organization, Yancey sought a slaveholders' revolt from within the Democracy. In 1848, Yancey focused his efforts on removing popular sovereignty from southern political discourse and substituting the Calhoun common-property doctrine for it. The Alabamian staunchly opposed any intimation that Mexican settlers could determine the future of slavery. Furthermore, he insisted that the federal government had the obligation to protect slaveholders' rights to take slaves into any territory. Beginning in December 1847, Yancey and his Alabama associates began advocating their own doctrine on the slavery issue, which became known as the Alabama Platform. He demanded that southerners refuse to vote for any presidential candidate who did not explicitly disavow any intention to interfere with slavery in the territories. More specifically, Yancey considered the Cass doctrine a fraud—essentially the Wilmot Proviso couched in language designed to deceive the southern populace. The Alabama Platform, as crafted by Yancey and future Supreme Court Justice John A. Campbell, repudiated the presidential candidacy of Cass and his interpretation of popular sovereignty.

Yancey and Campbell's platform consisted of four statements that affirmed southern rights in the territories and, indeed, in the Union. First, they denied congressional power to prohibit slavery in the territories. The second plank of the platform stipulated that the people of a territory could prohibit slavery only when drafting their constitution. At any time prior to the conferral of statehood, slavery was protected by the federal constitution. Though a territorial legislature could not exclude slavery, the platform did not expressly prohibit legislation such as slave codes—a logical inconsistency. Third, the platform instructed Alabama's delegates to the Democratic national convention to withhold support for any candidate who refused to repudiate the Wilmot Proviso and the Cass doctrine. Finally, in its most controversial plank, the platform dictated that the federal government had the obligation to protect the institution of slavery in the Mexican Cession.[32] In sum, Yancey and Campbell had crafted the most proslavery statement of their time regarding slavery in the territories.

Yancey expressed the most comprehensive and vehement attack against the presidential candidacy of Cass and his version of popular sovereignty of any southern politician. He reminded his audience that Cass had once supported the Wilmot Proviso, speciously calling the Michigan senator a "leading advocate" of the infamous measure. Cass's opinion that the residents within a proposed cession could determine the status of slavery for themselves, even before Americans had a chance to emigrate there, smacked of antislavery sentiment.

In assessing the character of the native Mexican people, Yancey echoed the racialized sentiments of Buchanan, who had argued that they would never allow slavery in their midst because to them, "as we are assured by the letters of Gen. Cass and Mr. Buchanan, 'the negro does not belong socially to a degraded race.'" Democracy and republican government belonged in the hands of white men, according to Yancey, an opinion with which southerners and many northerners alike would have concurred.[33]

The Alabama Platform received the unanimous approbation of the state's Democratic convention in February 1848, bolstered by Yancey's impassioned oratory in defense of southern rights in the territories and assertions that the Cass doctrine violated the Constitution. Having denounced Cass and the doctrine of self-government, the Alabamian revealed that his fellow southerners should rally around Supreme Court Justice Levi Woodbury of New Hampshire for the Democratic nomination. Yancey claimed that Woodbury opposed "both federal and popular interference with slavery in the Territories, and that he believed that the people of a Territory could only legislate on a subject when they met to frame a constitution preparatory to admittance as a State into the Union." Though Yancey and his close friend Senator Dixon Lewis had received private assurances from Woodbury that he opposed the Wilmot Proviso and the Cass doctrine, they could never seem to coax a public statement along these lines from the justice. Although considered a frontrunner for the nomination, Woodbury never mustered much support outside of the Deep South—and most of that came from the Yancey faction in Alabama.[34]

The enthusiasm for the Alabama Platform and its bold defense of southern rights marked a step forward for radical southern rights advocates against those seeking a moderate course. Yancey intended to build his movement among those individuals who remained skeptical of Cass and his Nicholson letter. A number of southerners viewed Cass, Dickinson, and other northern Democrats as, in the words of a Georgia editor, "trimmers between downright Abolitionism, and the true Democratic States-Right doctrine." Pressing ahead, Yancey relied on the groundswell of proslavery and expansionist sentiment in southern legislatures to advance the Alabama Platform. Legislatures in Alabama, Georgia, Florida, and Virginia passed resolutions in the early months of 1848 insisting that the citizens of the states had a right to bring slaves into any new territory acquired from Mexico.[35]

At first blush, these resolutions seemed to discredit the Cass doctrine as they upheld the traditional southern conception of popular sovereignty—that the people could permit or prohibit slavery only when they drafted a state constitution. Yancey and his associates, however, miscalculated on two crucial points. In supporting Levi Woodbury for president, they rallied behind a candidate who refused to make public his views on the slavery question. Woodbury drafted a letter on the slavery issue that, by comparison, made the Nicholson letter look crystal clear. The Supreme Court justice penned broad platitudes of strict construction of the Constitution, but he equivocated on the issue of slavery in the territories.[36] More importantly, Yanceyites underestimated the ability of moderate southern Democrats to craft their own interpretation of the Nicholson letter—or simply ignore Cass's implication that territorial legislatures could regulate slavery.

Southern Democrats desperate to hold their party together also took a perilous course of prevarication on the meaning of the Cass doctrine. Northern Democrats, according to a New Orleans writer, had "almost *en masse*, come forward to sustain the constitutional rights of the South—to declare that Congress has *no right* to prescribe what social institutions the people of a territory shall or shall not have." The correspondent, like many of his fellow Democrats, deferred comment on when the people could make their decision—or even which people could take part in the process. In many respects, like Yancey those individuals eager to restore party unity selectively read the Nicholson letter. And Cass played along by lending a degree of ambiguity to its meaning. When a Florida delegate to the Democratic National Convention asked for clarification on whether Cass believed that territorial legislatures possessed the right to permit or prohibit slavery, Cass "referred the Floridian to the Nicholson letter—the very document he had been asked to clarify."[37]

The debate over the meaning of the Cass doctrine gained added significance at the Democratic National Convention at Baltimore in May. A palpable tension shrouded the convention, as two sets of New York delegates demanded recognition, paralyzing business for several days as leaders sought desperately to achieve a compromise. But the antislavery allies of Martin Van Buren—the Barnburners—would ultimately bolt from the convention. At the same time, other state delegations maneuvered feverishly on behalf of their preferred candidates for nomination. Yancey came ready for battle, intending to introduce his Alabama Platform on the convention floor. The delegates took a step, however, that incensed him and other southern ultras: they agreed to choose nominees for president and vice president before they agreed on a platform. An apoplectic Yancey well understood the meaning of the development; his chances of advancing the Alabama Platform if someone such as Cass or Buchanan were nom-inated had markedly decreased. To his mind, the convention sought concilia-tion and compromise over principle; moderation had trumped southern rights. Delegates placed three candidates before the convention—Cass, Buchanan, and Woodbury, and on the fourth ballot they nominated Cass for the presi-dency. In the balloting, the sixty-six-year-old Michigan senator carried all the states in the Old Northwest, five southwestern states, and Virginia.[38]

With Cass's nomination secured, the convention moved to draft a platform, but at a convention marred by dissent, especially the debacle over New York's delegation, most delegates desired to craft a mild and conciliatory statement of Democratic Party faith. The platform committee drafted a document that reiter-ated the usual principles of platforms past. On the slavery question, it took only the broadest stance by asserting that Congress had no power to interfere with slavery in the states and, in a glancing blow to the supporters of the Wilmot Pro-viso, declared "that all efforts of the Abolitionists or others made to induce Con-gress to interfere with the questions of slavery, or to take incipient steps in rela-tion thereto," threatened the Union. The platform made no mention of territorial self-government as the alternative to the Wilmot Proviso. Yancey, already in-censed by the nomination of Cass, immediately rose to protest the wording of the platform, which he argued imperiled southern rights in the territories by its vagueness on the slavery question. He would later write, "When Gen. Cass was nominated the great deed of wrong and injury to the South was consummated; and could only have been alleviated by a bold and decided expression of consti-tutional principles on the part of the Convention." But as Yancey must surely have recognized by the time the platform committee presented its work, few delegates spoiled for a fight over the slavery issue.[39]

Speaking for the minority of delegates unsatisfied with the platform's indis-tinct stance on slavery in the territories, Yancey introduced an amendment de-signed to clarify the party's position: "*Resolved further*, That the doctrine of non-interference with the rights of property of any portion of the people of this confederacy, be it in the States or Territories, by any other than the parties inter-ested in them, be the true republican doctrine recognized by this body." Yancey had again erred badly in proposing the poorly crafted amendment, as it by no means clarified his position on the slavery question. Members of the Virginia delegation rejected the ambiguous statement, maintaining that "Mr. Yancey's amendment surrendered the very doctrine he had contended for," the inability of territorial legislatures to prohibit slavery. Delegates from North Carolina and

Georgia concurred. Even if one assumed Yancey's intent to uphold the spirit of his Alabama Platform, John Slidell of Louisiana posited, the resolution "would rebuke the opinions of Gen. Cass, and be inconsistent with itself." The delegates rejected the statement by a vote of 216–36, though five southern state delegations voted in favor of the amendment. A disgusted Yancey left the convention floor with a fellow Alabamian and the Florida delegation in an exhibition of political theater in the face of the inevitable more than a serious protest of the convention's actions. Democrats soon adopted the platform by a unanimous vote—in an effort to show party unity—and adjourned to celebrate their work.[40]

Southern Democrats had never completely trusted Cass, while southern Whigs had reveled in pointing out his chameleon-like stance on the slavery question. As the Democrats left Baltimore with Lewis Cass as their presidential nominee, Whigs journeyed to Philadelphia to nominate a candidate of their own and reckon with the slavery issue themselves. Northern Whigs could argue that the Cass doctrine gave slavery a chance to expand to the Mexican Cession, whereas the Wilmot Proviso specifically forbade it. The South, however, presented Whigs with a significant challenge. In order to gain votes in the slave states, they had to field a candidate who would appear safer on the slavery issue than the northerner Cass. Enter Zachary Taylor, the hero of Buena Vista. Nominating the general, whose reputation transcended petty partisan differences as well as the vexing slavery issue, proved a political masterstroke. A career soldier whose political beliefs remained largely shrouded from public knowledge (as well as from his supporters) Taylor seemed the ideal Whig candidate. Northern Whigs could point to his distinguished military career, while southern Whigs could portray the Louisiana slaveholder as a southern man who would safeguard the institution of slavery. All sides believed that Taylor the president could neutralize the slavery issue and return the political system to stasis.

A significant number of Whig stalwarts North and South believed that Taylor "could give them what Jackson had given the Democrats two decades earlier: the domination of southern politics."[41] Using the Cass doctrine as another weapon with which they fought the Democrats, southern Whigs lambasted popular sovereignty as proof that Democratic leadership on the slavery question had abjectly failed. Whigs from both sections predicted with great prescience that it would result in a perpetual struggle over the extension of slavery. Yet the party divided on the meaning of the Democratic doctrine. While northern Whigs interpreted the Cass doctrine to mean that settlers in the territories could *establish* slavery where it did not exist, southern Whigs argued that the

Cass doctrine allowed the settlers to *prohibit* the institution, even before Americans could emigrate west. The argument bore striking resemblance to the Calhounite position, a similarity that blurred party lines and further complicated an already complex argument over the status of slavery in the cession. Like the opposition, Whigs ran a Janus-faced campaign in 1848. Respecting presidential politics, America in 1848 was already a nation divided. All Whigs highlighted their candidate's status as a military hero to an adoring public. Northern Whigs, however, focused on Taylor's belief that principled congressional leadership on the slavery issue would ultimately honor the people's will. Southern Whigs asserted that their candidate, a southerner and a slaveholder himself, would guard southern rights, whereas Cass and his perverted principle of popular sovereignty would violate them.

Democrats pilloried the opposition for "Taylor's cowardly silence" since the party had chosen to offer no platform and the candidate was as silent as the tomb about his political principles. Privately, Taylor had ridiculed the Democrats for their position on the expansion of slavery. Before the Democratic convention, he wrote his former son-in-law, Jefferson Davis, "Cass, Buchanan, & Dallas in defining their position in their letters addressed to the public in relation to [slavery in the territories], bid for the votes of the Slave holding portions of the Union; which I apprehend will have the effect to prevent the election" of any of the three. Even some Calhounites who opposed the Cass doctrine questioned Taylor's position—or lack thereof. Southern Democratic newspapers mocked the Whig offensive against Cass and territorial self-government. A Virginia editor assured the Whigs that "the whole Democracy of Virginia, and ourselves, are satisfied with the ticket that floats at our masthead." Would the Whig nominee equally satisfy those who demanded a defense of southern rights, he asked? A Charleston correspondent and Calhoun supporter wrote that some southerners inexplicably believed that neither the Wilmot Proviso nor territorial self-government would endanger slavery in the states, and "for anything that we know, Gen. Taylor may be one of these, and may not even be opposed to the Wilmot Proviso, as Gen. Cass professes to be."[42]

The Whig Party's silence on the slavery issue exposed them to attack from the opposition, but silence proved golden. A hero fresh from the battlefields of Mexico was proving to be more popular and viable than party platforms. Meanwhile, Whigs pounced on the popular sovereignty platform of the Democrats. In a lengthy diatribe against the opposition, Whig senator Willie P. Mangum of North Carolina dismissed the Cass doctrine as a "manifest evasion." He accused Cass of selling different versions of his doctrine to the North and the South in an effort to gain votes, even charging his campaign with distributing separate biographical sketches in both sections that differed subtly on issues relating to slavery in the territories. "General Cass, in the 'Nicholson letter,'" Mangum concluded, "has evaded the only 'real issue' on this subject, and left the public wholly in the dark in regard to his opinions."[43]

Democrats scrambled to defend Cass against the Whig accusations and to depict the Nicholson letter as a solid affirmation of southern rights and Jacksonian principles by resorting to the antebellum hobbyhorse of constitutional theory. Southerner party members seized on an important statement in the Nicholson letter; while Cass "concedes to the people of the territories the right to regulate the [slavery] question for themselves, he does it with the qualification 'under the general principles of the constitution,' and the 'relations they bear to the confederacy.'" They could contend, therefore, that since the Constitution guaranteed equal protection to American citizens' property, and since the territories belong to the states as a whole, Cass's "clear and palpable meaning" was to uphold the traditional southern formula for legislating on slavery in the territories. The settlers could determine the status of slavery when they drafted a constitution and sought admission to the Union. According to Cass's most ardent southern supporters, no reasonable observer could contend that he meant otherwise. Any ambiguity in the Nicholson letter stemmed from interpretation of the clause "under the general principles of the constitution," and far less so from his statements regarding when a territory could decide the slavery question. The extension of slavery had proven too explosive for Congress to address, so Democrats like Cass had asserted the people's right to determine the issue. But when the issue of *when* the people could decide became too explosive for Congress to address, Democrats called on the Supreme Court to determine the meaning of popular sovereignty. The Constitution and its interpreters, which in the absence of a national consensus meant ultimately the Supreme Court, would dictate the terms of application for territorial self-government.[44]

Not all southern Democrats, however, could so easily dispose of the questions surrounding the Nicholson letter. Proslavery Democrats knew what they wanted the Cass doctrine to mean, but they also knew that many northern Democrats interpreted the candidate's position as essentially antislavery. Few people perceived it at the time, but the calculus of bisectional politics, which led parties to endorse one idea in the North and another in the South, had begun to corrode the party system by utilizing political obfuscation to create artificial intraparty unity. The Baltimore convention confirmed that the Democrats would play this most dangerous game. Their strategy led northerners like James Tallmadge—the congressman whose amendment to the Missouri bill almost thirty years earlier inflamed sectional tensions—to assert that *"Cass,* had danced around the circle—& settled down, under a pledge to *Slavery* and Southern interests." Conversely, southerners like Calhoun insisted that Cass's stance "made concessions, which surrender everything, as far as territories are concerned; and in which the South cannot acquiesce without endangering her safety."[45]

Southern Democrats desperately wanted to interpret the Cass doctrine as an affirmation of their long-held belief that a territory could permit or prohibit slavery only when admitted to the Union. "My *own notion is that the Territorial Legislature* while legislating *as such* and for the Territory and for territorial purposes *has no right* to pass a law to prohibit slavery," North Carolina Democrat James C. Dobbin wrote to Howell Cobb. "Because if we adopt that doctrine we at once practically exclude the slaveholder forever."[46] Therein lay the problem for slaveholders. As Dobbin illustrated, if southerners had any chance at expanding slavery into the Mexican Cession under the American flag, they had to prevent prospective territorial legislatures in the region from passing legislation prohibiting slavery. Dobbin, and many other southerners, knew full well that the population currently residing within the cession would never support the establishment of slavery. Therefore, the Cass doctrine would not give southerners enough time to emigrate west before the antislavery settlers passed positive laws prohibiting slavery.

The Mexican ban on slavery presented proslavery leaders with a quandary they had never before faced. Before discussion of the Mexican Cession and Oregon had ensued in the mid-1840s, all of the nation's major territorial acquisitions included places where slavery existed and where slaveholders could emigrate without fearing for the legal status of their slaves. Local control over slavery seemed less threatening to southerners when slaveholders lived in the territory. But southerners could not accept the possibility that antislavery native Mexicans could determine the status of slavery in the Mexican Cession. Southerners would evaluate Cass and the Democrats—as well as the Whigs—on their ability to protect southern institutions and rights, a test that made the interpretation of territorial self-government all the more significant. Absent a concrete definition of the Cass doctrine, southern Democrats could only resort to what northern and southern party members agreed upon—the "principle that Congress shall not legislate for new territories." Despite or because of the fact that the Whigs had dodged the slavery question in their own convention and through the nomination of Taylor, party regulars pummeled the Democrats on the Cass doctrine. Particularly in the South, Whigs unceasingly exposed and exploited the inconsistency of the Democratic stand on slavery in the territories. Virginia Whigs likened the Cass doctrine to a statement "that a territory is sovereign." Other Whigs accused the Democrats of evading the real questions concerning the expansion of slavery—an amazing charge given that their own party had no platform and an evasive presidential candidate. According to them, Cass and the Democrats had crafted a platform that deferred the hard decisions concerning the status of slavery in the Mexican Cession to a later date.[47]

In an effort to bolster southern support for Cass, Stephen A. Douglas of Illinois, a rising star in Democratic politics, embarked on an early summer tour of the South to rally the party faithful and to gauge southern support for Cass. From Mississippi, he wrote the candidate a summary of his meetings with southern party leaders. North Carolina, Douglas affirmed, would vote for Cass "unless Taylor should be nominated by the Whigs." South Carolina, as expected, seemed unlikely to go for the Democrats. The news from Georgia and Alabama, however, seemed generally positive. Alabama's Democrats had repudiated the ultra politics of Yancey and fallen in behind the nominee. In Mississippi, "the Democrats are in the best of spirits & the Whigs give up the contest." Douglas made no mention of Florida and Whiggish Louisiana, two states where Cass faced trouble. In a rousing speech in New Orleans in early June, Douglas warned his fellow Democrats that Taylor's election by no means guaranteed the protection of slavery. His silence on issues surrounding slavery extension and the Wilmot Proviso posed too great a risk for southern voters. Cass had made his stand clear, Douglas implied. His southern tour provided Cass with much needed information concerning how southerners had received his nomination and the principles of the Nicholson letter. Yet Douglas issued Cass a cryptic warning: "Write no more letters. The South are satisfied with your views on the slavery question, as well as others." Perhaps Douglas meant Cass to read his words at face value, perhaps he meant to suggest that Cass follow Taylor's silent example, but he almost certainly meant to discourage the candidate from further complicating the already difficult situation surrounding the interpretation of the Nicholson letter.[48]

During the late spring and summer of 1848 the issue of race and territorial self-government resurfaced, as a significant number of southerners raised objections to allowing the Mexican population to determine the status of slavery.

The discussion of how to settle the slavery issue in the Mexican Cession had gained greater urgency with ratification of the Treaty of Guadalupe Hidalgo in May 1848 as partisans asked who should have the right to determine whether the institution would pass into the cession or stop at the boundary of Texas. In racialized rhetoric, southerners made clear their belief that only free white men should possess power over the future of slavery. "Shall the few ignorant Mexicans now living in the country have the power of excluding the Southern people from settling amongst them with such property, as they choose to carry with them," a Columbus, Georgia, correspondent asked John C. Calhoun.[49]

The argument of those individuals who questioned the Cass doctrine based on the ability of the Mexican population to prohibit slavery in the territorial phase assumed two forms. The more benign, and less common, reasoning suggested that Congress should defer granting New Mexico and California an elected territorial legislature, allowing time for the people's democratic instincts to "ripen." Forty years earlier, southerners had vehemently objected to the northerners' suggestions that the people of the Louisiana Purchase—including the foreign population—could not legislate for themselves. But the settlers of the Louisiana territory posed no threat to the institution of slavery. The native inhabitants of the Mexican Cession, it was asserted, did not desire the extension of slavery into New Mexico and California.[50]

In its more common form, the debate assumed a derogatory tone against the native population and their ability to participate in territorial governance—not to mention republican government itself. One of Calhoun's associates flatly stated, "Congress has no authority to give the right of voting in conquered territory to Indians, negroes, or mixed breeds, in making constitutions or laws to Govern." Blatantly using the issue of race to drive voters away from Cass and the Democrats, a Virginia Whig editor wrote that the Nicholson letter meant that the Mexican residents "can prohibit slavery and will do so, and in fact having as much authority to act as the people of the *States*, they may even prohibit the introduction of *white* people within their domain." Allowing the residents of the Mexican Cession to assume sovereignty similar to that possessed by the states, the writer argued, would jeopardize the rule of white Americans. "Is this what Southern Democrats mean? Is it their object to establish a Black republic in our South Western border! [*sic*] And is it for that reason, they are so enthusiastic for Cass?"[51]

Southern Democrats responded by denying that the Cass doctrine granted the power to legislate on slavery in the earliest stages of territorial existence— that the candidate indeed upheld the southern interpretation of popular sovereignty. A Georgia Democrat sought to assuage his fellow southerners that the doctrine of "territorial sovereignty" did not mean that the "mixed races of New Mexico and California" had the power to prohibit slavery. Those who construed the Cass doctrine as a grant of sovereignty to the Mexican settlers failed to note the claim in the Nicholson letter that power would only be exercised "under the general principles of the constitution." Indeed, the *Richmond Enquirer* maintained, "the Nicholson letter was written to discuss the power of Congress to exclude Slavery in the Territories, and to show that Congress possessed no such power; it does not directly touch upon the powers of a Territorial Legislature over slavery."[52]

While southern and northern Democrats alike continued to finesse the meaning of popular sovereignty, another alternative to the Wilmot Proviso emerged in the Senate. In the closing weeks of the first session of the Thirtieth Congress, Whig Senator John M. Clayton of Delaware moved to form a select committee to settle the issues surrounding the problems related to Oregon and the Mexican Cession. With Jesse Bright of Indiana, Daniel S. Dickinson, and Calhoun, the Clayton committee drafted a plan to establish territorial governments for Oregon, New Mexico, and California. Under the Clayton Compromise, the prohibition of slavery enacted by Oregon's provisional government would stand until the territorial legislature passed its own law either permitting or prohibiting the institution. In essence, the Clayton Compromise ratified the principle of popular sovereignty in Oregon. For New Mexico and California, however, the committee resolved on a much different course of action. The bill prohibited the territorial legislatures from passing any law permitting or prohibiting slavery. Any slave brought into either territory would have the express right to sue for freedom in the territorial courts, with the ultimate right of appeal to the Supreme Court. In other words, the Clayton Compromise left the decision of whether slavery could exist in the Mexican Cession to the federal judiciary. "Constitutionalization of the struggle over slavery in the territories had at last been pursued to its logical conclusion," a historian of the period has argued.[53]

The Clayton Compromise and the Cass doctrine of popular sovereignty had much in common—a point that some contemporaries recognized. By vesting in the Supreme Court final authority over slavery in the Mexican Cession, Clayton's bill meshed with Cass's principle that popular sovereignty had to be guided by and honor the principles of the Constitution. A Virginian expressed his opinion that the Nicholson letter was "identical" to the Clayton Compromise.[54] Georgia Whig and U.S. senator John M. Berrien believed that the bill upheld the traditional southern interpretation of popular sovereignty, thereby protecting southern rights. Indeed, most southerners who lent support to the Clayton bill echoed Berrien's claim that by denying territorial legislatures the right to legislate on slavery, it upheld southern equality in the territories.

Though certainly not identical in form, the two plans for adjusting the slavery question certainly bore similarities. First and most apparent, the Clayton bill affirmed the principle of popular sovereignty in Oregon. The Oregon territorial legislature had prohibited slavery before Clayton drafted his bill. Like Cass and the Democrats, the compromise equivocated on the issue in New Mexico and California. By referring the decision of the legality of slavery to the federal courts, the plan essentially upheld Cass's statement that any action on the slavery question had to conform to the Constitution. Under the Clayton Compromise, the Supreme Court would almost certainly rule on the constitutional issues surrounding slavery in the territories. Put another way, the justices would define the meaning and limits of popular sovereignty.

Northerners trembled at the thought that the Supreme Court, with its proslavery majority, would rule on the slavery question. A New York editor called the plan "a perfect specimen of arrant political cowardice."[55] Antislavery northerners charged that the compromise opened the door for slavery by allowing slaveholders to enter and remain in the cession with their property until the courts ruled on the issue. Few if any antislavery partisans seemed to trust that the courts would rule on their side. People from both sections saw a more ominous flaw in the Clayton Compromise, however. Clayton's plan assumed that either northerners or southerners would acquiesce in the decision of the Supreme Court as final and binding. Given the superheated atmosphere surrounding the slavery issue, partisans in both sections questioned whether people on the losing side of the issue would accept the court's decision.

The most decisive opposition to the Clayton Compromise, however, came from southern Whigs, especially a group of eight congressmen led by the diminutive Alexander Stephens of Georgia. Fearful that the compromise could hurt Taylor's prospects in the upcoming presidential election and perhaps hopeful that the slaveholder Taylor would do more for his section, Whigs from the South blocked the Clayton bill. The bill unfairly forced southerners to engage in litigation to secure the right to carry slaves into the territory. "This seems very much like legislating the South out of her rights," a Tennessee Whig insisted. Stephens and his associates in the House of Representatives likewise contended that slavery in the Mexican Cession could exist only by congressional authority. David Outlaw, a Whig congressman from North Carolina, rejected the Clayton bill as a blow against southern rights. "My impressions were against it," he confided to his wife, "because I regard it as no compromise at all but a surrender of the whole territory to the North."[56]

All speculation on the Clayton bill, however, proved moot, as the legislation met a fate similar to the effort to extend the Missouri Compromise line to the Pacific Ocean. The Senate passed the bill by a vote of 33–22, but the House of Representatives killed the bill when Stephens introduced a motion to table the legislation. Most observers believed that the compromise would fail for want of support among northern representatives. But Stephens, Outlaw, and six other southern Whigs combined to oppose the bill. The Clayton Compromise died by a vote of 112–97. Had Stephens and his seven southern Whig colleagues voted yea, the Clayton Compromise might well have passed by the slimmest margin, but he took the occasion to defend his own peculiar understanding of the constitutional status of slavery in the territories. Slavery, the Georgian insisted, could legally exist in a federal territory only by congressional fiat. Stephens, too, feared that the Clayton bill jeopardized Taylor's own stance on the slavery issue because some Democrats had endorsed the plan. So Stephens and seven other southern Whigs combined with all of the northern Whigs and over half of the northern Democrats to kill Clayton's bill. The bitter debate over the Clayton Compromise showed yet again how the politics of slavery could blur, if not obliterate, party lines over the issue of the expansion of slavery.[57]

With the Clayton Compromise unceremoniously buried by the House of Representatives, both parties reverted to their established plans for dealing with slavery in the Mexican Cession. Democrats had to burnish their candidate's reputation and his plan for territorial self-government, especially among skeptical southerners. Stephen Douglas's warning that Taylor could defeat the southern Democrats appeared increasingly prescient, and other Democrats took notice. "I hope the South will see that their interests require them to stand fast for our Candidate," a northern Democrat wrote to a colleague. "If he is defeated by their fault it seems to me there will not soon if ever be another national candidate." The Whigs assaulted Cass and popular sovereignty with renewed vigor, forcing southern Democrats to further obscure the meaning of their candidate's message. A Virginia Whig journal accused Cass and his associates of using "bungling illustrations" to explain the meaning of the Nicholson letter. Democratic opponents struck back with complicated logic, arguing that the Whigs themselves had misconstrued Cass's words when he wrote that "in the mean time," presumably the point between territorial formation and admission to statehood, the people of the territories should manage their "internal concerns." Whigs failed to recall that the people themselves had no voice in selecting their territorial officers in the first grade of government, the *Richmond Enquirer* replied. Furthermore, the Cass doctrine only meant to give territorial legislatures the power to *regulate* slavery, not to *abolish* it.[58]

Southern Democrats settled on two critical points in interpreting the meaning of popular sovereignty. First, they reaffirmed that the power to establish or prohibit slavery existed only when a territory drafted its constitution and sought admission to the Union as a sovereign state. Second, slave-state Democrats concluded that territorial legislatures could only pass laws regulating slavery. Cass proposed to limit congressional authority to the creation of territorial governments and to allow territorial legislatures to pass laws regulating slavery as they saw fit, but the "power to regulate the institution of slavery, implies the existence of such an institution to be regulated, and is wholly distinct from, and by no means includes, the power to *prohibit it*."[59]

From Democrats in the South, Cass faced a confusing array of signals about his chances to carry the region. His equivocal standing among southern Democrats reflected the uncertainty surrounding his position on the all-important slavery question. Cass received a letter from a Jackson, Mississippi, correspondent urging him to support President Polk's Oregon message, which advocated extension of the Missouri Compromise, if he had any hope of carrying the state. One Virginian, however, advised him to oppose the message in order to sway the state's voters. An exasperated Cass sought clarification from Mississippi Senator Henry S. Foote, but found little hope of gauging the true pulse of southern opinion. A Virginia representative expressed more favorable sentiments, assuring Cass that the South would give "generous support" to his campaign. "All reflecting men, whose party bias does not overcome their devotion to their country and the Union," John Y. Mason wrote, "must see, and do see, that the association of the Democratic party, is now the only hope of the Union."[60]

The fire-eater Robert Barnwell Rhett, however, captured the division in southern opinion on Cass. "I feared, and I think I had reason to fear," the South Carolinian said, "that the Southern Democrats might be divided as to the rights of the South, by a portion of them supporting this doctrine." Although Cass loyalists in the South gamely declared that "neither in the Nicholson letter nor any where else, that we have seen, has [he] declared himself in favor of Territorial Sovereignty," they simply could not shape public opinion in their favor. The attacks of southern Whigs, ultra states' rights advocates, and, to a certain degree, the language of the Nicholson letter itself, proved crippling to the southern Democrats' bid to prove their candidate would best protect the institution of slavery and southern interests in the West. The statements of Democratic speechmakers that Cass had taken the "true Southern ground" on the slavery question failed to impress or persuade a sufficient number of southern voters. Alexander Stephens best characterized southern sentiment on the Cass candidacy: "Shall it be said that the South can not trust their peculiar interest in the hands of a cotton and sugar planter of Louisiana, but they must look for a man in Detroit, who has not a feeling in common with them?"[61]

In the end, Cass could not overcome the odds stacked against him in the South. The Whigs had succeeded in running a bisectional campaign that mobilized the party faithful in support of an extremely popular candidate with no stated principles in the North and South. Aside from the clear benefits of Taylor's war record, Whigs had raised too many questions about Cass's sincerity in protecting southern rights, skillfully attacking the Nicholson letter. Taylor won the national popular vote by 4.8 percent. Though he won in the South by only 2.8 percent, Taylor carried eight southern states to Cass's seven. The Whigs proved strongest in the southeastern states, adding Florida, Georgia, and Louisiana to the upper South states they had carried in 1844. Cass carried Texas, Missouri, Arkansas, Mississippi, and Alabama, but many Democratic stalwarts in the South stayed home on Election Day. Taylor, on the other hand, invigorated the southern Whig base especially. Taylor gained more actual votes than had Henry Clay in 1844 in every southern state save Maryland.[62]

The political moves designed to redefine popular sovereignty so as to appeal to antislavery and partisans alike led to confusion within the Democracy, which was illustrated by an alleged conversation quoted in a Boston journal. In the month before the election, two Democrats—a man from Cleveland and another from Louisiana—met aboard a steamboat traveling west from Buffalo. On deck, the Cleveland man enthusiastically endorsed Cass as the right choice for president, assuring his traveling companion that the candidate opposed the extension of slavery and favored the Wilmot Proviso. Puzzled at the Ohioan's speech, the Louisianan replied, "We are both Cass men, sir, but I see you are advocating his election on wrong grounds." On the contrary, the man insisted, Cass's Nicholson letter repudiated the Wilmot Proviso and protected southern interests in the territories. With that, the discussion ceased.[63] Cass and the Democrats necessarily played a dangerous game in 1848 and lost. They tried to court voters in different sections of the Union by trying to obscure the implications of popular sovereignty and lending a double meaning to their own platform. The Whigs, bolstered by a war hero candidate, played the same game and won by taking no clear-cut position on the question of slavery restriction.

Southern Democrats bitterly received news of their candidate's defeat. "Strange as it may seem," a Georgia editor wrote, "although the victorious chief is a Southern man, yet the South is the vanquished party." The southern endorsement of Taylor would prove "a suicidal policy." Taylor would finally have to break his silence on the slavery question, which would prove whether southerners had rightly placed their trust in one of their own. While Cass emerged defeated from the election of 1848, no one knew whether his doctrine of popular sovereignty would reemerge as an alternative to the Wilmot Proviso or whether the election had killed it, too.[64]

"SHALL THE CONQUERED GOVERN

THE CONQUEROR?"

Popular Sovereignty in
the Mexican Cession

Lewis Cass and the Democrats took a considerable time licking the wounds they received at the hands of the triumphant Whig party in November 1848. On the surface, the southern electorate had repudiated the Democratic hobbyhorse of popular sovereignty and the party's efforts to prove itself safe on the slavery question. Zachary Taylor, a hero of the Mexican War and a Louisiana slaveholder, received sufficient support from the Whigs to overcome indignant antislavery opposition and ascend to the presidency. He won election not by standing on an ambiguous platform, but by endorsing no platform at all. Taylor did not need a policy; his war record electrified the voters who carried him to victory over the feckless Cass. Whig pundits accused Cass and the Democrats of crafting an indecisive and evasive campaign message regarding the Wilmot Proviso and slavery in the territories. But Taylor's Whigs revealed nothing about their ideas, leaving many wondering if they or the president-elect had a plan at all. In the South, uncertainty reigned; southerners emerged from the 1848 canvass increasingly concerned that the rising tide of antislavery sentiment in the North would spur Congress to block the extension of slavery to the West. They feared, too, that the North had the political power to do it. Two years of internecine party struggle over slavery left southern Democrats questioning the future of their bisectional party. Southern Whigs, on the other hand, prayed that the victor of 1848 would stand for southern rights in the territories.

The South would soon experience bitter disappointment, as President Taylor, in a move southerners found almost inexplicable, endorsed immediate statehood for the territories in the Mexican Cession—a move that virtually assured no further extension of slavery. Taylor's actions and the ubiquitous Wilmot Proviso provoked a true crisis of the Union in 1849–1850, which centered on the extension of slavery and in turn federal authority over the South's peculiar institution. For thirty years, southerners of all political parties had retreated from the once-accepted notion that Congress had authority over the extension of slavery, a position the South had accepted—implicitly or explicitly—in the Northwest Ordinance of 1787. The debate over slavery in California and New Mexico represented a culmination of the ongoing struggle regarding federal authority over slavery in the territories. Though Henry Clay's Compromise of 1850 would provide a framework for escaping the slavery extension controversy, in no small part by using the popular sovereignty formula in the Mexican Cession, it failed to satisfy a number of southerners because of its implication that Congress did possess the right to legislate for the territories with regard to their peculiar institution. The interminable debate over slavery extension had transformed then united southern opinion on the issue. "Sir, it is no longer a mere question of party policy in the South," said Whig Senator Willie P. Mangum of North Carolina, responding to Clay. "An overwhelming proportion of our people believe that this Government has no power to touch the subject of slavery in either the States or in the Territories."[1]

WHILE citizens puzzled over the president-elect's potential course, the seemingly inexorable debate over slavery in the Mexican Cession continued to trouble the national councils. With possession of the cession secured and people both within the territory and in the states clamoring for the extension of American law and institutions over the newly acquired Mexican lands, congressional leaders perceived the gravity of the situation and the need to settle the slavery issue. Under Mexican law, however, slavery did not exist anywhere in the cession except in the form of peonage, which little resembled the institution that existed in the American South.[2] In the Mexican system, peons technically contracted themselves to a master for a meager wage. In practice, however, the institution effectively bound peons and their issue into a labor relation similar to that of slavery. Antislavery and proslavery partisans argued over whether the Mexican law prohibiting slavery prevailed under American rule, as antislavery politicians posited, or if slavery followed the flag, as proslavery leaders like John C. Calhoun insisted.

The slavery debate that had raged during the election year continued into the lame duck second session of the Thirtieth Congress. In his final message to Congress, President James K. Polk chided legislators for failing to provide territorial governments for California and New Mexico and encouraged them to act promptly lest conditions deteriorate in the West. The lack of stable territorial governments in the western territories threatened the stability and security of the region. Polk lamented that the slavery issue had delayed the creation of territorial governments. Calling for popular sovereignty in the territories, the president argued that "no duty imposed on Congress by the Constitution requires that they should legislate on the subject of slavery, while their power to do so is not only seriously questioned, but denied by many of the soundest expounders of that instrument."[3] Polk's statement revealed how the interpretation of popular sovereignty and federal power had divided the Democracy; the president did not necessarily deny congressional authority over the extension of slavery, but instead said their opinion was not required. Likewise, by calling the constitutionality of congressional authority into question, he foreshadowed the day when the Supreme Court would define which version of popular sovereignty would prevail.

Polk recognized the incalculable value of California, a vast, fertile territory of immense natural resources and strategic importance that had quickly emerged as the jewel of the Mexican Cession, to the newly continental nation. Almost two years earlier, settlers had found gold at Johann Sutter's mill along the banks of the American River, provoking an overwhelming influx of prospectors who moved west to find wealth.[4] New Mexico, on the other hand, seemed far less impressive—a territory dominated by cattle grazing and the ages-old Spanish seigniorial system of agriculture, a situation by no means suited for plantation agriculture. Indeed, some observers believed that slavery could never flourish in the Mexican Cession because of the land, the climate, and the inhabitants who would almost surely prohibit slavery by their territorial laws and state constitutions. An army officer visiting New Mexico in 1846 had observed that the "profits of labor are too inadequate for the existence of negro slavery." In California, some believed that the gold rush would work against its extension. Not only did the influx of white laborers to the gold mines seemingly militate against the use of slave labor, but the hostility of the native Mexicans as well as the whites emigrating to the region placed slaveholders at a disadvantage. Emigrants from the free states almost assuredly would tip the balance in favor of a free California, long before Congress would act on the subject. Popular sovereignty, it seemed, would almost certainly work against proslavery interests unless the southern form of popular sovereignty—in which territories could determine the status of slavery only when in constitutional convention—prevailed. Though slaves might well prove excellent mine laborers, Georgia politician Wilson Lumpkin stated, slaveholders would not "under existing circumstances run the risque of loosing [sic] the slaves." Unless Congress could provide some sort of protection for slave property in the Mexican Cession, significant southern emigration seemed unlikely.[5]

For antislavery followers who believed that slavery could never exist profitably in the region, the question of the expansion of slavery to the Mexican Cession seemed an abstract notion dreamed up by ultra southerners seeking to augment their power in the nation. Their increasing hatred of the institution, however, led them to make a stand against its expansion, even as they thought the question an abstract one. Southerners, however, viewed the question of the profitable existence of slavery in the cession as hardly an abstraction. They sought to secure their rights in the face of a perceived onslaught against their peculiar institution and their section. Proslavery politicians continued to accuse northerners of attempting to deprive the South, in the words of Texas Democrat Louis T. Wigfall, of "the common conquest and purchase" of the Mexican Cession. Southerners could not predict what course Taylor would take with regard to the slavery issue, which revealed the fact that some questioned the proslavery credentials of Louisiana's favorite son. "Unless they can show a united and bold front," a northern observer predicted, "it is generally thought Gen. Taylor will go against them." Southerners like Andrew Jackson Donelson, the nephew of Old Hickory, could only express hope that Taylor would adopt a compromise

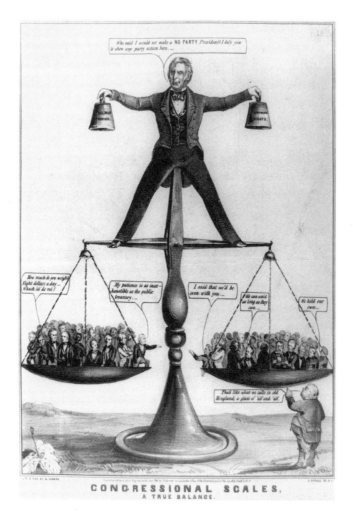

Southerners had voted for the Hero of Buena Vista, Zachary Taylor, not only for his wartime exploits but also for his status as a Louisiana slaveholder. Taylor attempted to balance northern and southern interests, but in the end he infuriated both sections. (Library of Congress)

proposal similar to the Clayton Compromise or endorse the Cass doctrine by allowing the territories to settle the matter for themselves.[6]

Many political spectators, however, predicted that while Taylor would not openly endorse the Wilmot Proviso, neither would he veto it. Even some southern Whigs had begun to question their leader's resolve on the slavery issue. Nevertheless, southerners remained deeply divided over the slavery issue. Calhoun's efforts to create a southern caucus in Congress and issue an address to the southern people to promulgate his opinions on settling the slavery issue had foundered amid the familiar divide between southern moderates and ultras, on the one hand, and, on the other, the persistence of partisan politics. Southerners had not yet abandoned the two-party Jacksonian political system that had protected southern interests for a generation. Vice President George M. Dallas observed the proceedings of the southern caucus, noting that Calhoun seemed unable to convince many of his colleagues to adopt an ultra southern stance that even hinted at the prospect of disunion over the slavery issue.[7]

While Calhoun's effort to rally the South failed, northern Democrats redoubled their efforts to assuage both antislavery and proslavery partisans. At the beginning of the congressional session, Stephen A. Douglas of Illinois introduced a bill that organized the entire Mexican Cession into one giant state of California, thereby bypassing the territorial stage. Though he had served in Congress for only four years—two terms in the House of Representatives before the Illinois state legislature elected him senator—the short, rotund dynamo from Chicago had earned a reputation as an ardent supporter of westward expansion. As a good Jacksonian Democrat, he also had come to endorse the doctrine of popular sovereignty. In the current session of Congress, the Illinoisan had considered taking a more orthodox approach, providing separate bills creating the territories of California and New Mexico. Douglas became convinced, however, that any territorial bill would fail because of the latest sectional dispute over constitutional interpretation on when a territory could permit or prohibit slavery. In order to organize the cession, he concluded, Congress had to grant immediate statehood to the entire Mexican Cession and let the people decide for themselves the status of slavery within their constitution.[8]

Douglas's ingenious plan addressed the political realities of the day while fulfilling his ultimate goal of extending American law and institutions over the Mexican Cession. Most significantly, the Douglas bill provided for self-government but rendered moot the discussion of when a territory could exercise its sovereignty over the slavery issue. The Douglas plan preserved the best part of the Cass doctrine by removing the issue of slavery from congressional deliberation, while it jettisoned the vexing question of when a territory gained the right to legislate on slavery.

Though Douglas's bill might have appealed to those looking for a way to organize the cession without renewing the contentious debate over slavery, southern senators soon raised objections. Douglas knew that his bill faced an uphill battle in the Senate and almost insurmountable opposition in the House of Representatives. Passage depended on committing the bill to the Committee on Territories—which Douglas chaired—where it would receive a favorable reading, but John M. Berrien, a veteran Whig senator from Georgia, outfoxed the Little Giant by using a parliamentary maneuver to derail the legislation. Berrien reminded his senate colleagues that the Judiciary Committee, which he chaired and which he knew would resist the bill, traditionally received statehood bills. Berrien won his point, and within four weeks the Judiciary Committee had issued an unfavorable report on the Douglas bill. The legislation, according to the committee, proposed to create a state out of a vast territory sparsely inhabited by people unfamiliar with American institutions and "unfitted" to assume the burden of self-government.[9] Given the present circumstances, the committee argued, statehood for California in the form it took in Douglas's bill seemed a poor idea.

Douglas could only stand by as a combination of proslavery and antislavery blocs dismantled his effort to organize the Mexican Cession and remove the slavery issue from congressional deliberation. Northerners remained committed to extending the Wilmot Proviso over the western territories. Slave-state radicals, on the other hand, advanced a new argument in their efforts to protect what they perceived as southern rights in the territories. In the past (most notably in the Louisiana Purchase) southerners had ridiculed northerners who insisted on a period of "territorial pupilage," where foreign residents of a territory could become Americanized. Believing as they did that Mexicans residing in the cession were hostile to slavery, they now insisted that the natives in the newly acquired territories could not govern themselves. Besides this explanation of why Congress should delay California statehood, however, southerners protested that they had not been given sufficient time to emigrate west themselves and influence the governments and thus governance of the cession. In the new zero-sum game of territorial expansion, where the Missouri Compromise line between slavery and freedom did not exist, southerners would have to engage in a footrace to ensure that proslavery citizens would control the destiny of the Mexican Cession. The future of slavery in the West, northerners and southerners agreed, depended on which section controlled the process of popular sovereignty. Ironically, voters had rejected this very solution at the polls in 1848.

Some political leaders observed that ultras on both sides of the slavery issue had maneuvered against Douglas's bill to gain advantage on the slavery question. Vice President Dallas lambasted the southern members of the Senate Judiciary Committee. The committee's argument that the "people of New Mexico & California are too barbarous," he confided to his diary, "seem to me mere spurious pretexts, devised by an acute and ingenious mind in order to keep those territories open to Slavery." Indeed, Dallas sensed the true purpose behind the opposition to the Douglas bill. In a conference with President Polk, Calhoun had frankly admitted that southerners opposed California statehood because slaveholders had been denied the opportunity to emigrate to the region with their slaves. He conceded, too, that California would certainly enter as a free state, rankling southerners who viewed the entire statehood movement as a northern plot to prevent the expansion of slavery. The president reminded Calhoun that the people themselves possessed the right to determine the status of slavery, but such reasoning would not suffice for the South Carolinian, who believed that the equal rights of slaveholders in the territories merited federal protection.[10]

Douglas would have to compromise on the terms of his bill if California statehood would have any chance of passing through Congress in early 1849, but he lacked southern support both in Congress and in the court of public opinion. "No man can be blind to the fact," a Georgian wrote, "if called on to form a State Constitution now, the people of California will exclude slavery. In doing this they will also fix the fate of New Mexico." Though Calhoun had failed to rally sufficient support for his "Southern Address," a significant number of southerners agreed with his contention that the Douglas plan excluded southern slaveholders from having a stake in the future of the Mexican Cession. The Polk administration saw great benefit in admitting California as a state bypassing the territorial stage, but the president and his advisers considered the size of the state as proposed by Douglas as prohibitively large. Better to secure statehood for California alone, the cabinet concluded, and defer deliberations on New Mexico for a later date. Of course, separating New Mexico from California cast off one of the benefits of the original Douglas plan—by organizing the entire cession as one state, the bill potentially would have neutralized the debate over slavery in the territories. Nevertheless, Polk prevailed on a reluctant Douglas to amend his bill.[11]

The revised legislation provided for the immediate admission of California and the delayed admission of New Mexico, almost certainly a recognition of the fact that California would become a free state. By delaying statehood for New Mexico, however, southerners could theoretically gain a foothold in the territory. For a fleeting moment, passage of the amended bill seemed possible. Supporters lauded the Douglas's effort to extend self-government to the residents of the Mexican Cession. "We go for the principle of non-intervention," the Democratic *Washington Union* declared. "We cannot obtain it in the territorial form. We must, then, seek it in the form of States—leaving the people themselves to frame their own constitution, and to seek admission into the Union as States."[12] Like Douglas, the *Union*'s editor recognized that the Cass version of popular sovereignty had failed to mend the sectional breach within the Democratic Party. Indeed, when Cass had initially suggested in the Nicholson letter that territorial legislatures could pass laws permitting or prohibiting slavery, Democrats faced a firestorm of opposition from southern party regulars who argued that "squatter sovereignty" would allow the native Mexicans to prohibit slavery in California and New Mexico before Americans could emigrate west. By sidestepping the territorial phase and admitting California and New Mexico as states, Congress could obviate the difficulty over when a territory could legislate on slavery while preserving the right of the people to settle the matter when drafting a constitution.

Though southerners had rejected the superheated rhetoric of Calhoun's Southern Address and his veiled threats of disunion, they nonetheless felt threatened by northern attacks on slavery and its westward expansion. In this atmosphere of fear and suspicion, they renewed their opposition to the Douglas bill. "The bill assumes that it is a mere point of honor for which the South is contending, and not for an actual bona-fide participation in the territory," an associate wrote to Georgia congressman Howell Cobb. "Be that as it may, the question is will even the point of honor or equality be saved by a practical surrender of the whole territory to the North."[13] Northern Democrats like Douglas and James Buchanan believed that slavery could never take root in the cession. Accordingly, they sought a way for the South to maintain its honor and its constitutional scruples. If enough southerners had concurred, the bill might have passed, but the fact that southern politicians demanded a real chance at emigrating to California and New Mexico indicates that they believed slavery might thrive there in some form. Of course, Douglas and Buchanan may have correctly perceived that the point or principle of the matter was more important that the possibility that slavery might be successfully extended to those climes.

Both parties strongly desired to extricate themselves from the increasingly dangerous and volatile slavery extension issue. A group of southern Whigs in the House of Representatives had closely followed the deliberations across the Capitol and latched onto the idea of immediate statehood as an ingenious way to solve the territorial crisis and preserve harmony within their party. Polk and Douglas in effect sold their plan to southern Whigs, who were anxious to settle the issue before Taylor took office, as a way to defuse the explosive Wilmot Proviso and secure southern rights in name, even if not in practice. Most everyone surmised that California would enter the Union as a free state regardless, and the Douglas plan effectively killed the debate over the Wilmot Proviso. If northern and southern Democrats, with southern Whigs also on board, could unite behind the Douglas bill, moderation would have prevailed and Congress could for the moment dispense with the slavery issue.[14]

With Douglas's bill mired in contentious Senate negotiations, the proponents of immediate statehood looked to Virginia Whig congressman William Ballard Preston's proposal to admit the entire cession as a single state of California. Borrowing the language of Douglas's original legislation, Preston entreated moderate Whigs and Democrats to give careful consideration to his bill; legislation he argued would settle the long-standing crisis over slavery in the territories by letting the people of California draft their own constitution and select their own institutions as they saw fit. Preston mocked the notion that the people of California could not erect their own government and therefore needed a period of "territorial tutelage." Illustrating the stakes involved in delaying the organization of California, Preston thundered, "Tutelage! You, in the great day and great hour of this question—are you to stop, like a mere pedagogue, to teach New Mexico and California the A B C of political liberty, while the destruction of an empire and a government might learn you the last lesson of its overthrow?"[15]

Moderate southerners from both parties endorsed the Preston bill because it upheld their belief in congressional nonintervention with slavery. Quoting the words of James Madison during the Missouri crisis, Democrat James McDowell of Virginia said, "The right of Congress to control the territories being given from the necessity of the case and in suspension of the great principle of self-government, ought not to be extended further nor continued longer than the occasion might fairly require." McDowell endorsed the Preston bill as a sure way of ensuring southern rights while upholding the principle of nonintervention. As for Preston himself, he represented the sentiments of those who had grown weary of the incessant turmoil over the Wilmot Proviso. *"I want repose,"* Preston exclaimed, *"and the bill now offered gives finality to the question. I want the question ended."*[16]

Though the moderates desired a speedy resolution of the territorial issue, northern Whigs and southern ultras would not let the matter be put to rest. Revealing divisions even within the southern Democracy, party members voiced opposition to the Preston bill denouncing it as the Wilmot Proviso cloaked in the mantle of compromise. Southern ultras who hoped to form a separate southern rights party uprising indicated that the continued agitation of the slavery question only benefited the Democratic party in the South. They repeated claims that immediate statehood would allow Indians, blacks, and native Mexicans to deny Americans the right to carry their slaves into the cession. Preston's most intractable opposition came from northern Whigs who insisted that Congress apply the Wilmot Proviso to the Mexican Cession. Two last-minute amendments, one of which added the Proviso to the bill, derailed his efforts to avoid the issue. With the moderating intent of the bill destroyed, not one member of the House voted for passage. Preston's original bill never came up for a vote. The lame duck Congress would pass no legislation for California or New Mexico statehood, leaving the issue for the next Congress and the new president. Thus the slavery issue would continue to threaten the stability of the Whig party, just as it stood poised to claim the presidency for only the second time in the party's brief existence.[17]

To Zachary Taylor, the Whigs in Congress left either the glory of solving the slavery issue or the misery of the continued stalemate. Whig and Democratic stalwarts had hoped to neutralize the slavery question before it destroyed their respective parties, but found their pleas for unity drowned out by extreme antislavery and proslavery voices. A majority of southerners distrusted Calhoun and the southern ultras, while they kept faith in the Jacksonian party system that had elected one of their own to the presidency. The debate over popular sovereignty's meaning had fueled the rise of extremism; a proposal for compromise made by northern doughfaces had instead created a crisis over the extension of slavery and constitutional theory surrounding federal authority in the territories. Northern antislavery ultras believed that the moral dimension of their cause transcended party; southern ultras increasingly wanted to destroy the bisectional party system itself.

All eyes fixed on the new president for some clue, some direction as to how he would settle the Wilmot Proviso controversy. Taylor's inaugural speech gave them nothing. In his "exceptionally brief and bafflingly vague" address, the new president gave no indication of the course he would take on the slavery in the territories; indeed, he made no explicit mention of the issue. Surveying the new administration, former president John Tyler wrote to his eldest son, "For the settlement of our territorial difficulties we must look to the territories themselves. They must organize governments for themselves as Congress will not do so for them." Tyler believed that slavery had paralyzed Congress and perhaps the new president; he, too, had no indication of what Taylor might do with regard to the situation in California and New Mexico.[18]

Within the month, however, Taylor had settled on a plan for organizing the Mexican Cession—and for altering the course of American politics. Seeking to revivify Whiggery, the president, Kentucky Governor John J. Crittenden, and John M. Clayton devised a "foolish and utopian initiative" (as one historian has put it) to create a new political party that would build consensus on issues that had traditionally divided the old parties and sections of the Union.[19] Of course, the most fractious issue in American politics remained: the extension of slavery. Popular sovereignty, Cass style, had failed miserably, as had other efforts to neutralize the Wilmot Proviso. Accordingly, Taylor decided to assume the substance of the Preston bill as executive policy, thereby circumventing congressional deliberation on the proposal and also bypassing the thorny territorial phase over which northerners and southerners had fought about the meaning of popular sovereignty. The president, however, advocated creating two states out of the Mexican Cession—California and New Mexico.

In April 1849, Thomas Butler King, a Whig congressman from Savannah, Georgia, embarked for California at the president's direction to encourage its residents to draft a constitution and seek prompt admission to the Union. Though the administration explicitly instructed King to avoid the question of slavery in his discussions with leaders in California, no doubt existed that the Taylor plan would result in its admission as a free state. At the same time that Taylor's envoy embarked for California, the president sent an emissary to New Mexico on an identical assignment and third official to Deseret to urge the Mormons to join the state of California. In one grand mission, Taylor intended to eliminate contention over slavery in the territories. By November, Taylor and his associates had succeeded in persuading the Californians to petition for statehood as a free state. New Mexico would not draft a constitution for another six months, but at least the process had commenced. Southerners had learned that the president intended for California and New Mexico both to become free states.[20]

Taylor's plan left southern Whigs crestfallen. He had confirmed what some Whigs had suspected even months before the inauguration: the president would almost certainly not oppose the Wilmot Proviso. Over the course of his first year in office, the president confirmed that he would not oppose the proviso if Congress passed it. Taylor himself dismissed the possibility that the proviso would even reach his desk; his plan for immediate statehood would obviate the need for any such antislavery action. His belief that Congress would never send him the proviso reaffirmed a position he had taken during his summer tour of the northern states. In a speech given at Mercer, Pennsylvania, in late August, Taylor declared, "The people of the North need have no apprehension of the further extension of slavery."[21]

For southerners already skeptical of the president's reliability on the slavery question, the northern tour—and especially his antislavery pronouncement at Mercer—confirmed their worst suspicions, for it "explained the purpose of King's mission to California and placed the man whom they had promised would never betray his fellow slaveholders squarely against slavery expansion." For the interests of Whig party unity as well as bipartisan hopes for a calm, considered settlement to the slavery question, Taylor's remarks proved disastrous. The southern Whigs "lapsed into bitter silence" as Taylor appeared to ally himself with the antislavery branch of the party. Southern Democrats excoriated the president for betraying his section and depriving slaveholders of equal participation in the territories won by common blood and treasure. Taylor's actions confirmed slave-state Democrats' campaign rhetoric better than they could have dreamed. If the southern states had rallied behind Lewis Cass, Tennessee Congressman Andrew Johnson stated, he would have won election and "then all would have been safe."[22]

Taylor either misunderstood or dismissed the hostile nature of southern public opinion against the mélange of American settlers—squatters to the minds of southerners—and native Mexicans drafting constitutions and seeking admission to the Union before southerners themselves could enter the territories. To his mind, the statehood plan had preserved the South's constitutional rights by allowing the citizens of California and New Mexico to draft constitutions as they pleased. However that may be, the plan "dodged the contested issue of the South's right to carry slaves into the commonly held territories." In doing so, Taylor revealed his true belief that the institution should and could not expand beyond its current boundaries. The protracted and seemingly intractable controversy surrounding the slavery extension question posed an immediate threat to the Union and was an obstacle to his vision of a new party coalition "unencumbered with old issues or old allegiances." Most southerners in either party had no interest in Taylor's chimerical political vision, but they did care deeply about the extension dispute. Taylor betrayed them by depriving the South of a long territorial phase that would allow slaveholders and proslavery advocates to settle in New Mexico and California. In sum, the president had dismissed the evolving southern interpretation of popular sovereignty, which southerners rightly considered critical to the extension of slavery to the Mexican Cession.[23]

Even before Taylor's summer tour, pro- and antislavery activists had commenced making preparations for a battle over the slavery issue. As Georgia Senator Herschel V. Johnson commented, the Taylor plan would prove nothing less than "a circuitous mode of cheating the South out of her rights and gaining the object of the Provisoists." Calhoun's unsuccessful southern rights movement, which had culminated in the pronouncement of his Southern Address, may not have united the South under a nonpartisan proslavery banner, but southerners continued to look warily at northern movements against slavery in the territories. A number of southern state legislatures and citizens' organizations issued resolutions condemning the Wilmot Proviso and asserting southern rights in the newly acquired territories. They affirmed that the right to prohibit slavery belonged, in the words of the Missouri General Assembly, "exclusively to the people thereof, and can only be exercised by them in forming their Constitution for a State government, or in their sovereign capacity as independent States." Of course, Taylor's plan would have done exactly this, but would have resulted in the restriction of slavery given the antislavery majorities in California and New Mexico territories.[24]

Galvanized in opposition against the Taylor plan, Democrats took the offensive on the slavery issue. The *Washington Union*, the official Democratic newspaper, led the call in the press for replacing the Taylor plan with the sound Democratic doctrine of popular sovereignty, which seemed to suggest that southerners still had allies in the North. After all, if northern Democrats had fully supported the Wilmot Proviso, they would have heartily endorsed Taylor's actions, which would have produced the same outcome. "We propose the ground of NON-INTERVENTION; by which we mean that Congress shall abstain from all legislation in relation to the subject of slavery in the new territories; leaving it to the people of the territories themselves to make the necessary provision for their eventual admission into the Union, and to regulate their internal concerns in their own way."[25]

The latest pronouncements in support of popular sovereignty, however, marked a subtle retreat from the Cass doctrine. In the latest discussions over slavery in the territories, northern Democrats backpedaled on when the citizens of a territory had the right to regulate their internal concerns. According to its supporters, nonintervention retained the promise to extricate Congress from jurisdiction over the dreaded slavery issue, while returning the nation to its first principles of popular sovereignty and consent of the governed. In the case of the Mexican Cession, according to the *Union*'s Thomas Ritchie, the doctrine left to the courts all matters concerning the prohibition of slavery in the territories which was essentially the aim of the Clayton Compromise of 1848, which would have given the Supreme Court the ultimate authority to adjudicate the slavery issue. Again, leaders appealed to the judiciary to determine the meaning of popular sovereignty because they could not solve it for themselves without destroying party unity.

The dispute over slavery extension revealed that the two-party system remained firm within the South, even as party ties between the sections had weakened considerably. Slave-state Democrats maintained that they had provided a safe way to dispose of the question of restriction in 1848, but southerners had chosen one of their own rather than to entrust the safety of the institution to an outsider. Now the Whig president, a southern slaveholder, had inexplicably abandoned their interests in the territories. The "relentless exploitation of sectional prejudices" during the 1848 campaign meant that tensions remained high between the northern and southern wings of the Democracy. Southern Democrats reminded their constituents that in the 1848 presidential contest "the Northern Democracy proved true to Southern interests," but now northern Democrats had become wary of extending a hand of friendship across the Mason-Dixon Line and a southern Whig had betrayed their trust. Northern Democrats had endorsed the Cass doctrine at considerable danger to their own electoral prospects at home, only to see southerners rebuff their overtures. Nevertheless, party stalwarts hoped to renew the enthusiasm for popular sovereignty, especially with the increasing dissatisfaction among southerners toward the Taylor administration. In 1848, Democrats had unsuccessfully defined the doctrine as a bisectional compromise designed to unify the party and neutralize the Wilmot Proviso. But the party failed to convince either southerners or anti-slavery northerners of its efficacy. Their attempts to placate the antislavery and proslavery wings of the party by applying multiple meanings to popular sovereignty had produced a seemingly insoluble problem. In 1850, moderate northern Democrats such as Lewis Cass and Daniel Dickinson renewed their efforts to establish popular sovereignty as national policy. This time, however, they worked especially hard at convincing southerners that electing one of their own versus voting for the safety of slavery by upholding nonintervention had cost them dearly. The South would remain center stage in the debate over popular sovereignty.[26]

Having returned to the Senate, Cass again defended the doctrine he had advanced in the Nicholson letter almost two years before, accusing his opponents of resorting to "inconsistency, amounting to dishonesty" in order to discredit his concept of popular sovereignty. Those who maintained the constitutionality of the Wilmot Proviso, he argued, must also believe that Congress possessed the power to "direct all the internal territorial legislation at its pleasure, without regard to the will of the people affected by it." Drawing from classic Jacksonian principles, Cass denied both suppositions. The Wilmot Proviso, according to Cass, was patently unconstitutional. Furthermore, the idea that Congress could dictate local laws for territories or states denied the nation's heritage. Americans had risen in rebellion against the British because the mother country refused to let the colonies rule on their own internal concerns. Had the U.S. government created its own colonial system in the West that it could rule at its own will, Cass asked rhetorically? "This dispute divided one empire," he proclaimed. "Let us take care that a similar assumption does not divide another."[27]

Cass's defense of popular sovereignty resonated with moderates on the slavery issue, but the continuing dispute between northerners and southerners over its interpretation exacted a toll on the impetus for compromise. By hearkening to the nation's revolutionary heritage, Cass sought to give the Democratic Party's doctrine added legitimacy. Many southern Democrats who rallied behind the Cass banner in 1848 lamented that their candidate had not taken the White House, believing they had missed their opportunity to unite with sympathetic northerners and secure the safety of slavery in the West. A Georgian inveighed against President Taylor's policy, writing that "The South . . . has been betrayed, and basely betrayed, and that too by her own sons." Others, however, saw the stiffening resistance of northern Democrats, including the defection of some to the free-soil movement, as a clarion call for the southern rights platform.[28]

Yet in the face of the bellicose pronouncements of ultra proslavery and anti-slavery leaders, northern Democrats like Cass and Daniel Dickinson rallied once again in favor of popular sovereignty. Soon after Cass issued his letter to Thomas Ritchie defending the principles in the Nicholson letter, Dickinson moved to galvanize his New York supporters to make another attempt at insti-tuting his favored doctrine—an important sign for moderation considering that the Free Soil Party had originated with disaffected New York Democrats. Like Cass, Dickinson appealed to the nation's revolutionary heritage in a bid to win the support of recalcitrant northerners who threatened to give up any chance at compromise with the South. Popular sovereignty, Dickinson reminded his audi-ence, upheld the right of self-government while rejecting the "tyrannical prece-dent of that living compound of scrofula and gold-lace, called George III."[29] Dickinson, who had always taken a more straightforward position on the popu-lar sovereignty issue than had Cass, argued that the people of the territories possessed the same sovereignty as the residents of the states. Using classic Jacksonian rhetoric, Dickinson maintained that American citizens did not lose their right of self-government by virtue of emigrating to the territories. Yet the New York senator offended southerners who believed that the North had con-spired to prevent southerners from sharing in the common conquest of the Mexican Cession by concluding that the people of California had already de-cided against slavery, and that the people of the states must respect their deci-sion as final and binding.

Southerners despised what they perceived as a two-front assault on south-ern rights: the northern Democrats' insistence that territorial legislatures could exercise popular sovereignty over slavery and President Taylor's endorsement of a free California and New Mexico. Yet they faced a quandary; as Herschel Johnson noted, "We admit the right of a people in forming a State Constitution to establish or eschew slavery. Then, ought we to oppose and how?" Southern-ers agreed that they could not stand idly by as California became a free state, with New Mexico poised to follow suit, but they disagreed on how to proceed. Like Johnson, some puzzled at how to oppose a free-state constitution for Cali-fornia when the South had always upheld the sanctity of self-government in the drafting of organic law. Others, who tended to ally with Calhoun, viewed the sit-uation more pragmatically. "I feel a most solemn conviction that the South must arouse from its negative position and assume that of the lion," a Tennessean wrote to Calhoun, or California "will be cut off from us & the doom of our chil-dren sealed." More experienced politicos viewed the situation in less apocalyptic terms. Mississippi Senator Henry S. Foote intimated that southerners could not hope to gain a foothold in California, but that they should insist on the admission of New Mexico only when a sufficient number of Americans had emigrated to the territory to apply for statehood. In the meantime, Congress should prohibit the native New Mexicans from legislating on the subject of slavery. Foote implied that southerners would have to populate the territories in order to hold their power in Congress and the nation.[30]

Many southerners blamed the California situation on the Taylor administration's efforts to encourage a statehood movement among the native population and the few American squatters on the ground. In the president's defense, historian David Potter has noted, "by leaving the question of slavery to local decision, Taylor was really adopting a kind of popular sovereignty." Actually, the president had done nothing less than advocate the *southern version* of popular sovereignty, that citizens of a territory had the right to draft a constitution with or without slavery as they saw fit without congressional intervention. But because southerners had not emigrated to California and New Mexico, and because the residents there held antislavery beliefs, the South could not rely on its standard constitutional rhetoric to produce a proslavery outcome—something that had never happened before. The struggle for southern "political sovereignty" would not prevail with adoption of the Taylor plan, no matter how closely it resembled southern political dogma.[31]

Consequently, southerners attacked the *process* by which California seemed ready to apply for statehood, not the *principle* that a territory could exercise self-government in drafting a constitution. Renewing an argument first suggested by Robert J. Walker and James Buchanan in 1847, a number of southerners attacked the notion that foreigners could decide the fate of slavery in the Mexican Cession using highly racialized rhetoric. In one of the more blatantly racist pronouncements against the California free-state movement, a proslavery commentator lamented the fact that the cession had become "the resort of Mexicans and South Americans of every hue and race, of Sandwich Islanders and even Chinese." Yet northerners sought to bar "the people of the fifteen Southern States and of that particular class to which Washington, Jefferson, Madison, Henry, Pinckney, Rutledge and Carroll belonged; that class from which the people of the North and South have elected a large majority of their Presidents." To the writer, the North had abandoned years of sectional conciliation and compromise in a mad effort to purge the territories of slavery. He argued that the Northwest Ordinance had its proslavery corollary—the Southwest Ordinance, which had provided for an equitable distribution of the nation's territories between the North and South. But now the North sought to renege on generations of compromise. Calling the northern efforts to bar slavery in the territories an "incendiary plot" of the "surviving fragments of the fallen houses of Braintree and Kinderhook"—referring to the antislavery leaders John Quincy Adams and Martin Van Buren—the correspondent echoed a growing cadre of southerners who believed that the South needed its own political coalition since both political parties had abandoned southern interests.[32]

Nonetheless most southerners still embraced their party affiliations while maintaining that opposition had perverted popular sovereignty by allowing native Mexicans to determine the status of slavery in the cession. After the residents of California elected delegates to draft a constitution in August 1849, southerners fumed at what they deemed a "mongrel convention." Their criticism only intensified when, on September 10, the convention officially added a slavery prohibition clause to their draft constitution. It seemed that the South had lost its battle against the antislavery advocates. They resorted to what seemed the last line of defense, lambasting the members of the convention as foreigners unfit to draft organic law and accusing the convention of admitting foreigners to its councils. The fact that the convention adopted the antislavery clause unanimously only deepened their suspicion of the convention's work, according to the *Richmond Enquirer*. Ultimately, the journal blamed the California situation on President Taylor. "Such are the 'glorious fruits,'" it scorned, "which the South is to reap under the administration of a 'Southern President.'"[33]

Once again the issue of slavery in the territories loomed over a newly elected Congress, as the nation's representatives gathered in Washington in December 1849. The election of a speaker of the House of Representatives portended the conflict ahead, when for three weeks the lower chamber failed to elect a leader. Gridlock paralyzed the House, leaving it unable to function.[34] So far most southerners had rebuffed the efforts of radicals to foment disunion, but one could foresee the future. The poisonous atmosphere in Washington, so vividly evinced by the battle for the speakership in the House, further troubled political observers as both sides stood ready to defend their beliefs on whether slavery could or would exist in California and New Mexico.

Resolutions from southern state legislatures poured into Washington demanding equal rights for southern slaveholders in the territories. Southern Democrats had emerged victorious in many state elections during the fall of 1849, riding the wave of indignation against the Taylor plan. The Missouri General Assembly decried the agitation over slavery in the West and raised the familiar refrain that territories could legislate on slavery only when drafting a state constitution. Observant southerners, however, had already noted that with respect to California and New Mexico, maintaining that popular sovereignty existed only in a constitutional convention would not suffice. Northern Democrats had hailed the California constitutional convention as a "triumphant confirmation" of the Cass doctrine. Southerners would have to attack constitution making in California as illegitimate in order to halt the process of creating a free state. As Missouri Congressman James S. Green wrote to his constituents, they could stand by the "old and long cherished doctrine of the Democratic party"— nonintervention, but they also must insist on the right of citizens from all the states to enjoy the benefits of the new territories. The precipitous move of the California statehood supporters threatened that right. In spite of the cries of a number of southern leaders, many already believed in the inevitability of a free state of California.[35]

The president confirmed their fears when he delivered special messages to Congress explaining his administration's efforts to promote immediate statehood for California and New Mexico, refuting the claims of those who denied the legitimacy of the California constitutional convention and defending his decision to send emissaries encouraging them to draft constitutions and seek immediate admission to the Union. Congress had proven unable to settle the issue without violent debate and interminable delay, so like a true general the president had taken charge, charting a way out of the Wilmot Proviso and popular sovereignty quandaries. Taylor, however, denied that either he or his representatives had actively influenced the formation of statehood movements in the territories, a truthful claim with respect to California, but not New Mexico. More importantly, Taylor disputed the charges of those who characterized the citizens of the cession as a conquered population. He observed that a significant number of American citizens had moved to the territories and had a right to draft a constitution as they saw fit. Although Taylor's proposition seemed reasonable, he had perhaps unwittingly raised an even more contentious issue by arguing that Congress had the power to prohibit slavery in the territories. Furthermore, his language suggested that he would not veto a congressional prohibition of slavery—essentially the Wilmot Proviso—if Congress passed such legislation. In other words, Taylor believed the Wilmot Proviso constitutional but unnecessary, as the territories could establish or prohibit slavery once they became states.[36]

Southerners excoriated the president for his message and his administration's actions, believing that he had conceded the antislavery argument and placed their section in a precarious position. North Carolina Whig Representative Thomas Clingman broke ranks with his president over the plan for immediate statehood. "The idea that conquered people should be permitted to give law to the conquerors," he exclaimed, "is so preposterously absurd, that I do not intend to argue it." A Texas Democrat likewise attacked the president's actions, implying that if Cass had been elected president, he would have rallied to the southern cause. Southerners had erred in electing one of their own, he claimed, believing wrongly that Taylor would stand up for their interests. The Democratic doctrine of nonintervention, he suggested, would have protected southern rights far better than the active intervention and machinations of the Taylor administration.[37]

Democrats across the nation rallied to defend their party and vindicate its 1848 platform in the midst of Taylor's controversial actions. In a lengthy address to his colleagues, Senator Cass reaffirmed the substance of the Nicholson letter. The Michigan legislature had placed Cass in a political quandary when it had instructed him to vote for the Wilmot Proviso. Cass, of course, completely opposed it, insisting on his own formula for dealing with slavery in the territories. Though the Michigan senator probably wished to avoid the discussion over slavery, by late January he recognized the impossibility of maintaining silence.[38] Cass repeated the theme that had become common among proponents of popular sovereignty—that the United States fought a war of revolution against Great Britain for precisely the same principles at stake in the present debate over slavery in the territories. He portrayed the battle as nothing less than a fight for the "human rights" of citizens residing in the cession. "Are not the people of the territories competent to manage their own affairs," Cass asked his colleagues. "Are they not of us, and with us?—bone of our bone, and flesh of our flesh?"[39]

Cass provided an exhaustive defense of popular sovereignty in an effort to convince shaken southerners that popular sovereignty and the Democracy provided surer protection of their rights than did a Louisiana slaveholder. He reiterated that the Constitution did not give Congress the power to pass laws concerning slavery in the territories, in spite of the precedents of the Northwest Ordinance and the Missouri Compromise, both of which avowed congressional authority over slavery in at least part of the national domain. Cass disputed the authority of the Northwest Ordinance because it had become law under the Articles of Confederation, ignoring the fact that the Congress created by the Constitution of 1787 had reaffirmed the law. The Missouri Compromise, Cass argued, "was not a legislative precedent," but a "political expedient, which adjusted a fearful controversy."[40] He sought once again to rally support for his theory of popular sovereignty, though he bowed to political expediency by refusing to define when and how a territorial legislature could pass laws concerning slavery. Cass expressed fear for the safety of the Union and portrayed himself as the voice of moderation as forces on both sides of the slavery issue threatened to tear apart the nation.

Cass identified the essence of popular sovereignty—that Americans who emigrated to the territories still possessed the basic political rights of their fellow citizens residing in the states. National citizenship and the rights of an American citizen, Cass implied, did not cease or change when he became a resident of a territory. The issue of citizenship itself—a troubling matter of constitutional interpretation in antebellum America—remained unsettled, but Cass insisted that Americans in the territories had the same natural right to self-government as those in the states.[41] But therein lay the heart of Calhoun's reasoning, too; the South Carolinian maintained that a slaveholder, by virtue of his American citizenship, had the legal right to carry slaves into American territory without fear of risking ownership. The vastly different reasoning behind an antislavery and proslavery vision of popular sovereignty, undergirded by the basic political rights of an American citizen, plagued the precise definition of popular sovereignty itself and foreshadowed an increasingly bitter conflict between North and South over the meaning of individual, state, and federal authority.

The moderate southern Democratic press generally praised Cass's speech and its firm stand against congressional intervention with slavery in the territories. His implication that territorial legislatures possessed the right to legislate on the slavery question and his contention that the Californians had rightfully exercised their right to draft a free-state constitution offended a few southern observers, but most of the southern press chose to ignore the ambiguity. The Taylor administration's baffling course left them few alternatives. Southerners still had a stalwart friend in Lewis Cass, a Georgia editor declared. Some Democrats accused President Taylor of stealing the Cass doctrine for his own political purposes. "It is a singular coincidence, that while Cass was making this fine speech in the Senate, Taylor, in his message, then being read in the House, was signifying his consent to the great doctrine of NON-INTERVENTION, opposed and misrepresented by his whig friends in the last Presidential canvass." And yet it seemed that little of the rancorous debate over the doctrine itself had abated, which was suggested by the nearly complete southern silence on the part of Cass's pronouncement that addressed popular sovereignty. The ability of the Cass doctrine to serve as an acceptable compromise remained doubtful.[42]

Amid the intensifying rancor over the slavery question, moderates in the North and South concluded that only a broad-based, sectionally balanced compromise could preserve the Union. Yet southern ultras insisted on delivering an ultimatum to northerners: honor southern rights or face disunion. Since October 1849, the momentum for a southern rights convention to be held at Nashville the following June had increased, with six southern states dispatching delegates to the meeting. Such ominous developments worried Henry Clay, the seventy-two-year-old senator from Kentucky who had shepherded compromises through Congress in 1820 and 1833. Sensing the onset of a true crisis of the Union, he took the lead in devising a way to avert the coming crisis of 1850. Clay's meeting on January 21 with Daniel Webster, in which he convinced his famed colleague to aid him in promoting a compromise plan and his subsequent introduction of a far-reaching settlement of the difficulties between the North and South have become the stuff of historical legend. Clay's compromise plan, which he delivered to the Senate on January 29, proposed eight resolutions, each designed to placate the North and the South on the troublesome questions concerning slavery and the westward expansion of the institution. Two of the resolutions directly affected slavery in the territories. First, Clay proposed to admit California to the Union with its free-state constitution. Second, Clay called for congressional nonintervention respecting slavery in the remainder of the Mexican Cession by establishing territorial governments without reference to the institution. In doing so, however, he contended that slavery would most likely never exist in the region; therefore, he considered congressional intervention "inexpedient." Furthermore, Clay clearly stated that he hoped that California and New Mexico would never admit slavery within their boundaries. He would not oppose statehood, however, if either or both territories did permit slavery because "then it will be their own work, and not ours, and their posterity will have to reproach them, and not us for forming constitutions allowing the institution of slavery to exist among them."[43]

For the next eight months, Congress and the nation would debate the Clay compromise plan in a highly charged discourse that itself repeatedly threatened to derail any effort at conciliation. More specifically, Americans debated the virtues and the complications of nonintervention, inasmuch as Clay had settled upon using the idea of self-government as the preferred means to defuse the

Wilmot Proviso controversy. Clay's interpretation of popular sovereignty proved vague and elusive, however, presumably because he believed that slavery would never exist in the region. Like Cass and the northern Democrats, he provided no answers for how or when the territorial governments erected in New Mexico and Deseret would settle the slavery question.

Clay's compromise package did have the effect of deflating the radical states' rights movement, whose members had hoped to unite their section at the Nashville Convention in June 1850. Some states held elections for delegates in the early months of 1850, but only five states would send official delegations to Tennessee; six slave states ignored the call completely. Southern Whigs abandoned the call first, choosing to follow the lead of Clay and leaving the southern Democrats who had supported the initiative tainted with the "odor of disunion." The southern rights leaders overestimated the southern electorate's indignation at the North since most had no interest in resurrecting the specter of nullification or disunion. At the same time, they underestimated the strength of partisan ties and the persistence of moderation—however strained—within the South.[44]

Though states' rights radicals saw their hopes for a southern rights political movement evaporate, Democrats in the South did not tamely accept Clay's compromise measures. Quite the opposite. Much to the chagrin of the Great Pacificator, southerners pounced on the plan as soon as he uttered the last words of his speech. Two Mississippi Democrats—Henry S. Foote and Jefferson Davis—expressed their dissatisfaction with the Kentuckian's plan. Foote flatly rejected Clay's reasoning that slavery did not exist by law in the Mexican Cession. To his mind, "the treaty with the Mexican republic carried the Constitution, with all its guaranties, to all the territory obtained by treaty." He also expressed resentment at Clay's contention that slavery would probably never enter the cession. Let time and the people of the states decide the question, Foote maintained. After insisting that Clay yield the floor for a response to his political "set speech" on the compromise measures, Davis denied that the eight resolutions constituted any sort of compromise. The Mississippi senator preferred extension of the Missouri Compromise line as the only way the South could hope to share equally in the settlement of the cession. Davis demanded that Congress adopt extension, with a positive declaration that citizens had a right to possess slaves south of the line.[45]

Davis had arrived at another critical conclusion that radical southerners would make about the extension of slavery and popular sovereignty in the Mexican Cession: without some dividing line between slavery and freedom acting as a corollary to local self-determination, the South would lose the new West. Some northern Democrats, including James Buchanan, had embraced extending the line in 1848 before Lewis Cass attempted to ride popular sovereignty to victory. Even James K. Polk had endorsed the idea as the safest means of defusing the Wilmot Proviso crisis. Now Davis agreed, because a line of division would do what the northern version of popular sovereignty would not: open at least part of the cession to slavery during the territorial phase. Yet the Mississippi senator added his own proviso to extension of the Missouri line by demanding "the specific recognition of the right to hold slaves in the territory below that line."[46] The Thomas amendment of 1820, which had established the 36 degrees, 30 minutes line, had not expressly stipulated, but merely implied, the right to hold slaves south of the boundary. Southern rights men might endorse extension of the line, but they desperately wanted some federal guarantee for the future of slavery, proving their rather ironic belief that states' rights needed federal protection when it came to the extension of slavery and anticipating Davis's position in 1860.

Southerners outside of Washington joined in a chorus of opposition against the Clay proposal. The compromise, according to a Georgia editor, "concedes all the Provisoists ask—that the territories are already free—all that the abolitionists contend for—that Mexican law in the territories, is paramount to the constitution." Clay's second resolution, with its assertion that slavery would most likely never exist in the cession and with its implication that the Mexican laws prohibiting slavery remained in force, particularly offended southerners. Some rejected Clay's expression that congressional legislation was *inexpedient*; they deemed it *unconstitutional*. "It is of no avail that the second resolution proposes to erect territorial governments, without saying any thing about slavery," the *Richmond Enquirer* stated; "the right of Congress to regulate it is conceded, and it is declared by the same resolution not to exist in the land."[47]

Though the criticism aimed at Clay stemmed chiefly from his resolution on slavery in the territories, some southerners reprised their disingenuous argument that California's free-state constitution did not represent the will of the people. "A mere handful of men should never be allowed to appropriate to themselves a vast extent of territory," a New Orleans Democrat argued. Southerners maintained that the "gold diggers in California are not *bona fide* inhabitants but mere adventurers" who had no lasting stake in the land. Perhaps more importantly, a number of southerners contended that the mixed-race native population of California had no right to participate in drafting a state constitution. "Her constitution," a Georgian wrote, "was made by those who had no right to make it." Just days after Clay delivered his compromise speech, the Georgia legislature passed resolutions of its own stating that Congress had no authority to prohibit slavery in the territories and that people of all the states had the right to emigrate to the territories with their slave property. In Louisiana, Governor Isaac Johnson repeated sound southern Democratic doctrine, declaring that the "inhabitants of the territories have a clear and indisputable right to settle this question according to their own wishes, when ready for admission into the Union as a state." Any congressional interference, he contended, would meet with solid resistance from the South.[48]

Clay had concluded his presentation of the compromise measures with an appeal for northern magnanimity, but many southerners believed his plan asked for far more concessions from their section than from the North. He averred that northerners must make "a more liberal and extensive concession than should be asked from the slave States" because they held the preponderance of power in the Union.[49] Though northerners viewed slavery as an abstraction, southerners faced the palpable reality of the institution and the danger and discontent stirred by fanatics who sought to abolish the peculiar institution. To the minds of many men from his own section, however, Clay had surrendered southern constitutional rights to the North in return for little to nothing.

Southern opinion on the extension of slavery into the territories once again had divided along familiar lines. Three factions—essentially those that had divided the South in the election year of 1848—reappeared: moderate Democrats who supported the Cass version of popular sovereignty, southern Whigs who supported—however reluctantly—the Clay compromise, and Calhounite radicals who demanded federal protection of slavery in the territories. Within these broad distinctions lay numerous variants of how specifically to settle the issue of slavery extension, but essentially the moderates and the Calhounites once again battled over how to protect best the rights of the South.[50] Of course, the argument raged on over when a territory gained sovereign power over slavery.

Once again, Cass offended southerners with his pronouncements on popular sovereignty. First, he asserted that slavery would never exist in the Mexican Cession. Second, Cass blurred the line between state and territorial sovereignty by stating that "the people of the Territories have just the same right to govern themselves as the people of the States have." Cass qualified his second statement by insisting that by territories he meant organized communities, but he would not define the term precisely, implying that the federal courts might well have to adjudicate the issue. Jefferson Davis immediately chastised Cass for his statements on popular sovereignty. "His doctrine, which acknowledges sovereignty in any community which may by accident or design be planted on territory belonging to the States, I always rejected." As Cass asserted his belief that the people of the territories had the right to legislate on the slavery question prior to drafting a constitution, more conservative southerners attempted to refute his claims. Once again southerners lashed out at northern Democrats who, to their minds, had fundamentally altered the meaning of popular sovereignty.[51]

A North Carolina Whig congressman wryly explained the predicament that southern Democrats faced in 1850 concerning slavery in the territories. They had demanded that Congress could not legislate on slavery for the territories, but that the people alone possessed the right when drafting a constitution. When California presented a constitution prohibiting slavery, though, southern Democrats cried foul. "What is not a little remarkable upon this subject too," David Outlaw wrote to his wife, "is the fact that the Democracy, whose candidate Gen. Cass, avowed before and has since reiterated the same opinion, that the people of the territories alone have the power to legislate, are the loudest in their denunciations—against their own doctrines."[52] Outlaw captured the dilemma facing southern Democrats. California had followed the southern plan of popular sovereignty, by prohibiting slavery in their constitution. Proslavery Democrats now could only object by disputing the right of native Mexicans to take part in constitution making and by arguing that an insufficient number of Americans lived in the territory.

And so they did. Southerners mocked the notion that the native Mexican population in the new American Southwest could have a hand in telling citizens of the states what property they could and could not bring into the territories. "Shall these *conquered people* be allowed to dictate such terms as will exclude one half of her *conquerors* from enjoying their acquired immunities within her limits," a Georgia commentator wrote. Southerners derided "Cass's proviso" because they feared it would deny their section equal participation within the territories. Others sought to seize control of the debate over popular sovereignty's meaning by reaffirming the South's traditional interpretation of the doctrine. Whig Senator John Bell of Tennessee, for example, introduced his own set of compromise resolutions that affirmed specifically that the people of a territory gained sovereignty when seeking admission to the Union. Bell considered California a lost cause, providing in his plan for admission with the free-state constitution presented to Congress. But he sought to save New Mexico for the South by defining when the territories gained sovereignty.[53]

As the debate over Clay's compromise measures continued through the spring of 1850, numerous southerners had become convinced Congress would have to settle on some form of popular sovereignty in order to solve the crisis. "We know that whenever the settlement does take place," a New Orleanian wrote, "it must be done on the ground advocated first by General Cass." Kentucky Governor John J. Crittenden, a Whig who supported the Taylor administration's plan to settle the slavery issue, expressed his belief "that the slavery question must soon be settled, & that upon the basis of admitting Calafornia [sic] & establishing Territorial governments without the Wilmot proviso." To Crittenden's mind, the nation had unwisely rejected Taylor's "pacific policy" to bypass the territorial phase, but any overall plan that reaffirmed congressional nonintervention seemed likely to gain the approval of Congress.[54]

Most southerners, however, made clear that they would not stand for squatter sovereignty—or the rule of a small and inchoate community of squatters on the public domain. The rule of law and order as well as the spirit of equality demanded that all decisions on the slavery issue rest with an elected territorial assembly charged with drafting a constitution. The Calhounites demanded that southern politicians repudiate squatter sovereignty. "The doctrine of absolute sovereignty in the inhabitants of a territory," Representative Daniel Wallace of South Carolina declared, "in every petty province of a mother country, is repugnant to all past history."[55] The Calhounites voiced the concern of most southerners that squatters and native Mexicans had seized control of the statehood process in California—and an equally motley group threatened to do the same in New Mexico. By implying that the Mexicans were essentially vassals, however, they came perilously close to portraying the United States as a colonial power, offending numerous advocates of nonintervention, including Lewis Cass, who justified popular sovereignty by invoking the memory of America's revolution against Great Britain.

The Clay compromise as well as President Taylor's initial proposal to settle the slavery issue each contained the essence of popular sovereignty, though observers could quibble about finer—though critical—points of how to interpret and implement the doctrine. Nevertheless, southerners remained divided over the compromise plan and the principle of popular sovereignty. Expressing support for Clay's work, John Tyler wrote to an associate, "I do not see that anything better can be done." Like President Taylor's plan, the Clay compromise

left the slavery matter "open to the selection of the people themselves in convention." Under the present circumstances, the South could not expect much
better. A Georgia editor expressed similar resigned support: "By the compromise we get territorial governments, and non-intervention on the slavery question for the Territories. That is something."[56]

The debate between southern moderates and ultras continued, as the latter
could not muster even tepid support for the compromise emerging in Congress.
In the Senate, Jefferson Davis remained a stalwart opponent of Clay's bill, especially because of its implication that Mexican laws against slavery trumped the
rights of American citizens, including slaveholders. He declared himself willing
"to leave the question to be decided according to the great cardinal principles of
the Democratic party; that the people inhabiting a territory, when they come to
form a State constitution for themselves, can do as they please," but spurned
both the implication that Mexican law prevailed in the cession or the idea that
territorial legislatures could prohibit slavery.[57] Northern Democrats had altered
the meaning of popular sovereignty to curry antislavery favor, he believed. Furthermore, the Mississippi senator flatly rejected Clay's contention that slavery
could never exist in the region. The people themselves could decide that question by emigrating there with or without slaves.

Though Davis attacked the compromise based on specific provisions that he
deemed odious to southern interests and rights, other legislators questioned
whether the package of resolutions even made up a compromise. Democratic
Representative James Seddon of Virginia wrote to his constituents that the compromise demanded great concessions from the South and at no expense to the
North—"not even the poor boon of equal privilege and simple protection of our
property in the Territories of Utah and New Mexico, the least valuable of our
new acquisitions." Others predicted that the people of the territories, namely
any southern slaveholders who might choose to settle in the West, would not
stand for any infringement of their rights and would establish or prohibit slavery as they saw fit, regardless of any congressional dictate. Southern ultras felt
that the compromise had hoodwinked the moderate leaders of their section and
lulled them into a dangerous complacency. Lamenting the "decadence of the
Southern spirit" to resist the compromise measures, Senator Robert M. T.
Hunter of Virginia decried the efforts of northerners to "dragoon the South into
fastening this act of submission on herself and by her own vote."[58]

Meanwhile, those southern Democrats willing to brook Clay's plan demanded concessions in exchange for their support. First, Clay agreed to drop

his insistence that Mexican law would prohibit slavery in the cession and instead adopt popular sovereignty. Second, at the suggestion of Mississippi Democrat Henry S. Foote, Clay acquiesced in the creation of an "Omnibus" bill that placed all of his measures in one bill, thereby requiring the Senate to accept or reject the entire package. The Omnibus combined California statehood and popular sovereignty in New Mexico in "a formal quid pro quo for the admission of California that Taylor, almost all northern Whigs, and Clay himself abhorred."[59] But Clay needed southern support if compromise would prevail.

The Omnibus bill instead solidified opposition among northern and southern ultras, leaving moderates to despair of their efforts to secure a bisectional adjustment. Facing discord over the Omnibus bill as well as heightened criticism over the correct interpretation of popular sovereignty, Cass exacerbated problems by clarifying his position. In a rare moment of self-deprecation for the Michigan senator, Cass stated that it seemed the Nicholson letter "is so dark that every man may read it his own way, or, in fact, no way at all." Cass finally and emphatically stated that the Nicholson letter asserted the doctrine that territorial governments could legislate on the slavery issue. Over the course of 1850, he had come to define the doctrine in less ambiguous terms. Four months later, during the fiercest deliberations over the compromise, the senator left no doubt of his opinion on the interpretation of popular sovereignty, but always left open the possibility that the Supreme Court could rule on the issue. The inhabitants of the territories "will always have a legislature which will reflect their wishes; and, if they desire slavery, they will have it, and if they do not, they will exclude it, unless prevented by the Constitution." While Cass left open the possibility of a legal challenge to popular sovereignty, he left no doubt that he believed it not only constitutional, but also the wisest policy to avert disunion.[60]

For three years politicians and political observers had debated the real meaning of the Nicholson letter. Had Cass merely reiterated the established principle of popular sovereignty or had he redefined it? In the Nicholson letter, Cass had strongly *implied* that territorial legislatures had the power to permit or prohibit. When a veritable firestorm erupted over the issue, it seemed that Cass and other supporters of the doctrine hedged on a precise definition. But Congress paid scant attention to Cass's ultimate clarification of the Nicholson letter, for the opponents of popular sovereignty already knew its true meaning, while supporters could either embrace his latest pronouncement or continue to ignore the implications of vesting power over slavery in territorial governments.

As if the proponents of the Omnibus bill did not have enough problems to contend with, a new front emerged in the battle over the Mexican Cession. In May 1850, the residents of New Mexico Territory had elected a constitutional convention that promptly drafted a document prohibiting the institution of slavery. Though few observers expected the New Mexico statehood movement to succeed, the actions taken by the territory's antislavery faction received an indignant response from southerners and heightened concerns about the compromise bill in the Senate. The movements in New Mexico seemed only to confirm that northerners sought to *convert the Territories into States*, before the south has a chance to gain a foothold in them."[61]

Efforts to secure compromise faced far greater challenges than the tenuous statehood movement in New Mexico. The summer of 1850 turned chaotic, as the Senate debate over the Omnibus bill grew increasingly acrimonious. Then, on July 9, President Taylor died unexpectedly. In the short term, the president's death created instability and uncertainty as to the prospects of achieving compromise. But thoughtful observers knew that Taylor had stubbornly opposed the Clay compromise, especially after the Kentucky senator had broken ranks with the administration over the preferred mode of sectional adjustment. Taylor's death removed a formidable obstacle in the way of compromise. Accordingly, intrigue swirled regarding the course that Vice President Millard Fillmore would take now that he assumed Taylor's office. The new president took only two weeks to chart a new course, ultimately deciding to throw his administration's support behind Clay's Omnibus package.[62]

"Close quarters. Neck and neck, and the omnibus under whip and spur, and on the outside track. Looks bad—looks awful—looks mighty squally for the vehicle, and the freight, and the passengers," wrote a witty *New York Herald* correspondent. Even with President Fillmore's support for the bill and his influence among key senators, the impetus for compromise—at least that proposed by Clay—seemed in peril. In spite of the plaintive appeals for moderation and the seemingly endless speeches in favor of an adjustment, the Omnibus met its fate on July 31, when opponents of the compromise package in the Senate succeeded at killing the bill through a procedural maneuver. Physically and mentally broken, Henry Clay retreated to Newport, Rhode Island, while his supporters contemplated their next move. A perceptive Tennessee representative recognized perhaps the only tactic left to save any of Clay's efforts: pass each proposition separately. Clay had opposed the Omnibus strategy all along, but southern Democrats had forced his hand. Instead, he preferred the method he

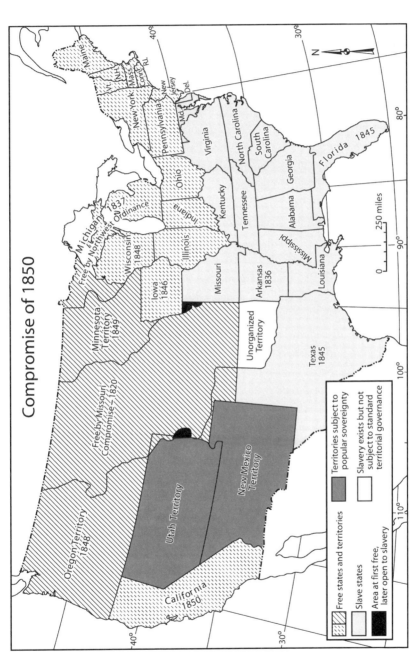

The Compromise of 1850 (map by Clifford Duplechin)

himself had used in 1820 to get the Missouri Compromise through an intransi-
gent Congress—separate passage of the components.[63]

In Clay's absence, Stephen Douglas assumed control of the compromise
movement, proposing to secure passage by breaking the ruined Omnibus bill
into its constituent parts. The Illinois senator knew that he could obtain passage
of individual measures by utilizing sectional and partisan blocs in the Senate.
The plan stood a great chance of success, but it completely defeated Clay's original purpose—to broker a truly bisectional compromise. Douglas recognized
that the possibility for give and take had long since passed, but he knew that
northerners and southerners would rally for the parts of the proposal that they
liked. His maneuver ensured passage, but did so through parliamentary tactics
and not through a sincere desire for compromise.[64] Success came with added
danger, for once again the slavery issue had disrupted already attenuated traditional party allegiances. North and South increasingly became antagonistic parties themselves with respect to the extension of slavery.

Nevertheless, by September 16 Douglas had gained passage of the separate
bills through the Senate and the House, where Douglas himself had correctly
predicted a bruising battle for passage. The bills comprising the Compromise of
1850 arrived at President Fillmore's desk the next day and received his signa-
ture. Congress had instituted popular sovereignty in all of the Mexican Cession
except California, which became a free state much to the chagrin of southerners. Interestingly, the debate over the popular sovereignty provision took an unexpected turn in the House of Representatives, where Georgia Representative
Robert Toombs made a last-ditch effort to erase any doubt that the Mexican
laws prohibiting slavery had ceased with American acquisition of the territory.
Toombs sought to nullify explicitly Mexican law and bar territorial legislatures
from prohibiting slavery in one sweeping amendment. Toombs's maneuver did
not succeed; indeed, the wording of the final bill seemingly granted territorial
legislatures the right to prohibit slavery if they so desired.[65] Popular sovereignty had prevailed, and had become law with respect to the Mexican Cession.
The territories of New Mexico and Deseret possessed the right to permit or
prohibit slavery as they saw fit.

On the surface, the nation rejoiced in the settlement of the difficult problems
concerning slavery in the Mexican Cession through a compromise effort that
touched the existence of the institution both in the territories and in the states.
Popular sovereignty had prevailed, though nobody knew which version had
been sanctioned. Southerners feared that popular sovereignty in practice meant

the prohibition of slavery. "The authors and inventors of the doctrine frankly and honestly avowed that its practical operation and result was identical with [the Wilmot] proviso," an Alabama jurist wrote. "It secured to the Northern States, by 'masterly inactivity,' all the fruits of the Mexican law; and correspondingly with this, excluded the South." Jefferson Davis lamented the passage of the popular sovereignty provision as a defeat for southern interests. He had opposed the "odious doctrine" because he "never knew what it meant." The Mississippian likewise abhorred the notion that squatters on the land could deny southern slaveholders the right to enter the territories with their property. Nevertheless, most all southerners acquiesced in the compromise plan and seemed to welcome an end to the crisis.[66]

Questions concerning the application of the compromise abounded, however, as observers pondered the finality of the compromise and the meaning of the measures concerning slavery in the territories. When a group of Georgia citizens queried former vice president George M. Dallas about the compromise measures and their impact on slavery in New Mexico, he predicted in his reply that the Supreme Court would eventually decide the issue of whether Mexican laws prohibiting slavery in the cession would prevail. In other words, the compromise could not dispose of all the issues concerning slavery in the territories, nor could it define popular sovereignty. Historians, too, have asked questions about the finality of the Compromise of 1850, especially whether the Thirty-First Congress crafted a settlement designed to apply to all territories present and future. From the vantage point of 1850, it seemed that Congress had settled all issues concerning slavery in the Mexican Cession or had deferred them to the judiciary. It seems that few, if any, leaders had given much consideration to future territorial acquisitions or to the remaining unorganized territory of the Louisiana Purchase. And in the case of the latter, the Missouri Compromise prohibition of slavery north of 36 degrees, 30 minutes had unquestionably settled the issue. The recrudescence of the issue of slavery in the territories less than four years later would place all established precedent in doubt.[67]

"A RECURRENCE TO FIRST

PRINCIPLES"

Kansas-Nebraska and
Popular Sovereignty

The Compromise of 1850 settled the question of slavery expansion in the vast Mexican Cession, and though southerners had chafed at the admission of California as a free state and the seemingly inevitable passage of New Mexico toward the same course, most acquiesced in the outcome. In most of the South, traditional party allegiances had survived in spite of the unmistakable fact that the slavery issue continued to divide the nation into sectional blocs. The compromise that Stephen A. Douglas had shepherded through Congress scotched any impetus for disunion, even as ultra southerners vainly exploited dissatisfaction with the law to organize a second southern convention to contemplate secession. Moderates carried the day and the heirs of the Calhounite mantle missed their chance to unite the South and deliver the North an ultimatum on the slavery issue.[1]

Southern acquiescence, however, could not mask the growing divisions within the national Democratic Party—and the American political system. A surge of protest in the aftermath of the compromise among antislavery members of the party who became known as the anti-Nebraska Democrats would give way to a momentary lull as moderate southerners tried to solidify the shaken foundations of their political parties. The Kansas-Nebraska Act of 1854, however, completely altered the political landscape. Southerners would rally behind the legislation sponsored by Illinois senator Stephen A. Douglas; indeed, the demands they made on Douglas in exchange for southern support of the bill shaped its contours. In 1854, southerners warmed to popular sovereignty, realizing that it could give their section something it could not otherwise have: slavery in Kansas. But they paid a mighty price. Outrage over the repeal of the Missouri Compromise line gave rise to an "Anti-Nebraska" movement that rallied antislavery northerners against doughfaces and southerners. Moreover, the indignation over Kansas-Nebraska lent a greater sense of urgency to the race for Kansas and Nebraska between proslavery and antislavery partisans. Northerners and southerners would compete for control of those territories. Though Nebraska would remain securely a free territory, Kansas Territory became a battleground over the future of slavery and the meaning of popular sovereignty in ways no one could have predicted. Even before the Kansas-Nebraska debate, party lines within the South had blurred considerably, thereby strengthening unity among southern rights politicians. Northern party lines, on the other hand, remained more distinct. With the bill's passage came the weakening of the northern Democracy and the unity of southerners behind their version and vision of popular sovereignty. Popular sovereignty—the elegantly simple affirmation of the people's right to govern their own domestic affairs—would face its ultimate test on the plains of Kansas.

EVEN AFTER passage of the Compromise of 1850, key southern politicians continued to express consternation over what the South had given away for the sake of national unity. Mississippi's Jefferson Davis embarked on a statewide speaking tour in an effort to galvanize southern opposition to the compromise. California had gained statehood, he insisted, through the efforts of antislavery partisans. More importantly, its admission to the Union illustrated the danger of squatter sovereignty, by which transient Americans combined with the native Mexicans, Indians, and other immigrants from foreign lands had seized control of the constitution-making process and drafted an antislavery document. By enacting the compromise, Congress practically endorsed the actions of these "'squatters' upon the soil." In his judgment, it had endorsed popular sovereignty in its most odious form, allowing a motley assortment of settlers to exercise self-government. A year after denouncing California statehood and in the midst of the election season of 1852, Davis continued to assail popular sovereignty as a doctrine that injured southern rights and interests. "The intangible, ever-changing doctrine of non-intervention," he said, "receiving as many interpretations as there were varieties of sectional policy, demoralized the South, and bore down the best and bravest of our Northern friends."[2]

Davis and his allies argued that popular sovereignty had divided rather than united the Democracy—and the nation. According to Davis, defending the nebulous doctrine against the charges of antislavery politicians had forced northern Democrats to abandon their bisectional overtures in order to save face at home, thereby weakening the party with the strongest ties between North and South. At the same time, southerners like Davis believed that the doctrine imperiled southern rights by allowing the first settlers on the ground to determine the status of slavery for all time. Behind Davis's attack on popular sovereignty lay his belief that the South would have fared better with an extension of the Missouri Compromise line. Undergirding southern discontent lay the fact that popular sovereignty no longer guaranteed the expansion of slavery. Yet many southern Democrats had inched toward an alternative even less palatable to their northern brethren: the federal government must protect the sanctity of slave property in the territories.

For a short time both the Democratic and Whig parties in several southern states divided into Union and Southern Rights factions as a direct response to the compromise and perceived threats to the extension of slavery. In Alabama, Mississippi, and Georgia, Whigs and pro-compromise Democrats united on a unionist platform while the remaining Democrats morphed into a southern states' rights coalition. Southern rights leaders argued that exclusion of slavery from the territories portended a crisis that would not only threaten the southern racial and economic order, but would also imperil the rights of free white southern men. They cautioned the slaveholder "that if he allowed the territories to become re-creations of the northern states, he could thereafter migrate to them only at the cost of giving up his own egalitarian, democratic world for a socially stratified society swept by the gales of class conflict and unbridled meliorist ferment." The Jacksonian parties, to the minds of southern rights men, had jeopardized southern safety for the chimerical promise of bisectional comity. In this respect, the southern rights movements of 1850–1852 foreshadowed the destruction of the Jacksonian political system.[3]

Yet persistent patriotism, an aversion to radicalism, and a vehement rejection of disunion among a majority of the southern electorate overwhelmed any effort by southern separatists. Unionist sentiment prevailed; fealty to party *and* section remained. In sum, most southerners still believed that the status quo provided sufficient protection and that the Compromise of 1850, however imperfect, had provided a satisfactory settlement. Desperate for peace on the slavery issue, the Democrats in 1852 sought to restore party harmony by endorsing compromise and conciliation and thereby banishing the specter of disunion. The rush to restore harmony left the Whigs badly wounded as Democrats captured moderate ground. Over the course of 1852, Union and Southern Rights Democrats in the South reunited in hopes of attaining electoral success in the fall. Southern Democrats buried their differences over the compromise, now endorsing the plan as sufficient protection for southern interests in the territories. All eyes focused on the 1852 presidential campaign.[4]

Yet Democratic operatives advanced two old warhorses for the presidential nomination—Lewis Cass of Michigan and James Buchanan of Pennsylvania. The young but politically experienced Stephen A. Douglas emerged as the third candidate. All carried significant liabilities. Cass's refutation of the southern interpretation of popular sovereignty earned him the enmity of key slave-state politicians. The Michigan senator exacerbated the problem when he reiterated his stance on the Senate floor in March, affirming that the "first settlers" of a territory inevitably influenced the community's "political and social system." Southerners like Jefferson Davis, to whom Cass directed his remarks, viewed this latest statement as further evidence that the author of the Nicholson letter endorsed squatter sovereignty. Only southern unionists exhibited any enthusiasm for Cass's candidacy. Antislavery northerners opposed Cass because they believed he had pandered to the South for votes. The politics of slavery had virtually destroyed his presidential aspirations because leaders in both sections mistrusted his motives. New York businessman and Democrat Erastus Corning confided to a friend that Cass stood no chance of carrying the Empire State in 1852 for "reasons which you can well understand"—a veiled reference to the Michigan senator's equivocal stand on slavery.[5]

The difficulties that the three frontrunners of 1852 faced in securing the nomination stemmed from an internecine conflict within the national Democracy between establishment leaders like Buchanan and Cass and an insurgent cadre of younger leaders represented by Douglas. The Young America faction scorned the "Old Fogies"—as the movement referred to them—for their utter lack of leadership in domestic and foreign policy. The establishment in turn viewed Douglas and his managers with contempt for running an overt presidential campaign and daring to challenge the Democratic leadership.[6]

The southern Democracy may have reunited by the election year, but the proceedings of the national convention in Baltimore in June revealed the party's still fragile condition on the slavery question. Its platform endorsed the Compromise of 1850 as a permanent solution to the question of slavery in the territories. Eager to end the internecine struggle over slavery, the platform committee proclaimed that Democrats would "resist all attempts at renewing, in congress or out of it, the agitation of the slavery question."[7] For forty-nine ballots, Cass, Douglas, and Buchanan jockeyed for advantage, but none could gain the necessary two-thirds of the delegate votes. In the end, the Democrats turned to a dark horse, Franklin Pierce of New Hampshire, a candidate backed by southerners who viewed the Mexican War veteran as safe on southern rights and by northerners as an acceptable alternative to the trio of Cass, Douglas, and Buchanan.

In the weeks before the Baltimore convention, Pierce had enthusiastically accepted the Compromise of 1850. "If the compromise measures are not to be substantially and firmly maintained," Pierce wrote in a public letter, "the plain rights secured by the constitution will be trampled in the dust."[8] Both North and South had to stand behind the compromises made in the turbulent summer of 1850 for the sake of the Union, not to mention for the future of the Democratic Party. Six years earlier, the one-time representative and senator from New Hampshire had endorsed the popular sovereignty doctrine; he now defended it as a candidate for president. Pierce trounced the Whig candidate Winfield Scott in the November election, carrying an overwhelming majority of the electoral vote. For a fleeting moment it seemed that moderation had prevailed and the Compromise of 1850 might well have settled the slavery question. But candidate Pierce's hopes for party unity and national harmony would face serious challenges once he became President Pierce.

Just as the new president took office in March 1853, a discussion had commenced over the organization of a vast territory in the center of the transcontinental nation—what became known as Nebraska. The large unincorporated portion of the Louisiana Purchase, spanning roughly from the northern boundary of present-day Oklahoma to the Canadian border and including land between the Missouri River and the Rocky Mountains, had escaped the attention of Washington for years, as many leaders viewed the domain as an Indian territory. The desire to construct a transcontinental railroad along with the inexorable westward push of settlers on the frontier led people both in the West and in Washington to reconsider the future of the vast region.[9]

No one had taken more interest in the settlement of the vast territory than Stephen Douglas. The Illinois senator had first introduced legislation to organize Nebraska Territory in 1844 in a multipronged effort to organize territories in the remainder of the Louisiana Purchase and Oregon, as well as prepare for construction of a transcontinental railroad. Building the railroad would bring a host of settlers eager to take up residence along the line, many of whom would be eligible for free homesteads provided by the federal government and would engage in farming. The breathtaking scope of Douglas's design, a master plan to settle the remainder of the West, bore more than a faint resemblance to Jefferson's plan for an agrarian republic. The senator would connect the Great Plains to the industrial East, with Chicago at its center, by laying iron rails through the center of the republic. For ten years, Douglas refused to give up hope on his plan, even in the face of formidable odds and considerable sectional rancor.[10] Yet southerners would look askance at his agenda for growth, for yet again it seemed that northerners intended to make the West an extension of the free soil Northeast, thereby assuring the political supremacy of North over South.

While Senator Douglas continued to seek support for organizing Nebraska in Washington, residents in western Missouri and Iowa began to push on their own for organization of the territory. The Missourians, in particular, eagerly sought organization of the territory in order to exploit its natural resources and establish homesteads. Though the initiative remained quite popular in western Missouri, Senator David Rice Atchison raised objections to the organization of Nebraska on the grounds that the Missouri Compromise would prohibit slavery in the prospective territory. Atchison, an uncouth, rough-hewn, but influential frontier Democrat from Platte County, Missouri, raised objections to the Nebraska bill at the close of the second session of the Thirty-Second Congress. With "no prospect, no hope for a repeal of the Missouri compromise, excluding slavery from that Territory," the senator confessed that he could not vote for any bill organizing Nebraska.[11]

Atchison condemned the Northwest Ordinance and the Missouri Compro-

Illinois Senator Stephen A. Douglas and his associates had secured
passage of the Compromise of 1850. Four years later, his Kansas-
Nebraska Act, its invalidation of the Missouri Compromise line, and its
extension of popular sovereignty to the territories pleased
slaveholders—but at great cost. It alienated the North, split the
Democratic Party, and led to the emergence of the antislavery
Republican Party. (Library of Congress)

mise as twin "irremediable" errors that previous congresses had passed against
the spirit, if not the letter, of the Constitution. Given the apparent inviolability of
the Missouri Compromise it seemed, to his mind, that slaveholders would simply have to acquiesce in the prohibition. But in the summer of 1853, Atchison
clarified his position in a series of speeches given in his home state, demanding
that any bill organizing Nebraska embrace the doctrine of popular sovereignty.

"I am willing that the people who may settle there, and who have the deepest interest in this question, shall decide it for themselves," he declared. Missourians had long supported the principle of popular sovereignty in memorials to Congress and numerous public meetings, especially during the contentious congressional session of 1849–1850. Now Atchison demanded that Congress apply the same standard to the Nebraska territory. Almost certainly unconscious of the implications of his statement, the senator had raised the pivotal question of whether the Compromise of 1850, with its endorsement of popular sovereignty, had superseded the Compromise of 1820.[12]

Missourians wasted no time in making their sentiments known to Congress and the nation. In a series of public meetings held in the heart of Atchison's political power base, citizens' committees endorsed "leaving questions of local policy to be settled by the citizens of the territory when they form a state government."[13] In other words, they endorsed the concept of popular sovereignty as defined by the South. Furthermore, their motives in supporting the organization of Nebraska became clear. First, western Missourians expected to supply a significant number of residents for the territory and therefore desired to carry slavery there. Second, many feared that a free Nebraska would prove hazardous to slaveholders in Missouri itself, as runaway slaves could cross the border into freedom. The latter issue would gain significance as the debate over Nebraska proceeded.

Douglas closely monitored the developments in western Missouri, maintaining contact with Atchison as the proposal to organize Nebraska gained momentum. During the latter months of 1853, Douglas had begun organizing his own thoughts on how to revivify his plan for western settlement and the construction of a transcontinental railroad that would pass through Nebraska. The senator knew that he needed southern and western support to achieve his goals, but realized that the Missouri Compromise prohibition on slavery north of 36 degrees, 30 minutes represented a significant obstacle. Ever the astute politician, Douglas believed that the principles of the Compromise of 1850, namely popular sovereignty, could assuage southerners and westerners and ensure their support for organizing Nebraska Territory. The senator, however, also recognized that violating the principles of the Missouri Compromise's slavery ban almost certainly would infuriate antislavery northerners. Douglas hoped to mollify all parties and interests by a sleight of hand; he would endorse popular sovereignty in Nebraska and remain silent on the Missouri Compromise. The senator staked his project on the belief that "all will be willing to sanction and affirm the principle established by the Compromise measures of 1850" and would ignore the Missouri Compromise.[14]

The Thirty-Third Congress opened its first session on December 5, 1853, with the Nebraska issue at the top of its agenda. Senator Augustus Dodge of Iowa introduced legislation to organize Nebraska Territory—essentially the same bill that had failed in the previous session. But the Senate referred the legislation to Douglas's Committee on Territories, and in the course of three weeks the chairman reworked the Dodge bill to his liking. Meanwhile, the press began speculating on the course the Douglas committee and Congress at large would take with regard to Nebraska. A well-informed correspondent to the *Richmond Enquirer* captured perfectly the negotiations occurring behind the scenes. Missouri's two senators—Atchison and the venerable Thomas Hart Benton—were in the midst of a battle over who would control the state's politics. Benton favored the immediate organization of Nebraska with the Missouri Compromise ban on slavery intact, while Atchison, the "faithful champion of the South," favored popular sovereignty. "Peopled by immigrants from Missouri, and, by the fertility of its soil inviting the labor of the negro, Nebraska, if allowed the free exercise of its own discretion, will soon apply for admission into the Union as a slave State," the writer predicted.[15] By all indications the people of Missouri, especially along its western border, favored the Atchison plan.

On a national scale, southern Democrats latched on to the proslavery Nebraska movement with a two-fold objective: to repeal the hated thirty-four-year-old Missouri Compromise and potentially open Nebraska to slavery and to reaffirm southern power within the Democracy. Atchison's connections with three prominent southern Senate leaders known as the F Street Mess—South Carolina's Andrew Pierce Butler, with Robert M. T. Hunter and James M. Mason of Virginia—would come to represent a formidable force for affirming southern rights in Nebraska Territory. In sum, they would counter proslavery losses in the Mexican Cession with the extension of slavery in Nebraska. Popular sovereignty, the doctrine that southerners alternatively endorsed and hated depending on conditions in the field, would overturn the Missouri Compromise ban on slavery in the territory.

Antislavery proponents recognized immediately that the impetus for sanctioning popular sovereignty in Nebraska might well result in a proslavery victory. "While so much zeal is evinced in behalf of the rights of the South, there is some danger that the rights of the North may be overlooked," a New Jersey editor warned. "It may be that the glories of the compromise of 1850 have so

Virginia Senators James M. Mason (left) and Robert M. T. Hunter (right) had demanded that northerners recognize southern rights in the territories, thereby emerging as two powerful proponents of a more doctrinaire southern defense of slavery and definition of popular sovereignty. (Library of Congress)

dimmed those of its Missouri namesake that it may be forgotten that by the latter agreement Nebraska must be nothing but free territory."[16] Northerners and southerners perceived the stakes of the coming debate over Nebraska just as clearly as their fellow citizens in Missouri. The great question became clear: would popular sovereignty supersede the Missouri Compromise ban on slavery in Nebraska? Another question loomed, too: which version of popular sovereignty would prevail?

On January 4, 1854, the Senate Committee on Territories affirmed that the Compromise of 1850 had indeed invalidated the Missouri Compromise, though the report specifically avoided explicit repeal. Writing for the committee, Douglas argued that the compromise measures "were intended to have a far more comprehensive and enduring effect than the mere adjustment of the difficulties arising out of the recent acquisition of Mexican territory." As the author of the Utah and New Mexico legislation, he argued that it established a new precedent for territorial organization. The Douglas report endorsed the Cass formula for popular sovereignty by allowing the people, "by their appropriate representatives," to legislate on "all questions pertaining to slavery in the territories." Presumably the Missouri Compromise ban on slavery would remain in effect until the territorial legislature provided otherwise. In sum, Douglas had reshaped the Dodge bill to incorporate the compromise principles without explicitly repealing the Missouri Compromise. But would northerners and southerners accept the disingenuous proposal?[17]

Even before Douglas introduced his version of the Nebraska bill, political observers in the South had intimated that they would support the organization of Nebraska only under the terms of the Compromise of 1850. The *Richmond Enquirer* accused the North of repudiating the Missouri Compromise in 1850, only to claim its validity in respect to Nebraska in 1853. Of course, northern restrictionists intended precisely that. The Missouri Compromise did not apply to the Mexican Cession; accordingly Congress had provided a different means of organizing Utah and New Mexico. Passage of the Compromise of 1850, according to antislavery partisans, did not nullify the Missouri Compromise. Northern Democrats and southerners, however, saw the matter quite differently. The compromise measures had established popular sovereignty as the preferred policy of territorial organization. Congress should defer to the wishes of the people on the slavery question. Supporters of the compromise principles saw the Douglas bill as a test of "how far gentlemen are willing practically to enforce their acquiescence" in popular sovereignty. "Before this bill gets through Congress," a Florida editor predicted, "the South will have an opportunity of seeing who among the members of both Houses construe the Compromise of 1850 as a settlement of the slavery difficulty."[18]

Why had the South come to embrace the principles of the Compromise of 1850, when a substantial number of southerners expressed skepticism four years earlier? Put simply, conditions in 1854 differed greatly from those the South faced in 1850. Then popular sovereignty seemed calculated to prevent slavery from entering the Mexican Cession. California had drafted a free-state constitution without congressional sanction, embodying the idea of squatter sovereignty, as southerners derisively labeled the doctrine. New Mexico seemed poised to follow suit with its own free-state movement, supported by native Mexicans and a small number of Americans who had moved west to exploit the region's natural resources. Southerners believed that they had *lost* access to the Mexican Cession because of popular sovereignty. But in Nebraska, south-

erners could *gain* a foothold for slavery only by implementing popular sovereignty. The Missouri Compromise prohibition on slavery stood on solid legal
footing, unlike the Mexican prohibition on slavery in the cession. Proslavery
partisans recognized that popular sovereignty could potentially circumvent the
thirty-four-year ban on slavery in the remainder of the Louisiana Purchase.
Though southerners seemed to embrace the fundamentals of the Nebraska report, they soon recognized that the plan had a significant flaw. Douglas's implication that the Compromise of 1850 had superseded the Missouri Compromise
provided insufficient protection for southern interests. Only by explicitly repealing the Compromise of 1820 could the South truly have a chance of extending
the slave domain into Nebraska. At this point, the impetus for repeal mixed with
the familiar politics of slavery to create a concerted movement to rescind the
Missouri Compromise line.

Days after the Senate Committee on Territories released its report on the
Nebraska bill, the *New York Herald*, a northern Democratic newspaper with pro-
southern proclivities, maintained that it contained an "artful dodge"—perhaps a
clever pun directed at the bill's original sponsor. Few, if any, accepted Douglas's
effort to avoid contention over the Missouri Compromise. The failure to repeal
the slavery prohibition equaled a tacit endorsement of the Wilmot Proviso, the
Herald argued. Southerners could not have agreed more. Indeed, they saw an
effort among antislavery advocates to reopen the wounds that the Compromise
of 1850 had purportedly closed. "The compromise measures will soon again be
in jeopardy," a Louisiana writer opined. Southerners espoused the belief—sincere or not—that the compromise achieved four years earlier had settled the
slavery question permanently and had, in spirit, supplanted the Missouri Compromise. Facing northern opposition to the expansion of slavery, as well as pressure within the South to stand firm on the issue, southern politicians in Washington began to move for an explicit repeal of the Missouri Compromise's ban
on slavery.[19]

Most interestingly, the impetus for repeal came from southern Whigs seeking to rejuvenate their moribund party by proving themselves safer on slavery
extension than their Democratic adversaries. They recognized that the Douglas
bill left much to chance in its explicit refusal to annul the slavery ban from 1820.
Additionally, the Whigs hoped to capitalize on southern skepticism of the Douglas formula for popular sovereignty. The Illinois senator had followed Lewis
Cass's definition of the doctrine by insisting that territorial legislatures could
prohibit or permit slavery at their pleasure. The bill of January 4, 1854, clearly

expressed the Cass version of the doctrine. Even southern Democrats hoped to amend that portion of the bill. Southerners demanded that the "people of Nebraska shall have the privilege of admitting or excluding Slavery, when they form a State constitution," a Georgia journalist declared.[20] Many southerners continued to express their opposition to squatter sovereignty, whereby a select few individuals could take the reins of government and prevent slaveholders from sharing the territory, insisting that citizens could determine the future of slavery only when drafting a constitution.

Two members of Congress took the lead in proposing the repeal of the Missouri Compromise's slavery ban—a Whig senator from Kentucky and a Democratic representative from Alabama. On January 16, Senator Archibald Dixon introduced an amendment that provided for the repeal of the ban on slavery. Answering charges that he sought to embarrass the Democrats, Dixon declared, "I know no Whiggery, and I know no Democracy. I am a pro-slavery man. I am from a slaveholding State; I represent a slaveholding constituency; and I am here to maintain the rights of that people whenever they are presented before the Senate."[21] Yet Dixon and the Whigs surely hoped to resuscitate their failing party by proving themselves safer on slavery than the Democrats, but their actions also bear witness that the preservation of slavery and southern rights came before party considerations. And because the Whigs' national alliance had all but disintegrated, they had little to lose and perhaps much to gain in the fluid politics of slavery.

In an unprecedented effort to prove himself and his party safe on slavery, Dixon went a step beyond repeal. In what one historian has rightly called "one of the most extreme proslavery pieces of legislation ever aired in Congress," the Dixon amendment also stipulated that American citizens had the right "to take and hold slaves within any of the Territories of the United States or of the States to be formed therefrom."[22] Dixon's proviso, which essentially upheld the Calhounite doctrine of positive protection for slavery, could not conceivably gain the support of a majority in the Senate, but his move to repeal the Missouri Compromise's ban on slavery enjoyed the support of southerners from both parties. Recognizing that he would have to incorporate repeal into the Nebraska bill, Douglas consulted with his Whig colleague and received permission to take charge of the movement for repeal.

Even before Dixon introduced his amendment to the Senate, an Alabama representative anticipated the impetus for repeal and acted in the House of Representatives. At the request of Douglas, the freshman Democrat Philip Phillips introduced his own amendment to repeal the Missouri Compromise's ban on slavery. Unlike the Dixon effort, in which the Kentucky Whig proposed to jettison self-government in the territories, Phillips built his proposal on the doctrine. Written just days after Douglas introduced the Nebraska bill, the amendment stipulated that "the people of the Territory through their Territorial legislature may legislate upon the subject of slavery in any manner they may think proper not inconsistent to the Constitution of the United States, and all laws inconsistent with this authority or right shall, from and after the passage of this act, become inoperative void and of no force and effect."[23]

In sum, the Phillips amendment had two aims. First, it unequivocally endorsed the Cass/Douglas version of popular sovereignty. Phillips, a Deep South congressman, had sanctioned the right of elected representatives in the territories to legislate on slavery. Furthermore, the amendment had received the approbation of that southern quartet known as the F Street Mess, all friends of Douglas, all powerful advocates of southern rights, and all individuals who would play a pivotal role in selling the Douglas bill to President Pierce and his administration.[24] Undeniably, southerners continued to maintain different beliefs about the popular sovereignty doctrine, but Phillips had taken a significant step toward placating all southern interests. To his endorsement of popular sovereignty, Phillips added the important caveat that any act of a territorial legislature could not conflict with the Constitution, thereby creating an opening for the judiciary to decide ultimately the meaning of popular sovereignty and the fate of slavery in the territories. Second, the amendment voided the Missouri Compromise's ban on slavery, but in more equivocal language than Dixon would use in his amendment just days later.

The movement for repeal became a *sine qua non* for southern support; without voiding the restriction on slavery in Nebraska, Douglas could not muster sufficient votes to pass his bill. Phillips and Douglas had attempted to assuage southerners with some success, yet the oblique wording on the repeal of the slavery restriction troubled others. Dixon's language regarding the Missouri Compromise proved far more acceptable to the South. After the Kentucky senator presented his amendment, Douglas knew that he would have to endorse the explicit repeal of the Missouri Compromise restriction on slavery. All the while, southerners in Congress surely knew that they had seized the initiative on the Nebraska bill and the future of slavery.

Northern Democrats seemed willing to broker a deal with the southern wing of their party in order to pass the Nebraska bill and achieve the heretofore elusive goal, they hoped, of removing the slavery question from political discourse. Party stalwarts called on Lewis Cass to endorse repeal of the slavery ban, but the aging Michigan senator characteristically equivocated on the Nebraska bill and the Dixon amendment. Certain newspapers reported that Cass would "not only vote for the repeal of the Missouri compromise as far as it interferes with the compromise of 1850," but that he would also declare the slavery ban unconstitutional. On the contrary, Cass vigorously denied the *New York Herald*'s report, for in private he advised President Pierce to oppose the repeal effort for fear that it would irreparably fracture the party. Cass may well have deplored the idea of repeal, but he also bore personal animosity toward Douglas, who in the opinion of the elder senator had unfairly and unceremoniously appropriated the popular sovereignty doctrine for himself. Accordingly, the elder senator kept silent for some time, refusing to lend either his name or his support to the Nebraska bill.[25]

Meanwhile, Douglas worked behind the scenes to craft a revised bill and secure the necessary southern support, but southern public opinion left no doubt of the course that the Illinois senator would have to take. "Does [the Compromise of 1850] render null and void the Missouri Compromise of 1820, which, if left in operation, will prohibit slavery in Nebraska and commit a gross outrage upon the South?" the *Richmond Enquirer* asked. "We do not entertain a doubt on the subject." In order to protect the rights of all citizens—slaveholders included—Congress needed to remove itself from the slavery debate and "throw its decision upon the courts and the people who may occupy the Territory, when it shall be sufficiently populated to be admitted as a State into the Union." Indeed, a number of southerners demanded explicit repeal because without it, they feared that the judiciary might strike down slavery in Nebraska based on the Compromise of 1820.[26]

After consulting with Archibald Dixon as well as his southern Democratic colleagues, Douglas prepared a revised Nebraska bill that included repeal of the Missouri Compromise. The senator, however, faced opposition from the president, who concurred with Cass's assessment of repeal and had pledged to oppose the effort. Pierce did not hold to that position for long; convinced by his attorney general, Caleb Cushing, that the slavery restriction in the Missouri Compromise was unconstitutional, the president hoped the judiciary would intervene. His cabinet prepared an amendment to the Nebraska bill stipulating that "the rights of persons and property shall be subject only to the restrictions and limitations imposed by the Constitution of the United States and the acts giving governments, to be adjusted by a decision of the Supreme Court of the United States."[27] In its ultimate outcome, the ponderous amendment bore resemblance to the unsuccessful Clayton Compromise of 1848, which would have left the status of slavery in the Mexican Cession in the hands of the Supreme Court. The president may have thought, too, that certain southerners would support a measure that would refer the issue to the southern-dominated Supreme Court. Douglas would have acquiesced in the amendment, but Atchison and his southern colleagues rejected the effort. They demanded direct repeal.

With one day left before he intended to deliver his revised bill to the Senate, Douglas faced the seemingly impossible task of convincing Pierce and the cabinet to accept a more direct form of repeal. At the behest of key southern senators, Secretary of War Jefferson Davis arranged an extraordinary Sunday meeting that has become legendary in the history of the effort to organize Nebraska. The pious president normally refused to conduct business on the Sabbath, but Davis convinced him of the necessity to discuss the legislation.[28] That afternoon, Douglas, Davis, and a number of southern legislators met with Pierce at the White House. The president must have faced one of the most surreal experiences of his young presidency as the most influential southern Democrats in Congress, and the most influential northern Democratic senator, confronted the titular head of their party with an ultimatum for repeal. Pierce capitulated. But because the president "had a way of changing his mind when later advice was given," Douglas insisted that Pierce place his assent in writing.[29] The next day, Douglas presented the revised bill to the Senate. And amazingly, Pierce simultaneously declared that he considered support of the new bill a test of party faith. In sum, he staked the success of his presidency and the future of his party on the Douglas bill.

Douglas doubly surprised his colleagues when he took the Senate floor on Monday, January 23. The senator's revised bill contained two provisions that fundamentally altered the original legislation. First, the bill delivered on his promise to his southern colleagues by declaring the eighth section of the Missouri Compromise "inoperative." He had inserted the amendment drafted at the White House the previous day. Second, the senator stunned his colleagues by dividing Nebraska into two territories—Kansas to the south and Nebraska to the north. Douglas claimed that agents from the Nebraska territory, and especially from Iowa, had petitioned for division of the vast land. Though no explicit proof has ever surfaced, the record suggests that Douglas and the people in Missouri and Iowa advocated division of the territory as a corollary to the repeal of the Missouri Compromise. "The object of this construction of the compromise of 1850, and the introduction of two territories instead of one," the *New York Herald* noted, "is understood to be one territory for the North and the other for the South." Kansas would lie west of Missouri and would likely become a slave state. With its proximity to the free state of Iowa, Nebraska would almost certainly become a free state. Regardless of geography, the bill declared that "all questions pertaining to slavery in the new Territories, and in the new States to be formed therefore, are to be left to the decision of the people residing therein, through their appropriate representatives."[30]

Douglas had succeeded at protecting the principle of popular sovereignty against the Whigs' maneuver, but as would soon become apparent only at great cost to the unity of the Democracy. One week later, the Little Giant rose in the Senate to explain his Kansas-Nebraska bill to his constituents and to the nation. But he also sought to defend the bill against a strident attack from northern antislavery advocates. A group of six senators led by Salmon P. Chase of Ohio had issued an "Appeal of the Independent Democrats in Congress to the People of the United States," accusing Douglas of serving a "Slave Power" conspiracy that sought to extend its domain. The reticence of Cass and Pierce, at least initially, to endorse repeal because it threatened Democratic unity had proved prescient. Chase and his associates condemned the repeal of the Missouri Compromise ban on slavery and called on northern Democrats to resist Douglas, the Pierce administration, and the southern Democrats who had made their power play. Douglas responded with a vituperative attack against the appeal of Chase and his allies as well as other opponents of his bill. On the "holy Sabbath, while other Senators were engaged in attending divine worship, these Abolition confederates were assembled in secret conclave, worship plotting by what means they should deceive the people of the United States, and prostrate the character of brother Senators." Of course, Douglas omitted that he and his associates had conducted business on the same Sabbath day, when they called on President Pierce at the White House.[31]

The senator spoke with incredulity as he described the efforts of those who opposed applying popular sovereignty to Kansas and Nebraska. The Compromise of 1850, he maintained, had superseded the Missouri Compromise. Northern antislavery Democrats had no one to blame but themselves for the repeal of the Missouri Compromise. "The first time that the principles of the Missouri compromise were ever abandoned, the first time they were ever rejected by

Congress, was by the defeat" of Douglas's own provision to extend the Missouri Compromise line to the Pacific Ocean. "By whom was that defeat effected?" Douglas asked. "By northern votes, with Free-Soil proclivities."[32]

The magnanimity of Democrats from both North and South had led politicians to propose extending the compromise line, Douglas suggested. Now he aimed to restore the "great principle of self-government" by affirming the right of the people in the territories to decide whether or not they desired slavery. Furthermore, he insisted on the right of sovereignty during the territorial phase, of course with the ubiquitous proviso that their actions conform to the Constitution. Congress simply could not, nor should it, attempt to establish the domestic institutions of the territories. Douglas used his own state as an example of how congressional interdiction of slavery had failed. Congress failed to prohibit slavery in Illinois Territory in spite of the Northwest Ordinance "because the people there regarded it as an invasion of their rights." Finally, Douglas maintained, his bill would return the nation and his party to their democratic principles of self-government and popular sovereignty.[33]

Southerners generally hailed Douglas's effort as an assertion of their section's rights. Douglas and the southern Democrats of 1854 had vindicated the Old Republicans of the 1820s, who had argued that the Missouri Compromise had unconstitutionally conceded power over slavery in the territories to the federal government. The voices of a small, though vocal, cadre of southern rights advocates thirty years before had now become mainstream opinion in the South. Douglas's southern colleagues hailed the establishment of self-government, "the redeeming feature of the Compromise bill of 1850," as the resurrection of sound Democratic doctrine and the guarantor of southern rights. Georgia Senator Robert Toombs best explained the southern position, maintaining that the North had long ago rendered the Missouri Compromise a dead letter. "They have adhered to its prohibitory provisions, but uniformly and nearly unanimously trampled its principles under foot so far as the South was to be benefited by it." Conversely, Toombs praised Douglas for recognizing the Compromise of 1850 as a "compact" recognized by North and South. Howell Cobb of Georgia lauded the bill as a "doctrine worthy of the democratic party." Acknowledging that in times past the South had divided over popular sovereignty, Douglas responded, "Our southern friends have only to stand firm & leave us of the North to fight the great Battle. . . . The great principle of self government is at stake & surely the people of this country are never going to decide that the principle upon which our whole republican system rests is vicious & wrong." Douglas appreciated the plaudits of his southern colleagues but recognized that he needed more from their section.[34]

At first glance it seemed that southerners had gained mightily from allying with Douglas to repeal the Missouri Compromise and establish popular sovereignty as national policy, but some slave-state observers viewed the situation warily. "I perceive a new storm is to break out in Congress and the country by the organization of the Nebraska Territory," former president John Tyler wrote. "As customary, I presume it is to end, as has heretofore been the case, in the despoilment of the South." Tyler feared that the abolitionists would move strongly against the Douglas bill's proponents. Indeed, his sentiment reflected a growing fear in what southerners perceived as an ongoing movement by abolitionist fanatics against southern rights. "Let the power of meddling with the domestic institutions of the States and Territories be taken away from Congress, and fanatics will cease to send men to Congress for the sole purpose of mooting this dangerous question," a southern correspondent cried.[35]

Southern commentators portrayed the actions and words of the abolitionist vanguard as hypocritical. "The natural religion of Abolitionism is all laid aside, and the South is appealed to in the name of the binding obligation of the Missouri Compromise—an act of Congress," a South Carolinian remarked. "It is a prodigious fall from the clouds, for such high-reaching spirits as the Freesoilers."[36] Of course, the North surely did not have the monopoly on hypocrisy; many southerners endorsed the Douglas bill in spite of its definition of popular sovereignty chiefly because it seemed to portend a proslavery victory.

Not only did proslavery advocates accuse their northern opponents of rank duplicity, but they also charged them with abridging the Constitution. Southern rights advocates advanced a more potent argument. The tenth amendment to the Constitution vested in the people the power of determining whether slavery would exist in a newly created state. Because Congress had no right to prohibit slavery in an existing state, they argued, the citizens of a territory about to enter the Union and acting in a sovereign constitutional convention, must have the right to craft their organic law free from federal intervention. This latitudinarian extension of the tenth amendment to an embryonic state owed much of its intellectual pedigree to John C. Calhoun, who had argued that Congress could not deny statehood based on the status of slavery in the territory. Southern rights proponents added a corollary, however, as increasingly they insisted that the federal government must afford any slaveholding citizen of any existing state who moved to a territory constitutional protection of his chattel property. In sum, the proponents of slavery in the territories had created a constitutional muddle. These ardent states-rights advocates seemingly transformed slavery from a purely local to a national institution. In order to protect slaveholders' due process, the federal government now had to affirm that state laws recognizing the lawful ownership of slaves extended to the federal territories. Increasingly, southerners relied on convoluted constitutional theories that simultaneously sanctioned circumscribed and expansive uses of federal authority.[37]

Southerners as well as other proponents of territorial control of the slavery issue had begun to craft a nuanced argument that supported the Kansas-Nebraska bill based on the Anglo-American heritage of popular sovereignty. Political theorists had long used the term to describe the will of the people to form and direct their own political affairs and institutions. During the Kansas debate, supporters of the bill appropriated the term—and the rich history behind it—to bolster their claim that the legislation would return the nation to first principles. Accordingly, writers hearkened back to classical political theorists such as Edmund Burke, John Locke, and others to legitimate the doctrine, which increasingly became known as popular sovereignty. They lauded the Kansas-Nebraska bill because it made "a clean sweep of all sectional compacts, dictated by trading aspirants for the Presidency," and left the issue of slavery in the territories "directly in the sovereignty of the people." "We have an opportunity now of restoring the constitution to its original vigor, and of vindicating the great principle of self-government," a New Orleans Democrat wrote, "and we will do both by passage of the Nebraska act." According to its southern supporters, the doctrine of popular sovereignty had the promise to end the bitter sectional quarrel because it respected states' rights and local control over domestic affairs. It respected the Constitution. And in the spirit of Jacksonian democracy, it respected the vox populi.[38]

In sum, the Kansas-Nebraska bill enjoyed southern support for several reasons. First, the South's political leaders had succeeded in forcing Douglas to include an explicit repeal of the 1820 ban on slavery; second, the legislation affirmed the principle of popular sovereignty. The two actually worked in tandem. Without popular sovereignty as the organizational principle in Kansas and Nebraska, southerners could have no hope of extending slavery into the region. Of course, without repeal of the 36 degrees, 30 minutes line not even popular sovereignty could prevail. Southerners could—and did—remain divided on the interpretation of popular sovereignty even though Douglas had sent strong signals that he believed that territorial legislatures could settle the issue. Nevertheless, many slave-state Democrats believed they had reaffirmed southern rights and southern power with considerable success.

Though the Kansas-Nebraska bill received substantial support in the South, contrarians raised concerns about the bill and its meaning. Former Alabama Senator Jeremiah Clemens emerged as an opponent of the bill, predicting that with its passage, a "floodgate will be opened, and a torrent turned loose upon the country which will sweep away in its devastating course every vestige of the compromise of 1850." Equal participation, to the most ardent southern rights men, meant that the North could potentially use popular sovereignty as an antislavery weapon. Clemens declared himself "fully against the doctrines of Gen. Cass's Nicholson letter," because it sanctioned squatter sovereignty. Now Douglas, who had become the chief proponent of popular sovereignty, wanted to repeal the slavery prohibition in the Missouri Compromise and replace it with squatter sovereignty. Clemens predicted that the courts would have to determine the constitutional interpretation of popular sovereignty. John Minor Botts, a former Whig congressman from Virginia, excoriated Douglas and his "mischievous and pernicious" effort to repeal of the slavery ban, prophesying that the bill would merely reopen the corrosive slavery question and destroy the benefits of the Missouri Compromise, which had provided relative peace for thirty-four years.[39]

In the Senate, Sam Houston of Texas emerged as one of the most vocal critics of the Kansas-Nebraska bill. Standing against the Pierce administration and much of the Democratic Party, the colorful senator dismissed the legislation as folly. Like other opponents of the bill, Houston predicted that it would "convulse the country from Maine to the Rio Grande." Not only did he believe the bill would reopen the debate over slavery in a most dangerous form, for a mere abstraction, but he also concluded that Douglas misinterpreted the true meaning of popular sovereignty. Houston would not "apply the principle to the Territories in their unorganized and chrysalis condition."[40]

Yet southern supporters of the legislation greatly outnumbered the bill's slave-state opponents. Under normal circumstances, one would surmise that the Whigs would have stood in opposition to the Democratic measure. But the politics of slavery had again blurred party lines and further radicalized the debate in the South. After all, a Whig—Archibald Dixon of Kentucky—had first proposed the repeal of the Missouri Compromise's prohibition of slavery.[41] Not all southern Whigs warmly endorsed the Kansas-Nebraska bill, but they recognized that a majority of the South saw the bill as a bold defense of slavery and southern rights. Even at the risk of further muddling party lines, they had to support the bill in order to maintain their credibility in the South.

Even as southerners gave solid support to the Kansas-Nebraska bill, significant questions lingered about the exact—and correct—interpretation of popular sovereignty. Optimists lauded the end of restriction and hoped that Missourians would migrate to and populate the territory and use popular sovereignty to establish slavery there. Pessimists, however, could not shake the suspicion that popular sovereignty equaled squatter sovereignty. Several factors provoked a response from wary southerners. After maintaining a long but studied silence on the Douglas bill, Cass delivered an address to the Senate regarding the measure in late February. The Michigan senator confessed that he did not support the movement for repeal, instead hoping that Douglas and his allies would remain silent on the Missouri Compromise. He endorsed popular sovereignty, though his language seemed equivocal at times. With advancing age and in infirm health, the senator had gained a reputation for labored oratory, which only became worse when he tried to convince both sections that popular sovereignty would serve their interests. Cass declared that the citizens of the territories "are their own masters, under the Constitution, as much as the people of a State, and are the property of no man." Of course, he added the phrase "under the Constitution" to signal that in the future, the courts might well have to decide the true meaning of popular sovereignty. In sum, the senator called for a return to the "true principles" of the Constitution as outlined in his Nicholson letter some six years earlier.[42]

In a clear indication of how politicized popular sovereignty had become between North and South, Cass's latest attempt to clarify the doctrine incensed southern Democrats. In terms perhaps clearer than ever before, the senator affirmed that he never meant for his doctrine to sanction the introduction of slavery in the territories. Likewise, he never believed that slavery would enter either Kansas or Nebraska, just as it would never enter the Mexican Cession. Cass merely intended the principle of popular sovereignty to affirm the equality of the territories and their citizens to the existing states and their citizens. For southern senators and just about anyone else who read the Cass speech, his words rang hollow. Indeed, the southern press interpreted his remarks to mean that slavery could enter the territories only "by positive enactment of the territorial legislature." They considered such a position anathema, insisting it was a "question belonging properly to the Supreme Court of the United States, and

not to Congress." Even supporters of popular sovereignty lamented the senator's speech. "Gen. Cass' gingerly speech was a source of profound regret to
me," a correspondent wrote to Stephen Douglas. "He spoke as if annoyed &
frightened at the resurrection of his own offspring." For the sake of the Democratic Party, many politicians and spokesmen pleaded for unity. Southern Democrats rallied behind the bill and its author, entreating their fellow citizens to
unite in support of its passage. "As usual with the unfortunate and fated South
we have split into any number of factions upon this Bill," a Georgia Democrat
lamented. Other observers predicted disaster if the South abandoned the
Kansas-Nebraska bill. Without unity on the issue, "the South is certain to lose
by a division among her representatives."[43]

Notwithstanding criticism leveled from the North or the South, two facts became evident even in the early stages of the debate: not only had Douglas unquestionably eclipsed the Michigan senator as the leading advocate of popular
sovereignty, but he had done so with the support of numerous southern Democrats, and increasingly with the approval of southern Whigs. Many southerners
saw the Kansas-Nebraska bill as perhaps the best deal they could obtain under
present circumstances. Nevertheless, ultra states' rights southerners pushed
further, voicing concerns about the Douglas bill and upholding the common
property doctrine first advanced in the late 1840s by John C. Calhoun. Moderates seemed willing to ignore the possibly untoward implications of the bill and
popular sovereignty. Robert Toombs of Georgia defined popular sovereignty in
the traditional southern way, arguing that the power to prohibit slavery came
only when a territory became a state. "Every citizen of each State carries with
him into the Territories this equal right of enjoyment of the common domain,"
Toombs declared, but the "inchoate society of the Territories" could do nothing
more than protect the rights of property—the people residing therein could not
legislate against a particular type of property until they assumed statehood.[44]
Toombs's logical inconsistencies mirrored those of his states' rights compatri-
ots; what made an "inchoate society" able to pass a territorial slave code, but not
pass a law prohibiting slavery? In their increasingly strained constitutional theories, ultra southerners contended that citizens of existing states could possess
slaves in the territories by virtue of the protections afforded them in their home
state. Absent positive federal protection of slavery in the territories, southerners
intimated that states rights could extend beyond the physical boundaries of an
individual state and into the federal territories, which the federal government
held in trust for all.

Others chose to ignore the long-standing dispute over when territories could exercise popular sovereignty, even though the truth became clearer over the course of the congressional debate. Virginia Senator Robert M. T. Hunter proposed to leave the matter alone, since proponents of the bill differed on its interpretation. Hunter and many of his colleagues increasingly rested their support of the bill on their belief that the courts would ultimately decide the proper interpretation of popular sovereignty. "There is a difference of opinion amongst the friends of this measure, as to the extent of the limits which the Constitution imposes upon the Territorial Legislatures," Hunter said. The senator invoked the Clayton compromise in saying, "I am willing to leave this point, upon which the friends of the bill are at difference, to the decision of the courts." Antislavery northerners, however, had prepared an ingenious plan to discredit the doctrine by defining it in terms that the South could not accept. The amendments contemplated by the antislavery forces would, in the words of a Texas correspondent, "test the sincerity of southerners, now, as to the non-intervention of Congress with respect to slavery in the territories." Salmon P. Chase of Ohio, the leader of northern opposition to the bill, proposed an amendment specifically granting territorial legislatures the right to prohibit slavery, an effort that one southern journal termed "insidious and mischievous." Chase and his associates clearly wanted to imbue popular sovereignty with an antislavery interpretation in an effort to strip the bill of southern support.[45]

Two southern senators—Andrew Pierce Butler of South Carolina and Albert Gallatin Brown of Mississippi—took the Ohioan's bait and disparaged the notion that territorial legislatures could determine the status of slavery. In perhaps his weakest statement yet about popular sovereignty's meaning, Cass reminded them that "the power of the people of the Territories to legislate upon their internal concerns, during the period of these temporary governments, is most clearly given in this bill, if the Constitution permits it." Though Butler vigorously disagreed with Cass's interpretation of popular sovereignty, he pronounced himself, with Hunter of Virginia, "perfectly willing to leave it under the Constitution, to be decided by the law tribunals of the country." Now even the most doctrinaire southerners believed that Congress could never satisfactorily define popular sovereignty. Critics of the doctrine had long accused its proponents of shrouding its true meaning in order to maintain bisectional support. But given statements from Cass and Douglas, among others, it seemed more plausible that the supporters of popular sovereignty defined the doctrine clearly, but always subjected their interpretation to the ultimate decision of the

Supreme Court—a point on which both the North and South could agree. When legislators used the phrase *subject to the Constitution*, they meant *subject to the Supreme Court*.[46]

Another critical issue directly related to the implementation of popular sovereignty surfaced in the Senate debate. Previous legislation organizing territories had given territorial governors, as well as Congress, the right of veto over local legislation. Both provisions threatened the free exercise of popular sovereignty since the president appointed territorial governors and Congress could nullify the laws passed by a territorial legislature. Douglas proposed amending the bill to give territorial legislatures the right to override a governor's veto and to strip Congress of its right to review and nullify legislation.[47] The unprecedented move would ensure the status of popular sovereignty in the territories and indisputably remove Congress from any deliberations over the future of slavery in the West—which was precisely the aim of the senator from Illinois.

Over the previous two months, the debate in the Senate had addressed at great length numerous points concerning the meaning and implementation of popular sovereignty in Kansas and Nebraska, but Douglas worked assiduously to preserve the cornerstone of his legislation, keep the bill on track, and prevent any effort to delay its passage. By the end of February, the senator signaled that he would move to bring the measure to a vote, culminating a months-long process of spirited debate and intense backroom negotiations. Beginning on March 2 and spilling over into the next day, the senators engaged in final deliberations before the vote. Leaders from both the North and the South delivered their final arguments over the merits of the Douglas bill. Southern senators repeated the now-familiar refrain that the North had long ago abandoned the principles of the Missouri Compromise when they deemed it expedient, only in the present to characterize it as a sacred compact. "Will any one dare to rise here to-day and say that the principle of the bill is not the American principle—the principle upon which our whole system of government is based—the right of the people to govern themselves," exclaimed Whig senator William C. Dawson of Georgia.[48] Why, he asked, should senators object to the very idea of self-government that their Revolutionary forebears had embraced? Other senators echoed his claims, while members of the northern antislavery caucus again decried the repeal of the Missouri Compromise.

At eleven-thirty in the evening on March 3, over ten hours after the Senate had convened, Douglas rose to give his final defense of the bill. Throughout the long day, the Illinois senator had listened to criticism from his northern colleagues and bided his time waiting to respond. The unmistakably nettled Douglas gave a three-hour-long speech that for sheer vitriol rivaled the address in which he introduced the Kansas-Nebraska bill. After addressing a few ancillary criticisms, the senator turned his focus to the "great principle involved in the bill"—popular sovereignty. Senators from the North had accused Douglas of reigniting the slavery debate by repealing the Missouri Compromise's ban on slavery and substituting popular sovereignty. He flatly rejected their allegation; indeed, "from 1820 to 1850 the abolition of congressional interference with slavery in the Territories and new States had so far prevailed as to keep up an incessant agitation in Congress, and throughout the country, whenever any new Territory was to be acquired or organized." His bill would calm the fury over slavery in the territories by placing it in the hands of the people concerned, not fanatics in the North and South.[49]

Douglas asserted that the Compromise of 1850, which he played a pivotal role in shepherding through Congress, was a "general principle of universal application" for addressing the slavery issue. The Kansas-Nebraska bill, he argued, followed the principles passed into law in 1850 and sanctioned by both parties in their campaign platforms in 1852. Betraying exasperation with the northern members of his party, the Illinoisan defended himself against charges that he did the bidding of the Slave Power. Douglas engaged in a curt dialogue with Whig William Seward of New York over the Missouri Compromise and its status as a compact between the sections. He excoriated Massachusetts Free Soil Senator Charles Sumner and Salmon Chase—both of whom had ceaselessly attacked the bill and upheld the Missouri Compromise. To them, Douglas replied, "The Missouri compromise was interference; the compromise of 1850 was noninterference, leaving the people to exercise their rights under the Constitution." He predicted that passage of the Kansas-Nebraska bill would forever destroy "all sectional parties and sectional agitations," effectively silencing men like Seward, Chase, and Sumner as well as the proslavery fanatics of the South. Moderation in the nation would prevail if popular sovereignty prevailed in Congress. On that note, Douglas concluded his remarks early in the morning of March 4.[50]

The debate continued for several more hours as Sam Houston of Texas made one final plea for maintaining the Missouri Compromise. At five o'clock in the morning, after seventeen hours of continuous debate, the Senate passed the Kansas-Nebraska Act by a vote of 37–14. Southern Democrats and Whigs united to support the bill; only Houston and John Bell of Tennessee voted nay. Fourteen northern Democrats voted for the bill, while four voted nay. The Democrats had held together, though not without a struggle. As for the Whig party, however, the vote revealed a fatal division between its northern and southern wings. Nine southern Whigs voted for Douglas's bill, while six northern Whigs voted against it. Three Whigs from the North had left the Senate floor. Nevertheless, the bill would have passed without any southern Whig support. Douglas had succeeded brilliantly in steering his legislation through the Senate. The governor of North Carolina wrote the senator, expressing the "proud satisfaction" of North Carolinians and southerners in general with his "statesmanlike and patriotic" efforts to affirm the principle of popular sovereignty. A Virginia editor called the bill the "greatest triumph that the South and the Constitution has ever had." Southerners congratulated themselves on the fact that they had combined "with a unanimity unprecedented in the annals of legislation, to approve a principle in '54 about the propriety of which she was divided in '50."[51]

With great parliamentary acumen, more than a little deception, and astonishing disregard for northern public opinion, the Little Giant had convinced enough of his colleagues that popular sovereignty would prove safe for their respective interests. Removing the slavery issue from Congress would purportedly quiet the increasingly bellicose political discourse; allowing the people in the territories themselves to determine their own course with regard to slavery would uphold the American tradition of self-government. But he knew full well that northerners and southerners did not interpret popular sovereignty in the same way; just as Douglas had secured passage of the Compromise of 1850 by exploiting sectional blocs, in 1854 he used the ambiguity of popular sovereignty to push the Kansas-Nebraska Act through the Senate.

But the astute politician also knew that the biggest battle would come in the House of Representatives, where recalcitrant northern Democrats might well buck the administration and oppose the legislation. Regardless of the potential outcome, Douglas knew that he would not achieve a landslide victory in the lower house. Supporters urged Douglas and the friends of the bill to keep the issue in front of the public. "Popular Sovereignty will win, if it is thoroughly & properly discussed & understood," a supporter wrote to Douglas. The leading voices for popular sovereignty stressed the common-sense nature of the doctrine—self-government should apply to slavery in the territories as much as it did to any other American institution. "Ultimately, the social institutions of all Territories seeking and obtaining admission into this Union must be moulded and fashioned by the people thereof when they possess a sufficient population to entitle them to take rank as States," the *New York Herald* declared. It became axiomatic among the supporters of popular sovereignty that the doctrine embodied the essence of American politics and the nature of people as political actors. Settlers in the territories would naturally take responsibility for determining their own ways of life and domestic institutions. Conversely, they would resent any effort from a distant federal government to direct them otherwise. So characterized, popular sovereignty seemed eminently wise.[52]

Southern advocates linked popular sovereignty with the states' rights doctrine that their section had embraced for years. Emboldened by the movement to repeal the Missouri Compromise ban on slavery, southerners lashed out at those who believed that men in Washington could determine whether slaves would pass into the territories. The federal government had no power "to prevent a Southern man from carrying his slaves to any Northern latitude he might select," a New Orleans editor stated, "provided the local authority of State or Territory permitted him to locate his habitation within their limits." No person who had a "correct understanding of State rights" and the Tenth Amendment to the Constitution could declare otherwise.[53]

One of the most impassioned defenses of popular sovereignty came from a Georgia Democrat writing under the pseudonym of Cato. Recognizing that northerners sought to exploit divisions in the South over the doctrine and believing that the law represented the best means of holding together the national Democracy, Cato entreated his fellow southerners to stand firm for the right of the people to determine the status of slavery in the territories for themselves. Antislavery newspapers in the North noted strains of southern unity that was revealed by dissent in the slave states over the squatter sovereignty variant of self-government in the territories. Though a significant contingent of southern leaders rejected the notion of squatter sovereignty—that the first settlers on the ground could forever determine whether to permit or prohibit slavery—Cato expressed little concern of such an eventuality. He wrote, "in future territory acquired by this government, under the great principle of non-intervention and the sovereign right of the people to make their own laws, wherever slavery will be found advantageous there it will go."[54]

Moderate southern Democrats saw the necessity of maintaining intersectional party ties, if for no other reason than one should keep his friends close, but his enemies even closer. They warned the people of the South that if they rejected popular sovereignty, they would "place slavery at the mercy of a growing number of representatives of the free States," which would be "the most critical and dangerous position it could possibly occupy." Astutely recognizing the diminishing power of the South in the halls of Congress, especially the House of Representatives, these moderates believed the Democratic Party and its historical affinity for entertaining southern demands stood as perhaps the last means by which the South could maintain its influence in the federal government. In a letter to Douglas, New York Governor Horatio Seymour had expressed concern that antislavery Democrats sought "to abolitionize the rank & file of the party." Furthermore, the governor predicted that "Southern men will yet realize that they committed an error in remaining passive spectators of a ruthless crusade against" northern moderate Democrats. The most stalwart southern party regulars seemed to believe the claims of northern Democrats like Seymour and tried to impress on their fellow southerners that they could not abandon the party. The South would fare far better by placing the future of slavery in the hands of local communities that would act in their own best interests, rather than in Congress, where an ever-growing phalanx of antislavery politicians sought to end the institution.[55]

Like Douglas, careful political observers in the South knew that the Kansas-Nebraska bill faced stiff opposition in the House of Representatives. Southern Democrats rallied the party faithful by appealing to the virtues of popular sovereignty while seeking to rebut claims that the bill would foist squatter sovereignty on the South. "Some profess to support the Nebraska bill because the doctrine of Squatter Sovereignty is embodied in it, others support it because the doctrine is not admitted in the bill," a Georgia editor observed, but Democratic regulars in the South, however, did not see those differences of opinion as an insurmountable obstacle. They believed, in the words of Cato, that if "any doubt arises upon the constitutionality of a territorial law the tribunal of judgment is not Congress but the Supreme Court." On this point both northern and southern Democrats could agree. "The extreme pro slavery, as well as the antislavery men, will still desire to fight out the battle on the compromise and slave extension issues," a New York Democrat wrote, "but the moderate men of both parties will resolve to leave over those points to be discussed and settled on their own legitimate ground"—namely the territorial legislatures and, on appeal, the Supreme Court.[56]

While the nation debated the merits and meaning of popular sovereignty, the House of Representatives labored over the Kansas-Nebraska bill. A close Douglas associate, fellow Illinoisan William A. Richardson, had introduced the bill on March 21, but a recalcitrant New York Democrat, Francis B. Cutting, used a parliamentary maneuver to bury the legislation under a mountain of other bills before the House. The bill's supporters fought valiantly, but the Cutting amendment to commit the bill to the full House, where it would rank below forty-nine other bills, succeeded on a close vote. The Cutting amendment showed the House managers of the Kansas-Nebraska bill that they faced an uphill battle to bring the bill to the floor, let alone to secure its passage. Fortunately for Douglas, who maintained an almost constant presence in the House chamber while the representatives considered his bill, his associates proved equal to the task. The senator as well as representatives from the Pierce administration placed intense pressure on House Democrats to clear quickly other legislation so that they could debate the legislation.[57]

By early May, Richardson had brought the bill before the House for debate, though it seemed that the opposition might kill it yet through a myriad of objections to the way in which supporters had introduced the legislation. Finally, Alexander Stephens of Georgia broke the parliamentary logjam. The Georgia Whig, who expressed "a deep interest in the success of the measure as a Southern man," had emerged as an ardent supporter of the legislation. Stephens believed it the best possible deal the South could obtain; that while slavery might never gain hold in either Nebraska or Kansas, the nation could gain more territory in the future—perhaps in Cuba or elsewhere in the Caribbean. Establishing popular sovereignty as the principle by which the residents of the territories would judge where slavery would or would not pass could greatly benefit the South in the future. Given his support of popular sovereignty, Stephens worked assiduously to ensure that the Kansas-Nebraska bill received a floor vote. On May 22, the House passed the Kansas-Nebraska Act by a vote of 113–100. Southern Democrats provided nearly unanimous support, but without help from southern Whigs the bill would have failed. Thirteen southern Whigs provided "the critical margin of victory," while seven colleagues voted against the bill. The House vote confirmed the split within the Whig party nationally and within the South. For the Democrats, however, the House vote revealed sharper differences between the northern and southern wings of the party. The northern Democracy divided evenly—forty-four representatives voted yea and forty-four voted nay. Democrats in New England and the northern states of the Old Northwest provided significant opposition to Kansas-Nebraska. On May 30, President Pierce signed into law the bill that he had reluctantly thrown his administration's support behind and had made a test of party faith.[58]

Supporters hailed the vote with a jubilant response. "The contest in the House was close and hot but we whipped the opposition out and carried the measure by 13 majority," Stephens exclaimed. "Nobody says anything now against it but the abolitionists. Let them howl on—'Tis their vocation." John Tyler hailed the outcome as a vindication of the nation's Revolutionary heritage of self-government and affirmed that the South would back the outcome, stating, "they desire a rule of universal application to all the Territories, which will prevent the busy intermeddling of Congress, and allow it some moments free from eternal agitation to look to the great interests of the country." Stalwart supporters of the act announced a "recurrence to first principles" and "the triumph of a great principle over temporizing expedients—of the constitution over sectional fanaticism, and of popular sovereignty over the usurpations of Congress."[59]

Many southerners found much to support in the Kansas-Nebraska Act. First, by securing the repeal of the Missouri Compromise's ban on slavery, it had the potential to open free territory to slaveholders. It also removed a restriction that had irked southerners for thirty-four years. To no small number of proslavery and states' rights advocates, the Kansas-Nebraska Act restored the nation to constitutional principles. Indeed, one New York Whig remarked acidly that southerners supported the bill in spite of squatter sovereignty "because it repeals the Missouri Compromise."[60] Southerners certainly embraced repeal, but many found other merits in the legislation. Second, it removed Congress from the business of determining where slavery could or could not exist and placed the decision in the hands of the people involved. By extension, it set a useful principle for the future: Congress could no longer meddle with slavery in the territories. More pragmatically, the law seemed likely to add Kansas to the Union as a slave state. Regardless of whether slavery would ever flourish in Kansas and Nebraska, the South had gained mightily by removing the issue from the hands of an increasingly antislavery Congress.

Contrarians questioned whether the South would ever benefit from the principles of the Kansas-Nebraska Act. In reality, some feared a northern backlash. Popular sovereignty had radicalized southern politics; now it seemed certain to do the same in the North. "This act may give more quiet to the South but it will be the protest for the formation of a new party at the North," a friend confided to Georgia Governor Herschel V. Johnson. "Now is the time to unite the South with the great west, our only safety depends on that union." Other southerners advised heightened vigilance against abolitionists, who roundly criticized the bill as a violation of the sacred compact struck in the Missouri Compromise. "Our Southern friends must be up and stirring," future Caribbean filibuster

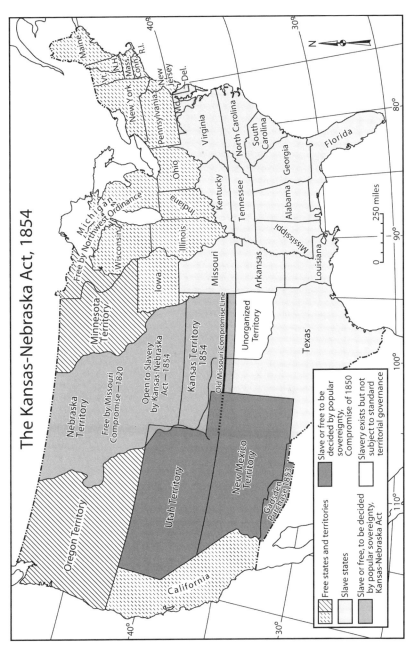

The Kansas-Nebraska Act, 1854 (map by Clifford Duplechin)

William Walker wrote to David Atchison. "Virginia, Tennessee and Kentucky ought to send her hardy sons out to claim their rights and maintain them too."[61]

Though a few southern politicians feared a northern backlash or meddling from abolitionists, other opponents claimed that the act legalized squatter sovereignty, which would bar the South from the territories just as effectively as would the Wilmot Proviso. Certain southern Whigs charged their Democratic rivals with embracing the notion that mere squatters could prohibit slavery. "[The Democrats] tell us, they contend for the principle, that Congress has no right to legislate on the subject of slavery," remarked an Arkansas Whig, "appearing to forget that the admission of this principle necessarily admits the right of the squatter to legislate the people of the south out of any territory we now possess, or may hereafter acquire."[62] The very principle embodied in the Kansas-Nebraska Act, opponents argued, had in 1850 lost California to the South.

Irrespective of concerns that the Kansas-Nebraska Act would injure the South, a substantial majority of southern citizens believed their section had won a signal victory, at least on principle and quite possibly in practice. Although hardly anyone expected Nebraska to become a slave state, Kansas presented an altogether different possibility. If populated by Missourians and other slaveholders from the region, the territory might well sustain a slave culture similar to that of its eastern neighbor. Even if Kansas became a free state, the South had won a symbolic victory. Passage of the legislation vindicated their principles of states' rights and local control of domestic issues and institutions.[63]

Stephen Douglas had succeeded at affirming popular sovereignty with respect to slavery in the territories as the law of the land. The ebullient senator celebrated his victory by proclaiming the triumph of "self-government, state rights, & constitutional liberty" embodied in the act. More importantly for the ardent expansionist, passage of the act now paved the way for the settlement of a vast portion of the nation's territorial domain. He could now concentrate on issues like homestead policy and a transcontinental railroad, which would encourage economic development and bind the West to the rest of the Union. Unfortunately for Douglas's hopes and aspirations, the Kansas-Nebraska Act did not quiet the debate over slavery in the territories. In fact, it seemed to have inaugurated a race between North and South over which section would gain control of the two territories. In other words, the settlement of Kansas and Nebraska and the doctrine of popular sovereignty became equated with the battle for sectional supremacy. A correspondent who had traveled to Kansas saw the coming migration as a chess game between the sections. "The territories of Kansas and Nebraska being free from constitutional clogs and thrown open to the competition of North and South," he wrote, "no one who understands the philosophy of Yankee enterprise can doubt the result for a moment." Some southerners admitted that the "Abolitionists will compass sea and land heaven & hill to prevent the establishment of slavery" in Kansas.[64]

The first indication that the Kansas-Nebraska Act had achieved anything but its goal of promoting sectional harmony and an end to the struggle over slavery in Congress came with the November 1854 elections for Congress. Northern Democrats suffered a horrendous electoral defeat in the midterm elections, while southern voters rewarded their Democratic legislators by returning them to Congress. In the North, the Democrats lost sixty-six of ninety-one congressional seats, while the southern Democrats lost only four seats out of sixty-seven. In sum, voters decimated the northern Democracy while the southern wing of the party remained strong, a fact that did not bode well for the future of a bisectional Democratic Party. The Whigs, on the other hand, disintegrated. In several key southern states, Whig politicians fell to their Democratic rivals. By the end of the election season, the party had virtually "bled to death." The bleeding would continue—figuratively within the political parties and literally on the plains of Kansas.[65]

"MOVES ON THE POLITICAL

CHESS-BOARD"

Southerners Redefine
Popular Sovereignty

The footrace between antislavery and proslavery forces to gain control of Kansas had commenced even before President Franklin Pierce signed the Kansas-Nebraska Act into law, but it gained vigor and urgency once popular sovereignty became the national policy for territorial organization. The federal government had officially created the territories of Nebraska and Kansas; the former would almost certainly become a free state while southerners hoped they could add the latter to the slave state column. Southern Democrats who had derided the northern Democratic version of popular sovereignty in the late 1840s warmed to it in 1854 because it made possible the impossible by permitting slavery where the Missouri Compromise had banned it. In sum, southerners initially believed that slavery had a legitimate chance to exist and thrive in Kansas Territory, but the repeal of the thirty-four-year restriction on slavery and the implementation of popular sovereignty obscured significant long-term challenges presented by the new policy.[1]

Popular sovereignty created a zero sum contest for the future of slavery in Kansas in which one side would win and the other would lose. A high-stakes challenge over slavery in Kansas opened the possibility of fraud and chicanery from partisans on both sides of the issue. Southerners had accused the North of swindling slaveholders in California and New Mexico. Would northerners and southerners follow the rules of popular sovereignty in Kansas? More importantly, what were the rules? More than any other proponent of popular sovereignty, Stephen Douglas left the question open by giving credence to both interpretations—that territorial legislatures could prohibit slavery before statehood or only when a territory drafted a constitution and sought admission to the Union. Many people in the North and South increasingly believed that the Supreme Court would someday decide which interpretation would prevail. In 1857, the Supreme Court did intervene, through the case of *Dred Scott v. Sandford*. The majority opinion of Chief Justice Roger B. Taney upheld the southern version of popular sovereignty, but antislavery northerners quickly made clear their disdain for the Court's pronouncement and their intention to ignore it.

Finally, given the highly charged atmosphere surrounding the slavery debate, one could legitimately question if the losing side would abide by the will of the majority. Would, or more importantly, could popular sovereignty work? Most southerners continued to insist that settlers could prohibit slavery only when drafting a state constitution, while northerners interpreted popular sovereignty to mean that territorial legislatures could ban slavery whenever they pleased. The infamous Lecompton Constitution of 1858 marked the high tide of proslavery efforts to impose a version of popular sovereignty on the Kansas territory and by extension the nation, but the crass manipulation of the political process in Kansas made a mockery of any semblance of reverence for constitutionalism. The Lecompton fiasco ended in failure for proslavery stalwarts, as Douglas and the northern Democrats in Congress blocked the proslavery document. Never again would southern Democrats trust their northern brethren, or place their faith in the doctrine of popular sovereignty. After Lecompton, slaveholders believed only one option remained for the security of their rights and their property: federal protection for slavery in the territories.

WHILE southern Democrats flocked to the popular sovereignty standard in 1854, northern Democrats proved much more reserved about the doctrine. State legislatures in key southern states hailed popular sovereignty as a bold affirmation of the Compromise of 1850, asserting that "the question whether slavery shall or shall not form a part of their domestic institutions is for them alone to determine for themselves." Southern Democrats especially approved of the Kansas-Nebraska Act as a repeal of the "mis-named 'compromise' of eighteen hundred and twenty" and the victory of popular sovereignty and congressional noninterference with slavery in the territories. Howell Cobb of Georgia praised the bill because it "affirmed the great principle of popular sovereignty" and "pledged Congress to the admission of Nebraska and Kansas, with or without slavery, as the people of those territories might declare for or against slavery, in the organization of their State Constitutions." Cobb's comments nicely captured the southern view of popular sovereignty and the best hopes of his section that Kansas would become a slave state. In the simplest terms, the democratic and moderate principle of popular sovereignty would restore sectional harmony, maintain the balance between free and slave states, and ensure the permanent ascendancy of the Democracy.[2]

Popular sovereignty worked almost exactly as planned in Nebraska Territory, producing the result that the territory's residents desired: a free territory and a free state. The residents themselves did not want the institution, and slaveholders had no desire to immigrate to the territory. During the congressional debate over the Kansas-Nebraska bill, a Nebraskan sent a memorial to Congress endorsing popular sovereignty as an antislavery doctrine. The writer, however, made clear that "the philanthropist need not be alarmed, as I believe there has never been, nor do I suppose there ever will be, a single slave residing in the Territory of which I am writing."[3] Because nobody believed that slavery would ever exist in Nebraska, few resorted to extraordinary actions, chicanery, or other dubious measures to affect the outcome. No competition between proslavery and antislavery forces emerged in the territory. In Nebraska, popular sovereignty operated successfully; only a handful of slaves resided in Nebraska, prior to 1861 when the territorial legislature passed a bill prohibiting slavery in the territory—over their governor's veto. Consensus within Nebraska on the slavery issue emerged in the territory's earliest days and never waned, making popular sovereignty appear sensible and unproblematic. Conditions in Kansas could not have differed more.

Supporters on both sides of the slavery issue in Kansas quickly mobilized to influence the outcome of the race to make the territory a free state or a slave state. Territorial candidates committed to a "Southern Rights" platform carried the election for a delegate to Congress in the fall of 1854. Four months later, Missourians flooded the territory and elected a proslavery territorial legislature.[4] Antislavery supporters rejected the results of the fraudulent election when they learned that the proslavery votes cast in March 1855 exceeded the eligible voters twofold. Proslavery Missourians, they argued, had committed fraud and made a mockery of popular sovereignty to ensure that Kansas would become a slave state. Without doubt, Missourians fully intended to use their power to sway the territorial government in favor of a proslavery policy.

What is more, situations on the ground in Kansas had led to a great inversion in the beliefs of proslavery and antislavery partisans in their respective interpretations of popular sovereignty. Proslavery Missourians flooded the nascent territory on a series of election days, beginning in November 1854, seeking to gain proslavery control of the territorial government. By March 1855, proslavery partisans had influenced the election of a territorial delegate to Congress and ensured a friendly territorial legislature. Four months later, at territorial Governor Andrew Reeder's suggestion that the legislature move to "temporarily prohibit, tolerate or regulate Slavery in the Territory," the proslavery body responded by passing a harsh slave code. Proslavery leaders had embraced a version of popular sovereignty that gave territorial legislatures wide latitude in regulating slavery. Of course, southerners had always agreed that a territory could regulate, but not prohibit slavery. But after passage of the slave code, free state Kansans protested bitterly against what they termed a violation of the rights of free men. By co-opting the machinery of territorial government through fraudulent electoral means, proslavery Missourians had reduced antislavery residents of Kansas to "the veriest slaves and serfs"—to use the words of free-state leader Charles Robinson. With the territorial legislature firmly in proslavery hands, Robinson and his fellow free-state partisans took a cue from the southern interpretation: bypass the territorial phase by creating an antislavery (and extralegal) government that would draft a constitution prohibiting slavery and seek admission to the Union.[5]

Once again, competing visions and interpretations of popular sovereignty had muddled the meaning of self-government in the American territories. Popular sovereignty in the territories seemed a perfect idea in theory. In practice settlers found numerous problems that they would have to address and redress in order to create a government. Aside from the certain election frauds perpetrated by proslavery forces in Kansas, the nation's patchwork system of electoral laws confounded efforts to create a uniform system in a territory peopled by emigrants from across the nation. Residency requirements varied from state to state, and jurisdictions administered the electoral process differently.[6] Ensuring a fair, uniform, and equitable election would have proved challenging even in the least politically charged atmosphere. In Kansas, however, proslavery Missourians had made a farce of honest elections by brazenly crossing the border to vote in territorial elections. Southerners seemed to accept the fact that the territorial legislature in Kansas would likely determine the future of slavery, but in 1854 they believed that the proslavery forces had control of the territorial legislature and that they would make the territory a slave state. The first territorial census revealed that nearly two-thirds of the residents hailed from Missouri and other southern states, with the remaining third coming from the North. The numbers, however, obscured another demographic reality: a meager slave population. Two factors contributed to the lack of slaves in the territory. Poorer farmers who did not own slaves moved to Kansas to seek cheap land and economic sufficiency. More importantly, the Missourians who resided on the border between their state and Kansas felt reluctant to move west with their slaves until they had secured the future of slavery in the territory. Southerners residing on the border appealed to their fellow citizens to move west in order to make Kansas a slave state. "As to the security of negro property," a Lexington, Missouri, correspondent wrote, "that will depend on the aid we get from Southern States." The writer asserted that if only "500 to 1000 at most pro-slavery men . . . would move to Kansas with their slaves," their presence "would settle the matter beyond question."[7]

Slaveholders who looked to settle in Kansas, however, wanted assurances that the territorial government would take a favorable stance toward slavery. Of course, southern radicals had identified this problem in 1849 and 1850 when they insisted on federal protection for slave property in the Mexican Cession. Absent federal protection, slaveholders remained reticent to emigrate, leading to a self-fulfilling prophecy of doom for slavery in Kansas. Slaveholders demanded security for their property and their future before they would move west, something they could not achieve without manipulating the popular sovereignty formula to their advantage. Only one other option remained: to influence the creation of the territorial government by crossing the border to vote. Missourians did precisely that.

Mobilization of the antislavery movement in the territory further complicated the already unstable situation in Kansas. After passage of the Kansas-Nebraska Act, antislavery proponents in New England were determined to send settlers west to secure the territory against slavery. Organizations such as the New England Emigrant Aid Company, backed by powerful northeasterners, mobilized in the spring and summer of 1854. In spite of a miniscule number of emigrants during the first year of the enterprise, their very presence galvanized free soil supporters and inflamed the South. "We should not allow the Abolitionists to Colonise [*sic*] Kansas by emigrant societies without making the effort to counteract it by throwing in a Southern population," Jefferson Davis wrote.[8]

By the summer of 1855, southerners recognized that the Kansas issue and thus popular sovereignty had become far more complicated that they had anticipated. Familiar divisions reemerged in the South, as ultra proslavery advocates called for a sectional political party to resist any attack on southern rights in the territories. Facing reelection as governor of Georgia, Herschel V. Johnson implored his Democratic friends to stay true to their party and to the policy of popular sovereignty. He reminded Georgia Democrats that many of their northern brethren had worked diligently to pass the Kansas-Nebraska Act. "Did they not aid the South in repealing the Missouri restriction, under which she had writhed for thirty years, as degrading to her equality and violative of the constitution," he asked? Johnson urged southerners to wait and see what happened in Kansas, leaving open the possibility that the South could resort to stronger action should Congress refuse to admit Kansas should it submit a proslavery constitution.[9]

Moderate southern Democrats stood by popular sovereignty even as its application in Kansas Territory became increasingly problematic. They understood that the principle gave their section the best possible chance at securing Kansas as a slave state. A Mississippi correspondent lauded Stephen Douglas for protecting the rights of southerners in the territories through popular sovereignty and expressed hope that both northerners and southerners would "let the Territories settle their own affairs without the intervention of Congress." Although many southerners stood by popular sovereignty, they also made clear that the South would not allow the free soil elements entering Kansas to seize control of the territorial government solely for the purposes of prohibiting slavery. Just as southerners had viewed immigrants to California and New Mexico as squatters on the land and not bona fide citizens, so too they rejected the legitimacy of those who settled in Kansas under the auspices of emigrant aid societies. At a rally in Milledgeville, Georgia, Democrats made clear their interpretation of popular sovereignty. The people of Kansas "have the right, when the number of their population justifies it, to form a republican State constitution, with or without slavery, as they may determine," the committee stated. If Congress refused to admit Kansas with a proslavery constitution, there would exist "just cause for the disruption of all the ties that bind the State of Georgia to the Union."[10]

As the opponents of slavery continued to settle in Kansas, southerners more carefully—and more forcefully—asserted their version of popular sovereignty against the antislavery vanguard. The presence of New England free soil immigrants not only challenged proslavery residents but southerners in the states who sought to protect slaveholders' interests in the new territory. The South had assailed antislavery Mexicans five years before, arguing that the conquered had no right to govern the conqueror. Accusing American citizens as squatters, however, made the South look paranoid and hypocritical. Leading southerners had consistently and adamantly insisted on equal rights for Americans in the territories. Therefore most southerners instead sought to send proslavery citizens into Kansas to control the local government and secure the territory for the South's peculiar institution. Few disagreed that slaveholders needed to immigrate to the territory if the institution of slavery stood any chance of survival, with the support of a proslavery majority in the territorial legislature. If northerners gained control of the territorial government, they would surely seek to prohibit slavery as soon as possible. Although southerners denied their right to enact such a prohibition, maintaining control of the Kansas territorial government removed any doubt about the future.

Southern politicians again accused northern Democrats of trying to change the substance of the popular sovereignty doctrine by affirming the power of territorial legislatures to prohibit slavery, even though proslavery leaders in Kansas sought to use the legislature to permit slavery. "The true doctrine was incorporated in the Utah bill of 1850," a Richmond editor argued, "declaring the right of the people of the territories *in organizing a State government preparatory to admission into the Union*, and not before, to decide the question of slavery or no slavery for themselves." Lewis Cass and many northerners now endorsed the idea of what southern Democrats called "squatter sovereignty," which affirmed the right of territorial legislatures to exclude slavery. The editor argued that Douglas upheld the former, while Cass and many northerners affirmed the latter. Squatter sovereignty, according to the editor, "means no more nor less than the power of congress through its creatures, the territorial legislatures, to legislate upon the subject of slavery—which is held an absurdity among all State Rights politicians." As conditions in Kansas deteriorated in late 1855 and early 1856, southerners shifted tactics yet again, defending their interpretation of popular sovereignty in order to maintain slavery's toe hold within the territory. Fearing that the South was losing the battle, they realized that whichever interpretation of the doctrine prevailed would determine the future of slavery in Kansas.[11]

The winter of 1855–1856 saw the battle in Kansas shift from rhetorical bombast to force as pro- and antislavery forces violently clashed within the territory. The fraudulent election of a proslavery territorial legislature in March 1855 galvanized free-state forces into creating a shadow government opposed to slavery within Kansas and hostile to the increasingly belligerent proslavery body seated in the territorial capital of Lecompton. Indeed, democracy in Kansas assumed a farcical nature as the free-state partisans sought to create their own government and delegitimize the proslavery government at Lecompton. By January 1856, antislavery voters had drafted and ratified a constitution and elected their own governor and legislature. The free-state partisans frequently threatened outright resistance to the officially recognized Lecompton government, though they rarely acted. Instead, they engaged in a "form of brinksmanship that threw the proslavery faction off balance and more than once goaded them into acts of repression which discredited their own cause." Throughout the first six months of 1856, however, both sides clashed not in legislative halls, but in combat on the ground. Both sides skirmished outside the free-state stronghold of Lawrence, but ultimately they dispersed. In May 1856 the situation escalated when the proslavery sheriff of Douglas County, Kansas, sought to arrest recalcitrant free-state citizens. His posse of Missourians, having failed to detain their quarry, returned to and ransacked the city of Lawrence. The day after the "Sack of Lawrence," South Carolina Representative Preston Brooks marched up to the desk of Charles Sumner, his Massachusetts colleague, and proceeded to beat Sumner senseless. Sumner had delivered a strong philippic just two days before, "The Crime against Kansas," in which he excoriated Stephen A. Douglas and the Slave Power for perverting the idea of popular sovereignty by using it to legalize slavery in Kansas. In his tirade Sumner personally assailed Douglas and Andrew P. Butler, a South Carolina senator who was related to Brooks. Bleeding Kansas had spilled over into Congress; now antislavery individuals talked, too, of Bleeding Sumner.[12]

Popular sovereignty had begat not orderly democracy in Kansas and sectional peace in Congress, but turmoil and violence. Andrew Reeder, the territorial governor, fled Kansas in disguise. His successor, Wilson Shannon, begged Pierce to authorize the use of federal troops to quell the disorder. The president flatly refused, siding with the proslavery territorial government and vowing not "to volunteer interposition by force to preserve the purity of elections, either in state or territory." But every day that Kansas continued to bleed, and every day that the Pierce administration and its lieutenants on the ground in the territory failed to gain control of the explosive situation, Republicans gained strength as a political party opposed to the farce of popular sovereignty and the Slave Power. The Democratic *New York Herald* could dismiss reports coming from Kansas as "Black Republican balderdash," but they still swayed public opinion and still led many northerners to believe that popular sovereignty seemed doomed to failure.[13]

The presidential election of 1856 would in many ways serve as a referendum on Kansas-Nebraska and popular sovereignty. It soon became clear that the turmoil in and over Kansas had gravely weakened the Democratic Party, especially in the free states. Enactment of the Kansas-Nebraska Act had caused considerable disruption in the national two-party political system while popular sovereignty "had not provided a common ground but a battle ground." Antislavery Democrats and Whigs fled their old parties and came together under a new political banner called the Republican Party, which completely rejected popular sovereignty calling it a formula for disaster. The newly formed party criticized self-government in the territories as an insidious and cowardly means of avoiding discussion of the slavery question. To Republicans' minds, the doctrine of Stephen Douglas ignored the moral dilemma of extending slavery while it upheld the absurd claim that Congress had no power to legislate for the territories.[14]

Viewing with great alarm the development of a sectional antislavery party, southerners expressed resentment and vehemently rejected attacks on southern morality. "We believe our institutions to be as moral, rightful and expedient as those of the North," a Virginian wrote. "But we are no propagandists, and we do not set ourselves up, like Massachusetts, as a model and a pattern for other people." The writer portrayed the South as eminently tolerant and democratic; indeed, he implied that northerners intended to impose their will on other free Americans, rather than staying true to the quintessentially American principle of self-governance. According to many southerners, the Northern antislavery activists ultimately sought to violate the terms of state equality and equal rights for all free Americans. The Kansas-Nebraska Act and popular sovereignty, southerners asserted, returned the nation to its heritage of self-government, whereas antislavery activists and abolitionists sought to force slaveholding Americans to give up their domestic institutions. In a touch of biting criticism, the *Richmond Enquirer* stated, "Were the Federal Government to enact a law preventing Massachusetts from sending Sharp's rifles to Kansas, all would admit the iniquity of the law. Yet the exclusion of Southern slaves is alike in principle, and far more iniquitous in practice." The southern defense of its interpretation of the Constitution and popular sovereignty became increasingly strident amidst the rising antipathy toward slavery.[15]

Southern moderates and their northern allies sought to quiet the increasingly bellicose debate by pointing to popular sovereignty as the best means of compromise on the slavery question. Yet they made their arguments in an atmosphere where compromise had increasingly become a pejorative indication of weakness. While the doctrine steered a moderate path between the ultra opinions in the North and the South, according to moderate Democrats it also represented not a compromise as such but a fundamental axiom of American political institutions—the right of the people to govern themselves. In early 1856, Douglas worked closely with southern Democrats to boost northern support for popular sovereignty, encouraging them to ally with their northern brethren and reunite the Democracy. Several notable southern political leaders responded by extolling the virtues of popular sovereignty as a moderate, pragmatic, and essentially American solution to the slavery issue. "In the Kansas bill it was provided that this vexed question of slavery should be left—where the blood of the Revolution put it," Howell Cobb cried before a New Hampshire audience, "where the constitution leaves it; where the great principle of self-government leaves it—to be decided by the people of Kansas, subject only to the constitution of the United States."[16] Cobb argued that neither the people of his native Georgia nor any other state had the right to tell the settlers of Kansas whether to prohibit or permit slavery. Moderate southern Democrats who believed that the ascendancy of a sectional antislavery party threatened the power and security of their section fell back on popular sovereignty as a way to defend their interests within the political system. Mindful of circumstances in Kansas and the determined resolve of northerners to halt the spread of slavery in Kansas, radical southerners increasingly rejected the doctrine, which they believed had unwittingly and ultimately become a tool for halting the expansion of slavery. Southern ultras pointed to another American political axiom—the sanctity of property—to legitimize federal protection of slavery.

Southerners threw down the gauntlet to the antislavery leaders who had increasingly attacked the South for perpetuating an immoral institution. In the wake of the Kansas fiasco and the rise of abolitionism, political antislavery forces had expanded their arguments beyond the familiar bounds of constitutional interpretation in order to rebuke slaveholders on moral grounds. These attacks southerners would not abide. "Whenever the South takes the distinct ground that her institutions are righteous, honorable and expedient, as those of the North, she will find her defence easy," the editor of the *Richmond Enquirer* wrote. "Until she does this, until she asserts her equality in morality, as well as in right, she invites, nay, she justifies, the attacks of abolition." Southern politicians sought to impress on their wavering northern Democratic allies that popular sovereignty presented the best way to navigate safely the issue of slavery in Kansas. In a letter to the Tammany Society of New York, Governor Herschel Johnson, a southern Democratic moderate, implored northerners to cease their criticism of popular sovereignty. "Why should the Abolitionists and Free-Soilers rail against the Kansas-Nebraska act?—They had repudiated the Missouri Compromise in 1850, why insist upon it now," he asked. "Its repeal does not, ipso facto extend the area of slaveholding territory. Its only effect is, to open the territory to emigrants from every State in the Union, upon terms of equality."[17]

Politicians in both sections now sadly recognized that the Kansas-Nebraska Act had fractured the Democracy. When the party of popular sovereignty met in Cincinnati for its national convention in June 1856, leaders and delegates anticipated a protracted fight over the presidential nomination as well as the platform. The convention marked the first time that a national party held its meeting in the West, which was a nod to the growth of the nation and the political power of the western states. Based on the press coverage of popular sovereignty as it played out in Kansas, one might have expected a battle over how the platform would address the doctrine. The delegates, however, unanimously endorsed the plank supporting popular sovereignty and the Kansas-Nebraska Act. The language of the platform suggested that the resolutions committee had accepted the southern version of popular sovereignty. It upheld congressional noninterference with slavery, while proclaiming that the people of any territory, "acting through the legally and fairly expressed will of a majority of actual residents, and whenever the number of their inhabitants justifies it; to form a Constitution, with or without domestic slavery, and be admitted into the Union upon terms of perfect equality with the other states."[18] The popular sovereignty plank artfully addressed the issues surrounding the doctrine's operation in Kansas by addressing the recent election frauds. Perhaps more importantly, it suggested that territories exercised their true popular sovereignty when writing a constitution—and not before. In sum, the platform carefully balanced sectional concerns in order to present a united front on popular sovereignty and slavery in the territories.

The delegates quickly and harmoniously approved the platform, but the contest over who would receive the presidential nomination proved more contentious. Northerners would take their stand against Kansas-Nebraska by striking at the Pierce administration, while southerners would uphold his and Douglas's efforts to plant popular sovereignty in the territory. Southerners made clear their preference for Pierce, with Douglas as their second choice should the incumbent fail to gain sufficient votes. But with the ongoing Kansas debacle in mind, northern Democrats refused to support Pierce's renomination. In the afternoon of the fourth day of the convention, the delegates began the laborious process of nominating candidates and casting ballots. James Buchanan of Pennsylvania emerged as the frontrunner, with Pierce and Douglas considerably behind in the voting. After fourteen ballots, the delegates adjourned for an evening of closed-door politicking. The next morning revealed that a deadlock had emerged between Buchanan and Douglas. After intense debate and a handwritten plea from Douglas for party unity, enough delegates shifted their votes to push Buchanan over the top. During the final vote, several southern delegations expressed their support for Douglas and his efforts to provide for popular sovereignty in Kansas, making clear that they expected the Democracy to stand firm for the doctrine.[19]

The greatest praise for Douglas and popular sovereignty came from William E. Preston of Kentucky, who gave an impromptu speech supporting the Illinoisan and his doctrine. Preston lauded the efforts of northerners like Douglas who had worked to repeal the Missouri Compromise's ban on slavery, "which for thirty years, had produced festering discontent at the North and the South." When Buchanan accepted the nomination ten days later, the party nominee endorsed the Kansas-Nebraska Act and popular sovereignty. Buchanan had not always looked with favor on the doctrine; for years, he advocated extending the Missouri Compromise line to the Pacific Ocean. Now, however, with the nomination of his party secured and the expressed support of the delegates for popular sovereignty, Buchanan could only offer praise for the doctrine derived "from the original and pure fountain of legitimate political power."[20]

Two other political parties—both new and both composed of dissidents from the Democratic and the defunct Whig parties—settled on their nominations for the coming election. Just ten days after the Democratic convention adjourned, the nascent Republican Party opened its convention in Philadelphia with delegates present from only four Upper South slave states. Its platform not only denied the right of territorial legislatures to regulate slavery, but affirmed the "right and imperative duty of Congress" to prohibit the institution in the territories. Ever since the Kansas-Nebraska Act became law, Republicans attacked the "monstrous fraud" of popular sovereignty, accusing southerners and their doughfaced northerner toadies of seeking to create territorial governments "of such character that the people cannot possibly keep slavery out." Ironically on one point Republicans and radical southerners concurred: the battle for or against slavery, if played by the rules of Douglas's popular sovereignty formula that would allow territorial legislatures to determine the institution's fate, would hinge on the proclivities of the initial residents of a territory. Republicans feared that a small cadre of proslavery partisans would doom Kansas to slavery; southern radicals believed that Yankee abolitionists would doom it to freedom.[21]

The most explosive component of the emerging Republican critique of popular sovereignty addressed the moral imperative of halting the extension of slavery. Beginning in 1854, Republican politicians, most notably an Illinois lawyer and former Whig congressman named Abraham Lincoln, objected to popular sovereignty because it effectively denied the humanity of slaves. Faced with opposing a doctrine rooted in the American revolutionary heritage, Lincoln and the Republicans asserted that popular sovereignty affirmed the freedom of white Americans at the expense of denying slaves any natural rights. "But if the negro, upon soil where slavery is not legalized by law and sanctioned by custom, *is* a man," Lincoln argued, "then there is not even the shadow of popular sovereignty in allowing the first settlers upon such soil to decide whether it shall be right in all future time to hold men in bondage there." Furthermore, Lincoln and the Republicans presented their own version of the revolutionary heritage by accusing Douglas and the Democrats of reversing the Founders' condemnation of slavery. In speeches at Springfield and Peoria, Illinois, in October 1854, Lincoln castigated those who had perverted the "sacred right of self-government" into a means of extending slavery into Kansas and Nebraska. Using the moral condemnation of slavery extension that had emerged among nascent Republicans and Independent Democrats, Lincoln argued, "When the white man governs himself that is self-government; but when he governs himself and also governs *another* man, that is *more* than self-government—that is despotism." Lincoln had made clear his belief in the republican vision of self-government, but not as Stephen Douglas and the South had defined it.[22]

Over the course of the 1856 election season, Republicans would openly endorse the free-state cause in Kansas and denounce the perfidy of popular sovereignty, blaming Pierce and the Democrats for Bleeding Kansas and accusing them of thwarting the will of the majority of the settlers there.[23] The platform decried the violence in Kansas, and they predicted that it would end only with the admission of the territory as a free state. John C. Frémont won the nomination of the Republicans, and the party committed itself to rejecting the Kansas-Nebraska Act and the doctrine of popular sovereignty.

The third party that nominated a presidential candidate in 1856, the American, or Know-Nothing Party, also addressed the popular sovereignty issue. In the South, many former Whigs joined the Know-Nothing ranks after the disintegration of the former organization. In the past, southern Whigs had advanced negative, but thoughtful, critiques of self-government in the territories. In 1856, the southern Know-Nothings resorted to the familiar politics of slavery by resurrecting the old Whig charge that popular sovereignty equaled squatter sovereignty. Know-Nothings in the South reminded the electorate that squatters in California had "assembled without law or authority, in a mob—called a Convention and formed a Constitution prohibiting slave owners forever from the whole Territory of California. This was Squatter Sovereignty in its worst form."[24] Democrats, according to southern Know-Nothings, had caused the disaster in Kansas by repealing the Missouri Compromise and substituting popular sovereignty, which gained nothing for the South. Indeed, the doctrine deceived many southerners into believing that North and South could unite based on self-government. Popular sovereignty, according to the Know-Nothings, bore different meanings in the two sections. Better to secure part of the West for slave-holding interests via the Missouri Compromise line than to lose everything by popular sovereignty, they argued. More alarming for the South, the repeal of the Missouri Compromise had united antislavery citizens and fostered the creation of the Republican Party, a sectional organization fundamentally opposed to the South and its interests. In spite of their objections to the Democratic platform, southern Know-Nothings flocked to the party when their own fledgling organization collapsed amid its own sectional disputes. They came to realize that the South faced a common sectional enemy—the Republican Party.

Though the Know-Nothings achieved little in using the squatter sovereignty issue to advance their own partisan interests, southerners had to confront northern efforts to secure Kansas against slavery, which led some in the South to conclude that squatter sovereignty might prevail. Slave state supporters of the doctrine, however, continued to rally to the defense of self-government in Kansas despite all that had transpired there. "The people who bona fide settle the territories North and South, by their fairly expressed will, are to determine the character of their institutions," a Georgian wrote. "This is popular—or as our American friends see fit to call it—'squatter sovereignty.'" Alexander Stephens, who had provided critical support for passage of the Kansas-Nebraska Act and who became a Democrat after the collapse of the Whig party, made clear to his fellow southerners that popular sovereignty did not permit squatters to rule. He firmly endorsed the traditional southern view that "when admitted as a State the said territory or any portion of the same shall be received into the union with or without slavery as their Constitution may prescribe at the time of their admission." Stephens denied the allegations of Know-Nothings and other opponents of popular sovereignty that the doctrine allowed squatter rule. "Neither the Kansas, nor the Utah bill, nor the New Mexico bill, recognized any such doctrine," he insisted. "For all the powers exercised by the Territorial Legislatures of all these territories emanated from Congress—they exercised them by permission and by grant from Congress and not by sovereign right."[25]

Democratic leaders canvassed the nation to secure support for Buchanan in the coming election and to encourage the party faithful to stand behind popular sovereignty. Douglas maintained a grueling speaking schedule in his home state. The senator knew that the strife over Kansas had divided the Democrats in Illinois and elsewhere. Anti-Nebraska Democrats had united with the new Republican Party in opposition to popular sovereignty and to the extension of slavery. Douglas sought to rally the electorate and counteract the inroads made within the Democracy by party dissidents and Republicans. By the end of September, he felt confident enough to inform Buchanan that Illinois would vote Democratic in the presidential election. In New York, former senator Daniel Dickinson once again took to the hustings to support Democrats and popular sovereignty, all the while lambasting abolitionists for their efforts to stir sectional discontent and for opposing the principles of self-government. Of course, Dickinson never doubted that Kansas would become a free state; indeed, he argued that popular sovereignty would secure the outcome. "They admit that man is capable of self-government in New York and Massachusetts," Dickinson said mockingly, "but if he gets out into Kansas they would put a kind of political baby-jumper about him, to protect him from himself and learn him to walk, before they would trust him to make the attempt."[26]

The efforts of key Democratic leaders paid off, as their party won the presidency and both houses of Congress. The Democrats won every southern state except Maryland. Nevertheless, the vote revealed significant problems for the party, as Buchanan received a plurality, not a majority of the popular vote. In the North, Democrats had carried only five free states. The presence of three parties diluted the party's voter base, an alarming sign for southerners given that one of the parties had no interest in courting the southern electorate. Furthermore, the Republicans had made significant strides in the North, carrying eleven states for Frémont. In fact, if Pennsylvania and either Illinois or Indiana had voted Republican, he would have become president.[27] The Democrats' troubles did not end with the election, because Buchanan now had to devise a plan to govern the nation and resolve the contentious Kansas issue. Though the president-elect endorsed popular sovereignty during the election, he had equivocated on how it would operate. In some instances, he supported the southern view of the doctrine; in others, Buchanan suggested that territorial legislatures could settle the matter. In a speech given at Wheatland, Buchanan's Pennsylvania home, the president-elect declared his support for "the doctrine which is the very root of all our institutions." Popular sovereignty recognized the right of "a majority of the people of a Territory, *when about to enter the Union as a State*, to decide for themselves whether domestic slavery shall or shall not exist among them."[28] Buchanan extolled the idea of popular sovereignty as the democratic way of settling the slavery issue, but he offered no clue as to how he believed it should operate in real time on the ground. Supporters of popular sovereignty, as well as Buchanan, added the key phrase "subject only to the Constitution" or "under the principles of the Constitution" to any description of popular sovereignty. In reality, he faced almost insurmountable division between northern Democrats who demanded the new president chart a drastically different course than his predecessor and southern Democrats who expected the "Old Public Functionary" to uphold slaveholders' rights in the territories. Furthermore, statements from southern fire-eaters indicated that they stood poised to repudiate the Democracy and indeed the entire Jacksonian party system if leaders did not address and redress their concerns over slavery.

But finally, a decade after the Wilmot Proviso had provoked the reintroduction and reformulation of the popular sovereignty doctrine, Democrats themselves began to challenge and attempted to clarify the ambiguity of their party's keystone policy. In the aftermath of the 1856 election, the *New York Herald* asked, "'Subject only to the constitution!' What does that mean? How far does the constitution allow the people of a Territory to go in their legislation upon slavery?" Democrats could not agree upon a single answer to that most significant question regarding popular sovereignty. Lewis Cass and Daniel Dickinson had stated that territorial legislatures could enact legislation with regard to slavery whenever they pleased. Southern Democrats rejected that interpretation, asserting that territories could act on slavery when drafting a constitution. Anyone who had read the 1856 Democratic Party platform had to conclude that the party supported the latter interpretation. Douglas seemed intent on avoiding the issue as best as he could. Though Democrats had differing interpretations of popular sovereignty, a problem that intensified as events in Kansas spiraled out of control, most party regulars assumed that the Supreme Court would ultimately decide what definition would prevail. The true meaning of the phrase "subject only to the Constitution" lay in the assumption that the Court would have to interpret the meaning of popular sovereignty. The *Herald* stated defiantly that Buchanan's first duty would be to "give us his official interpretation of squatter sovereignty."[29]

The new president would not have the chance to define popular sovereignty for the nation, in what he surely considered a welcome relief from a task that no moderate politician wanted to touch. For some time, Congress and presidents alike had attempted to defer the question and to refer it to the judiciary. The Kansas-Nebraska Act itself twice declared that territorial citizens could legislate on slavery "subject only to the Constitution of the United States." In other places, it adapted the language of the Clayton Compromise, which left "all cases involving title to slaves and 'questions of personal freedom'" to the "adjudication of local tribunals, with the right of appeal to the Supreme Court of the United States." In December 1856, the Supreme Court heard for the second time a case that most political observers believed would settle the interpretation over popular sovereignty. The case involved a Missouri slave named Dred Scott, who had sued his current owner, John F. A. Sanford, for his freedom based on the fact that his previous owner had kept him in the state of Illinois and Wisconsin Territory even though both jurisdictions prohibited slavery. Scott and his attorneys argued that his residence in Illinois and Wisconsin had made him free. The case made its way slowly through the judicial system, finally arriving on appeal at the Supreme Court in February 1856.[30]

The justices of the Supreme Court faced two questions regarding Scott's case, one of which had direct bearing on slavery in the territories. First, the Court would have to decide if Scott, a slave, had the right to sue in court. The issue centered on whether a slave held citizenship. If Scott was a citizen of the state of Missouri, he clearly possessed the right to sue his owner in court, but if he did not he lacked legal standing to bring litigation. Second, the justices would determine whether Scott's residence in Illinois and Wisconsin Territory invalidated his master's ownership. To address this issue the Court had to determine whether a territory—in this case, Wisconsin—had the right to pass laws prohibiting slavery.[31]

For a time, it seemed that the justices would confine their ruling to a determination on Scott's case for freedom. By February 1857, however, the Court decided to rule on the constitutionality of the Missouri Compromise, almost certainly desiring to settle the question of slavery in the territories. Rumors from the capital indicated a majority of the justices wanted to issue an "emphatically pro-southern decision." Perhaps no one hoped more for a judicial determination on popular sovereignty than James Buchanan. The president-elect, who desperately wanted to end the slavery dispute, saw in *Dred Scott v. Sandford* a perfect opportunity to dispose of the issue at the outset of his administration. Buchanan crossed the line of propriety, however, by communicating directly with several justices on the Supreme Court regarding the case and discussing the emerging decision with Chief Justice Roger B. Taney. The president knew on his inauguration day the substance of the decision that Taney, the man who would administer the oath of office, would imminently deliver. The two men even engaged in a brief conference during the ceremonies, which led to speculation afterward that they had colluded on the decision. Buchanan's inaugural address later fueled those suspicions. The new president began his address with platitudes about the American system of government and the cherished principle of self-government. The election had "excited to the highest degree" the passions of the electorate, but "when the people proclaimed their will, the tempest at once subsided, and all was calm."[32]

Buchanan then made the logical leap from the vindication of self-government in the presidential canvass to popular sovereignty in the territories. "What a happy conception, then, was it for Congress to apply this simple rule—that the will of the majority shall govern—to the settlement of the question of domestic slavery in the Territories," he exclaimed. Buchanan acknowledged that a "difference of opinion" existed regarding when a territory could exercise popular sovereignty, but dismissed it as "a matter of but little practical importance." He

Chief Justice Roger B. Taney's infamous opinion in the case of *Dred Scott v. Sandford* declared that neither Congress nor territorial legislatures could prohibit slavery in the territories, therefore giving judicial approbation to the radical southern version of popular sovereignty. (Library of Congress)

could dismiss the problem because he knew of the Supreme Court's impending decision. It "is a judicial question, which legitimately belongs to the Supreme Court of the United States, before whom it is now pending, and will, it is understood, be speedily and finally settled." Subtly but unmistakably, Buchanan had revealed that the Court would make a pronouncement on the constitutionality of the Missouri Compromise and the meaning of popular sovereignty—something that many people had already anticipated. He did not, however, reveal which way the Court would rule, though he almost certainly knew from his correspondence with Justices John Catron and David Grier that it would declare the Compromise of 1820 unconstitutional. Buchanan declared that he would "cheerfully submit" to the Court's decision, adding somewhat disingenuously, "whatever this may be."[33]

Two days later, Chief Justice Taney delivered the decision of the Supreme Court in *Dred Scott v. Sandford*. The eighty-year-old jurist, his voice barely audible, read the opinion of the Court in its chambers in the Capitol. On the first question the justices faced, the Taney opinion declared that a "free negro of the African race, whose ancestors were brought to this country and sold as slaves, is not a 'citizen' within the meaning of the Constitution of the United States."[34] Therefore, Scott had no right to bring suit in a federal court. Most startling, the opinion affirmed that neither a slave nor a free black could ever hold American citizenship, regardless of emancipation. Taney further complicated matters by addressing the issue of state versus national citizenship, thereby converting the issue of Scott's alleged citizenship in Missouri to his standing as a citizen of the United States. In other words, he nationalized the issue of Scott's citizenship. The chief justice then declared that blacks could not hold state citizenship either. Taney had to do so for his opinion to have any meaning, because under the diversity of citizenship clause in the Constitution if one state granted citizenship to a slave another had to recognize it. In sum, Dred Scott held neither state nor national citizenship and therefore had no standing to sue in court.

At first glance, the citizenship issue seems to have little to no bearing on the interpretation of popular sovereignty, but to Taney's mind the latter built on the former. Indeed, the Supreme Court could have ended its ruling with invalidation of Scott's original suit and declined to address the issue of slavery in the territories. Taney fully intended, however, to rule on the Missouri Compromise restriction and by extension popular sovereignty. He began the second part of the decision with a summation of the nation's territorial history. Under the Articles of Confederation, the national government accepted certain cessions of land from the states on behalf of the confederacy and pledged to act as their common agent in administering the national domain. The territories, therefore, belonged to the states as common property. In reasoning closely akin to the theories of John C. Calhoun, Taney asserted that the Constitution of 1787 largely maintained the relation of the federal government to the territories. The new government, too, acted as a common agent for the states, holding the territories for the equal enjoyment of its citizens.[35]

The chief justice anticipated criticism from those who believed that Article Four, Section Three of the Constitution—the "needful rules and regulations" clause—gave Congress the expressed power to legislate for the territories on all matters, including slavery. Taney took the narrow interpretation of the clause long held by southerners that it referred only to the administration and disposition of federal property. And yet like generations of southerners—and northerners for that matter—he vacillated when confronted with the exigencies of territorial administration. The clause certainly did not grant to Congress the "despotic and unlimited power over persons and property" in the territories as some implied. But citing an 1842 Supreme Court case involving the Territory of Florida, Taney affirmed that the federal government did possess the power to enable creation of territorial governments. He sanctioned the traditional practice of assigning territorial grades, or stages of government, based on the population of a territory and its ability to govern itself. "In some cases a Government, consisting of persons appointed by the Federal Government, would best subserve the interests of the Territory, when the inhabitants were few and scattered, and new to one another," Taney explained. "In other instances, it would be more advisable to commit the powers of self-government to the people who had settled in the Territory, as being the most competent to determine what was best for their own interests." In other words, the question of who governs depended on conditions afield.[36]

But when slavery entered the equation, the chief justice drew the sharpest distinction between local and federal authority. The government's role as a common agent for the states limited its jurisdiction as well as that of any territorial government it created. The Fifth Amendment, Taney argued, guaranteed the right of property to an American citizen regardless of where he resided. Accordingly, an act of Congress "which deprives a citizen of the United States of his liberty or property, merely because he came himself or brought his property into a particular Territory of the United States, and who had committed no offence against the laws, could hardly be dignified with the name of due process of law."[37] Because Congress could not confer a power that it did not itself possess, a territorial legislature could not prevent a citizen from the enjoyment of his property within a territory. Taney therefore concluded that the Missouri Compromise restriction was unconstitutional and therefore void. In substance, then, the Taney court used federal authority to protect slavery in the territories while denying the right of Congress to legislate against its extension.

Not only had the Supreme Court declared the Missouri Compromise restriction unconstitutional, but it implicitly had also defined popular sovereignty, a fact not always recognized by scholars. If taken at its word, the *Scott* decision dealt a fatal blow to the Cass/Douglas definition of the doctrine and upheld the most radical southern interpretation of federal power over slavery in the territories.[38] In doing so, it substantiated the Calhoun common-property doctrine regarding slavery in the territories, which had increasingly become the southern version of popular sovereignty. With the Taney opinion, the Supreme Court defined popular sovereignty as the right of the people in a territory to determine the status of slavery when they drafted a constitution and asked for admission to the Union—and not a moment before. Territorial legislatures could presumably pass laws to regulate slavery, such as slave codes, but they could not prohibit slavery or restrict the right of a person to hold slaves as property within any territory.

For the first time in the nation's history the Supreme Court, by a vote of 7–2, had invalidated a major piece of federal legislation. "The decision just made in the *Dred Scott* case, an obscure African, by the Supreme Court of the United States," a Maryland editor wrote, "is probably the most important that ever emanated from that highest tribunal of our country." Scott's name had become inextricably linked with the slavery issue; his case had given the Supreme Court the opportunity to define popular sovereignty. More important to the moment, the Court had delivered "a final adjudication" on the slavery issue, "one which is in accordance with the great principle of popular sovereignty in regard to slavery in the Territories." Radical southerners hailed the decision as a vindication of southern rights, insisting that the court's opinion "is equally fatal to Congressional Intervention and Squatter Sovereignty, and opens before the South a clean and unobstructed field for the propagation of its institutions." Abolitionists had threatened to negate the spirit of the Kansas-Nebraska Act by imposing squatter sovereignty, but the Supreme Court had ruled for states' rights and a strict construction of the Constitution, thereby restoring the true meaning of popular sovereignty as it bore shape in their mind. Southerners believed the

Taney court had vindicated their rights in the territories and had relieved their section from the "moral stigma" of slavery restriction. Simply put, the court had upheld their equality in the Union.[39]

Northern and southern Democrats initially united in approval of the decision and its meaning for the restriction of slavery in the territories. The Taney opinion absolved them of the duty to define the doctrine, thereby allowing the legislative branch to maintain the policy of nonintervention with the vexing slavery issue. Many Democrats saw the opinion as a fatal blow against the young Republican Party. A Maryland journal acknowledged the "indiscreet and suicidal ravings among some of those who *know no law* except that of their own violent self-will and passions," but concluded that even the Republicans would have to abide by the Court's definition of popular sovereignty. Other observers held hope that the case marked the end of the slavery dispute and the Republican Party itself. The Supreme Court's decision, a Georgia editor declared, "crushes the life out of that miserable political organization." Indeed, the virulent response of the Republicans to the decision in *Dred Scott v. Sandford* "had the effect of uniting the Democracy behind the Court." Democrats in the North and South could come together against their common enemy and declare that popular sovereignty—the democratic and Democratic doctrine—had prevailed. Or so the party's luminaries hoped.[40]

The two great free-state proponents of popular sovereignty, however, did not share in the enthusiasm of the southern Democracy because the decision shattered the alluring ambiguity of their cherished doctrine. Lewis Cass had to respond cautiously given his position as secretary of state in the Buchanan administration. Prior to the inauguration, he had contended to Buchanan that territorial legislatures could pass laws concerning slavery, though he also hoped that the Supreme Court would settle the matter.[41] Consequently, when the Court handed down the *Dred Scott* decision, Cass could offer little objection to its endorsement of the southern position. Of course, Douglas had long ago succeeded the elderly and infirm Cass as the chief proponent of popular sovereignty. Though the Taney court had rejected Douglas's position on the doctrine, the Little Giant held his tongue on the matter, choosing to study the issue carefully and let others—especially the Republicans—make intemperate remarks before he would issue his own pronouncement on the decision and its implications for popular sovereignty. Douglas broke his silence in June with a major address delivered in Springfield, Illinois, on the strife in Kansas, the ongoing problems with the Mormons in Utah, and most importantly, the *Dred Scott* decision. The senator warmly endorsed the Court's invalidation of the Missouri Compromise, but he strained to express his opinion on the decision's meaning for popular sovereignty. Ever the master of circumlocution, Douglas argued that he could find no contradiction between his and the Supreme Court's definition of popular sovereignty. In his attempt to resolve the differing interpretations, Douglas resorted to an idea that others had expressed during the debates over slavery in the Old Northwest and in Missouri, but one for which he later would become famous— or infamous. He argued that the right of a person to hold slaves in a territory "necessarily remains a barren and a worthless right, unless sustained, protected and enforced by appropriate police regulations and local legislation." Any regulations depended "entirely upon the will and wishes of the people of the territory as they can only be prescribed by the local legislatures. Hence the great principle of popular sovereignty and self-government is sustained and firmly established by the authority of this decision."[42]

In one respect, Douglas spoke of a different issue than that which the Supreme Court addressed. Nothing in the decision suggested that a territorial legislature could not pass laws regulating slavery; it simply declared that they could not prohibit the institution. More importantly, Douglas raised a critical point by noting that the people in any territory—but especially in Kansas— could easily find ways to realize a de facto prohibition of slavery and thereby circumvent the spirit of *Dred Scott*. Southerners excoriated Douglas for his position, even though some of their own had already arrived at the same conclusion. Just four months before the Supreme Court ruled, South Carolina Representative James L. Orr anticipated Douglas's 1858 Freeport Doctrine by declaring that slavery could not exist where "local legislation and local police regulations" did not protect the sanctity of slave property.[43]

President Buchanan seemed virtually undeterred by the *Scott* decision from his endorsement of popular sovereignty in Kansas. Nothing in Taney's opinion invalidated the right of a territory to draft and ratify its own constitution. Therefore, Buchanan vowed to ensure a fair and free plebiscite on a prospective state constitution. Thinking he had found an able lieutenant to faithfully discharge his orders, the president dispatched former Secretary of the Treasury Robert J. Walker to Kansas as its territorial governor. Meanwhile, the territorial legislature at Lecompton had called for the election of a constitutional convention in June.

With popular sovereignty defined by the Supreme Court and with Buchanan resolved to regain control of Kansas politics, the administration faced the task of putting theory into practice. Southerners welcomed the pronouncements of Buchanan and the Supreme Court, but feared the vicissitudes of victory. Betraying a belief that the South would lose Kansas to the abolitionists, Louisiana Senator Judah P. Benjamin implored the Buchanan administration to consider the expansionist impulse of the South in other areas. "Let your policy be directed to affording to the South legitimate expansion," he wrote to Cass, "and she will forget all about Kansas, as unworthy of a struggle, whilst her individual energies can be bent on her development in regions where our future is plainly marked out for us." Not all southerners looked to expansion in the Caribbean as a panacea for the nation's sectional disputes, but an increasing number believed that Kansas would become a free state regardless of the Court's decision or Buchanan's best intentions. Republicans seemed intent on halting the spread of slavery at any cost, and free soilers had gained a perhaps decisive foothold in Kansas. Others made clear that the South could ill afford to let down its guard, even with the resounding victory of *Dred Scott*. Jefferson Davis reiterated his denunciations of the "dangerous innovation" of squatter sovereignty. Though Davis and most southerners hoped that the Supreme Court had sounded the death knell for squatter sovereignty, they looked west to Kansas warily.[44]

Events in Kansas reached a crescendo in the summer of 1857, as deliberation over a proslavery constitution intensified and the Buchanan administration sent a new territorial governor to impose order. Walker, who had only reluctantly agreed to take charge in Kansas and steer the chaotic territory toward statehood, faced immediate difficulty. To the president and his cabinet, he seemed a perfect fit; as "a Northerner by birth, a Southerner by adoption, and a Union man by conviction," the diminutive but resolute Walker possessed the necessary credentials to unite people of disparate opinions and quiet the discontent in Kansas.[45] Walker firmly endorsed popular sovereignty, but he also believed that conditions in Kansas would never accommodate slavery. In 1856, he had made the controversial assertion that Kansas would become a free state because of its climate and soil as well as the mass of northern immigration that brought laborers to the new territory. Kansans would not need slaves for labor when they could hire European immigrants and northern day laborers, Walker posited.

Largely because of his opinions on slavery in Kansas, southerners coolly received news of Walker's appointment. Some southerners insisted that Walker depart from the practice of his "treacherous" predecessors, maintaining "nothing short of a genuine and strict neutrality" on the slavery issue. Other moderates in both sections implored the South to give Walker a chance to oversee a fair and neutral application of popular sovereignty in the territory. Almost immediately, however, the governor ingratiated himself with the free-state partisans in Kansas. In his inaugural address, Walker repeated his claim that Kansas lay beyond an "isothermal" line that would prevent slavery from developing in the region. Walker also addressed the recent action of the territorial legislature to organize a constitutional convention. Popular sovereignty would fail in Kansas, the new governor insisted, "unless the Convention submit the constitution to a vote of all the actual resident settlers of Kanzas [sic], and the election be fairly and justly conducted, the constitution will be and ought to be rejected by Congress." Northern newspapers and antislavery editors in the territory alike received Walker's words as an affirmation of their hope that Kansas would become a free state.[46]

Elections for the constitutional convention came and passed with none of the drama of earlier canvasses in the territory. The problem, however, came from the fact that few people voted in the election at all. The call for the convention had breathed new life into the floundering free-state movement, which in spite of pleas from Democrats and Republicans, vowed to boycott the June elections. Instead they demanded ratification of their Topeka constitution. Other voters in the territory simply did not register. Most of the voters for the sixty delegates came from proslavery strongholds. Accordingly, most of the delegates were proslavery Democrats who had immigrated to Kansas from the Upper South states. The convention, however, soon made clear that it had no intention of submitting their work to the people for a referendum. Some even took the extreme position that because the *Dred Scott* decision had invalidated the traditional version of popular sovereignty, the convention would not submit the constitution to the voters.[47]

In spite of the fact that Walker's pronouncement demanded that the constitution must receive a fair up or down vote—which all but defined the traditional southern version of popular sovereignty—radical southerners almost immediately broke with Walker over his inaugural address remarks. They argued that the new governor had no intention of ensuring the fair and impartial expression of the people's will. In step with the Lecompton convention, Laurence Keitt of South Carolina called Walker's demand that voters ratify the constitution "unprecedented, and intended only to restore [Kansas] to black republicanism." Some southern Democrats accused Buchanan of breaking his promise to southerners to protect their rights; instead the administration had "irredeemably sold" the South down the river to curry northern favor. Moderate southerners rejected the fulminations of their fire-eating brethren. In the past, constitutional conventions may not have submitted their work to the voters for ratification, but the Kansas-Nebraska Act had set a new precedent. "The distinct ground of this Act is—and a more important ground was never taken—that the people of a territory have a right to say in their constitution what shall be the character of their domestic institutions," a Georgia moderate wrote in opposition to the fire-eaters' criticisms. "How can they say this? In no other way so effectually as by a direct vote of themselves."[48]

Key Democrats, most especially Stephen Douglas and Lewis Cass—the chief proponents of popular sovereignty, feared for the governor's position. They knew that the future of popular sovereignty as a successful means of settling the slavery question—and a united Democratic party—hinged on the outcome of the Lecompton constitutional convention and the subsequent vote on the document it drafted. Not only did the governor need to make sure that Missourians did not cross the border and vote fraudulently, but he also needed to convince the free-state Kansans not to boycott the election as they had done in past canvasses. Douglas praised Walker's call for popular ratification of a state constitution, citing that his position "commanded the approbation of the whole country, with the exception of a small party at the South" who intended to make the new governor a "scape goat" for their dissatisfaction with the Buchanan administration.[49]

Like Douglas, Cass believed that Walker had to ensure a vote free of fraud in order to achieve stability in Kansas. At the same time, the secretary of state communicated with key southern allies in an effort to galvanize support for the administration and for true popular sovereignty in Kansas. Robert Toombs praised Cass for instructing Walker to ensure a fair vote on any prospective constitution, stating his belief that most southerners had no issue with submitting the constitution to a popular vote. "This course though not necessary to the validity of the act unless required by lawfull [sic] authority," he wrote to Cass, "yet, is more conformable to the more recent practice, & under the peculiar circumstances of Kansas I should consider the most prudent & proper policy." Walker, however, had committed an error that southerners could not ignore. "He has usurped the authority to decide what people, what voters shall have the right to vote on this constitution." Toombs insisted that the territorial legislature—elected by the people themselves—possessed the right to determine who could or could not vote in the election. As a federal appointee, Walker's course was "in direct contravention of the doctrine of non-interference." Popular sovereignty could not prevail with the governor's interference. "Shall he fix the qualifications of voters in Kansas," Toombs asked, "or shall the people in Kansas be free to form their institutions according to their own will?"[50]

Under the guise of regaining their strict constitutional scruples, but in reality merely seeking to give the upper hand to the threatened proslavery Lecompton faction in Kansas, radical southerners averred that the constitutional convention itself had the sovereign authority to approve the document. Of course, they chose this tactic because the proslavery forces firmly controlled the convention. Likewise, the ultras knew that a majority of the bona fide voters of Kansas opposed the extension of slavery to their territory. Once again, a fight had ensued over the means by which popular sovereignty would operate. And it had nothing to do with the wishes of the citizens of Kansas Territory; it had everything to do with the battle over slavery and its future in the West—and the battle for sectional supremacy. Now southern fire-eaters advanced their most disingenuous position on popular sovereignty; by rejecting Walker's call for a free and fair election and instead endorsing the fiat of a constitutional convention, the radicals verily proclaimed that they sought to establish slavery in Kansas regardless of the popular will.

Southerners like Toombs and Keitt undoubtedly realized that the popular vote in Kansas would reject a proslavery constitution, but if the constitutional convention and the territorial legislature ratified the document, slavery would almost certainly prevail. The opponents of squatter sovereignty had once focused on the right of territorial legislatures to prohibit slavery; now they expanded their criticism to the dishonest proposition that popular ratification of a constitution constituted squatter sovereignty. The *Dred Scott* decision had not ended the popular sovereignty debate; it had inaugurated a perverse debate over the meaning of democracy and the future of slavery in the West. At the same time, it ushered in a new era in southern politics as the radicals, with their increasingly convoluted positions on territorial independence and state making had exiled themselves from the Jeffersonian-Jacksonian political mainstream.

Cass anguished over how to address Toombs's concerns. The Buchanan administration scarcely needed another prominent critic of its policy toward Kansas, but it desperately needed southern allies. In a stunning repudiation of the Buchanan administration and the Democratic establishment, Democratic state conventions in three southern states had already passed no-confidence resolutions against Walker. The *New York Herald* called the conventions a dec-

laration of "open war" between the southern ultra Democrats and the administration. Cass conferred with Secretary of the Treasury Howell Cobb, who advised him to reply that "we do not approve of any dictation to the people of
Kansas about the qualification of voters & that Walker himself in his communi-
cations disclaims such purpose." Jefferson Davis praised Cass for his services to
the southern states in dealing with the Walker imbroglio, even as he warned
him that Congress would have to approve of the Kansas constitution, a subtle
implication that southerners had all but abandoned the principle of popular sovereignty and Democratic party allegiance when the future of their peculiar institution lay in the balance. Surely southerners would define fraud liberally; if the
constitutional convention wrote an antislavery charter, the South would cry foul.
"The game is now plain," the president wrote while on vacation in Bedford
Springs, Pennsylvania. "The assaults on Walker were intended to reach the administration."[51]

Some southerners had indeed grown impatient with Buchanan's handling of
the affairs in Kansas. Once again, they argued that the northern wing of the
Democratic Party had reneged on past promises made to the South. Popular
sovereignty in Kansas seemed on the brink of becoming a repeat of what happened in California seven years earlier, when a group of antislavery squatters—
according to southerners—had taken control of the territorial government,
drafted an antislavery constitution, and stealthily gained admission to the Union
as a free state. Southerners in the states as well as in Kansas called for restrictions on voting rights in the territory to ensure that only bona fide settlers had a
voice in the formation of a constitution—precisely the position that Walker had
taken when calling for the constitutional referendum! Yet Toombs repeated his
claims that Walker had engaged in "executive interference with the popular will
in Kansas," a direct attack on President Buchanan's policy. Not all southerners
openly criticized Buchanan and the popular sovereignty policy. According to a
South Carolinian residing in Kansas who advanced yet another position on the
mechanics of popular sovereignty, the southern settlers supported popular ratification of the state constitution, but "with a restriction, requiring at least, six
months residence in the Territory, so as to cut out all those who are denomi-
nated here as the 'carpet sack gentry' from the North, who have doubtless been
imported by the aid societies."[52]

During the contentious summer of 1857, the Buchanan administration stood
firm on popular sovereignty and behind Governor Walker. Events in Kansas,
however, continued to deteriorate. The free-state shadow government head-

quartered some twenty miles west of Lecompton in Topeka resolved to do everything in its power to disrupt the work of the Lecompton convention. They had refused to take part in the June election of delegates to the constitutional convention, but participated in the fall election of a new territorial legislature and won control of the body. Incensed at the results of the election, the proslavery Lecompton constitutional convention finished work on a proslavery constitution in November. Having first resolved to submit their work directly to Congress and ignore Governor Walker's instructions to seek popular ratification, the delegates relented at the behest of moderates who forged a compromise plan. The Lecompton convention would submit the seventh article of the charter—which addressed the slavery issue—to voters for ratification. Voters could choose a constitution with slavery or without slavery, the convention contended. Actually, Kansans had no such choice. If they approved the slavery article, Kansas would become a slave state complete with a slave code akin to that of Missouri and Kentucky. Rejection of the article would prohibit the future importation of slaves, but would not affect the status of slaves currently residing in the territory. One way or the other, slavery would remain in Kansas.

The Lecompton constitution presented northern Democrats with a dilemma. If they rejected the convention's version of ratification, the South would erupt in opposition to federal interference in the affairs of Kansas. If they accepted popular sovereignty Lecompton style, they would face the wrath of voters at home. Either outcome would cause an irreparable breach between the northern and southern wings of their party. In his first annual message to Congress, the president declared that the Lecompton convention had "fairly and explicitly referred to the people whether they will have a constitution 'with or without slavery,'" therefore complying with the principle of popular sovereignty. But either way the people of Kansas voted, the slaves already in the territory and their issue would remain enslaved. By endorsing only partial submission of the Lecompton constitution to the people, Buchanan had reneged on the spirit, if not the letter, of his promise to ensure a free and equitable constitutional election. "Looking back, knowing the ultimate consequences of Buchanan's policy decision," one historian has remarked, "it stands as one of the most tragic miscalculations any President has ever made."[53]

Some consequences of Buchanan's endorsement of the Lecompton convention became immediately apparent. Douglas leapt to his feet after the Senate clerk had finished reading the president's message, announcing his opposition to the administration's course regarding Lecompton. The following day, the Illinois senator delivered a speech on the Senate floor, rebuking Buchanan for his startling and demoralizing endorsement of the Lecompton convention. The man whom some had predicted would become the "great pacificator between the policy of the administration and the uncompromising attitude of hostility assumed by Governor Walker" broke with his president. The proslavery convention's prescription for ratification threatened to make a mockery of popular sovereignty, Douglas argued, by submitting only a part of the constitution to the people for a vote. If "the President be right in saying that, by the Nebraska bill, the slavery question must be submitted to the people, it follows inevitably that every other clause of the constitution must also be submitted to the people."[54]

Douglas saved his most vituperative criticism for the manner in which the convention delegates had framed the question of whether slavery would or would not exist in Kansas. To him and many northerners, the convention gave Kansans no choice at all; regardless of the outcome of the vote slavery would remain. "Is that the mode in which I am called upon to carry out the principle of self-government and popular sovereignty in the Territories—to force a constitution on the people against their will," Douglas asked. The indignant senator had broken with the president in bold fashion, completely scorning and discrediting Buchanan's motives and actions with respect to the Lecompton fiasco. Douglas took the matter personally, believing that the administration had perverted his popular sovereignty doctrine. "I have spent too much strength and breath, and health, too," Douglas declared before his fellow senators, "to establish this great principle in the popular heart, now to see it frittered away." The Little Giant's break with Buchanan "plunged the party into confusion and consternation," as leaders sought to calculate their next step. Douglas particularly lamented the inevitable loss of his southern allies, but he believed that Buchanan's policy left him no other choice but to oppose the work of the Lecompton convention and risk the break with the South.[55]

Southern Democrats reacted with disgust at their erstwhile ally, hypocritically suggesting that Douglas discredited his own doctrine by attempting to dictate to Kansans how they should ratify their own constitution. Indeed, ultra southerners had done precisely the same when they rejected a plebiscite on the constitution and affirmed Congress's right to reject the document if necessary. "It is with regret," a Baltimore editor wrote, "that we find this distinguished man now, at this moment, when he should be firm in support of his own measure, deliberately arraying himself against it, and virtually declaring that the Kansas-Nebraska act is a failure." "That Senator Douglas is in and with the Northern party," the *Charleston Mercury* maintained, "is no longer questioned." John Tyler declared his dismay with Douglas's break with the president, arguing like many other southerners that the Illinois senator had basically invalidated his own doctrine. "Douglas, I see, has taken ground against the Lecompton Convention, and yet nothing is plainer than that, by his own admission, the convention was the creation of the popular will, as far as the voting class could make it so, and that is the only standard to which we can refer."[56]

Voters in Kansas did receive the chance to vote on the entire Lecompton constitution, but only after some complicated maneuvering by Acting Governor Frederick Stanton. Walker had left Kansas for Washington, never to return, to plead his opposition to the Lecompton convention. Stanton let the initial election continue, but scheduled a second referendum in which residents would vote on the whole constitution and not just Article VII. On December 21, 1857, voters ratified the Lecompton constitution with the seventh article by a vote of 6,226–569. The free-state supporters boycotted the December election that they considered fraudulent. Southerners hailed news of the vote while the northern Democrats bided their time until the next canvass, when Kansans would vote on the entire document. On January 4, 1858, they voted en masse against ratification of the Lecompton constitution by the overwhelming vote of 10,226–162.[57] This time, the proslavery faction boycotted the election. The entire affair had caused irreparable damage to the president's reputation and to the stability of the Democratic party. Nonetheless, the Buchanan administration proceeded by referring the Lecompton constitution to Congress for ratification and disregarding the January 4 vote. The South, however, feared defeat at the hands of the anti-Lecompton Democrats. The administration's allies desperately tried to convince southerners that the Democratic Party remained the last bulwark of security for their section. Many in the South could not forgive Douglas's opposition to the Lecompton convention's handiwork. To their minds, Douglas had committed himself to squatter sovereignty just as Lewis Cass had during the debate over the Compromise of 1850. Douglas had finally shown his true colors. Southerners could no longer trust the Little Giant as a defender of their rights. Equally ominous, the vehement resistance from northern Democrats to the Lecompton constitution had shaken their trust in their party. Douglas and the northern Democracy had betrayed the South and her interests by interpreting popular sovereignty as an antislavery principle that would bar slaveholders from the plains of Kansas.[58]

By 1858, the last national political organization had divided along sectional lines, in no small part because North and South could no longer agree to disagree over the meaning of popular sovereignty. Douglas maintained his position, arguing that the January 4 vote had established conclusively that "the Lecompton Constitution is not the act of the people of Kansas, and that it does not embody the popular will of that Territory." Southern Democrats, too, vociferously defended the work of the Lecompton convention as a true embodiment of popular sovereignty. Congress thrust itself into one of the most heated deliberations in its history over admitting Kansas to statehood with the Lecompton constitution—the product of popular sovereignty and congressional nonintervention. In the lower house in particular, anti-Lecompton Democrats rebelled against the president, threatening to block the admission of Kansas. Southerners witnessed the proceedings with indignation. Governor Joseph E. Brown of Georgia declared, "If Kansas is rejected by a direct vote I can see no other course for Georgia to take but to stand by her rights, upon her platform, and act, or confess to the world that she has backed down from her solemn pledges."[59]

With Congress deadlocked, the Democracy all but destroyed as a viable national party, and threats of disunion surfacing, an Indiana Democrat developed an ingenious—if outrageous—means of circumventing the Lecompton crisis. A bill presented by Representative William H. English of Indiana would submit the Lecompton constitution to another popular vote after Congress intervened again changing the land grant provided to the territory. Under the English plan, voters would have the choice to gain statehood with slavery if they agreed to a vastly reduced federal land grant. If they opposed the change, Kansas would have to wait until it had a population of 93,000—the minimum population to gain a representative in Congress—to reapply for statehood. This farcical land grant subterfuge allowed Kansans to take another vote on the constitution, this time sanctioned by the federal government. Most politicians recognized that the Kansans would reject the constitution and delay admission.[60] Though radical southerners opposed the English bill, most moderates acquiesced owing to the fact that the Lecompton constitution would inevitably fail in Congress.

The English bill, which passed Congress on April 30, 1858, allowed southern politicians to save face in some small way. Voters would not technically reject the constitution because of slavery, but because of the land grant reduction. On August 2, Kansans went to the polls yet again and resoundingly defeated the congressionally amended Lecompton constitution. Southerners lamely portrayed the English bill as a technical victory for the South. In the months after the Lecompton vote, Jefferson Davis made several speeches in Maine and in his home state of Mississippi lauding the English bill as a vindication of southern rights. Technically, according to Davis, Congress had admitted Kansas as a slave state. The Kansans themselves had rejected its offer of admission because of the terms stipulated for the circumscribed land grant. To Davis's mind, the English bill preserved the power of the Democratic Party by protecting equal rights for the South. The Mississippi senator's optimism did not obscure the incredibly weak bargain Congress had struck, but politicians saw no better way to extricate themselves from the Kansas imbroglio.[61]

ONE COULD ARGUE that popular sovereignty actually worked in Kansas because a majority of bona fide settlers within the territory opposed the institution of slavery and when it became the thirty-fourth state on January 29, 1861, Kansas entered the Union under an antislavery constitution. The *outcome* may have represented the will of the people, but the *process* proved catastrophic. The interminable conflict over the meaning of popular sovereignty itself, and its meaning for the future of slavery in the territories destroyed the bisectional unity of the Democratic Party—and ultimately contributed in a fundamental way to sectionalism and ultimately disunion. Northern and southern Democrats had so alienated one another over the meaning of the very principle that was to remove the slavery question from national politics that both sides ended up losing. Northerners lost a national political coalition that had managed, if not neutralized, the slavery controversy since the 1830s. Southerners, whom Calhoun had correctly perceived as a minority within American politics by mid-century, had alienated and lost key northern allies. Few doughfaces remained in Congress after 1858. Southern radicals could cry foul, blame the abolitionists for stoking antislavery fervor, damn popular sovereignty as an antislavery weapon, and threaten disunion as they pleased—and they did—but their minority cadre no longer had any allies in the North. Only one recourse seemed to remain: unite the entire South under a states' rights, proslavery banner that would question the value of Union itself.[62]

Meanwhile, Republicans saw Democratic discord and southern separatism as manna from heaven. For four years they had condemned the Kansas-Nebraska Act as the violation of a sacred compact—the Missouri Compromise—and had heaped scorn on popular sovereignty as a proslavery contrivance. But the way in which popular sovereignty played out in Kansas gave them a victory greater than if the sacred compact had survived. The debate over popular sovereignty had divided the Democracy, galvanized Republican ranks, and still had not opened Kansas to slavery. As southerners abandoned the doctrine en masse, and as the Democratic Party slouched toward Charleston and its unceremonious final curtain at the national convention of 1860, the Republicans stood poised for victory. The demise of popular sovereignty had provided that opportunity. Americans would again govern themselves and elect Abraham Lincoln president. And the war came.

Epilogue

The Demise of Popular Sovereignty
and the Crisis of the Union

By the fateful election year of 1860, the issue of popular sovereignty and the extension of slavery into the western territories had well nigh destroyed any semblance of unity in the Democratic Party, the last national political organization binding North and South together. Northern Democrats insisted they would no longer truckle to the southern wing of their party, while southern Democrats denounced their former allies for embracing the antislavery cause. For the South, the disruption of the Democracy acutely boded ill, as the organization had long connected slaveholders and states' rights advocates with key northern allies. But southerners heaped special scorn upon Stephen Douglas; his condemnation of the Lecompton constitution thoroughly discredited the senator among the South's Democratic faithful. Many of them resolved to crush his presidential aspirations in the upcoming canvass. In fact, Douglas had misread the situation in both sections of the country. He correctly perceived that northern Democrats no longer would protect southern interests at their own political peril, yet he still clung to his ambiguous version of popular sovereignty, believing that moderate northerners and southerners could ultimately prevail in the crisis over the extension of slavery—and the crisis of the Union. Southern Democrats, however, flatly refused to compromise on the doctrine once the Supreme Court had sanctioned the southern version of popular sovereignty. If Douglas believed he could restore the doctrine's bisectional appeal, he did so in vain. Once defined, popular sovereignty became a rigid principle that divided northern and southern Democrats.

Southerners, however, had found no security in their victory over the meaning of popular sovereignty. Implacable resistance from Republicans—and much hostility from northern Democrats—had led a growing number of southerners to endorse a federal slave code for the territories. For much of the 1850s, southern radicals had seemingly cast aside their states' rights scruples, demanding that the federal government uphold the right of slaveholders to carry their human chattel to the western territories. Paradoxically, the ultras now argued that only federal law could preserve the doctrine of states' rights. Republicans cried that the southern victory in *Dred Scott* had shattered the myth of states' rights ideology by using the Constitution to support the Calhounite theory that slavery followed the flag.[1] Opposition to popular sovereignty southern-style had negated any benefit that slaveholders might have gained from the Supreme Court's 1857 ruling. They believed that regardless of Supreme Court pronouncements or the blandishments of the few northern Democrats who remained tied to a political system passing into history, the South had lost the battle over the extension of slavery, the meaning of popular sovereignty in the territories, and their vision of a confederated nation based on the principles of states' rights and localism.

STEPHEN DOUGLAS, who had invested so much in the ideal of self-government, continued to defend popular sovereignty as the only way to ensure the safety of the Union and the preservation of the Democratic Party. Desperately clinging to his favored principle, the Little Giant continued to promote a "strict adherence to the doctrine of popular sovereignty and non intervention by Congress with slavery in the territories as well as in the states" long after Kansas. Douglas made a mockery of the former and Congress and flagrantly violated the latter. Southerners who had once vigorously supported the Illinois senator now abandoned him, and they now viewed popular sovereignty as an antislavery doctrine. Desperately hoping to save his party—and his career— Douglas drafted a lengthy article for *Harper's Magazine* in September 1859, in which he defined popular sovereignty in the context of American political history. The Supreme Court had effectively gutted Douglas's formula for popular sovereignty by endorsing the southern interpretation of the doctrine, but now the Illinois senator resolved to challenge the Court's decision and justify his conception of popular sovereignty.[2]

In addition to the *Dred Scott* decision, another political factor motivated Douglas to write a defense of popular sovereignty. After the failure of the Lecompton Constitution, some Republicans had taken to the doctrine with an enthusiasm that troubled Douglas and the Democrats. Like southerners, they recognized that popular sovereignty had become an effective tool to prevent the spread of slavery, in no small part because it had prevented slavery from taking root in Kansas. In 1859, some Republicans called for an extreme version of popular sovereignty that would have allowed territorial residents to elect their own governor and judges, presumably to prevent the proslavery Buchanan administration from appointing officials sympathetic to slavery. Douglas recognized that if he had any hope of resurrecting popular sovereignty from the ashes of the Kansas conflagration, he had to neutralize this new Republican threat.[3]

Douglas had a reputation as a brilliant speaker and master debater, but "The Dividing Line between Local and Federal Authority" lacked his characteristic verve and logic. In forty pages of labored prose, the Little Giant presented his case for popular sovereignty. After laying out its different interpretations, Douglas launched into a history lesson designed to show that his doctrine upheld the central tenet of the nation's Revolutionary fathers—the right of the people to govern themselves. America's forebears had fought for independence to gain "Local Self-Government" in order to "make their own local laws, form their own domestic institutions, and manage their own internal affairs in their own way." The founders recognized that a "diversity of interests" regarding slavery existed and that only through compromise could the thirteen states join in a Union. Popular sovereignty, Douglas implied, had facilitated the creation of the Union itself by leaving the matter of slavery to local communities.[4]

For far too long, Douglas argued, the federal government had ignored the wisdom of its fathers by meddling in the local affairs of the territories. The Compromise of 1850 and the Kansas-Nebraska Act had restored the nation to its constitutional moorings, but the *Dred Scott* decision—or at least the interpretation others gave to it—threatened all that Douglas and the Democrats had gained. He asserted that the decision did not affect popular sovereignty in the territories, a contention that was easily dismissed by his critics. The Supreme Court had unquestionably challenged Douglas's contention that territorial legislatures could pass laws prohibiting slavery. On some occasions, most notably the Lincoln-Douglas Debates of 1858, the Illinoisan had fallen back on an idea that became known as the Freeport Doctrine, arguing that slavery could not exist where the people did not provide laws and aid for its protection. Other politicians had articulated the idea long before Douglas, but his statement gained immediate attention and prompt disdain from the South. Nonetheless, although Southern ultras would not admit it, they implicitly believed him. They concluded that if local communities would not respect the rights of slaveholders, the federal government would have to use its authority via a territorial slave code. In the *Harper's* article, however, Douglas moved away from the Freeport Doctrine and tried to portray the *Dred Scott* decision as sympathetic toward his version of popular sovereignty.[5]

The Douglas essay, with its all-too-familiar recitation of the dispute over popular sovereignty and its utter lack of new insight into the crisis, failed to persuade any of the senator's opponents. Indeed, they clamored for the chance to refute Douglas's argument. These rejoinders, gathered with Douglas's *Harper's* article, offer a panoramic view of the issue on which the presidential election of 1860 would turn: slavery in the territories. The southern Democratic press condemned the Illinois senator's defense of squatter sovereignty—as they viewed it—as "false in theory as it would be dangerous in practice should it ever be established as the policy of this government." The *Richmond Enquirer* labeled it an "incendiary document" designed to pacify antislavery northerners. Southerners now viewed the Douglas version, which had become poisoned by his Freeport Doctrine, as an antislavery tool that would deprive the South of "all her rights in the territories."[6]

Just as southern Democrats excoriated Douglas, so too did the Republicans, who accused the senator of ignoring both the will of the antislavery northerners and the moral crime inherent in perpetuating slavery. Horace Greeley, the editor of the *New York Tribune*, asserted that most Americans wanted to halt the spread of slavery into the territories rather than resurrect "a politician's dodge" designed to prevent sectional discord through a false sense of compromise. "The Sovereignty you defer to, is that of a political necessity, not that of the people of the Territories," Greeley charged. The editor took issue with Douglas's revisionist interpretation of history; for example, he used Thomas Jefferson's proposed Ordinance of 1784 to prove that the founding generation instituted popular sovereignty in the territories—or "new states," as Jefferson called them. Douglas did not admit, Greeley correctly noted, that the ordinance would have abolished slavery in any of the territories after 1800, completely ignoring Jefferson's proposal for gradual abolition in any states created out of the national domain. Likewise, Greeley claimed, Douglas glossed over precedents for federal legislation over slavery in the territories. In the Ordinance of 1784 and the Northwest Ordinance of 1787, Greeley concluded, history gave "two explicit affirmations by the Revolutionary Fathers, of the right and duty of Congressional Inhibition of slavery in the Territories."[7]

Southern Democratic stalwarts who had lashed out at Douglas after his break with the Buchanan administration found an ally in Attorney General Jeremiah Sullivan Black, who drafted a response to the popular sovereignty dispute that would have satisfied all but the most ardent southern radicals. The attorney general's rebuttal outlined the position that most southerners held after the failure of the Lecompton Constitution. Black, too, questioned Douglas's interpretation of history, but for far different reasons than Horace Greeley. The nation's history provided no precedent for the power of territorial legislatures to prohibit slavery, as Douglas asserted, or for congressional intervention, as Greeley argued. Focusing on the legal aspects of the popular sovereignty question, Black maintained that "the Constitution certainly does not *establish* slavery in the Territories, nor anywhere else. But the Constitution regards as sacred and inviolable all the rights which a citizen may legally acquire in a State." The Constitution was impartial on slavery in the territories, requiring both slaves and freedmen "to remain in *statu quo* until the *status* already impressed upon them by the law of their previous domicil [*sic*] shall be changed by some local competent authority," namely a constitutional convention.[8]

Not only did Black support the decision in *Dred Scott v. Sandford*, which upheld the right of an American citizen to hold slaves in any federal territory, but his words lent credence to the Calhoun theory that slavery followed the flag. Republicans, whom the attorney general called a "little band of ribald infidels," refused to abide by the decision. Douglas, too, seemed insistent on rejecting the definition supplied by the Supreme Court in favor of his view that territorial legislatures could prohibit slavery. Seemingly in an effort to turn back the clock to 1856, Black articulated the position southerners had held before the Lecompton fiasco had demonstrated that they had moved beyond that assertion—only a constitutional convention could determine the future of slavery within a territory preparing for admission to the Union. He accused Douglas of ignoring his own doctrine with respect to the Lecompton Constitution, for he had rejected the vote of a plebiscite on the slavery provision in the constitution because the convention did not allow popular ratification of the entire document. After the failure of Lecompton, the senator insisted that the territorial legislature could determine the status of slavery without submission of the question to the people. "Popular sovereignty in the last Congress meant the freedom of the people from all the restraints of law and order; now it means a government which shall rule them with a rod of iron," Black wrote. "It swings like a pendulum from one side clear over to the other."[9]

In pointing out the inconsistencies of Douglas's argument, Black advanced the southern contention that the Constitution protected the sanctity of personal property—including slavery—in the national domain. Southerners had felt vindicated after the *Dred Scott* decision, but the unrelenting assault on slavery by the North, especially by Republicans, led them to realize that popular sovereignty would never sufficiently secure their rights or guarantee the extension of slavery. Douglas's rejection of the Lecompton Constitution and his subsequent alienation from Buchanan Democrats convinced many southerners that popular sovereignty was at bottom and in essence an antislavery doctrine. Squatter sovereignty had triumphed over the true doctrine of popular sovereignty, according to the South. "Squatter Sovereignty," a New Orleans editor declared in 1860, "looks to *permanent exclusion* by hostile Territorial legislation."[10]

With northerners unwilling to accept the pro-southern popular sovereignty formula mandated by the *Dred Scott* decision and many fire-eaters shifting away from even Taney's definition of the doctrine, southerners believed they had but one alternative: to demand federal protection for slavery in the territories. Some ultra southerners had endorsed federal protection in the past, but most southerners repudiated the idea, instead standing by their conception of popular sovereignty. The hypocrisy of advocating a territorial slave code premised on congressional intervention in territorial governance deterred some southerners, but radicals bowed to changing circumstances by positing that the sanctity of states' rights and property necessitated federal action. On January 18, 1860, Albert Gallatin Brown, a Democratic senator from Mississippi, delivered a series of resolutions calling for federal protection of slavery in the territories and specifically demanding a federal slave code that would guarantee the sanctity of slave property in any territory. Two weeks later, Senator Jefferson Davis introduced a less bellicose set of resolutions affirming the constitutional right to hold slaves in the territories. Mississippi's other senator did not call for a federal slave code or for active federal intervention against antislavery forces in the territories, but insisted that the Senate use its power to "resist all efforts to discriminate" against slaveholders' rights in the territories. Regardless of the debate over the necessity and scope of a federal slave code, southerners clearly expressed their belief that popular sovereignty no longer offered them protection for slavery in the national domain.[11]

The debate played out over the spring and summer of 1860 in the cities of Charleston, Baltimore, Chicago, and Richmond, as partisans gathered in convention to select nominees for president. By the end of June, the last remnants of the old second party system would lay in tatters as a sectional campaign emerged between four men vying for the presidency. And whether addressed

HON. WILLIAM L. YANCEY.

By 1860, Alabama Senator William Lowndes Yancey led the radical southern vanguard against presidential candidate Stephen A. Douglas—and ultimately against a united Democracy. (Library of Congress)

implicitly or explicitly, slavery in the territories stood as the pivotal issue in each convention. First came the Democrats, who congregated in the sweltering city of Charleston to select a platform and standard-bearer. Stephen Douglas very much wanted the nomination; southerners desperately want to deny it to him. Alabamian William Lowndes Yancey set the tone for the southern repudiation of Douglas, describing him and his allies as "corrupt and abolitionized." Like ostriches, he went on, they buried their heads "in the sand of squatter sovereignty" unaware that "their great ugly, ragged abolition body was exposed."[12] The southern Democrats who came to Charleston remained convinced that their erstwhile northern allies had abandoned the rule of law and sectional comity by refusing to accept popular sovereignty as defined by the Taney court. In this respect, they argued, Douglas Democrats had practically gone over to the Republican side. As for Douglas, he had worked tirelessly to galvanize support among his northern allies for his version of popular sovereignty. He gained crucial support in the Old Northwest as well as in the chaotic New York caucus. In the end Douglas had only obtained enough support to produce a simple majority in his favor at Charleston, which fell far short of the longstanding Democratic tradition of a necessary two-thirds vote.

Meanwhile, the southern Democrats maneuvered for advantage. Seven state delegations threatened to withdraw from the convention should Douglas receive the nomination; four other states threatened at least partial withdrawal. With the Lecompton debacle and Douglas's Freeport Doctrine fresh in their minds, the southerners vowed to destroy Douglas's presidential aspirations, and they were prepared to demand enhanced protection for slavery in the territories. Although moderate southerners remained steadfast in their interpretation of popular sovereignty, it had become a moot point as radicals like Yancey had succeeded in convincing a majority of southern delegates that popular sovereignty equaled the end of slavery in the territories. Northern Democrats insisted that territorial legislatures possessed the sovereign power to prohibit slavery, and that the remaining territories would indeed prohibit the institution. By the convention's third day, southern delegates had not only rejected the "popular sovereignty heresy," but also threatened to withdraw if it remained in the platform.[13]

Over the course of forty years, the debate over slavery and the territories and the rightful interpretation of popular sovereignty had increasingly become constitutionalized, pitting competing notions of sovereignty and Union against one another. The battle within the Democracy had distilled the disagreement over popular sovereignty and the future of slavery into a simple form: Stephen

Douglas and the northern Democrats portrayed the southern assault on their doctrine as an assault on democracy itself, while southern Democrats believed that without positive protection for slavery in the territories, their liberty, rights, and way of life became imperiled. The crisis played out on the convention floor, as southern Democrats endorsed a platform report that affirmed the finality of the *Dred Scott* decision and reiterated the southern interpretation of popular sovereignty. Sovereignty commenced when the territories had sufficient population to draft a constitution; before that time, all citizens had an equal right to settle therein with slave property without the interference of either Congress or a territorial legislature. Finally, and perhaps most controversially, the report called on the federal government "to protect, when necessary, the rights of persons and property in the Territories."[14]

Douglas Democrats responded with their own platform report, which frankly admitted the party's serious divisions over popular sovereignty, but lamely addressed them by promising to "abide by the Supreme Court of the United States upon these questions of Constitutional law." Until then, the report reaffirmed the principle of popular sovereignty as defined in the party's 1856 platform. At this point, the convention descended into a cavalcade of speech-making; "one dull fellow after another" took the floor to speak on the competing reports and filibuster the coming vote that would likely end with the adoption of the northern resolutions. The substance of the southern position, however, became clear as delegates from the southern states lambasted the northerners' report, declaring that they no longer found security in the equivocations of Stephen A. Douglas and his northern allies. Even Murat Halstead, the intrepid convention correspondent from Ohio, decried the northern report as a "miserable and cowardly evasion." "Now, the majority report is at least tolerably honest," he wrote. "You can tell what it means." The northern Democrats had tried in vain to restore the ambiguity of popular sovereignty. Moreover, their call to abide by the decision of the Supreme Court rang hollow; after all, Taney and his associates made their position clear in 1857. Nevertheless, Douglas succeeded at securing victory for the northern report. Having won the battle, he then proceeded to lose the war. The delegations of South Carolina and the five Gulf South states withdrew from the convention. The southerners had bolted, while the northerners left Charleston on May 3 deadlocked and without a nominee. The disruption of the Democracy had finally come.[15]

Six weeks later, the Democrats reconvened in Baltimore in an attempt to salvage the remains of their shattered party. But when the Baltimore delegates refused to seat the Charleston seceders, Virginia and the Border State delegations promptly withdrew from the convention floor. Douglas received his nomination, but the makeup of the convention made unmistakably clear that he solely represented Democrats from the North. Even the candidate himself recognized the nature of his nomination, though he tried to put forth the semblance of unity. In a letter to the delegates charged with notifying Douglas of his nomination, he wrote that he had received "authentic evidence of my nomination by the [Regular] National convention of the Democratic Party." Douglas had crossed out the word Regular, indicating the schism that had breached the party, and replaced it with the word National.[16]

The southerners who had seceded from the Charleston Convention ultimately styled themselves as Constitutional Democrats, wholly opposed to popular sovereignty Douglas-style and committed to a territorial slave code. At their first, and ultimately unsuccessful, convention in Richmond, Virginia, which eleven months later would become the capital of the Confederacy, delegates railed against the Douglas Democrats. "The serpent of 'Squatter Sovereignty' must be strangled," one delegate cried. "What! are we to be told that we are not to go into the Territories and enjoy equal rights, when that principle has been settled by the Supreme Court of our country?"[17] Therein lay the problem for the Democratic Party: since 1850 they had prayed for the Supreme Court to define popular sovereignty. But northern Democrats despised and ignored Roger Taney's opinion. Meanwhile at Lecompton, southern Democrats had so perversely manipulated even their own version of popular sovereignty that bona fide Kansans could not choose a constitution of their own will. Answered prayers and gross manipulation had made a mockery of popular sovereignty.

The Democratic Party's fracture, and the coalescence of southern party regulars as Constitutional Democrats with John C. Breckinridge as their standard-bearer, did not necessarily bode well for the South and its interests. For a generation, southern Democrats had relied on a party structure that maintained political allegiances across the Mason-Dixon line. Furthermore, the arrangement had accentuated southern power by linking proslavery southerners with doughfaced northerners indifferent to the institution. From the vantage point of 1860, however, precious little of the old order remained. A series of events beginning with the Lecompton debacle and the split over popular sovereignty's meaning had shattered a thirty-year political compact, as slave-state Democrats could no longer claim that their party alliances would protect southern rights. Democratic strength in the South had relied on intersectional unity; now it seemed that bisectional party politics might well imperil the future of the South in the Union.[18]

Republicans fully expected to capitalize on the disruption of the Democracy and the fluid if not chaotic status of presidential politics. By summer, two contests had ensued: in the South, Constitutional Democrat John Breckinridge opposed the elderly Constitutional Unionist John Bell, a man and a party devoted to silencing the discord over slavery and restoring national unity. Indeed, the Constitutional Unionist platform made no mention of slavery in the territories or popular sovereignty; the topics hardly came up at their convention. In the North, Stephen Douglas battled against his old adversary Abraham Lincoln. The Republican platform emphatically rejected popular sovereignty as an affront to the antislavery designs of the founding fathers and derided the Taney court's definition of the doctrine as a "dangerous political heresy."[19] Republicans presented a united front at their Chicago convention and thereafter during the canvass, but once Lincoln won the election in November 1860, fissures appeared in their position.

Lincoln had long committed himself to halting the extension of slavery into the territories, and he had likewise dismissed popular sovereignty as a gross misrepresentation of the principle of self-government. Especially since Douglas had published his lengthy defense of the doctrine in *Harper's Magazine* and Lincoln had replied to it with contempt, it had become clear that the two men held fundamentally differing notions of how the founding generation had viewed the future of slavery. Whereas Douglas believed that the founders left the issue to local communities, Lincoln believed they had charted a path for its extinction by restricting it to the states where it had already existed. Indeed, to the minds of Lincoln and many of his fellow Republicans, popular sovereignty hardly upheld local self-government; it instead paved the way for the nationalization of the institution. Of course these differences had surfaced and become salient during the 1858 Lincoln-Douglas debates.[20]

But as the secession crisis wore on over the winter of 1860–1861, some Republicans called for at least a modicum of conciliation to aid southern Unionists in their opposition to immediate secession. And here during the secession winter, popular sovereignty breathed its last gasp as moderate Republicans looked for ways to keep the border states in the Union and thereby stem the tide of disunion. In late 1860, several factions emerged within Lincoln's party. Radical Republicans demanded that the president-elect and his circle of advisors stand firm against southern threats. But a group of moderates encouraged party leaders to offer some form of compromise, especially with respect to slavery in the territories, that would strengthen southern Unionists. By December 1860, Republicans both inside and outside of Washington had divided in support of or opposition to compromise.

More substantively, the young party had divided between those who believed the time had finally arrived to return the nation to its revolutionary heritage—as they defined it—and those who desired first to save the Union. By December, a sort of stalemate had emerged where conservative unionists in all the political parties sought to put the Crittenden compromise—with its restoration of the Missouri Compromise line and imposition of a federal slave code—to a popular referendum, but they were stymied by radical Republicans and southern ultras who opposed all compromises or pragmatic conciliation. Seeking to find middle ground, a committee of congressmen proposed a plan originally conceived by a Pennsylvania Republican that prohibited federal interference with slavery in the territories and instituted the southern version of popular sovereignty south of 36 degrees, 30 minutes. The Border State plan initially enjoyed support from moderate Republicans and southern Unionists, even though the latter preferred the Crittenden compromise. The ongoing stalemate between Confederate officials and the Buchanan administration over federal property in the southern states provoked fierce resistance among the Republicans; on January 7, when the Border State plan came up for a vote on the House floor, most Republicans abandoned it and the impetus for compromise.[21]

Despite the failure of the Border State plan, the debate revealed that some Republicans had taken to popular sovereignty as a means to preserve the Union. In an irony not lost on the doctrine's greatest champion, Stephen A. Douglas, moderate Republicans saw value in using popular sovereignty to assuage southern Unionists by upholding their states' rights constitutional scruples. At the same time, few if any Republicans believed that slavery would take root in the remaining territorial domain. Therein lay one of the two problems that beset the supporters of popular sovereignty in the secession crisis: Republicans recognized that popular sovereignty had become an effective tool to prevent the spread of slavery. But so too did southerners, which thereby rendered its use in a compromise formula fatal to any accord. The second problem came with the realization that moderate Republicans held little sway within their party. Even the most prominent Republican compromiser, secretary of state-designate William H. Seward, found his efforts to promote compromise stymied by the more radical wing of his party—and by President-elect Lincoln.[22]

The creation of three territories in the West just before Lincoln's inauguration proved that popular sovereignty had essentially become a guarantor of free
soil. In February, Congress voted to create three new territories in the West—
Colorado, Dakota, and Nevada. The enabling bills for each territory contained
no reference to slavery, a development that Stephen Douglas saw as an oblique
endorsement of popular sovereignty. Dakota Territory presented an interesting
case, being the last unorganized region within the Louisiana Purchase. Before
1857, the Missouri Compromise would have prohibited slavery within the territory, but the Supreme Court's invalidation of the compromise line mooted discussion of that legal technicality.[23]

Republicans in Congress had worked diligently to remove any shadow of a
doubt that slavery would never exist in the new territories. The bills had initially
contained language affirming the popular sovereignty principle, much akin to
the clause in the Kansas-Nebraska Act. Key Republican senators removed the
clause, however, in order to gain passage of the separate bills. Senator Benjamin
Wade, an influential Ohio Republican, revealed the reason: party factions within
both the House and Senate could not agree on the meaning of popular sovereignty. Accordingly, negotiators from both chambers agreed to remove the offending clause and remain silent on the slavery issue within the three bills.[24]

Douglas tried valiantly to save some remnant of his cherished doctrine, but
key Republicans as well as Douglas's Democratic opponents stripped the bills of
any overt reference to his version of popular sovereignty. In a carefully designed blow aimed at the Supreme Court, the Senate amended the bills to deny
the right of appeal to the Supreme Court on property issues. They sent a clear
message that Congress would not allow the Taney court to exercise its power of
judicial review to permit slavery in Colorado, Dakota, or Nevada. Again Douglas
opposed the amendment, calling out the Republicans for their effort to circumscribe the authority of the southern-dominated Supreme Court and enhance the
power of President-elect Lincoln. Republicans could play the political game to
their advantage now, Douglas averred, "but suppose, four years from now, there
should be a southern President; then are we to be called upon to change the law
again, to give a right of appeal from the territorial judges to the Supreme Court
of the United States? Are we to change the law and the territorial system according as the politics of the President may be changed?"[25]

Douglas suffered a final blow to his conception of popular sovereignty in the
territorial bills of 1860-1861, but in a way, the bills contained the idea of popular
sovereignty in its purest form. None of the three bills addressed the slavery is-

sue with regard to the powers of territorial legislatures or the judiciary. Slavery received no mention in the legislation, presumably leaving the matter to the people of the territories. Neither Congress nor the Supreme Court had a charge to implement or interpret popular sovereignty. Most important to the South, nobody believed that slavery would exist for a day within Colorado, Dakota, or Nevada. The territorial debate during the secession winter of 1860–1861 provided still more confirmation that popular sovereignty would not provide southerners with what they demanded—more slave states.

By now southern secessionists believed that northerners had corrupted the principle of self-government in the states, in no small part because they had corrupted self-government in the territories. Hindsight shows, however, that both northerners and southerners had transformed their ideas on the extension of slavery and the idea of popular sovereignty in numerous and labyrinthine ways to meet immediate political circumstances. By 1861, North and South stood for two different aims; the South demanded the perpetuation of slavery with federal protection, while the North stood for the eradication of the peculiar institution. Perhaps no better illustration of the chasm that had grown between North and South over popular sovereignty and the extension than the constitution of the Confederate States of America, ratified just seven days after the inauguration of Abraham Lincoln. In many ways, the document preserved the essence of republicanism as defined in the Constitution of 1787, but the emergent vision of southern republicanism placed slavery at its center. It also defined what for all intents and purposes became the Confederate version of popular sovereignty. Article Four, Section Three of the Confederate constitution gave Congress power "to dispose of and make all needful rules and regulations concerning the property of the Confederate States, including the lands thereof," a clear repudiation of the ambiguous "needful rules and regulations" clause of the U.S. Constitution. More importantly, the Confederate constitution provided that slavery "shall be recognized and protected by Congress and by the Territorial government; and the inhabitants of the several Confederate States and Territories shall have the right to take to such Territory any slaves lawfully held by them in any of the States or Territories of the Confederate States." The framers of the Confederate constitution settled the issues concerning popular sovereignty and federal authority over slavery in the territories for their generation and generations to come by removing it from the purview of Congress and political parties. In a slaveholders' republic, popular sovereignty meant slavery.[26]

Notes

Introduction

1. See Glover Moore, *The Missouri Controversy, 1819–1821* (Lexington: University Press of Kentucky, 1953), and Robert Pierce Forbes, *The Missouri Compromise and Its Aftermath: Slavery and the Meaning of America* (Chapel Hill: University of North Carolina Press, 2007).

2. Don E. Fehrenbacher, *Sectional Crisis and Southern Constitutionalism* (Baton Rouge: Louisiana State University Press, 1995), 111. See also Austin Allen, *Origins of the Dred Scott Case: Jacksonian Jurisprudence and the Supreme Court* (Athens: University of Georgia Press, 2006), 178–202 and passim.

3. For works dealing with early struggles over the issue of slavery in the territories, see Donald L. Robinson, *Slavery and the Structure of American Politics, 1765–1820* (New York: Harcourt Brace Jovanovich, 1971), 378–423; John Craig Hammond, *Slavery, Freedom, and Expansion in the Early American West* (Charlottesville: University of Virginia Press, 2007); and Matthew Mason, *Slavery and Politics in the Early American Republic* (Chapel Hill: University of North Carolina Press, 2006), 172–216 and passim.

4. Michael A. Morrison, *Slavery and the American West: The Eclipse of Manifest Destiny and the Coming of the Civil War* (Chapel Hill: University of North Carolina Press, 1997), is the standard work on slavery expansion and the debates of the 1840s and 1850s.

5. Ibid., 7.

6. Ibid., 8.

7. Don E. Fehrenbacher uses this term in his magisterial study of *Dred Scott v. Sandford*. See *The Dred Scott Case: Its Significance in American Law and Politics* (New York: Oxford University Press, 1978).

1. A Desire for Self-Government: Slavery in the Early American Territories

1. For a brilliant discussion of southern attitudes toward territorial expansion and American nationalism, see Drew McCoy, "James Madison and Visions of American Nationality in the Confederation Period: A Regional Perspective," in Richard Beeman, Stephen Botein, and Edward C. Carter II, eds., *Beyond Confederation: Origins of the Constitution and American National Identity* (Chapel Hill: University of North Carolina Press, 1987), 226–258.

2. For a general overview of the federal government's assumption of western lands, see Richard B. Morris, *The Forging of the Union, 1781–1789* (New York: Harper & Row, 1989), 220–244.

3. Arthur Bestor, "Constitutionalism and Settlement of the West: The Attainment of Consen-

sus, 1754–1784," in John Porter Bloom, ed., *The American Territorial System* (Athens: Ohio University Press, 1973), 28.

4. For a thorough discussion of this point, see Bestor, "Constitutionalism and Settlement of the West," 13–44. For Jefferson's Ordinance of 1784, see especially pp. 27–33. See also Robert Berkhofer, Jr., "The Northwest Ordinance and the Principles of Territorial Evolution," in Bloom, ed., *The American Territorial System*, 47–50; Peter S. Onuf, *Statehood and Union: A History of the Northwest Ordinance* (Bloomington: Indiana University Press, 1987), 55–56.

5. Galliard Hunt, ed., *Journals of the Continental Congress, 1774–1789,* 34 vols. (Washington, DC: Government Printing Office, 1904–1937), 26: 119 (hereafter cited as *JCC*).

6. Ibid., 247; "Jefferson's Observations on Demanier's Manuscript for the *Encyclopedie Methodique,*" 1786, in Julian P. Boyd et al., eds., *The Papers of Thomas Jefferson,* 34 vols. to date (Princeton, NJ: Princeton University Press, 1950–), 10: 58. See also Don E. Fehrenbacher, *The Dred Scott Case: Its Significance in American Law and Politics* (New York: Oxford University Press, 1978), 77; Donald L. Robinson, *Slavery and the Structure of American Politics, 1765–1820* (New York: Harcourt Brace Jovanovich, 1971), 379–380.

7. Peter S. Onuf, *The Origins of the Federal Republic: Jurisdictional Controversies in the United States, 1775–1787* (Philadelphia: University of Pennsylvania Press, 1983), 42. Historians have vigorously debated the differences between the Ordinance of 1784 and the Northwest Ordinance, specifically in relation to the question of self-government. For a useful guide to this debate, see R. Douglas Hurt, "Historians and the Northwest Ordinance," *Western Historical Quarterly* 20 (August 1989): 261–280.

8. The standard history of the Northwest Ordinance is Onuf, *Statehood and Union,* 58. For the text of the ordinance, see 60–64.

9. Ibid., 64.

10. *JCC,* 32: 334–343.

11. Nathan Dane to Rufus King, July 16, 1787, in Paul H. Smith et al., eds. *Letters of Delegates to Congress, 1774–1789,* 25 vols. (Washington, DC: Library of Congress, 1976–2000), 24: 358. For King's effort to ban slavery in the territories, see Robinson, *Slavery and the Structure of American Politics,* 380. Scholars have long debated this very point and have arrived at few concrete answers. Circumstantial evidence does shed some light on the insertion of the sixth article. Peter Onuf notes (*The Origins of the Federal Republic,* 42) that prohibition of slavery in the newly framed "neo-colonial" system of territorial government served twin purposes: first, as a tangible part of strengthening federal control over the territories; second, and more significantly, as a way to entice the emigration of New Englanders to the Northwest Territory. By 1787, Massachusetts and New Hampshire had ended slavery. The states of Pennsylvania, Rhode Island, and Connecticut had committed to gradual emancipation. A number of delegates to Congress, especially from the Northeast, surmised that settlers in the Northwest Territory would come from the states that had emancipated their slaves and consequently would not desire the institution. Yet the southern boundary of the territory—the Ohio River—served as the northern boundary of a vast territory once in the possession of the states of Virginia and North Carolina. North Carolina ceded its territory to the federal government in 1790; Virginia's land would become the state of Kentucky two years later.

12. William Grayson to James Monroe, August 8, 1787, in *Letters of Delegates to Congress,* 24: 393. For the southern position, see Lacy K. Ford, *Deliver Us from Evil: The Slavery Question in the Old South* (New York: Oxford University Press, 2009), 20–21; McCoy, "James Madison and Visions of Nationality in the Confederation Period," 230–239. For the controversy over the au-

thorship of the sixth article, see Paul Finkelman, "Slavery and the Northwest Ordinance: A Study in Ambiguity," in *Slavery and the Founders: Race and Liberty in the Age of Jefferson*, 2nd ed. (Armonk, NY: M. E. Sharpe, 2001), 41–42 and 209n13.

13. Dane to King, July 16, 1787, in *Letters of Delegates to Congress*, 24: 358. See also Dane to King, August 12, 1787, in ibid., 24: 401–403 and Staughton Lynd, "The Compromise of 1787," *Political Science Quarterly* 81 (June 1966): 229–230.

14. Lynd, "Compromise of 1787," 231. Lynd argues that this alteration in the ordinance represents not only a compromise on where slavery could or could not exist in the western territories, but also a compromise related to passage of the three-fifths ordinance being debated at the same time at the Constitutional Convention in Philadelphia. For the study of popular sovereignty, the former is of greater concern. For the suggestion of an implicit compromise, see ibid., 231–232. For the initial draft of the ordinance, see *JCC*, 31: 669–673.

15. *JCC*, 26: 247; Ford, *Deliver Us from Evil*, 21.

16. Finkelman, "Slavery and the Northwest Ordinance," 44–46, 51–55.

17. For the definitive discussion of this and other conflicting clauses within the Northwest Ordinance, see ibid., 44–49.

18. See George William Van Cleve, "Founding a Slaveholders' Union, 1770–1797," in John Craig Hammond and Matthew Mason, eds., *Contesting Slavery: The Politics of Bondage and Freedom in the New American Nation* (Charlottesville: University of Virginia Press, 2011), 117–137, quote on p. 121.

19. Act of May 26, 1790, ch. 6, 2 *U.S. Statutes at Large*, 123. The deed of cession is printed in Act of April 2, 1790, ch. 6, 2 *U.S. Statutes at Large*, 106–109, quote on p. 108. See also *Annals of Congress* (hereafter cited as *AC*), Senate, 1st Cong., 2nd Sess., 978, 985–988, 999–1000. The Southwest Ordinance applied initially only to the North Carolina cession—the future state of Tennessee. The future state of Kentucky remained part of Virginia until it became a state in 1792.

20. *AC*, House, 4th Cong., 1st Sess., 1301, 1305. For the Tennessee petition, see ibid., 892. On the issue of statehood, see ibid., 1299–1329. Because Kentucky remained part of the state of Virginia until its admission to the Union as a separate state, only Virginia could permit or prohibit slavery within its bounds. And because Kentucky never had a territorial phase, the decision rested undisputedly with the Kentuckians after 1792. See John Craig Hammond, *Slavery, Freedom, and Expansion in the Early American West* (Charlottesville: University of Virginia Press, 2007), 11–12.

21. *AC*, House, 4th Cong., 1st Sess., 1309; Act of June 1, 1796, ch. 47, 1 *U.S. Statutes at Large*, 491–492.

22. "Slavery, and the Exchange of Certain Donations of Land in the Northwestern Territory," May 12, 1796, *American State Papers* (hereafter cited as *ASP*): Public Lands, 1: 69, 68. For the context of this memorial and a discussion of internal debate over slavery in Illinois, see Nicole Etcheson, *The Emerging Midwest: Upland Southerners and the Political Culture of the Old Northwest, 1787–1861* (Bloomington: Indiana University Press, 1996), 15–26.

23. Arthur St. Clair to James Ross, December 1799, quoted in Etcheson, *Emerging Midwest*, 16. Etcheson addresses the Northwest Territory's complex political milieu in ibid., 15–26, 63–71, and passim.

24. *AC*, House, 5th Cong., 2nd Sess., 1277–1312; Andrew Ellicott to the Secretary of State, September 24, 1797, in Clarence Edwin Carter, ed., *The Territorial Papers of the United States* [hereafter cited as *Territorial Papers*]: *The Territory of Mississippi, 1798–1817* (Washington,

DC: U.S. Government Printing Office, 1937), 5: 5. For the reasons why southerners moved west, see Adam Rothman, *Slave Country: American Expansion and the Origins of the Deep South* (Cambridge, MA: Harvard University Press, 2005), 24–26 and passim.

25. *AC*, House, 5th Cong., 2nd Sess., 1306, 1308, 1310.

26. For a discussion of diffusion and its origins in the Upper South, see Ford, *Deliver Us from Evil*, 73–76, 106–107.

27. *AC*, House, 5th Cong., 2nd Sess., 1311, 1307.

28. Act of April 7, 1798, ch. 28, 1 *U.S. Statutes at Large*, 549–550; The Secretary of State to Andrew Ellicott, March 27, 1798, in Carter, ed., *Territorial Papers: The Territory of Mississippi, 1798–1817*, 5: 15–16.

29. For details on the partition of the Northwest Territory and creation of the state of Ohio, see "Application to Erect the Northwestern Territory into a State," *ASP*: Miscellaneous, 1: 325–329.

30. *AC*, House, 7th Cong., 2nd Sess., 473. For a discussion of the situation regarding slavery in the Northwest Territory, see Hammond, *Slavery, Freedom, and Expansion*, 96–150.

31. For a brief discussion of these factors, see Hammond, *Slavery, Freedom, and Expansion*, 103–113. See also Paul Finkelman, "Evading the Ordinance: The Persistence of Bondage in Indiana and Illinois," in *Slavery and the Founders*, 58–80.

32. "Indiana Territory," March 2, 1803, *ASP*: Public Lands, 1: 160. All of the relevant petitions are also compiled in Jacob Piatt Dunn, ed., *Slavery Petitions and Papers* (Indianapolis: Bowen-Merrill, 1893); "Second Report on Petition of the Vincennes Convention," February 17, 1804, in Dunn, ed., *Slavery Petitions and Papers*, 33; John Rice Jones to Judge [Thomas T.] Davis, January 21, 1804, in Carter, ed., *Territorial Papers: The Territory of Indiana, 1800–1810*, 7: 169. For the British question, see Finkelman, "Evading the Ordinance," 66.

33. "Report on the Petitions of 1805," February 14, 1806, in Dunn, ed., *Slavery Petitions and Papers*, 53. See also "Memorial from Randolph and St. Clair Counties, 1805," December 1805, in Dunn, ed., *Slavery Petitions and Papers*, 41–50, esp. p. 43. Measuring the true level of proslavery support in Indiana is impossible.

34. "Legislative Resolutions of 1807," January 21, 1807, in Dunn, ed., *Slavery Petitions and Papers*, 65–67; quotes from "Slavery in the Indiana Territory, September 19, 1807, *ASP*: Miscellaneous, 1: 485.

35. "Counter-Petition of Clark County [1807]," September 19, 1807, in Dunn, ed., *Slavery Petitions and Papers*, 77–78; Jacob Piatt Dunn, *Indiana: A Redemption from Slavery*, 2nd ed. (Boston: Houghton Mifflin, 1905), 359.

36. "House Report on the [Indiana Legislative Resolutions of 1807]," February 12, 1807, in Dunn, ed., *Slavery Petitions and Papers*, 67–68.

37. "Report on [Slavery in Indiana Territory]," November 13, 1807, in ibid., 79; Finkelman, "Evading the Ordinance," 68, 72–73.

38. Duncan MacLeod, *Slavery, Race, and the American Revolution* (Cambridge: Cambridge University Press, 1974), 103. See also Hammond, *Slavery, Freedom, and Expansion*, 115–123.

39. For a discussion of these issues, see Peter J. Kastor, *The Nation's Crucible: The Louisiana Purchase and the Creation of America* (New Haven, CT: Yale University Press, 2004), 19–75.

40. Ibid., 29–32. See also Jon Kukla, *A Wilderness So Immense: The Louisiana Purchase and the Destiny of America* (New York: Alfred A. Knopf, 2003).

41. John Edgar to John Fowler, September 25, 1803, in Carter, ed., *Territorial Papers: The Territory of Louisiana-Missouri, 1803–1806*, 13: 6–7, 7.

42. *Senate Journal*, 8th Cong., 1st Sess., 320–321; *AC*, House, 8th Cong., 1st Sess., 1054.

43. This argument would recur over forty-five years later with the acquisition of the Mexican Cession.

44. *AC*, House, 8th Cong., 1st Sess., 1058, 1061, 1073.

45. Ibid., 1063, 1066, 1062.

46. Ibid., 1060, 1064. See William J. Cooper, Jr., *Liberty and Slavery: Southern Politics to 1860* (New York: Alfred A. Knopf, 1982).

47. *AC*, House, 8th Cong., 1st Sess., 1063. See ibid., 1078–1079, 1193–1194; *AC*, Senate, 8th Cong., 1st Sess., 289–290; *AC*, House, 8th Cong., 1st Sess., 1229–1230.

48. See the speeches and roll call votes in *AC*, House, 8th Cong., 1st Sess., 1078, 1194–1195, 1207, 1229; *AC*, Senate, 8th Cong., 1st Sess., 290. John Craig Hammond discusses the vulnerability of the western territories in *Slavery, Freedom, and Expansion*, 30–54 and passim.

49. William C. Carr to John Breckinridge, July 7, 1804, in Carter, ed., *Territorial Papers: The Territory of Louisiana-Missouri, 1803–1806*, 13: 30.

50. For the final draft of the law, see *AC*, Appendix, 8th Cong., 1st Sess., 1293–1300; "Remonstrance of the People of Louisiana against the Political System Adopted by Congress for Them," December 31, 1804, in *ASP*: Miscellaneous, 1: 398, 397 (italics in the original).

51. For the Hillhouse amendment, see *AC*, Senate, 8th Cong, 1st Sess., 240. Quote of Sen. James Jackson of Georgia in Everett Somerville Brown, *The Constitutional History of the Louisiana Purchase, 1803–1812* (Berkeley: University of California Press, 1920), 113; Ford, *Deliver Us from Evil*, 106–107; "Remonstrance of the People of Louisiana," 399.

52. For an overview of Federalist opposition to westward expansion, see Gordon S. Wood, *Empire of Liberty: A History of the Early Republic, 1789–1815* (New York: Oxford University Press, 2009); for Louisiana, see Ford, *Deliver Us from Evil*, 106–111. For the effect of slavery on Federalist-Jeffersonian politics, see also David Hackett Fischer, *The Revolution of American Conservatism: The Federalist Party in the Era of Jeffersonian Democracy* (New York: Harper & Row, 1965), 159–167.

53. "Revision of the Political System Adopted for Louisiana," January 25, 1805, in *ASP*: Miscellaneous, 1: 417; *AC*, House, 8th Cong., 1st Sess., 1078, 1206–1207. For the loyalty of the Louisianans, see Brown, *The Constitutional History of the Louisiana Purchase*, 155–156.

54. "Revision of the Political System Adopted for Louisiana," 418.

55. "Remonstrance of the People of Louisiana," 400, 401, 404.

56. See "Importation of Slaves into the Territories," February 17, 1806, *ASP*: Miscellaneous, 1: 451; *AC*, 8th Cong., 2nd Sess., Appendix, 1674–1676, 1684–1686; "A Bill for the Government of Louisiana Territory," [January 22, 1810], in Carter, ed., *Territorial Papers: The Territory of Louisiana-Missouri, 1806–1814*, 14: 362–364; *AC*, House, 11th Cong., 2nd Sess., 1157, 1253; *AC*, House, 12th Cong., 1st Sess., 1279; Senate, 244; Appendix, 2310–2315.

57. Several cases concerning slavery and indentured servitude made their way to the Indiana Supreme Court as late as 1821.

58. Matthew Mason, *Slavery and Politics in the Early American Republic* (Chapel Hill: University of North Carolina Press, 2006), 150. For the congressional debate, see *AC*, House, 14th Cong., 1st Sess., 408, 1373; Senate, 31, 315; *AC*, House, 15th Cong., 2nd Sess., 306–307, 309, 311.

2. "Shall the Creature Govern the Creator?":
Self-Government and the Missouri Compromise

1. *Annals of Congress* (hereafter cited as *AC*), 15th Congress, 2nd Session, 1170.

2. Thomas Jefferson to John Holmes, April 22, 1820, in Merrill D. Peterson, ed., *Thomas Jefferson: Writings* (New York: Library of America, 1984), 1434.

3. See Peter Onuf, *Jefferson's Empire: The Language of American Nationhood* (Charlottesville: University Press of Virginia, 2000), 109–146; Robert Pierce Forbes, *The Missouri Compromise and Its Aftermath: Slavery and the Meaning of America* (Chapel Hill: University of North Carolina Press, 2007), 6–7.

4. See Glover Moore, *The Missouri Controversy, 1819–1821* (Lexington: University of Kentucky Press, 1953), 31–32.

5. "Application of Missouri for Admission into the Union as a State," November 21, 1818, *American State Papers*: Miscellaneous, 2: 557–558. The 1820 census lists Missouri as having a population of just over 66,586.

6. *AC*, House, 15th Cong., 2nd Sess., 1222. Few historians have probed the link between Arkansas and Missouri; see Don E. Fehrenbacher, *The Dred Scott Case: Its Significance in American Law and Politics* (New York: Oxford University Press, 1978), 101–102.

7. For Jefferson's claim, see Leonard L. Richards, *The Slave Power: The Free North and Southern Domination, 1780–1860* (Baton Rouge: Louisiana State University Press, 2000), 53–54. For Tallmadge's explanation, see Forbes, *Missouri Compromise and Its Aftermath*, 36. See also Daniel Walker Howe, *What Hath God Wrought: The Transformation of America, 1815–1848* (New York: Oxford University Press, 2007), 147–148.

8. Richards, *Slave Power*, 54; Moore, *Missouri Controversy*, 33.

9. See Forbes, *Missouri Compromise and Its Aftermath*, 33–41; Matthew Mason, *Slavery and Politics in the Early American Republic* (Chapel Hill: University of North Carolina Press, 2007), 177–188.

10. Northerners objected that the Constitution counted slaves as three-fifths of a human being for purposes of apportionment, thereby enhancing the slaveholding section's power in the halls of Congress. For a thoughtful discussion of the sectional balance of power, see Richards, *Slave Power*, 52–82. My interpretation of the politics surrounding the Missouri controversy draws from Mason, *Slavery and Politics in the Early American Republic*, 179–183; Forbes, *Missouri Compromise and Its Aftermath*, 32–68; Shaw Livermore, Jr., *The Twilight of Federalism: The Disintegration of the Federalist Party, 1815–1830* (Princeton, NJ: Princeton University Press, 1962), 88–112.

11. Forbes, *Missouri Compromise and Its Aftermath*, 50. For the tensions between the northern and southern Republicans, see Padraig Riley, "Slavery and the Problem of Democracy in Jeffersonian America," in John Craig Hammond and Matthew Mason, eds., *Contesting Slavery: The Politics of Bondage and Freedom in the New American Nation* (Charlottesville: University of Virginia Press, 2011), 227–246.

12. Forbes, *Missouri Compromise and Its Aftermath*, 49–50; Fehrenbacher, *Dred Scott Case*, 90–91. See Norman J. Risjord, *The Old Republicans: Southern Conservatism in the Age of Jefferson* (New York: Columbia University Press, 1965), 213–222.

13. Forbes, *Missouri Compromise and Its Aftermath*, 36; *AC*, House, 15th Cong., 2nd Sess., 1170.

14. *AC*, House, 15th Cong., 2nd Sess., 1170–1171. On the alliance between Tallmadge and Taylor, see Forbes, *Missouri Compromise and Its Aftermath*, 37–38; Moore, *Missouri Contro-*

versy, 38–44. New Yorkers played a role on both sides of the Missouri debate; the Empire State had commenced the process of abolition, but it would not be completed until 1827. See David N. Gellman, *Emancipating New York: The Politics of Slavery and Freedom, 1777–1827* (Baton Rouge: Louisiana State University Press, 2007), esp. 189–219.

15. *AC*, House, 15th Cong., 2nd Sess., 1171; Sean Wilentz, *The Rise of American Democracy: Jefferson to Lincoln* (New York: W.W. Norton, 2005), 225–226.

16. "Remarks on the Tallmadge Amendment," February 15, 1819, in James F. Hopkins et al., eds., *The Papers of Henry Clay*, 11 vols. (Lexington: University of Kentucky Press, 1959–1992), 2: 670. Unfortunately, the House reporter did not transcribe Clay's speech (or many of his speeches from this session of Congress). Historians have determined the thrust of his argument from the context of other speeches and from statements in the press.

17. Ibid.

18. *AC*, House, 15th Cong., 2nd Sess., 1182.

19. Livermore, *Twilight of Federalism*, 90. For a discussion of the Federalist course in the Missouri debates, see pp. 88–112.

20. Forbes, *Missouri Compromise and Its Aftermath*, 41; Wilentz, *Rise of American Democracy*, 227–228. The first scholar to make this distinction was Hermann von Holst, *The Constitutional and Political History of the United States*, 8 vols. (Chicago: Callaghan and Company, 1876–1904), 1: 364–365.

21. *AC*, House, 15th Cong., 2nd Sess., 1185, 1191.

22. Ibid., 1201.

23. Ibid., 1196–1197.

24. For the vote, see ibid., 1214–1215. For a sectional roll call analysis of the vote, see Moore, *Missouri Controversy*, 53.

25. *AC*, House, 15th Cong., 2nd Sess., 1222.

26. *AC*, House, 15th Cong., 2nd Sess., 1226, 1227; Onuf, *Jefferson's Empire*, 144. For Jefferson's conception of territories and states, see pp. 118, 143–145; *AC*, House, 15th Cong., 2nd Sess., 1227.

27. *AC*, House, 15th Cong., 2nd Sess., 1227.

28. Ibid., 1278–1279, 1228, 1229, 1281; see Act of March 2, 1819, ch. 49, 3 *U.S. Statutes at Large*, 493–496.

29. *AC*, Senate, 15th Cong., 2nd Sess., 273, 279–280; *Richmond Enquirer*, February 25, 1819; for the roll call vote on these questions, see *AC*, Senate, 15th Cong., 2nd Sess., 273.

30. See Robert J. Brugger, *Beverley Tucker: Heart over Head in the Old South* (Baltimore: Johns Hopkins University Press, 1978), 49–57; *St. Louis Enquirer*, April 7, 1819.

31. *St. Louis Enquirer*, April 7, 28, 1819, May 12, 1819. Italics in the original.

32. *St. Louis Enquirer*, April 21, 1819; *Missouri Gazette*, April 7, 1819; *St. Louis Enquirer*, April 21, 1819.

33. Forbes, *Missouri Compromise and Its Aftermath*, 40; *St. Louis Enquirer*, April 28, 1819; *Kentucky Reporter*, quoted in *St. Louis Enquirer*, June 9, 1819.

34. Moore, *Missouri Controversy*, 48; *St. Louis Enquirer*, June 23, 1819. The opponents of restriction actually misinterpreted the treaty; its provisions applied only to those residents who lived in Missouri under French rule. American law governed settlers who resided in the territory after the cession.

35. *St. Louis Enquirer*, May 19, 1819.

36. *Niles' Weekly Register*, August 14, 1819. Italics in the original. See also *Edwardsville Spectator*, June 9, 1819; *Edwardsville Spectator*, June 5, 1819.

37. *Niles' Weekly Register*, July 10, 1819.

38. Don E. Fehrenbacher discusses how the issue of slavery in the territories became increasingly "constitutionalized" in the antebellum era. See *Dred Scott Case*, 102–103, 135–151; *Niles' Weekly Register*, November 6, 1819. See also November 27, 1819.

39. *Richmond Enquirer*, November 23, 1819; See also *New-York Gazette & General Advertiser*, November 18, 1819; *New York Evening Post*, quoted in *Niles' Weekly Register*, November 27, 1819, November 6, 1819, November 27, 1819; *St. Louis Enquirer*, December 4, 1819.

40. See Herman V. Ames, ed., *State Documents on Federal Relations: The States and the United States* (1906; repr., New York: Da Capo Press, 1970), 196–203; *Richmond Enquirer*, December 21, 1819.

41. James Monroe to George Hay, December 20, 1819, quoted in Noble E. Cunningham, *The Presidency of James Monroe* (Lawrence: University Press of Kansas, 1996), 94; *Richmond Enquirer*, December 21, 1819.

42. Risjord, *Old Republicans*, 213–221. The best summary of Monroe's stance on Missouri is in Cunningham, *Presidency of James Monroe*, 93–104. Robert Pierce Forbes makes special effort to rehabilitate the president's reputation by overemphasizing Monroe's involvement in the crisis behind the scenes. See Forbes, *Missouri Compromise and Its Aftermath*, esp. 63–71; Forbes, *Missouri Compromise and Its Aftermath*, 64.

43. *AC*, House, 16th Cong., 1st Sess., 835, 832.

44. *AC*, Senate, 16th Cong., 1st Sess., 169–170, 175.

45. *Richmond Enquirer*, January 1, 1820.

46. *AC*, Senate, 16th Cong., 1st Sess., 222, 229.

47. Ibid., 943, 944, 945.

48. Ibid., 946. Stephen A. Douglas articulated this same concept over thirty-five years later in his debate with Abraham Lincoln at Freeport, Illinois.

49. *Richmond Enquirer*, January 8, 1820.

50. Mathew Carey, *Some Considerations on the Impropriety and Inexpediency of Renewing the Missouri Question* (Philadelphia: M. Carey & Son, 1820), 4, 38.

51. Forbes, *Missouri Compromise and Its Aftermath*, 40. For a fuller discussion of the emerging southern defense of slavery, see pp. 37–42; Mason, *Slavery and Politics in the Early American Republic*, 158–176. *AC*, Senate, 16th Cong., 1st Sess., 228–229; for more on Macon's efforts, see Mason, *Slavery and Politics in the Early American Republic*, 162–164; see *Richmond Enquirer*, January 1, 1820; Mason, *Slavery and Politics in the Early American Republic*, 159.

52. *AC*, House, 16th Cong., 1st Sess., 949; Fehrenbacher, *Dred Scott Case*, 103–104.

53. *AC*, House, 15th Cong., 2nd Sess., 1228; for the legislative history surrounding the link between Maine and Missouri's statehood, see Moore, *Missouri Controversy*, 86–90; for a detailed analysis of the motives behind the plan, see Forbes, *Missouri Compromise and Its Aftermath*, 62–68. In 1819, Arkansas Territory included the land that would become Indian Territory (present-day Oklahoma) by 1828.

54. Forbes, *Missouri Compromise and Its Aftermath*, 68; *AC*, House, 16th Cong., 1st Sess., 1140, 1160.

55. *Richmond Enquirer*, February 10, 1820; C. W. Gooch to David Campbell, February 16, 1820, Box 4, Campbell Family Papers, Rare Book, Manuscript, and Special Collections Library, Duke University, Durham, North Carolina; *AC*, House, 16th Cong., 1st Sess., 1111.

56. *AC*, House, 16th Cong., 1st Sess., 1237, 1502.

57. Ibid., 1320, 1327.

58. *Richmond Enquirer*, March 7, 1820; *AC*, House, 16th Cong., 1st Sess., 1368.

59. *AC*, House, 16th Cong., 1st Sess., 1383. For a discussion of the tenth president's beliefs on republican government and states' rights during the Missouri controversy, see Dan Monroe, *The Republican Vision of John Tyler* (College Station: Texas A&M University Press, 2003), 24–47.

60. *AC*, House, 16th Cong., 1st Sess., 1130, 1345.

61. Ibid., 1294–1295.

62. Ibid., 1377.

63. Carey, *Some Considerations on the Missouri Question*, 57; *Niles' Weekly Register*, January 29, 1820.

64. *Richmond Enquirer*, February 26, 1820, March 3, 1820; James Monroe to Thomas Jefferson, February 19, 1820, in Stanislaus Murray Hamilton, ed., *The Writings of James Monroe: Including a Collection of His Public and Private Papers and Correspondence Now for the First Time Printed*, 6 vols. (New York: G. P. Putnam's Sons, 1902), 6: 115–116.

65. James Madison to James Monroe, February 23, 1820, *Letters and Other Writings of James Madison, Fourth President of the United States*, 4 vols. (Philadelphia: J. B. Lippincott, 1865), 3: 168.

66. This account is based the diary of John Quincy Adams. See entry for March 3, 1820, in Charles Francis Adams, ed., *Memoirs of John Quincy Adams, Comprising Portions of His Diary from 1795 to 1848*, 12 vols. (Philadelphia: J. B. Lippincott, 1874–1877), 5: 4–11. See also Cunningham, *Presidency of James Monroe*, 103–104; *Memoirs of John Quincy Adams*, 5: 5; for the written response of Crawford, Calhoun, and Wirt, see their letter to James Monroe, March 4, 1820, in Worthington Chauncey Ford, ed., *Writings of John Quincy Adams*, 7 vols. (New York: Macmillan, 1913–1917), 7: 1–2; *Memoirs of John Quincy Adams*, 5: 6. Adams did not specify this in his written response to the president; see *Writings of John Quincy Adams*, 7: 1–2, for that letter.

67. See Forbes, *Missouri Compromise and Its Aftermath*, 89–95 and passim; Hammond, *Slavery, Freedom, and the American West*, 161–168; quote in Richards, *Slave Power*, 84. See pp. 84–86 for an explanation of "Randolph's pejorative." See also Moore, *Missouri Controversy*, 103–104. The epithet may be misspelled; Randolph may well have referred to "doe faces," suggesting the men had the nature of a timid female deer; Richards, *Slave Power*, 86. Italics in the original. See pp. 83–87 for details on the northerners who voted for the compromise bill.

68. From Mark Langdon Hill, Massachusetts-District of Maine, March 31, 1820, in Noble E. Cunningham, Jr., ed., *Circular Letters of Congressmen to Their Constituents, 1789–1829*, 3 vols. (Chapel Hill: University of North Carolina Press, 1978), 3: 1103; from John Holmes, Massachusetts-District of Maine, in ibid., 3: 1111; Richards, *Slave Power*, 87–88.

69. Hammond, *Slavery, Freedom, and the American West*, 167.

70. Henry Clay to Adam Beatty, March 4, 1820, in Hopkins et al., eds., *Papers of Henry Clay*, 2: 788.

71. For details on the effort to revive slavery in Illinois, see Eugene H. Berwanger, *The Frontier against Slavery: Western Anti-Negro Prejudice and the Slavery Extension Controversy* (Urbana: University of Illinois Press, 1967), 12–17; Hammond, *Slavery, Freedom, and the American West*, 157.

72. *Richmond Enquirer*, March 7, 1820; *Milledgeville Southern Recorder*, March 7, 1820; see Moore, *Missouri Controversy*, 108–111, for roll call analyses of the compromise votes; John C. Calhoun to A[ndrew] Jackson, June 1, 1820, in Clyde N. Wilson et al., eds., *The Papers of John C. Calhoun*, 28 vols. (Columbia: University of South Carolina Press, 1959–2003), 5: 164.

73. *St. Louis Enquirer*, March 25, 1820.

74. *Niles' Weekly Register*, October 21, 1820.

75. *AC*, House, 16th Cong., 2nd Sess., 1228.

3. "Forgotten Principles of Their Forefathers": Retreat from the Missouri Compromise

1. *Niles' Weekly Register*, March 11, 1820.

2. William M. Wiecek, *The Sources of Antislavery Constitutionalism, 1760–1848* (Ithaca, NY: Cornell University Press, 1977), 126; *Richmond Enquirer*, March 17, 1820.

3. *Richmond Enquirer*, March 7, 1820; Samuel Flagg Bemis, *John Quincy Adams and the Foundations of American Foreign Policy,* (New York: Alfred A. Knopf, 1949), 309–310; 321–322; for the interstate slave trade, see Steven Deyle, *Carry Me Back: The Domestic Slave Trade in American Life* (New York: Oxford University Press, 2005), 42–46 and passim.

4. *Richmond Enquirer*, March 7, 1820; for the Old Republicans, see Norman K. Risjord, *The Old Republicans: Southern Conservatism in the Age of Jefferson* (New York: Columbia University Press, 1965), 222–223; Nathaniel Beverley Tucker to James Monroe, August 4, 1819, quoted in Robert J. Brugger, *Beverley Tucker: Heart over Head in the Old South* (Baltimore: Johns Hopkins University Press, 1978), 57.

5. The standard biography of Taylor is Robert E. Shalhope, *John Taylor of Caroline, Pastoral Republican* (Columbia: University of South Carolina Press, 1980). For a superb sketch of Taylor's intellectual heritage, see Michael O'Brien, *Conjectures of Order: Intellectual Life and the American South, 1810–1860* (Chapel Hill: University of North Carolina Press, 2004), 785–799.

6. John Taylor, *Construction Construed, and Constitutions Vindicated* (Richmond: Shepherd & Pollard, 1820), 229; 292–293.

7. Ibid., 304, 303, 306. John C. Calhoun would draw on Taylor's logic in later years to craft his doctrine of the concurrent majority.

8. Glover Moore, *The Missouri Controversy, 1819–1821* (Lexington: University of Kentucky Press, 1953), 123; for the suitability of slave-based agriculture in Missouri and Arkansas, see William Rector to Josiah Meigs, April 14, 1819, in Clarence Edwin Carter, ed., *The Territorial Papers of the United States: The Territory of Arkansas, 1798–1817* (Washington, DC: U.S. Government Printing Office, 1937), 19: 67.

9. Richard H. Brown, "The Missouri Crisis, Slavery, and the Politics of Jacksonianism," *South Atlantic Quarterly* 65 (Winter 1966): 60; Charles S. Sydnor, *The Development of Southern Sectionalism, 1819–1848* (Baton Rouge: Louisiana State University Press, 1948), 132; Don E. Fehrenbacher, *Sectional Crisis and Southern Constitutionalism* (Baton Rouge: Louisiana State University Press, 1995), 22; Brown, "Missouri Crisis, Slavery, and the Politics of Jacksonianism," 61.

10. Don E. Fehrenbacher, *The Dred Scott Case: Its Significance in American Law and Politics* (New York: Oxford University Press, 1978), 116; see Louis Filler, *The Crusade against Slavery, 1830–1860* (New York: Harper & Row, 1960), esp. 10–27, 82–90 for a sketch of the origins of abolitionism.

11. See Richard H. Sewell, *Ballots for Freedom: Antislavery Politics in the United States, 1837–1860* (New York: Oxford University Press, 1976), 6–20, for the origins of the petition movement. For the standard (if somewhat idiosyncratic) history of the petition controversy, see William Lee Miller, *Arguing about Slavery: The Great Battle in the United States Congress* (New York: Alfred A. Knopf, 1996), 115–119. For the gag rule in the Senate, see George Rable,

"Slavery, Politics, and the South: The Gag Rule as a Case Study," *Capitol Studies* 3 (Fall 1975): 69–85; Daniel Wirls, "'The Only Mode for Avoiding Everlasting Defeat': The Overlooked Senate Gag Rule for Antislavery Petitions," *Journal of the Early Republic* 27 (Spring 2007): 115–138.

12. Martin Van Buren's famous definition of the Jacksonian Democratic Party, written to Thomas Ritchie in 1827, is quoted in Brown, "The Missouri Crisis, Slavery, and the Politics of Jacksonianism," 69. For the rise of southern Jacksonian Democrats, see William J. Cooper, Jr., *The South and the Politics of Slavery, 1828–1856* (Baton Rouge: Louisiana State University Press, 1978), 5–11.

13. For the history of Arkansas Territory and the statehood movement, see Lonnie J. White, *Politics on the Southwestern Frontier: Arkansas Territory, 1819–1836* (Memphis, TN: Memphis State University Press, 1964); Jack B. Scroggs, "Arkansas Statehood: A Study in State and National Political Schism," *Arkansas Historical Quarterly* 20 (Autumn 1961): 227–244.

14. *Little Rock Arkansas Gazette*, March 31, 1835.

15. White, *Politics on the Southwestern Frontier*, 164–167, 172; *Little Rock Arkansas Gazette*, April 7, 1835.

16. All 1830 census figures from U.S. Secretary of State, *Abstract of the Returns of the Fifth Census, Showing the Number of Free People, the Number of Slaves, the Federal or Representative Number; and the Aggregate of Each County of Each State of the United States*, 22nd Cong, 1st Sess., House Document 263 (Washington, D.C. 1832), http://www.census.gov/prod/www/abs/decennial/1830.htm.

17. *United States Telegraph*, February 18, 1835.

18. *Little Rock Arkansas Gazette*, May 12, 1835; ibid., May 26, 1835.

19. *Washington Globe*, November 2, 1835.

20. Ibid.; White, *Politics on the Southwestern Frontier*, 175–177; *Little Rock Arkansas Gazette*, December 29, 1835 (italics in the original). Whether Fulton may simply have made a mistake in his message to the territorial legislature or may have intended something more of his remarks is impossible to know. The fact that he had taken precisely the opposite point of view on the subject just two months earlier makes the issue more vexing.

21. *Journal of the Proceedings of the Convention Met to Form a Constitution and System of State Government for the People of Arkansas. . .* (Little Rock, AR: Albert Pike, 1836), 25; White, *Politics on the Southwestern Frontier*, 192; *Little Rock Arkansas Gazette*, April 12, 1836 (italics in the original).

22. *Congressional Globe* (hereafter cited as *CG*), 24th Cong., 1st Sess., 315.

23. Michael F. Holt, *The Rise and Fall of the American Whig Party: Jacksonian Politics and the Onset of the Civil War* (New York: Oxford University Press, 1999), 49–50.

24. Cooper, *The South and the Politics of Slavery*, 64. My interpretation of southern politics in what is commonly termed the Second American Party System comes from Cooper, *The South and the Politics of Slavery*, 43–97; Michael F. Holt, *The Political Crisis of the 1850s* (New York: John Wiley & Sons, 1978), 17–38; J. Mills Thornton, *Politics and Power in a Slave Society: Alabama, 1800–1860* (Baton Rouge: Louisiana State University Press, 1978), 20–39, among many other works.

25. *CG*, 24th Cong., 1st Sess., 315, 316; *Little Rock Arkansas Gazette*, April 26, 1836. In January 1837, the second session of the Twenty-Fourth Congress finalized the admission of Michigan to the Union, though the process had begun in the previous session in conjunction with Arkansas, which became a state in June 1836. A dispute over its northern boundary delayed Michigan's statehood.

26. *CG*, 24th Cong., 1st Sess., 346.

27. *CG*, 24th Cong., 1st Sess., 346, 346–347.

28. Ibid., 374.

29. Ibid., 533, 550–551. For Adams's account of the debate, see John Quincy Adams diary, June 13, 1836, *The Diaries of John Quincy Adams: A Digital Collection* (Boston: Massachusetts Historical Society, 2004), 603. For the roll call vote, see *CG*, 24th Cong., 1st Sess., 551. For a detailed roll-call analysis of the Arkansas vote in the House, see Thomas B. Alexander, *Sectional Stress and Party Strength: A Study of Roll-Call Patterns in the United States House of Representatives, 1836–1860* (Nashville: Vanderbilt University Press, 1967), 11–13, 130.

30. See Cooper, *The South and the Politics of Slavery, 1828–1856*, 43–97 and passim.

31. Sewell, *Ballots for Freedom*, 8. For a discussion of Calhoun's actions during the petition controversy, see John Niven, *John C. Calhoun and the Price of Union* (Baton Rouge: Louisiana State University Press, 1988), 200–207.

32. For the Vermont resolutions, see *Macon Weekly Telegraph*, January 8, 1838. *CG*, 25th Cong., 2nd Sess., 39; *Milledgeville Federal Union*, January 9, 1838.

33. John C. Calhoun to Nathaniel Beverley Tucker, January 2, 1838, in Clyde N. Wilson et al., eds., *The Papers of John C. Calhoun*, 28 vols. (Columbia: University of South Carolina Press, 1959–2003), 14: 45.

34. See Lacy K. Ford, *The Origins of Southern Radicalism: South Carolina, 1800–1860* (New York: Oxford University Press, 1988), 114–117. *CG*, 25th Cong., 2nd Sess., 55; John C. Calhoun to William Hendricks, January 4, 1838, in Wilson et al., eds., *Papers of John C. Calhoun*, 14: 53; *CG*, 25th Cong., 2nd Sess., 55.

35. Ibid.

36. *CG*, 25th Cong., 2nd Sess., Appendix, 22. For insight on Calhoun's call for southern unity, see Cooper, *The South and the Politics of Slavery*, 103–118; Niven, *John C. Calhoun and the Price of Union*, 206–207.

37. *CG*, 25th Cong., 2nd Sess., Appendix, 30, 37.

38. Thomas Hart Benton, *Thirty Years' View; or A History of the Working of the American Government for Thirty Years, from 1820 to 1850*, 2 vols. (New York: D. Appleton, 1854–1856), 2: 141.

39. *CG*, 25th Cong., 2nd Sess., Appendix, 22, 28 (italics in the original). See Fehrenbacher, *Dred Scott Case*, 122–123.

40. *CG*, 25th Cong., 2nd Sess., Appendix, 55.

41. Charles M. Wiltse, *John C. Calhoun: Nullifier, 1829–1839* (Indianapolis: Bobbs-Merrill, 1949), 373; *CG*, 25th Cong., 2nd Sess., Appendix, 60. For Clay's role in the debate of the Calhoun resolutions, see also Robert V. Remini, *Henry Clay: Statesman for the Union* (New York: W. W. Norton, 1991), 509–511.

42. *CG*, 25th Cong., 2nd Sess., Appendix, 59; Wiecek, *Sources of Antislavery Constitutionalism in America*, 188.

43. *CG*, 25th Cong., 2nd Sess., Appendix, 72, 61.

44. *CG*, 25th Cong., 2nd Sess., Appendix, 61.

45. Ibid., 64, 70.

46. For the final roll call on the Clay resolution, see ibid., 74; Fehrenbacher, *Dred Scott Case*, 123. See Rable, "Slavery, Politics, and the South," 75–77, for a discussion of division among southerners during the gag rule controversy. *CG*, 25th Cong., 2nd Sess., Appendix, 74.

47. See Wiltse, *John C. Calhoun: Nullifier*, 374. Wiltse correctly notes that Calhoun's resolutions addressed concrete issues facing the Union, not abstract constitutional theories. Yet he

stands on less solid ground when he argues that Calhoun's constitutional interpretation "was nearer to that envisaged by the founding fathers." *Richmond Enquirer,* January 2, 1838.

48. See Act of March 30, 1822, ch. 13, 3 *U.S. Statutes at Large,* 654–659.

49. See Sidney Walter Martin, *Florida during the Territorial Days* (Athens: University of Georgia Press, 1944), 258–277; "Report of the Committee on General Provisions, including the Subject of Domestic Slavery," December 11, 1838, *Journal of the Proceedings of a Convention of Delegates to Form a Constitution for the People of Florida, Held at St. Joseph, December 1838,* in Dorothy Dodd, ed. *Florida Becomes a State* (Tallahassee: Florida Centennial Commission, 1945), 170, 325.

50. For opposition to the Florida constitution, see *Boston Emancipator,* February 14, 1839, April 11, 1839; *Philadelphia National Enquirer,* July 18, 1839; Martin, *Florida during the Territorial Days,* 272; *CG,* 28th Cong., 2nd Sess., 273.

51. *CG,* 28th Cong., 2nd Sess., 283.

52. *Albany Journal,* quoted in *Boston Emancipator and Weekly Chronicle,* June 11, 1845. For Texas annexation, see Joel H. Silbey, *Storm over Texas: The Annexation Controversy and the Road to Civil War* (New York: Oxford University Press, 2005), 80–90 and passim. See also William W. Freehling, *The Reintegration of American History: Slavery and the Civil War* (New York: Oxford University Press, 1994), 162–165, for a brief but cogent statement of the southern position on Texas.

53. *CG,* 28th Cong., 2nd Sess., 284.

54. Ibid.; *CG,* 28th Cong., 2nd Sess., 284; Robert W. Johannsen, *Stephen A. Douglas* (New York: Oxford University Press, 1973), 220.

55. *CG,* 28th Cong., 2nd Sess., 286.

56. Ibid., 383.

57. *Macon Weekly Telegraph,* January 8, 1838.

4. "A Fit of Convulsions": The Wilmot Proviso and Slavery in the West

1. *National Intelligencer,* August 11, 1846.

2. William J. Cooper, Jr., *The South and the Politics of Slavery, 1828–1856* (Baton Rouge: Louisiana State University Press, 1978), 195; for the political considerations surrounding Texas, see ibid., 182–192. For the history of Texas annexation, see Joel H. Silbey, *Storm over Texas: The Annexation Controversy and the Coming of the Civil War* (New York: Oxford University Press, 2005). For the political and constitutional issues surrounding annexation, see Frederick Merk, *Slavery and the Annexation of Texas* (New York: Alfred A. Knopf, 1972), 121–151; Michael F. Holt, *The Rise and Fall of the American Whig Party: Jacksonian Politics and the Onset of the Civil War* (New York: Oxford University Press, 1999), 168–176; Michael A. Morrison, *Slavery and the American West: The Eclipse of Manifest Destiny and the Coming of the Civil War* (Chapel Hill: University of North Carolina Press, 1997), 13–38.

3. See Silbey, *Storm over Texas,* 47–48. For a discussion of Whig attitudes toward expansion, see Morrison, *Slavery and the American West,* 19–26.

4. See Resolution of March 1, 1845, no. 8, 5 *U.S. Statutes at Large,* 797–798. For the inclusion of the Missouri Compromise line in the joint resolution, see Merk, *Slavery and the Annexation of Texas,* 122–125, 152–153.

5. David M. Potter, *The Impending Crisis, 1848–1861*, completed and edited by Don E. Fehrenbacher (New York: Harper & Row, 1976), 25. For the context of the Oregon debate, see pp. 24–27. See also Yonatan Eyal, *The Young America Movement and the Transformation of the Democratic Party, 1828–1861* (Cambridge: Cambridge University Press, 2007), 127–135, 183–201, for competing opinions within the Democracy on slavery and Texas annexation. For the correct context of the famous phrase, see Edwin A. Miles, "'Fifty-four Forty or Fight'—An American Political Legend," *Mississippi Valley Historical Review* 44 (September 1957): 291–309.

6. See Leonard L. Richards, *The Slave Power: The Free North and Southern Domination, 1780–1860* (Baton Rouge: Louisiana State University Press, 2000), 144–147; 150–152. See also Morrison, *Slavery and the American West*, 53–58.

7. Milo Milton Quaife, ed., *The Diary of James K. Polk During His Presidency, 1845–1849*, 4 vols. (Chicago: A. C. McClurg, 1910), 2: 75; *Niles' National Register*, 15 August 1846. For the immediate effect of the proviso, see Chaplain W. Morrison, *Democratic Politics and Sectionalism: The Wilmot Proviso Controversy* (Chapel Hill: University of North Carolina Press, 1967), 3–20; Potter, *Impending Crisis*, 18–23.

8. Quoted in Potter, *Impending Crisis*, 21. Historians have carefully studied the origins of the proviso. Some argue that Wilmot authored the amendment alone, while others argue that he did the bidding of other angry northern antislavery Democrats. For the former, see Milo Milton Quaife, *The Doctrine of Non-Intervention with Slavery in the Territories* (Chicago: Mac C. Chamberlin, 1910), 13–16. For a persuasive version of the latter argument, see Eric Foner, "The Wilmot Proviso Revisited," *Journal of American History* 56 (September 1969): 262–279. For a more recent analysis that places Wilmot and his proviso in the context of Free Soil politics, see Jonathan H. Earle, *Jacksonian Antislavery and the Politics of Free Soil, 1824–1854* (Chapel Hill: University of North Carolina Press, 2004), 123–143.

9. *Baltimore American*, in *Niles' National Register*, August 15, 1846; Foner, "The Wilmot Proviso Revisited," 278; Morrison, *Slavery and the American West*, 54–55. See also Holt, *Rise and Fall of the American Whig Party*, 250–253.

10. William A. Hale to Henry Bedinger, January 26, [1846], Box 2, Bedinger-Dandridge Papers, Rare Book, Manuscript, and Special Collections, Duke University, Durham, North Carolina.

11. Ibid.

12. *Congressional Globe* (hereafter cited as *CG*), 28th Cong., 2nd Sess., 154. See also P. Orman Ray, *The Repeal of the Missouri Compromise: Its Origin and Authorship* (Cleveland: Arthur C. Clark, 1909), 170–172, esp. 172n240; Silbey, *Storm over Texas*, 11–13.

13. *New-Hampshire Patriot and State Gazette*, June 18, 1846.

14. *Niles' National Register*, January 16, 1847.

15. Quaife, ed., *Polk Diary*, 2: 308, 334–335; *Niles' National Register*, 23 January 1847.

16. Quaife, ed., *Polk Diary*, 2: 308, 284.

17. *Niles' National Register*, January 23, 1847; *Richmond Enquirer*, January 12, 1847; *Charleston Mercury*, in *Milledgeville Federal Union*, January 19, 1847.

18. *Charleston Mercury*, in *Milledgeville Federal Union*, January 19, 1847; Quaife, ed., *Polk Diary*, 2: 309; see also pp. 334–335.

19. Potter, *Impending Crisis*, 65; "1st Oregon Bill [speech draft]," [January 1847], Folder 67, James McDowell Papers #459, Southern Historical Collection, The Wilson Library, University of North Carolina at Chapel Hill. For the Oregon issue, see Quaife, *Doctrine of Non-Intervention*, 24. For the Burt amendment, see Potter, *Impending Crisis*, 65–66 and Morrison, *Democratic Politics and Sectionalism*, 32.

20. *CG*, 29th Cong., 2nd Sess., Appendix, 112, 113. Historians have debated the meaning of Leake's comments for years. Hermann von Holst first recognized the Leake statement as an early statement of popular sovereignty in his work, *The Constitutional History of the United States*, 8 vols. (Chicago: Callaghan and Company, 1876–1904), 3: 353. Milo Quaife disagreed, stating that "what Leake had in mind was not Squatter Sovereignty at all, but the ordinary doctrine among Southern politicians . . .of the lack of power in Congress to legislate upon Slavery in the Territories" (Quaife, *Doctrine of Non-Intervention*, 46). True, Leake did not advocate "squatter sovereignty," but he did propose a form of popular sovereignty that had existed since the settlement of the Louisiana Purchase.

21. *CG*, 29th Cong., 2nd Sess., Appendix, 244; *CG*, 29th Cong., 2nd Sess., 187–188; *Milledgeville Federal Union*, January 19, 1847. For the link between Rhett's speech and Calhoun's thoughts, see Charles M. Wiltse, *John C. Calhoun: Sectionalist, 1840–1850* (Indianapolis: Bobbs-Merrill, 1951), 295.

22. *CG*, 29th Cong., 2nd Sess., 454. In his speech, Calhoun made the amazing claim that he had suggested extension of the Missouri Compromise line to his fellow South Carolinian Burt, even though he disapproved of the principles behind the compromise itself. For the doctrinaire Calhoun to endorse extension of the Missouri line seems an ideological inconsistency. Of course, the North rejected this latest effort at magnanimity from the South—as Calhoun portrayed it—when its representatives in the House overwhelmingly voted against compromise.

23. Ibid., 455.

24. Potter, *Impending Crisis*, 61. My interpretation of Calhoun's territorial doctrine largely follows the work of Potter. Charles M. Wiltse gives Calhoun's speech in the Senate marginal treatment in his *John C. Calhoun: Sectionalist*, 305–307.

25. *Milledgeville Federal Union*, August 3, 1847; *New Orleans Louisiana Courier*, August 31, 1847; *Richmond Enquirer*, August 24, 1847, August 27, 1847.

26. "Speech at a Meeting of Citizens of Charleston, March 9, 1847," in Clyde N. Wilson et al., eds., *The Papers of John C. Calhoun*, 28 vols. (Columbia: University of South Carolina Press, 1959–2004), 24: 250. For the full text of the Charleston speech, see ibid., 24: 248–260. For a summary that emphasizes Calhoun's attack against party politics, see Wiltse, *John C. Calhoun: Sectionalist*, 308–311. Calhoun referred to the South's minority status in a follow-up speech to his February 19, 1847, resolutions; see *CG*, 29th Cong., 2nd Sess., 466–467. For a fuller discussion, see also Jesse T. Carpenter, *The South as a Conscious Minority, 1789–1861* (1930; Columbia: University of South Carolina Press, 1990), 77–126.

27. J. Mills Thornton III, *Politics and Power in a Slave Society: Alabama, 1800–1860* (Baton Rouge: Louisiana State University Press, 1978), 173. For the Alabama meeting see W[illiam] L[owndes] Yancey, *An Address to the People of Alabama* (Montgomery, AL: Flag and Advertiser Job Office, 1848), 9–10. For the Virginia Resolutions, see Joseph G. Rayback, *Free Soil: The Election of 1848* (Lexington: University Press of Kentucky, 1970), 113; Morrison, *Democratic Politics and Sectionalism*, 48–49. For the Georgia resolutions, see Morrison, *Democratic Politics and Sectionalism*, 51. For Alabama, see Eric H. Walther, *William Lowndes Yancey and the Coming of the Civil War* (Chapel Hill: University of North Carolina Press, 2006), 97–98.

28. John C. Calhoun to Duff Green, March 9, 1847, Wilson et al., eds., *Papers of John C. Calhoun*, 24: 260; James Buchanan to Charles Kessler et al., August 25, 1847, in John Bassett Moore, ed., *The Works of James Buchanan: Comprising His Speeches, State Papers, and Private Correspondence*, 12 vols. (Philadelphia and London: J. B. Lippincott, 1908–1911), 7: 386, 386–387; *New York Herald*, August 31, 1847.

29. *Niles' National Register,* August 28, 1847; *Richmond Enquirer,* September 3, 1847. See also *Milledgeville Federal Union,* September 14, 1847.

30. *Richmond Enquirer,* August 27, 1847.

31. *Washington Union, Buffalo Courier,* both quoted in ibid., September 18, 1847.

32. Jefferson Davis to Charles J. Searles, September 19, 1847, in Lynda L. Crist et al., eds., *The Papers of Jefferson Davis,* 12 vols. to date (Baton Rouge: Louisiana State University Press, 1971–), 3: 225; *Niles' National Register,* October 23, 1847. See also Rayback, *Free Soil,* 121–129.

33. For Dallas's presidential candidacy in 1848, see John M. Belohlavek, *George Mifflin Dallas: Jacksonian Patrician* (University Park: Pennsylvania State University Press, 1977), 86–90, 126–130. and Rayback, *Free Soil,* 13–14, 131–135.

34. "Great Speech of Hon. George M. Dallas, upon the Leading Topics of the Day, Delivered at Pittsburgh, Pa." (Philadelphia: Times and Keystone Job Office, 1847), 14.

35. Ibid., 15.

36. Ibid.

37. Ibid., 14.

38. Belohlavek, *George Mifflin Dallas,* 127–128; Morrison, *Democratic Politics and Sectionalism,* 87–88.

39. *Richmond Enquirer,* October 1, 1847; *New Orleans Louisiana Courier,* October 8, 1847; John Marshall to George M. Dallas, October 7, 1847, George Mifflin Dallas Political and Business Papers, Box 4, Folder 26, Historical Society of Pennsylvania, Philadelphia, PA; Ellis Lewis to George M. Dallas, October 7, 1847, ibid.

40. Quoted in Merk, *Slavery and the Annexation of Texas,* 10.

41. *Richmond Times,* quoted in the *Richmond Enquirer,* October 1, 1847; ibid.; "The Presidential Nomination," January 1, 1848, William Claude Tell Editorials, William L. Clements Library, University of Michigan, Ann Arbor, MI; "The Thirtieth Congress," November 20, 1847, in ibid. Regarding the problem of expansion in southern Whiggery, see Thornton, *Politics and Power in a Slave Society,* 133–139; for Whigs and territorial expansion, see Morrison, *Slavery and the American West,* 72–81.

42. *Greenville Mountaineer,* quoted in *Niles' National Register,* October 30, 1847; Montgomery Moses to George M. Dallas, October 23, 1847, Box 4, Folder 26, Dallas Papers.

43. *Washington Union,* quoted in *Niles' National Register,* October 2, 1847. David Potter brilliantly explains Polk's actions in *Impending Crisis,* 68–73. See also Eugene Irving McCormac, *James K. Polk: A Political Biography* (Berkeley: University of California Press, 1922), 612–631. Polk's most recent biographer gives scant attention to his support of extending the Missouri Compromise line to the Pacific. See Walter R. Borneman, *Polk: The Man Who Transformed the Presidency and America* (New York: Random House, 2008), 324, 333–334.

44. *Binghamton Democrat,* quoted in *New Orleans Louisiana Courier,* October 28, 1847.

45. James G. Birney to William Cullen Bryant, October 18, 1847, Box 13, James G. Birney Papers, William L. Clements Library, University of Michigan, Ann Arbor, MI.

46. *Richmond Times,* October 28, 1847.

47. James Buchanan to General James Shields, April 23, 1847, Moore, ed., *Works of James Buchanan,* 7: 286. For a discussion of American opinions and racial attitudes regarding the Mexican population, see Reginald Horsman, *Race and Manifest Destiny* (Cambridge, MA: Harvard University Press, 1981), 229–248 and passim.

48. James Buchanan to Charles Kessler et al., August 25, 1847, Moore, ed., *Works of James Buchanan,* 7: 387.

49. The Dallas speech is quoted in *Milledgeville Federal Union,* November 9, 1847.

50. Ibid.; *Richmond Enquirer*, October 19, 1847; *New York Herald*, November 28, 1847.

51. *S. Doc. Misc. No. 6*, 30th Cong., 1st Sess. (December 14, 1847). Serial Set No. 511. For the introduction of the resolutions in the Senate, see *CG*, 30th Cong., 1st Sess., 21, 26.

52. For the standard interpretations of Dickinson's resolutions, see Morrison, *Democratic Politics and Sectionalism*, 88–89; Potter, *Impending Crisis*, 71–72; Rayback, *Free Soil*, 116.

53. John C. Calhoun to H[enry] W. Conner, December 16, 1847, Wilson et al., eds., *Papers of John C. Calhoun*, 25: 18.

54. Ibid. Northern Whigs, too, had used the same racialized rhetoric.

55. *Milledgeville Federal Union*, December 21, 1847, December 28, 1847.

56. Hopkins Holsey to Howell Cobb, December 31, 1847, in Ulrich B. Phillips, ed., *The Correspondence of Robert Toombs, Alexander H. Stephens, and Howell Cobb* (Washington, DC: Government Printing Office, 1913), 92.

57. Ibid.

58. Lewis Cass to Aaron Hobart, September 30, 1847, Box 11, Lewis Cass Papers, William L. Clements Library, University of Michigan, Ann Arbor, MI. For Cass's actions in the fall of 1847 and his appeal as a potential candidate, see Willard Carl Klunder, *Lewis Cass and the Politics of Moderation* (Kent, OH: Kent State University Press, 1996), 175–176.

5. "Intended to Delude the South": Northern Democrats Redefine Popular Sovereignty

1. Nicholson had supported Cass's bid for the Democratic nomination in 1844, much to the chagrin of James K. Polk. See Charles Sellers, *James K. Polk: Continentalist, 1843–1846* (Princeton, NJ: Princeton University Press, 1966), 8–10. For the nominees and the status of the presidential campaign season in the latter months of 1847, see Joel H. Silbey, *Party over Section: The Rough and Ready Presidential Election of 1848* (Lawrence: University Press of Kansas, 2009), 45–85; Joseph G. Rayback, *Free Soil: The Election of 1848* (Lexington: University Press of Kentucky, 1970), 56–80.

2. For Cass's presidential aspirations in 1844, see Willard Carl Klunder, *Lewis Cass and the Politics of Moderation* (Kent, OH: Kent State University Press, 1996), 119–144. Wright unexpectedly died in August 1847 just as his name entered discussion over the nomination.

3. Michael A. Morrison, *Slavery and the American West: The Eclipse of Manifest Destiny and the Coming of the Civil War* (Chapel Hill: University of North Carolina Press, 1997), 85. For the tactics of southern political leaders on the slavery question after Wilmot, see William J. Cooper, Jr., *The South and the Politics of Slavery, 1828–1856* (Baton Rouge: Louisiana State University Press, 1978), 240–244.

4. See Lewis Cass to John Larwill, February 6, 1848, Box 20 [photostat], Lewis Cass Papers, William L. Clements Library, University of Michigan, Ann Arbor, MI; David M. Potter, *The Impending Crisis, 1848–1861*, completed and edited by Don E. Fehrenbacher (New York: Harper & Row, 1976), 71.

5. *Washington Union*, December 30, 1847.

6. Ibid.

7. Ibid.

8. Ibid. The best analysis of the state sovereignty question is Arthur Bestor, "State Sovereignty and Slavery: A Reinterpretation of Proslavery Constitutional Doctrine, 1846–1860," *Journal of the Illinois State Historical Society* (Summer 1961): 117–180. See also Francis S.

Philbrick, ed., *The Laws of Illinois Territory* (Springfield: Illinois State Historical Library, 1950), lvii and passim.

9. Morrison, *Slavery and the American West*, 87.

10. Ibid., 84.

11. *Washington Union*, December 30, 1847.

12. *Congressional Globe*, 30th Cong., 1st Sess., 157, 159, 160; *S. Doc. Misc. No. 6*, 30th Cong., 1st Sess. (January 12, 1848). Serial Set No. 511.

13. John C. Calhoun to Henry Gourdin, January [ca. 15], 1848, in Clyde N. Wilson et al., eds., *The Papers of John C. Calhoun*, 28 vols. (Columbia: University of South Carolina Press, 1959–2004), 25: 121.

14. Campbell P. White to Daniel S. Dickinson, February 2, 1848, Daniel S. Dickinson Correspondence, Modern Manuscripts Collection, Newberry Library, Chicago, IL.

15. *New York Herald*, January 1, 1848.

16. Ibid., January 24, 1848.

17. *Richmond Enquirer*, January 4, 1848; *New Orleans Louisiana Courier*, January 7, 1848; *Milledgeville Federal Union*, January 11, 1848; *Richmond Enquirer*, January 25, 1848.

18. *Milledgeville Federal Union*, February 1, 1848.

19. Henry L. Benning to Howell Cobb, February 23, 1848, in Ulrich B. Phillips, ed., *The Correspondence of Robert Toombs, Alexander H. Stephens, and Howell Cobb* (Washington, DC: Government Printing Office, 1913), 97 (italics in the original).

20. Edward A. O'Neal to George S. Houston, February 6, 1848, Box 1, George Smith Houston Papers, Rare Book, Manuscript, and Special Collections Library, Duke University, Durham, NC; *Milledgeville Federal Union*, February 1, 1848.

21. Quoted in *Washington Union*, December 30, 1847. For an incisive assessment of Walker's theories on slavery in the West, see Thomas R. Hietala, *Manifest Design: Anxious Aggrandizement in Late Jacksonian America* (Ithaca, NY: Cornell University Press, 1985), 27–32.

22. Klunder, *Lewis Cass and the Politics of Moderation*, 162; *Washington Union*, December 30, 1847.

23. Henry L. Benning to Howell Cobb, February 23, 1848, in Phillips, ed., *Correspondence of Toombs, Stephens, and Cobb*, 98. For Cass's southern strength, see R. F. Simpson to James L. Orr, March 7, 1848, Orr and Patterson Family Papers #1413 (microfilm), Southern Historical Collection, The Wilson Library, University of North Carolina at Chapel Hill.

24. I. E. Holmes to Mitchell King, July 13, 1848, Folder 20, in the Mitchell King Papers #400, Southern Historical Collection, The Wilson Library, University of North Carolina at Chapel Hill; *New Hampshire Sentinel*, January 6, 1848.

25. John C. Calhoun to Henry Gourdin, January [ca. 15], 1848, in Wilson et al., eds., *Papers of John C. Calhoun*, 25: 121.

26. *Charleston Mercury*, quoted in *Niles' National Register*, February 19, 1848. For Calhoun's directives, see Henry Gourdin to John C. Calhoun, January 19, 1848, in Wilson et al., eds., *Papers of John C. Calhoun*, 25: 135–136.

27. Morrison, *Slavery and the American West*, 211–212.

28. *CG*, 30th Cong., 1st Sess., Appendix, 868–873. For an analysis of Calhoun's objections to the "Bright amendment," a provision extending the Missouri Compromise line, which Indiana senator Jesse Bright appended to the Oregon bill, see John Niven, *John C. Calhoun and the Price of Union* (Baton Rouge: Louisiana State University Press, 1988), 315–317.

29. *CG*, 30th Cong., 1st Sess., 1061. Historians have generally ignored the strength of the movement to extend the Missouri Compromise line, even though its ultimate rejection played

a significant role in the development of popular sovereignty, a point that David M. Potter noted in *Impending Crisis, 1848–1861*, 56–57, 71–73.

30. *S. Doc. Misc. No. 37*, 30th Cong., 1st Sess. (January 27, 1848). Serial Set No. 511.

31. Eric H. Walther, *William Lowndes Yancey and the Coming of the Civil War* (Chapel Hill: University of North Carolina Press, 2006), 98.

32. For the Alabama Platform, see ibid., 102–103.

33. W[illiam] L[owndes] Yancey, *An Address to the People of Alabama* (Montgomery, AL: Flag and Advertiser Office, 1848), 7, 13.

34. *New York Express*, quoted in *Boston Daily Atlas*, May 24, 1848. For support of the Alabama Platform, see Walther, *William Lowndes Yancey*, 102; Yancey, *Address to the People of Alabama*, 17–20. See also Rayback, *Free Soil*, 141–142. For the Woodbury campaign, see Silbey, *Party over Section*, 47, 140–141.

35. *Macon Weekly Telegraph*, April 25, 1848. For the southern resolutions, see Yancey, *Address to the People of Alabama*, 20–21.

36. The Woodbury letter is printed in Yancey, *Address to the People of Alabama*, 28–29.

37. *New Orleans Louisiana Courier*, March 11, 1848; *New York Herald*, September 22, 1848; Klunder, *Lewis Cass and the Politics of Moderation*, 178.

38. For the Baltimore convention, see Silbey, *Party over Section*, 62–68, Klunder, *Lewis Cass and the Politics of Moderation*, 184–187.

39. Democratic Party Platform, 1848, quoted in Silbey, *Party over Section*, 158; Yancey, *Address to the People of Alabama*, 42.

40. Yancey, *Address to the People of Alabama*, 48; *Richmond Enquirer*, June 2, 1848; Yancey, *Address to the People of Alabama*, 49; for the vote, see Rayback, *Free Soil*, 194.

41. Cooper, *The South and the Politics of Slavery*, 245. My interpretation of the Whig position in 1848 is indebted to Cooper's book, especially pp. 225–268; Morrison, *Slavery and the American West*, 87–95, and Michael F. Holt, *The Rise and Fall of the American Whig Party: Jacksonian Politics and the Onset of the Civil War* (New York: Oxford University Press, 1999), esp. pp. 310–382.

42. Holt, *Rise and Fall of the American Whig Party*, 357; Zachary Taylor to Jefferson Davis, April 20, 1848, in Lynda L. Crist et al., eds., *The Papers of Jefferson Davis*, 12 vols. to date (Baton Rouge: Louisiana State University Press, 1971–), 3: 306–307; *Richmond Enquirer*, June 6, 1848; *Charleston Mercury*, quoted in ibid., June 27, 1848.

43. "Democratic Platform," Speech in the Senate, July 3, 1848, in Henry Thomas Shanks, ed., *The Papers of Willie Person Mangum*, 5 vols. (Raleigh, NC: State Department of Archives and History, 1950–1956), 5: 664, 661.

44. *Richmond Enquirer*, June 6, 1848.

45. James Tallmadge to Daniel Webster, June 16, 1848, in Charles M. Wiltse et al., eds., *The Papers of Daniel Webster*, 15 vols. (Hanover, NH: University Press of New England, 1974–1989), Series 1: Correspondence, 6: 298; John C. Calhoun to Henry Bailey, June [ca. 15], 1848, in Wilson et al., eds., *Papers of John C. Calhoun*, 25: 484.

46. James C. Dobbin to Howell Cobb, June 15, 1848, in Phillips, ed., *Correspondence of Toombs, Stephens, and Cobb*, 108 (italics in the original).

47. *Mobile Journal*, quoted in *Milledgeville Federal Union*, June 13, 1848; *Richmond Whig*, quoted in *Richmond Enquirer*, June 30, 1848. See also *Richmond Enquirer*, July 14, 1848, and *New Orleans Louisiana Courier*, July 4, 1848.

48. Stephen A. Douglas to Lewis Cass, June 13, 1848, Box 12, Cass Papers. For a summary of Douglas's southern tour and speech in New Orleans, see Robert W. Johannsen, *Stephen A.*

Douglas (New York: Oxford University Press, 1973), 232–233. See also *Milledgeville Federal Union*, July 4, 1848.

49. Mansfield Torrance to John C. Calhoun, June 19, 1848, in Wilson et al., eds., *Papers of John C. Calhoun*, 15: 493.

50. *Richmond Enquirer*, July 21, 1848. See also *Washington Union*, quoted in *Niles' National Register*, July 26, 1848. My discussion of how race impacted the debate over territorial self-government is influenced by Hietala, *Manifest Design*, 152–166, and Eugene H. Berwanger, *The Frontier against Slavery: Western Anti-Negro Prejudice and the Slavery Extension Controversy* (Urbana: University of Illinois Press, 1967), 60–77 and passim.

51. Fitzwilliam Birdsall to John C. Calhoun, July 31, 1848, in Wilson et al., eds., *Papers of John C. Calhoun*, 15: 645; *Richmond Whig*, quoted in *Charleston Southern Patriot*, August 4, 1848.

52. *Milledgeville Federal Union*, July 26, 1848; *Richmond Enquirer*, August 15, 1848.

53. Don E. Fehrenbacher, *The Dred Scott Case: Its Significance in American Law and Politics* (New York: Oxford University Press, 1978), 149. For a summary of the Clayton Compromise, see Holt, *Rise and Fall of the American Whig Party*, 335–337; Fehrenbacher, *Dred Scott Case*, 148–151. For the slavery issue in Oregon Territory, see Robert W. Johannsen, "Oregon Territory's Movement for Self-Government, 1848–1853," in *The Frontier, the Union, and Stephen A. Douglas* (Urbana: University of Illinois Press, 1989), 3–18; Johannsen, *Frontier Politics on the Eve of the Civil War* (Seattle: University of Washington Press, 1955), 16–17.

54. *Richmond Enquirer*, August 8, 1848.

55. *New York Herald*, July 20, 1848.

56. Andrew S. Fulton to William B. Campbell, August 10, 1848, Box 24, Campbell Family Papers, Duke University; David Outlaw to Emily B. Outlaw, July 23, 1848, Folder 5, David Outlaw Papers #1534, Southern Historical Collection, The Wilson Library, University of North Carolina at Chapel Hill. See also letter of July 19, 1848.

57. For the votes on the Clayton Compromise, see Holt, *Rise and Fall of the American Whig Party*, 336–337.

58. A. H. Redfield to Dutee J. Pearce, August 20, 1848, Box 12, Cass Papers; *Richmond Enquirer*, August 15, 1848. Emphasis in the original.

59. *Richmond Enquirer*, August 18, 1848 (italics in the original).

60. Lewis Cass to Henry S. Foote, September 18, 1848, Box 12, Cass Papers; John Y. Mason to Lewis Cass, September 25, 1848, in ibid.

61. *Milledgeville Federal Union*, October 10, 1848; *Macon Georgia Telegraph*, October 3, 1848; *Clarksville Northern Standard*, October 21, 1848; William W. Freehling, *The Road to Disunion: Secessionists at Bay, 1776–1854* (New York: Oxford University Press, 1990), 476–477.

62. For a popular and electoral vote analysis, see Silbey, *Party over Section*, 134–137. See also Holt, *Rise and Fall of the American Whig Party*, 368–369.

63. *Boston Daily Atlas*, October 9, 1848.

64. *Milledgeville Federal Union*, November 14, 1848.

6. "Shall the Conquered Govern the Conqueror?"
Popular Sovereignty in the Mexican Cession

1. *Congressional Globe* (hereafter cited as *CG*), 31st Cong., 1st Sess., 300. For southern rejection of congressional power over slavery in the territories, see George William Van Cleve, *A*

Slaveholders' Union: Slavery, Politics, and the Constitution in the Early American Republic (Chicago: University of Chicago Press, 2010), 242–257.

2. For peonage in New Mexico, see Howard Roberts Lamar, *The Far Southwest, 1846–1912* (New Haven, CT: Yale University Press, 1966), 27–28; Loomis Morton Ganaway, *New Mexico and the Sectional Controversy* (Albuquerque: University of New Mexico Press, 1944), 9–10.

3. *CG*, 30th Cong., 2nd Sess., 5. In the antebellum era, Congress met in a short winter session, which in an election year meant that Congress met in between the election and seating of its successor body. The situation became even stranger in a presidential election year, when the president remained in office for almost four months after the election of his successor.

4. See Leonard L. Richards, *The California Gold Rush and the Coming of the Civil War* (New York: Alfred A. Knopf, 2007), 8–14. For Polk's comments on California, see ibid., 4–5.

5. *H.R. Exec. Doc. No. 41*, 30th Cong., 1st Sess. (1848), Serial Set No. 517, 98; Wilson Lumpkin to John C. Calhoun, January 3, 1849, in Clyde N. Wilson et al., eds., *The Papers of John C. Calhoun*, 28 vols. (Columbia: University of South Carolina Press, 1959–2004), 26: 200. See also *New York Herald*, quoted in *Milledgeville Federal Union*, January 9, 1849.

6. Louis T. Wigfall to John C. Calhoun, January 4, 1849, in Wilson et al., eds., *Papers of John C. Calhoun*, 26: 202; J. Pugh to John Meredith Read, Sr., January 7, 1849, Folder 1, John Meredith Read, Sr. Papers, Rare Book, Manuscript, and Special Collections Library, Duke University, Durham, NC; Andrew J. Donelson to John C. Calhoun, January 5, 1849, in Wilson et al., eds., *Papers of John C. Calhoun*, 26: 203.

7. For the southern Whigs' fears about Taylor, and Calhoun's Southern Address, see David M. Potter, *The Impending Crisis, 1848–1861*, completed and edited by Don E. Fehrenbacher (New York: Harper & Row, 1976), 83–87; John Niven, *John C. Calhoun and the Price of Union* (Baton Rouge: Louisiana State University Press, 1988), 322–327; Roy F. Nichols, ed., "The Mystery of the Dallas Papers (Part II)," *Pennsylvania Magazine of History and Biography* 73 (October 1949): 492–495.

8. For Douglas's introduction of the California bill, see *CG*, 30th Cong., 2nd Sess., 21; Robert W. Johannsen, *Stephen A. Douglas* (New York: Oxford University Press, 1973), 241–242.

9. *CG*, 30th Cong., 2nd Sess., 191.

10. Entry of January 9, 1849, George M. Dallas Diary [December 4, 1848–March 6, 1849], George M. Dallas Papers, Historical Society of Pennsylvania, Philadelphia, PA; Milo Milton Quaife, ed., *The Diary of James K. Polk During His Presidency, 1845–1849*, 4 vols. (Chicago: A. C. McClurg, 1910), 4: 287–288.

11. *Milledgeville Federal Union*, January 30, 1849; Johannsen, *Stephen A. Douglas*, 244. See also James L. Huston, *Stephen A. Douglas and the Dilemmas of Democratic Equality* (Lanham, MD: Rowman and Littlefield, 2007), 68–70.

12. *Washington Union*, quoted in *Baltimore Sun*, February 16, 1849.

13. Hopkins Holsey to Howell Cobb, February 13, 1849, in Ulrich B. Phillips, ed., *The Correspondence of Robert Toombs, Alexander H. Stephens, and Howell Cobb* (Washington, DC: Government Printing Office, 1913), 150.

14. For the proposed alliance between the Democrats and southern Whigs, see William J. Cooper, Jr., "'The Only Door': The Territorial Issue, the Preston Bill, and the Southern Whigs," in William J. Cooper, Jr., et al., eds. *A Master's Due: Essays in Honor of David Herbert Donald* (Baton Rouge: Louisiana State University Press, 1985), 76–78.

15. *CG*, 30th Cong., 2nd Sess., 480. For the bill and Preston's speech, see pp. 477–480.

16. *CG*, 30th Cong., 2nd Sess., Appendix, 213, 478 (italics in the original).

17. For ultra opposition to the Preston bill, see Hilliard M. Judge to John C. Calhoun, April 29, 1849, in Wilson et al., eds., *Papers of John C. Calhoun*, 26: 384–386; Fitzwilliam Byrdsall to John C. Calhoun, February 28, 1849, in ibid., 326–328.

18. Potter, *Impending Crisis*, 415; John Tyler to Robert Tyler, March 5, 1849, in Lyon Gardiner Tyler, ed., *The Letters and Times of the Tylers*, 2 vols. (Richmond: Whittet & Shepperson, 1884–1885), 2: 462. For Taylor's address, see James D. Richardson, ed., *A Compilation of the Messages and Papers of the Presidents, 1789–1897*, 10 vols. (Washington, DC: Government Printing Office, 1896–1899), 5: 4–6.

19. Michael F. Holt, *The Rise and Fall of the American Whig Party: Jacksonian Politics and the Onset of the Civil War*. New York: Oxford University Press, 1999, 412–415.

20. The most detailed narrative of the Taylor plan is Holt, *Rise and Fall of the American Whig Party*, 437–475; see also Michael A. Morrison, *Slavery and the American West: The Eclipse of Manifest Destiny and the Coming of the Civil War* (Chapel Hill: University of North Carolina Press, 1997), 103–105.

21. Quoted in Holt, *Rise and Fall of the American Whig Party*, 444. For Taylor's antislavery statement at Mercer, see also Holman Hamilton, *Zachary Taylor: Soldier in the White House* (Indianapolis: Bobbs-Merrill, 1951), 224–225, 227–228.

22. Holt, *Rise and Fall of the American Whig Party*, 444; Potter, *Impending Crisis*, 87; Speech at Evans' Crossroads, Greene County, TN, May 26, 1849, in Leroy P. Graf et al., eds., *The Papers of Andrew Johnson*, 16 vols. (Knoxville: University of Tennessee Press, 1967–1996), 1: 503. For Taylor's eroding support among southern Whigs, see William J. Cooper, Jr., *The South and the Politics of Slavery, 1828–1856* (Baton Rouge: Louisiana State University Press, 1978), 275–278.

23. Morrison, *Slavery and the American West*, 106; Cooper, *The South and the Politics of Slavery*, 275.

24. Herschel V. Johnson to John C. Calhoun, July 20, 1849, in Wilson et al., eds., *Papers of John C. Calhoun*, 16: 510; *Niles' National Register*, April 25, 1849. For southern opposition, see *Milledgeville Federal Union*, February 20, 1849; *Niles' National Register*, February 21, 1849, March 14, 1849, April 25, 1849.

25. *Washington Union*, quoted in *Milledgeville Federal Union*, June 12, 1849 (italics in the original removed).

26. Anthony Gene Carey, *Parties, Slavery, and the Union in Antebellum Georgia* (Athens: University of Georgia Press, 1997), 103; *Niles' National Register*, June 13, 1849. See Henry L. Benning to Howell Cobb, July 1, 1849, in Phillips, ed., *Correspondence of Toombs, Stephens, and Cobb*, 168–172.

27. *Washington Union*, July 17, 1849.

28. *Milledgeville Federal Union*, July 24, 1849. See also Carey, *Parties, Slavery, and the Union in Antebellum Georgia*, 103–104.

29. "Speech at a Democratic Convention in Rome, NY," August 15–17, 1849, in John R. Dickinson, ed., *Speeches, Correspondence, Etc., of the Late Daniel S. Dickinson, of New York . . .*, 2 vols. (New York G. P. Putnam & Son, 1867), 1: 318.

30. Herschel V. Johnson to John C. Calhoun, July 20, 1849, in Wilson et al., eds., *Papers of John C. Calhoun*, 16: 510; Levin H. Coe to John C. Calhoun, August 20, 1849, in ibid., 27: 27; Henry S. Foote to John C. Calhoun, September 25, 1849, in ibid., 27: 66.

31. Potter, *Impending Crisis*, 92. The concept of "political sovereignty" with respect to the slavery issue is developed in Van Cleve, *Slaveholders' Union*, 273–275 and passim.

32. *Richmond Enquirer*, August 7, 1849.

33. *Augusta Republic*, quoted in *Milledgeville Federal Union*, November 30, 1849; *Richmond Enquirer*, November 20, 1849. For the constitutional convention, see Richards, *California Gold Rush and the Coming of the Civil War*, 69–77.

34. See Holman Hamilton, *Prologue to Conflict: The Crisis and Compromise of 1850* (Lexington: University of Kentucky Press, 1964), 34–42.

35. For the Missouri resolutions, see *S. Doc. Misc, No. 5*, 31st Cong., 1st Sess. (1849), Serial Set No. 581, 1–2; *Columbus Daily Ohio Statesman*, January 7, 1850; *St. Louis Daily Missouri Republican*, January 22, 1850.

36. For Taylor's message, see *CG*, 31st Cong., 1st Sess., 195; Richardson, ed., *Messages and Papers of the Presidents*, 5: 26–30. See also Holt, *Rise and Fall of the American Whig Party*, 474–475. For the Taylor administration's efforts to actively promote statehood for New Mexico, see Mark J. Stegmaier, *Texas, New Mexico, and the Compromise of 1850* (Kent, OH: Kent State University Press, 1996), 68–79.

37. *CG*, 31st Cong., 1st Sess., 202; ibid., 205–210.

38. See Willard Carl Klunder, *Lewis Cass and the Politics of Moderation* (Kent, OH: Kent State University Press, 1996), 241–243.

39. *CG*, 31st Cong., 1st Sess., Appendix, 59.

40. *CG*, 31st Cong., 1st Sess., Appendix, 71.

41. For the citizenship issue, see Harold M. Hyman and William M. Wiecek, *Equal Justice under Law: Constitutional Development, 1835–1875* (New York: Harper & Row, 1982), 95, 181–183.

42. *Milledgeville Federal Union*, February 5, 1850; *New Orleans Louisiana Courier*, February 5, 1850. For opposition to the Cass speech, see *Baltimore Sun*, February 2, 1850.

43. *CG*, 31st Cong., 1st Sess., 245, 249. For the Nashville Convention, see Thelma Jennings, *The Nashville Convention: Southern Movement for Unity, 1848–1851* (Memphis, TN: Memphis State University Press, 1980); Potter, *Impending Crisis*, 94–95, 104–105. Clay's third resolution dealt with the explosive issue of the boundary of Texas and New Mexico, which obliquely concerned slavery in the territories. See Stegmaier, *Texas, New Mexico, and the Compromise of 1850*. For the resolutions, see *CG*, 31st Cong., 1st Sess., 244–247.

44. Carey, *Parties, Slavery, and the Union in Antebellum Georgia*, 161. See also Elizabeth R. Varon, *Disunion! The Coming of the American Civil War, 1789–1859* (Chapel Hill: University of North Carolina Press, 2008), 223–225.

45. *CG*, 31st Cong., 1st Sess., 246, 249–250. For Davis's opinion on the compromise measures, see William J. Cooper, Jr., *Jefferson Davis, American* (New York: Alfred A. Knopf, 2000), 189–191.

46. Quoted in Cooper, *Jefferson Davis, American*, 190.

47. *Milledgeville Federal Union*, February 5, 1850; *Richmond Enquirer*, February 5, 1850.

48. *New Orleans Louisiana Courier*, February 16, 1850; *New York Herald*, January 11, 1850; *Milledgeville Federal Union*, February 5, 1850; *Richmond Enquirer*, February 8, 1850. For the Georgia resolutions, see Herman V. Ames, ed., *State Documents on Federal Relations: The States and the United States* (1906; repr., New York: Da Capo Press, 1970), 260.

49. *CG*, 31st Cong., 1st Sess., 246.

50. See *Savannah Republican*, March 21, 1850.

51. *CG*, 31st Cong., 1st Sess., 398, 402.

52. David Outlaw to Emily B. Outlaw, March 4, 1850, Folder 8, David Outlaw Papers #1534, Southern Historical Collection, The Wilson Library, University of North Carolina at Chapel Hill.

53. *Milledgeville Federal Union*, March 12, 1850 (italics in the original). For the use of "Cass's proviso," see Carey, *Parties, Slavery, and the Union in Antebellum Georgia*, 101. For Bell's resolutions, see *CG*, 31st Cong., 1st Sess., 436–439.

54. *New Orleans Louisiana Courier*, April 1, 1850; John J. Crittenden to Orlando Brown, April 30, 1850, Box 2, John J. Crittenden Papers, Rare Book, Manuscript, and Special Collections Library, Duke University.

55. *CG*, 31st Cong., 1st Sess., Appendix, 432.

56. John Tyler to Alexander Gardiner, May 29, 1850, in Tyler, ed., *Letters and Times of the Tylers*, 2: 484. See also Tyler to Henry S. Foote, May 21, 1850, ibid., 485–489; *Richmond Enquirer*, May 31, 1850; *Augusta Constitutionalist*, quoted in *New Orleans Louisiana Courier*, June 1, 1850.

57. *CG*, 31st Cong., 1st Sess., 1003.

58. *Richmond Examiner*, quoted in *Milledgeville Federal Union*, June 11, 1850; *New Orleans Louisiana Courier*, June 21, 1850; R. M. T. Hunter to George Booker, May 24, 1850, Folder 1, George Booker Papers, Rare Book, Manuscript, and Special Collections Library, Duke University. The claim that slaveholders would settle in the west regardless of congressional dictate anticipates Stephen A. Douglas's Freeport Doctrine, in which he claimed that, in spite of the Supreme Court's proslavery ruling in *Dred Scott v. Sandford*, people in the territories could prohibit slavery by declining to enact laws favorable to slavery.

59. Holt, *Rise and Fall of the American Whig Party*, 487. For Clay's reticence to join his proposals in one bill, see Hamilton, *Prologue to Conflict*, 62.

60. *CG*, 31st Cong., 1st Sess., 1120, 1121, 1122.

61. *Richmond Enquirer*, June 28, 1850. For the convention, see Ganaway, *New Mexico and the Sectional Controversy*, 49–54; Stegmaier, *Texas, New Mexico, and the Compromise of 1850*, 115–133.

62. For Fillmore's course after assuming the presidency, see Holt, *Rise and Fall of the American Whig Party*, 521–530.

63. *New York Herald*, July 31, 1850; Andrew Ewing to Edwin [?], August 2, 1850, Folder 1, Andrew Ewing Papers, Rare Book, Manuscript, and Special Collections Library, Duke University, Durham, NC.

64. For Douglas's efforts, see Johannsen, *Stephen A. Douglas*, 294–303.

65. For a fascinating analysis of this often overlooked effort and its implications of popular sovereignty in New Mexico, see Holt, *Rise and Fall of the American Whig Party*, 540–541. For the assertion that the compromise granted territorial legislatures power to permit or prohibit slavery, see Robert R. Russel, "What Was the Compromise of 1850?" *Journal of Southern History* 22 (August 1956): 292–309. David M. Potter takes issue with this contention in *Impending Crisis*, 117n45.

66. "Letter from John A. Campbell to his Excellency, H. W. Collier," ca. October 5, 1850, Box 1, Abraham Watkins Venable Scrapbook, Rare Book, Manuscript, and Special Collections Library, Duke University, Durham, NC; Speech at Raymond, October 26, 1850, in Lynda L. Crist et al., eds., *The Papers of Jefferson Davis*, 12 vols. to date (Baton Rouge: Louisiana State University Press, 1971–), 4: 135; Speech at Fayette, July 11, 1851, in ibid., 183–218.

67. George M. Dallas to R. L. McWhorter, Jas. R. Sanders, B. E. Spencer, A. S. Williams, W. L. A. Harris, John Dyson, and O. A. McLaughlin of Pinfield, GA, November 19, 1850, George Mifflin Dallas Political and Business Papers, Box 5, Folder 2, Historical Society of Pennsylvania, Philadelphia, PA. For the finality of the Compromise of 1850, see Milo Milton Quaife, *The*

Doctrine of Non-Intervention with Slavery in the Territories (Chicago: Mac C. Chamberlin, 1910), 98–99.

7. "A Recurrence to First Principles": Kansas-Nebraska and Popular Sovereignty

1. See Elizabeth R. Varon, *Disunion! The Coming of the American Civil War, 1789–1859* (Chapel Hill: University of North Carolina Press, 2008), 227–231.

2. Speech at Fayette, July 11, 1851, in Lynda L. Crist et al., eds., *The Papers of Jefferson Davis*, 12 vols. to date (Baton Rouge: Louisiana State University Press, 1971–), 4: 190; Speech at Jackson, June 9, 1852, in ibid., 271.

3. J. Mills Thornton, III, *Politics and Power in a Slave Society: Alabama, 1800–1860* (Baton Rouge: Louisiana State University Press, 1978), 209–210. For the Union and Southern Rights movements, see William J. Cooper, Jr., *The South and the Politics of Slavery, 1828–1856* (Baton Rouge: Louisiana State University Press, 1978), 304–321; for individual state histories, see Thornton, *Politics and Power in a Slave Society*, 204–227; Anthony Gene Carey, *Parties, Slavery, and the Union in Antebellum Georgia* (Athens: University of Georgia Press, 1997), 164–180; Christopher J. Olsen, *Political Culture and Secession in Mississippi: Masculinity, Honor, and the Antiparty Tradition, 1830–1860* (New York: Oxford University Press, 2000), 45–53.

4. See Cooper, *The South and the Politics of Slavery*, 317–322.

5. *Congressional Globe* (hereafter cited as *CG*), 32nd Cong., 1st Sess., 784; Erastus Corning to William A. Seaver, December 13, 1851, Box 13, Lewis Cass Papers, William L. Clements Library, University of Michigan, Ann Arbor, MI. For southern opposition to Cass's 1852 candidacy, see David M. Potter, *The Impending Crisis, 1848–1861*, completed and edited by Don E. Fehrenbacher (New York: Harper & Row, 1976), 141–142; Roy F. Nichols, *The Democratic Machine, 1850–1854* (New York: Columbia University Press, 1923), 48–49.

6. See Robert W. Johannsen, *Stephen A. Douglas* (New York: Oxford University Press, 1973), 345–373; James L. Huston, *Stephen A. Douglas and the Dilemmas of Democratic Equality* (Lanham, MD: Rowman and Littlefield, 2006), 97–98.

7. Kirk H. Porter and Donald Bruce Johnson, eds., *National Party Platforms, 1840–1960*, 2nd ed. (Urbana: University of Illinois Press, 1961), 17.

8. Quoted in Roy Franklin Nichols, *Franklin Pierce: Young Hickory of the Granite Hills* (1931; Philadelphia: University of Pennsylvania Press, 1958), 202.

9. The literature on the origins of the Kansas-Nebraska Act and the transcontinental railroad is voluminous and occasionally superfluous, but the essential studies are Potter, *Impending Crisis*, 145–154; James C. Malin, *The Nebraska Question, 1852–1854* (Lawrence, KS: n.p., 1953), 24–153 and passim; P. Orman Ray, *The Repeal of the Missouri Compromise: Its Origin and Authorship* (Cleveland: Arthur C. Clark Company, 1909), 72–108; Johannsen, *Stephen A. Douglas*, 390–395. For a historiographical review of the act, which pays attention to its origins, see Roy F. Nichols, "The Kansas-Nebraska Act: A Century of Historiography," *Mississippi Valley Historical Review* 43 (September 1956): 187–212.

10. See Johannsen, *Stephen A. Douglas*, 391–395; Michael A. Morrison, *Slavery and the American West: The Eclipse of Jacksonian Democracy and the Coming of the Civil War* (Chapel Hill: University of North Carolina Press, 1997), 142–143.

11. *CG*, 32nd Cong., 2nd Sess., 1113. See also William E. Parrish, *David Rice Atchison: Bor-*

der Politician (Columbia: University of Missouri Press, 1961), 121–131; Malin, *Nebraska Question*, 102–112.

12. *CG*, 32nd Cong., 2nd Sess., 1113; quoted in Parrish, *David Rice Atchison*, 126.

13. Resolutions of the Nebraska Convention at St. Joseph, Missouri, January 1854, quoted in Ray, *Repeal of the Missouri Compromise*, 170. For a detailed discussion of the St. Joseph Convention and the impact of western Missourians on the Nebraska situation, see Malin, *Nebraska Question*, 207–287.

14. Stephen A. Douglas to J. H. Crane, D. M. Johnson, and L. J. Eastin, December 17, 1853, in Robert W. Johannsen, ed., *The Letters of Stephen A. Douglas* (Urbana: University of Illinois Press, 1961), 271. See also Johannsen, *Stephen A. Douglas*, 399–402.

15. *Richmond Enquirer*, December 6, 1853.

16. *Trenton State Gazette*, December 8, 1853.

17. *S. Rep. No. 15*, 33rd Cong., 1st Sess., (1854), Serial Set No. 706, 1, 4.

18. *Richmond Enquirer*, December 6, 1853; *New York Weekly Herald*, January 7, 1854; *Tallahassee Floridian and Journal*, January 14, 1854.

19. *New York Herald*, January 14, 1854; *New Orleans Louisiana Courier*, January 18, 1854.

20. *Milledgeville Federal Union*, January 10, 1854. On January 10, Douglas added another section to the bill, which had been omitted in a "clerical error." Some scholars have claimed that the new section reinvented the bill. While his claim of omission is dubious, the additional section merely affirmed the principles in the Compromise of 1850 in clearer language. It did not fundamentally alter the bill's meaning as some have claimed. See Johannsen, *Stephen A. Douglas*, 408–409.

21. *CG*, 33rd Cong., 1st Sess., 240.

22. Michael F. Holt, *The Rise and Fall of the American Whig Party: Jacksonian Politics and the Onset of the Civil War* (New York: Oxford University Press, 1999), 809; *CG*, 33rd Cong., 1st Sess., 175.

23. Henry Barrett Learned, "The Relation of Philip Phillips to the Repeal of the Missouri Compromise in 1854," *Mississippi Valley Historical Review* 8 (March 1922): 303–317, quote on p. 310.

24. Ibid., 313. See also Johannsen, *Stephen A. Douglas*, 413.

25. *New York Herald*, January 18, 1854. For Cass's rebuke of the *Herald*, see Willard Carl Klunder, *Lewis Cass and the Politics of Moderation* (Kent, OH: Kent State University Press, 1996), 266. For Cass's consultation with Pierce, see Nichols, *Franklin Pierce*, 321–322; Johannsen, *Stephen A. Douglas*, 413.

26. *Richmond Enquirer*, January 24, 1854; *St. Louis Daily Missouri Republican*, January 22, 1854. See Robert R. Russel, "Congressional Issues over the Kansas-Nebraska Act," *Journal of Southern History* 39 (May 1963): 193.

27. Quoted in Nichols, *Franklin Pierce*, 321–322.

28. For Davis's role in arranging the meeting, see William J. Cooper, Jr., *Jefferson Davis, American* (New York: Alfred A. Knopf, 2000), 286–287.

29. Nichols, *Franklin Pierce*, 323.

30. *CG*, 33rd Cong., 1st Sess., 221–222; *New York Herald*, January 24, 1854; *CG*, 33rd Cong., 1st Sess., 222. For the division of Nebraska, see Malin, *Nebraska Question*, 309–310.

31. *CG*, 33rd Cong., 1st Sess., 277; address is printed in ibid., 281–282. See also Mark E. Neely, Jr., "The Kansas-Nebraska Act in American Political Culture: The Road to Bladensburg and the *Appeal of the Independent Democrats*," in John R. Wunder and Joann M. Ross, eds., *The Nebraska-Kansas Act of 1854* (Lincoln: University of Nebraska Press, 2008):13–46.

32. *CG*, 33rd Cong., 1st Sess., 277.

33. Ibid., 279.

34. *New Orleans Louisiana Courier*, February 2, 1854; Robert Toombs to W. W. Burwell, February 3, 1854, in Ulrich B. Phillips, ed., *The Correspondence of Robert Toombs, Alexander H. Stephens, and Howell Cobb* (Washington, DC: Government Printing Office, 1913), 342; Howell Cobb to Stephen A. Douglas, February 5, 1854, Box 3, Folder 5, Stephen A. Douglas Papers, Special Collections, Joseph Regenstein Library, University of Chicago, Chicago, IL; Stephen A. Douglas to Howell Cobb, April 2, 1854, Johannsen, ed., *Letters of Stephen A. Douglas*, 300.

35. John Tyler to Col. David Gardiner, February 2, 1854, in Lyon Gardiner Tyler, ed., *The Letters and Times of the Tylers*, 2 vols. (Richmond: Whittet & Shepperson, 1884–1885), 2: 509; *Milledgeville Federal Union*, February 7, 1854.

36. *Charleston Mercury*, quoted in *New Orleans Louisiana Courier*, January 29, 1854. See also *New York Herald*, January 29, 1854.

37. See Harold M. Hyman and William M. Wiecek, *Equal Justice under Law: Constitutional Developments, 1835–1875* (New York: Harper & Row, 1982), 132–140, 163–166; Don E. Fehrenbacher, *The Dred Scott Case: Its Significance in American Law and Politics* (New York: Oxford University Press, 1978), 135–147.

38. *New York Weekly Herald*, February 11, 1854; *New Orleans Louisiana Courier*, February 12, 1854. For use of the term "popular sovereignty," see Edmund S. Morgan, *Inventing the People: The Rise of Popular Sovereignty in England and America* (New York: W. W. Norton, 1988).

39. Jeremiah Clemens to John Van Buren, February 4, 1854, printed in *Trenton State Gazette*, February 9, 1854. See also John Van Buren to Jeremiah Clemens, February 3, 1854, Box 13, Lewis Cass Papers, Clements Library; *Richmond Enquirer*, February 21, 1854. For southern opposition to Kansas-Nebraska, see Avery O. Craven, *The Growth of Southern Nationalism, 1848–1861* (Baton Rouge: Louisiana State University Press, 1953), 192–205. Craven, however, exaggerates opposition in the South to the Douglas bill.

40. *CG*, 33rd Cong., 1st Sess., Appendix, 340, 338.

41. In *The Rise and Fall of the American Whig Party*, 814–816, Michael F. Holt argues that southern Whigs had contemplated opposing the bill precisely because it sanctioned repeal. For a fleeting moment, they sought to portray the Kansas-Nebraska bill as dangerous to sectional harmony and a needless attack on the great compact of 1820. The Free Soil attack on the bill dashed their hopes. Southern Whigs, however, had to defend slavery in order to maintain support at home. Southern Democrats had rallied behind southern rights; therefore, the Whigs could not afford but to follow suit and endorse repeal. See Cooper, *The South and the Politics of Slavery*, 350–353.

42. *CG*, 33rd Cong., 1st Sess., Appendix, 272, 279.

43. *Baltimore Sun*, February 28, 1854; S. W. Johnston to Stephen A. Douglas, March 24, 1854, Box 3, Folder 6, Douglas Papers; *Macon Georgia Telegraph*, February 28, 1854; *New Orleans Louisiana Courier*, March 8, 1854.

44. *CG*, 33rd Cong., 1st Sess., Appendix, 347. For the moderates' position, see Russel, "Congressional Issues over the Kansas-Nebraska Bill," 188–189, 201.

45. *CG*, 33rd Cong., 1st Sess., Appendix, 224; *Austin Texas State Gazette*, February 28, 1854; *CG*, 33rd Cong., 1st Sess., 420; *Richmond Enquirer*, February 21, 1854. See also Milo Milton Quaife, *The Doctrine of Non-Intervention with Slavery in the Territories* (Chicago: Mac C. Chamberlin, 1910), 111.

46. *CG*, 33rd Cong., 1st Sess., 423.

47. *CG*, 33rd Cong., 1st Sess., 520. See Johannsen, *Stephen A. Douglas*, 427–428; Russel, "Congressional Issues over the Kansas-Nebraska Bill," 203–204.

48. *CG*, 33rd Cong., 1st Sess., Appendix, 304.

49. *CG*, 33rd Cong., 1st Sess., Appendix, 326. See also Johannsen, *Stephen A. Douglas*, 428–432.

50. *CG*, 33rd Cong., 1st Sess., Appendix, 327, 337, 328.

51. David S. Reid to Stephen A. Douglas, March 16, 1854, Box 3, Folder 7, Douglas Papers; John M. Daniel to Stephen A. Douglas, March 16, 1854, in ibid.; *Tallahassee Floridian and Journal*, March 18, 1854. For the vote in the Senate, see *CG*, 33rd Cong., 1st Sess., 538. For vote analyses, see Holt, *Rise and Fall of the American Whig Party*, 819–820; Johannsen, *Stephen A. Douglas*, 432; Cooper, *The South and the Politics of Slavery*, 354.

52. S. W. Johnston to Stephen A. Douglas, March 24, 1854, Box 3, Folder 6, Douglas Papers; *New York Herald*, March 23, 1854.

53. *New Orleans Louisiana Courier*, April 2, 1854.

54. *Milledgeville Federal Union*, April 11, 1854. For northern recognition of southern dissent, see *Boston Daily Atlas*, April 29, 1854.

55. *Milledgeville Federal Union*, April 11, 1854; Horatio Seymour to Stephen A. Douglas, April 14, 1854, Box 3, Folder 6, Douglas Papers.

56. *Milledgeville Federal Union*, April 18, 1854, April 11, 1854; *New York Sun*, quoted in *Trenton State Gazette*, April 20, 1854.

57. For the Cutting amendment, see *CG*, 33rd Cong., 1st Sess., 701–703. The classic narrative of the once-neglected battle in the House over Kansas-Nebraska is Roy F. Nichols, *Blueprints for Leviathan: American Style* (New York: Atheneum, 1963), 104–120.

58. Alexander Stephens to W. W. Burwell, May 7, 1854, in Phillips, ed., *Correspondence of Toombs, Stephens, and Cobb*, 344; Holt, *The Rise and Fall of the American Whig Party*, 821. See the roll-call analysis in Thomas B. Alexander, *Sectional Stress and Party Strength: A Study of Roll-Call Voting Patterns in the United States House of Representatives, 1836–1860* (Nashville: Vanderbilt University Press, 1967), 85–90, 226–229. For a discussion of territorial expansion in the Caribbean and the slavery issue, see Robert E. May, *The Southern Dream of a Caribbean Empire, 1854–1861* (Baton Rouge: Louisiana State University Press, 1973), 59–60, 177–181 and passim.

59. Alexander Stephens to J. W. Duncan, May 26, 1854, in Phillips, ed., *Correspondence of Toombs, Stephens, and Cobb*, 345; John Tyler to Rev. William Tyler, February 2, 1854, in Tyler, ed., *Letters and Times of the Tylers*, 2: 510; *New York Herald*, May 27, 1854.

60. Solomon G. Haven to James M. Smith, May 16, 1854, Solomon G. Haven Papers, William L. Clements Library, University of Michigan, Ann Arbor.

61. William B. W. Dent to Herschel V. Johnson, June 13, 1854, Box 1, Herschel Vespasian Johnson Papers, Duke University, Durham, NC; William Walker to David Rice Atchison, July 11, 1854, David Rice Atchison Papers, Western Historical Manuscript Collection, University of Missouri at Columbia, Columbia, MO.

62. *Little Rock Arkansas Whig*, June 1, 1854.

63. See Nicole Etcheson, *Bleeding Kansas: Contested Liberty in the Civil War Era* (Lawrence: University Press of Kansas, 2004), 9–27.

64. Stephen A. Douglas to Indiana State Central Committee, August 8, 1854, Box 38, Folder 18, Douglas Papers; *Madison Wisconsin Patriot*, July 24, 1854; William Walker to David Rice Atchison, July 11, 1854, Atchison Papers.

65. Holt, *Rise and Fall of the American Whig Party*, 839. See also Cooper, *The South and the Politics of Slavery*, 359–360. The election statistics are taken from Potter, *Impending Crisis*, 175.

8. "Moves on the Political Chess-Board":
Southerners Redefine Popular Sovereignty

1. See Nicole Etcheson, *Bleeding Kansas: Contested Liberty in the Civil War Era* (Lawrence: University Press of Kansas, 2004), 30–31.

2. Herman V. Ames, ed., *State Documents on Federal Relations: The States and the United States* (1906; New York: Da Capo Press, 1970), 282, 285; *Milledgeville Federal Union*, June 19, 1855.

3. *S. Misc. Doc. No. 23*, 33rd Cong., 1st Sess. (1854), Serial Set No. 705, 3. Until recently, historians have usually ignored Nebraska's path to statehood, instead focusing on its wayward southern neighbor. Nicole Etcheson has explained how popular sovereignty succeeded in Nebraska; see "Where Popular Sovereignty Worked: Nebraska Territory and the Kansas-Nebraska Act," in John R. Wunder and Joann M. Ross, eds., *The Nebraska-Kansas Act of 1854* (Lincoln: University of Nebraska Press, 2008): 159–182.

4. The best treatment of the Bleeding Kansas period is Etcheson, *Bleeding Kansas*. For the elections of 1854 and 1855, see pp. 50–68. See also David M. Potter, *The Impending Crisis, 1848–1861*, completed and edited by Don E. Fehrenbacher (New York: Harper & Row, 1976), 199–224.

5. Quotes from Etcheson, *Bleeding Kansas*, 63, 68.

6. Etcheson, *Bleeding Kansas*, 51–52. For a survey of different voting processes in the antebellum era, see Chilton Williamson, *American Suffrage from Property to Democracy* (Princeton, NJ: Princeton University Press, 1960), 260–280.

7. *Milledgeville Federal Union*, March 4, 1856. For the origins of Kansas settlers, see Etcheson, *Bleeding Kansas*, 29.

8. *Milledgeville Federal Union*, March 4, 1856. For the origins of Kansas settlers, see Etcheson, *Bleeding Kansas*, 29; Jefferson Davis to William R. Cannon, December 7, 1855, in Lynda L. Crist et al., eds., *The Papers of Jefferson Davis*, 12 vols. to date (Baton Rouge: Louisiana State University Press, 1971–), 5: 141–142. See Etcheson, *Bleeding Kansas*, 35–38; Allan Nevins, *The Ordeal of the Union*, 2 vols. (New York: Charles Scribner's Sons, 1947), 2: 306–316.

9. Herschel V. Johnson to John W. Stoward, June 11, 1855, Box 1, Herschel Vespasian Johnson Papers, Rare Book, Manuscript, and Special Collections Library, Duke University, Durham, NC; Herschel V. Johnson to L. B. Smith, E. J. McGehee, John Ward, and R. H. D. Sorell, June 8, 1855; Johnson to Col. T. Lomax, June 21, 1855, in ibid.

10. C. S. Tarpley to Stephen A. Douglas, November 15, 1855, Box 3, Folder 14, Stephen A. Douglas Papers, Special Collections, Joseph Regenstein Library, University of Chicago, Chicago, IL; *Richmond Enquirer*, November 20, 1855.

11. *Richmond Enquirer*, February 5, 1856 (italics in the original).

12. Potter, *Impending Crisis*, 206. For a complete account of the political turmoil, see Etcheson, *Bleeding Kansas*, 50–102.

13. Quoted in Roy Franklin Nichols, *Franklin Pierce: Young Hickory of the Granite Hills* (1931; Philadelphia: University of Pennsylvania Press, 1958), 442; *New York Herald*, May 14, 1856.

14. Michael A. Morrison, *Slavery and the American West: The Eclipse of Manifest Destiny and the Coming of the Civil War* (Chapel Hill: University of North Carolina Press, 1997), 164; for Kansas-Nebraska, popular sovereignty, and the origins of the Republican Party, see ibid., 162–175; William E. Gienapp, *The Origins of the Republican Party, 1852–1856* (New York: Ox-

ford University Press, 1987); Eric Foner, *Free Soil, Free Labor, Free Men: The Ideology of the Republican Party before the Civil War* (New York: Oxford University Press, 1970), esp. 124–133.

15. *Richmond Enquirer*, March 11, 1856, March 28, 1856.

16. *Milledgeville Federal Union*, March 18, 1856. For Douglas's efforts, see Stephen A. Douglas to Howell Cobb, January 8, 1856; Douglas to James W. Singleton, March 16, 1856, in Robert W. Johannsen, ed., *The Letters of Stephen A. Douglas* (Urbana: University of Illinois Press, 1961), 346–347, 351.

17. *Richmond Enquirer*, March 14, 1856; *Milledgeville Federal Union*, August 5, 1856.

18. *Official Proceedings of the Democratic National Convention, Held in Cincinnati, June 2–6, 1856* (Cincinnati: Enquirer Company, 1856), 26. For a colorful description of the Cincinnati convention, see Roy F. Nichols, *The Disruption of American Democracy* (New York: Macmillan, 1948), 14–18. See also Nevins, *Ordeal of the Union*, 2: 456–460.

19. Morrison, *Slavery and the American West*, 177–178; *Proceedings of the Democratic National Convention*, 50–58. See also Nevins, *Ordeal of the Union*, 2: 459–460.

20. *Proceedings of the Democratic National Convention*, 70, 76.

21. Charles W. Johnson, *Proceedings of the First Three Republican Conventions of 1856, 1860, and 1864* (Minneapolis: n.p., 1893), 43; second quote in William E. Gienapp, *Origins of the Republican Party, 1852–1856* (New York: Oxford University Press, 1987), 75.

22. "Speech at Bloomington, Illinois, September 26, 1854," in Roy P. Basler, ed., *The Collected Works of Abraham Lincoln*, 9 vols. (New Brunswick, NJ: Rutgers University Press, 1953–1955), 2: 239; "Speech at Peoria, Illinois, October 16, 1854," in ibid., 266. For the Republican critique of popular sovereignty, see James L. Huston, *Stephen A. Douglas and the Dilemmas of Democratic Equality* (Lanham, MD: Rowman and Littlefield, 2007), 110–111; Morrison, *Slavery and the American West*, 164–172.

23. Gienapp, *Origins of the Republican Party*, 349–354.

24. *Milledgeville Federal Union*, August 5, 1856. For an excellent summary of the southern Know-Nothing position, see Avery O. Craven, *The Growth of Southern Nationalism, 1848–1861* (Baton Rouge: Louisiana State University Press, 1953), 240–242. The standard history of the party in the South is W. Darrell Overdyke, *The Know-Nothing Party in the South* (Baton Rouge: Louisiana State University Press, 1950).

25. *Milledgeville Federal Union*, August 19, 1856, October 28, 1856.

26. Stephen A. Douglas to James Buchanan, September 29, 1856, in Johannsen, ed., *Letters of Stephen A. Douglas*, 367–368; Speech at a Democratic Meeting at Brooklyn, October 21, 1856, in John R. Dickinson, ed., *Speeches, Correspondence, Etc., of the Late Daniel S. Dickinson, of New York*, 2 vols. (New York: G. P. Putman and Sons, 1867), 1: 533. For an account of Douglas's efforts, see Johannsen, *Stephen A. Douglas*, 535–539.

27. Morrison, *Slavery and the American West*, 185.

28. Speech at Wheatland, November 6, 1856, in John Bassett Moore, ed., *The Works of James Buchanan: Comprising His Speeches, State Papers, and Private Correspondence*, 12 vols. (Philadelphia and London: J. B. Lippincott, 1908–1911), 10: 97 (italics in the original).

29. *New York Herald*, December 28, 1856.

30. Act of May 30, 1854, ch. 59, 10 *U.S. Statutes at Large*, 277–290; quoted in Potter, *Impending Crisis*, 271.

31. The standard history of *Dred Scott v. Sandford* is Don E. Fehrenbacher, *The Dred Scott Case: Its Significance in American Law and Politics* (New York: Oxford University Press, 1978). For a brief recent summary of the case, see Earl M. Maltz, *Dred Scott and the Politics of Slavery*

(Lawrence: University Press of Kansas, 2007). For an alternative view that emphasizes the evolution of the Court's thought on self-rule and popular sovereignty, see Austin Allen, *Origins of the Dred Scott Case: Jacksonian Jurisprudence and the Supreme Court, 1837–1857* (Athens: University of Georgia Press, 2006), 178–202 and passim.

32. Fehrenbacher, *Dred Scott Case*, 311; Inaugural Address, March 4, 1857, in Moore, ed., *Works of James Buchanan*, 10: 105.

33. Moore, ed., *Works of James Buchanan*, 10: 106. For the letters of Catron and Grier, see 106–108n1.

34. Benjamin Howard et al., eds., *Reports of Cases Argued and Adjudged in the Supreme Court of the United States*, 67 vols. (Boston: Charles C. Little and James Brown and others: 1804–1861), 19: 393.

35. Ibid., 19: 434–437. For a discussion of the citizenship issue, see Fehrenbacher, *Dred Scott Case*, 335–364.

36. Ibid., 439, 449.

37. Ibid., 450.

38. See Fehrenbacher, *Dred Scott Case*, 379.

39. *Baltimore Sun*, March 9, 1857; *Charleston Mercury*, April 2, 1857; Kenneth M. Stampp, *America in 1857: A Nation on the Brink* (New York: Oxford University Press, 1990), 100.

40. *Baltimore Sun*, March 9, 1857 (italics in the original); *Augusta Constitutionalist*, March 15, 1857; Morrison, *Slavery and the American West*, 189.

41. See Willard Carl Klunder, *Lewis Cass and the Politics of Moderation* (Kent, OH: Kent State University Press, 1996), 296–297.

42. Quoted in Johannsen, *Stephen A. Douglas*, 569. The Mormon question assumed limited significance in the popular sovereignty debate because of the polygamy issue. Politicians in Washington questioned whether the settlers in Utah should have the right to exercise self-government, given their unorthodox religious beliefs and suspicions of some that the Mormon Church desired to establish a religious oligarchy in the territory. See Sarah Barringer Gordon, *The Mormon Question: Polygamy and Constitutional Conflict in Nineteenth-Century America* (Chapel Hill: University of North Carolina Press, 2001).

43. *Congressional Globe* (hereafter cited as *CG*), 34th Cong., 3rd Sess., 103–104. See also Stampp, *America in 1857*, 102–104.

44. Judah P. Benjamin to Lewis Cass, March 9, 1857, Box 14, Lewis Cass Papers, William L. Clements Library, University of Michigan, Ann Arbor, MI; Speech at Jackson, May 29, 1857, Crist et al., eds., *Papers of Jefferson Davis*, 6: 122.

45. Allan Nevins, *The Emergence of Lincoln*, 2 vols. (New York: Charles Scribner's Sons, 1950), 1: 145. For Walker's appointment as territorial governor, see Etcheson, *Bleeding Kansas*, 143–149.

46. *Charleston Mercury*, quoted in *New York Herald*, May 27, 1857; *Milledgeville Federal Union*, June 23, 1857; see Stampp, *America in 1857*, 165; *Inaugural Address of R. J. Walker, Governor of Kansas Territory* (Lecompton, KS: Union Office, 1857), 6; *New York Herald*, June 6, 7, 1857.

47. Etcheson, *Bleeding Kansas*, 141–158.

48. *New York Herald*, June 12, 1857; *New Orleans Crescent*, July 17, 1857; *Milledgeville Federal Union*, July 21, 1857.

49. Stephen A. Douglas to Robert J. Walker, July 21, 1857, Johannsen, ed., *Letters of Stephen A. Douglas*, 386.

50. Robert A. Toombs to Lewis Cass, July 28, 1857, Cass Papers. For Cass's instructions to Walker, see *Transactions of the Kansas State Historical Society*, 10 vols. (Topeka, KS: 1875–1908), 5: 323–324.

51. *New York Herald*, July 4, 1857; Howell Cobb to Lewis Cass, August 1, 1857, Cass Papers; Jefferson Davis to Lewis Cass, August 1, 1857, in ibid.; James Buchanan to Lewis Cass, August 5, 1857, in ibid.

52. Robert Toombs to Lewis Cass, August 11, 1857, Cass Papers; *Milledgeville Federal Union*, September 8, 1857. For contemporary examples of the comparison between Kansas and California, see *New York Herald*, July 4, 1857; *Charleston Mercury*, July 7, 1857.

53. First Annual Message, December 8, 1857, in James D. Richardson, ed., *A Compilation of the Messages and Papers of the Presidents, 1789–1897*, 10 vols. (Washington, DC: Government Printing Office, 1896–1899), 5: 453; Stampp, *America in 1857*, 282.

54. *New York Herald*, December 5, 1857; *CG*, 35th Cong., 1st Sess., 15.

55. Ibid., 16, 15; Johannsen, *Stephen A. Douglas*, 592.

56. *Baltimore Sun*, December 12, 1857; *Charleston Mercury*, December 15, 1857; John Tyler to Robert Tyler, December 14, 1857, in Lyon Gardiner Tyler, ed., *The Letters and Times of the Tylers*, 2 vols. (Richmond: Whittet & Shepperson, 1884–1885), 2: 541.

57. Potter, *Impending Crisis*, 318; Etcheson, *Bleeding Kansas*, 156–161. Of the 162 voters for Lecompton, 138 voted for the document with slavery and 24 for it without.

58. See Morrison, *Slavery and the American West*, 189–206.

59. Stephen A. Douglas to John W. Forney et al., February 6, 1858, Johannsen, ed., *Letters of Stephen A. Douglas*, 408; Joseph E. Brown to Alexander Stephens, March 26, 1858, in Ulrich B. Phillips, ed., *The Correspondence of Robert Toombs, Alexander H. Stephens, and Howell Cobb* (Washington, DC: Government Printing Office, 1913), 432.

60. See Etcheson, *Bleeding Kansas*, 168–189.

61. Potter, *Impending Crisis*, 324–325, 184; William J. Cooper, Jr., *Jefferson Davis, American* (New York: Alfred A. Knopf, 2000), 294–296.

62. See Elizabeth R. Varon, *Disunion! The Coming of the American Civil War, 1789–1859* (Chapel Hill: University of North Carolina Press, 2008), 305–310.

Epilogue: The Demise of Popular Sovereignty and the Crisis of the Union

1. See Michael A. Morrison, *Slavery and the American West: The Eclipse of Manifest Destiny and the Coming of the Civil War* (Chapel Hill: University of North Carolina Press, 1997), 191–193.

2. Stephen A. Douglas to James W. Singleton, March 31, 1859, in Robert W. Johannsen, ed., *Letters of Stephen A. Douglas* (Urbana: University of Illinois Press, 1961), 439. See Stephen A. Douglas, *The Dividing Line between Federal and Local Authority* (New York: Harper & Brothers, 1859). The best analysis of Douglas's *Harper's* article is Robert W. Johannsen, "Douglas, *Harper's Magazine*, and Popular Sovereignty," in *The Frontier, the Union, and Stephen A. Douglas* (Urbana: University of Illinois Press, 1989), 120–145.

3. See Johannsen, "Douglas, *Harper's Magazine*, and Popular Sovereignty," 123–124; Robert W. Johannsen, *Stephen A. Douglas* (New York: Oxford University Press, 1973), 706–707.

4. Douglas, *Dividing Line*, 8, 12.

5. See ibid., 26–28; Johannsen, "Douglas, *Harper's Magazine*, and Popular Sovereignty," 130–131.

6. *Nashville Union*, September 7, 1859; *Richmond Enquirer*, August 30, 1859; *New Orleans Delta*, September 15, 1859. For the general reaction of the South to the essay, see Avery O. Craven, *The Growth of Southern Nationalism, 1848–1861* (Baton Rouge: Louisiana State University Press, 1953), 302–303.

7. *New York Tribune*, October 15, 1859.

8. [Jeremiah S. Black], *Observations on Senator Douglas's Views of Popular Sovereignty, as Expressed in* Harper's Magazine, *for September 1859*, 2nd ed. (Washington, DC: Thomas McGill, 1859), 4, 5. Italics in the original.

9. Ibid., 6, 13.

10. *New Orleans Delta*, April 3, 1860. Italics in the original.

11. *Congressional Globe* (hereafter cited as *CG*), 36th Cong., 1st Sess., 404, 658. Some historians have claimed that Davis, too, proposed a federal slave code; others dispute the point. See William J. Cooper, Jr., *Jefferson Davis, American* (New York: Alfred A. Knopf, 2000), 305–306; William W. Freehling, *The Road to Disunion: Secessionists Triumphant, 1854–1861* (New York: Oxford University Press, 2007), 275–278.

12. William B. Hesseltine, ed., *Three against Lincoln: Murat Halstead Reports the Caucuses of 1860* (Baton Rouge: Louisiana State University Press, 1960), xv. For a comprehensive analysis of the Democratic convention, including a description of the city and the conditions, see Freehling, *Road to Disunion: Secessionists Triumphant, 1854–1861*, 288–308, and *Three against Lincoln*. For Douglas's efforts, see James L. Huston, *Stephen A. Douglas and the Dilemmas of Democratic Equality* (Lanham, MD: Rowman and Littlefield, 2007), 160–162.

13. Hesseltine, ed., *Three against Lincoln*, 35.

14. *Official Proceedings of the Democratic National Convention, Held in 1860 in Charleston and Baltimore* (Cleveland: Plain Dealer Job Office, 1860), 47. For the differences within the Democracy, see Huston, *Stephen A. Douglas and the Dilemmas of Democratic Equality*, 162–165; Morrison, *Slavery and the American West*, 219–229.

15. Ibid., 48; Hesseltine, ed., *Three against Lincoln*, 61.

16. Stephen A. Douglas to William H. Ludlow, R. P. Dick, R. C. Wickliffe, et al., June 27, 1860, in Johannsen, ed., *Letters of Stephen A. Douglas*, 494.

17. Hesseltine, ed., *Three against Lincoln*, 182.

18. See William J. Cooper, Jr., *Liberty and Slavery: Southern Politics to 1860* (New York: Random House, 1983), 263–264.

19. Platform printed in Hesseltine, ed., *Three against Lincoln*, 156–158. See also See Potter, *Impending Crisis*, 416–417; Hesseltine, ed., *Three against Lincoln*, 118–140.

20. See Ronald C. White, Jr., *A. Lincoln: A Biography* (New York: Random House, 2009), 298–301; Don E. Fehrenbacher, *Prelude to Greatness: Lincoln in the 1850s* (Stanford, CA: Stanford University Press, 1962), 78–83.

21. *CG*, 36th Congress, 2nd Session, 279. See also Russell McClintock, *Lincoln and the Decision for War: The Northern Response to Secession* (Chapel Hill: University of North Carolina Press, 2008), 116–117; Daniel W. Crofts, *Reluctant Confederates: Upper South Unionists in the Secession Crisis* (Chapel Hill: University of North Carolina Press, 1989), 201–207. A similar plan appeared during the Washington Peace Conference in February 1861.

22. Historians have amply chronicled the debate between Lincoln and Seward over compromise; for the most recent account, see McClintock, *Lincoln and the Decision for War*, 93–185.

See also William C. Harris, *Lincoln's Rise to the Presidency* (Lawrence: University Press of Kansas, 2007), 290–293.

23. *CG*, 36th Cong., 2nd Sess., 729, 765, 1005, 1207–1208, 1334–1335. Bills to create two other territories—Idaho and Arizona—did not pass. Idaho became a territory in 1863. Arizona was a Confederate territory from 1861 to 1863, when Union forces regained control of the region. For Douglas's response, see Johannsen, *Stephen A. Douglas*, 830–831.

24. *CG*, 36th Cong., 2nd Sess., 763–765.

25. Ibid., 1205.

26. "The Constitution of the Confederate States of America, March 11, 1861," quoted in Emory M. Thomas, *The Confederate States of America, 1861–1865* (New York: Harper & Row, 1979), 320. For analysis of the Confederate constitution, see Mark E. Neely, Jr., *Lincoln and the Triumph of the Nation: Constitutional Conflict in the American Civil War* (Chapel Hill: University of North Carolina Press, 2011), 237–240; George C. Rable, *The Confederate Republic: A Revolution against Politics* (Chapel Hill: University of North Carolina Press, 1994), 39–63.

Bibliography

Primary Sources

Manuscript Collections
Rare Book, Manuscript, and Special Collections Library, Duke University, Durham, NC
    Bedinger-Dandridge Papers
    George Booker Papers
    Campbell Family Papers
    John J. Crittenden Papers
    Andrew Ewing Papers
    George Smith Houston Papers
    Herschel Vespasian Johnson Papers
    John Meredith Read, Sr., Papers
    Abraham Watkins Venable Scrapbook
Historical Society of Pennsylvania, Philadelphia, PA
    George Mifflin Dallas Political and Business Papers
Special Collections, Joseph Regenstein Library, University of Chicago, Chicago, IL
    Stephen A. Douglas Papers
Modern Manuscripts Collection, Newberry Library, Chicago, IL
    Daniel S. Dickinson Correspondence
Southern Historical Collection, The Wilson Library, University of North Carolina at Chapel Hill
    James McDowell Papers
    Orr and Patterson Family Papers
    David Outlaw Papers
Western Historical Manuscript Collection, University of Missouri at Columbia
    David Rice Atchison Papers
William L. Clements Library, University of Michigan, Ann Arbor
    James G. Birney Papers
    Lewis Cass Papers
    Solomon G. Haven Papers
    William Claude Tell Editorials

Letterpress Collections
Adams, John Quincy. *The Diaries of John Quincy Adams: A Digital Collection*. Boston: Massachusetts Historical Society, 2004.
Adams, Charles Francis, ed. *Memoirs of John Quincy Adams, Comprising Portions of His Diary from 1795 to 1848*, 12 vols. Philadelphia: J. B. Lippincott, 1874–1877.
Basler, Roy P., ed., *The Collected Works of Abraham Lincoln*, 9 vols. New Brunswick, NJ: Rutgers University Press, 1953–1955.

Boyd, Julian P., et al., eds. *The Papers of Thomas Jefferson*, 34 vols. to date. Princeton, NJ: Princeton University Press, 1950–.

Crist, Lynda L., et al., eds. *The Papers of Jefferson Davis*, 12 vols. to date. Baton Rouge: Louisiana State University Press, 1971–.

Dickinson, John R., ed. *Speeches, Correspondence, Etc., of the Late Daniel S. Dickinson, of New York . . .*, 2 vols. New York G. P. Putnam & Son, 1867.

Ford, Worthington Chauncey, ed. *Writings of John Quincy Adams*, 7 vols. New York: Macmillan, 1913–1917.

Graf, Leroy P., et al., eds. *The Papers of Andrew Johnson*, 16 vols. Knoxville: University of Tennessee Press, 1967–1996.

Hamilton, Stanislaus Murray, ed. *The Writings of James Monroe: Including a Collection of His Public and Private Papers and Correspondence Now for the First Time Printed*, 6 vols. New York: G. P. Putnam's Sons, 1902.

Hopkins, James F., et al., eds. *The Papers of Henry Clay*, 11 vols. Lexington: University of Kentucky Press, 1959–1992.

Johannsen, Robert W., ed. *The Letters of Stephen A. Douglas*. Urbana: University of Illinois Press, 1961.

Letters and Other Writings of James Madison, Fourth President of the United States, 4 vols. Philadelphia: J. B. Lippincott, 1865.

Moore, John Bassett, ed. *The Works of James Buchanan: Comprising His Speeches, State Papers, and Private Correspondence*, 12 vols. Philadelphia and London: J. B. Lippincott, 1908–1911.

Phillips, Ulrich B., ed. *The Correspondence of Robert Toombs, Alexander H. Stephens, and Howell Cobb*. Washington, DC: Government Printing Office, 1913.

Quaife, Milo Milton, ed. *The Diary of James K. Polk during His Presidency, 1845–1849*, 4 vols. Chicago: A. C. McClurg, 1910.

Shanks, Henry Thomas, ed. *The Papers of Willie Person Mangum*, 5 vols. Raleigh, NC: State Department of Archives and History, 1950–1956.

Tyler, Lyon Gardiner, ed. *The Letters and Times of the Tylers*, 2 vols. Richmond: Whittet & Shepperson, 1884–1885.

Wilson, Clyde N., et al., eds. *The Papers of John C. Calhoun*, 28 vols. Columbia: University of South Carolina Press, 1959–2003.

Wiltse, Charles M., et al., eds. *The Papers of Daniel Webster*. 15 vols. Hanover, NH: University Press of New England, 1974–1989.

Newspapers

Albany Journal
Augusta Constitutionalist
Augusta Republic
Austin Texas State Gazette
Baltimore American
Baltimore Sun
Binghamton Democrat
Boston Daily Atlas
Boston Emancipator and Weekly Chronicle
Buffalo Courier
Charleston Mercury
Charleston Southern Patriot

Clarksville Northern Standard
Columbus Daily Ohio Statesman
Dover Delaware State Reporter
Edwardsville Spectator
Greenville Mountaineer
Kentucky Reporter
Little Rock Arkansas Gazette
Little Rock Arkansas Whig
Macon Weekly Telegraph
Milledgeville Federal Union
Milledgeville Southern Recorder
Mobile Journal
Nashville Union
New-Hampshire Patriot and State Gazette
New Hampshire Sentinel
New Orleans Crescent
New Orleans Delta
New Orleans Louisiana Courier
New York Evening Post
New York Express
New-York Gazette & General Advertiser
New York Herald
New York Tribune
Niles' National Register
Niles' Weekly Register
Philadelphia National Enquirer
Richmond Enquirer
Richmond Times
Richmond Whig
Savannah Republican
St. Louis Daily Missouri Republican
St. Louis Enquirer
St. Louis Missouri Gazette
Tallahassee Floridian and Journal
Trenton State Gazette
United States Telegraph
Washington Daily Union
Washington Globe
Washington National Intelligencer
Washington Union

Official Publications
American State Papers
Annals of Congress
Congressional Globe
H.R. Exec. Doc. No. 41, 30th Cong., 1st Sess. (1848), Serial Set No. 517
Senate Documents Misc. No. 6, 30th Cong., 1st Sess. (Serial 511)

S. Doc. Misc. No. 6, 30th Cong., 1st Sess. (14 December 1847). Serial Set No. 511

S. Doc. Misc. No. 6, 30th Cong., 1st Sess. (12 January 1848). Serial Set No. 511

S. Doc. Misc. No. 37, 30th Cong., 1st Sess. (27 January 1848). Serial Set No. 511

S. Doc. Misc. No. 5, 31st Cong., 1st Sess. (1849), Serial Set No. 581

S. Rep. No. 15, 33rd Cong., 1st Sess. (1848), Serial Set No. 706

S. Misc. Doc. No. 23, 33rd Cong., 1st Sess. (1854), Serial Set No. 705

Senate Journal

Secretary of State, U.S. *Abstract of the Returns of the Fifth Census, Showing the Number of Free People, the Number of Slaves, the Federal or Representative Number; and the Aggregate of Each County of Each State of the United States*, 22nd Cong, 1st Sess., House Document 263. Washington, DC, 1832.

U.S. Statutes at Large

Ames, Herman V., ed. *State Documents on Federal Relations: The States and the United States*. 1906; repr., New York: Da Capo Press, 1970.

Carter, Clarence Edwin, ed. *The Territorial Papers of the United States*. Washington, DC: U.S. Government Printing Office, 1937–.

Hunt, Galliard, ed. *Journals of the Continental Congress, 1774–1789*, 34 vols. Washington, DC: U.S. Government Printing Office, 1904–1937.

Richardson, James D., ed. *A Compilation of the Messages and Papers of the Presidents, 1789–1897*, 10 vols. Washington, DC: U.S. Government Printing Office, 1896–1899.

Smith, Paul H., et al., eds. *Letters of Delegates to Congress, 1774–1789*, 25 vols. Washington, DC: Library of Congress, 1976–2000.

Other Published Primary Sources

[Black, Jeremiah S.] *Observations on Senator Douglas's Views of Popular Sovereignty, as Expressed in* Harper's Magazine, *for September 1859*, 2nd ed. Washington: Thomas McGill, 1859.

Carey, Mathew. *Some Considerations on the Impropriety and Inexpediency of Renewing the Missouri Question*. Philadelphia: M. Carey & Son, 1820.

Cunningham, Noble E., Jr., ed. *Circular Letters of Congressmen to Their Constituents, 1789–1829*, 3 vols. Chapel Hill: University of North Carolina Press, 1978.

Dallas, George M. "Great Speech of Hon. George M. Dallas, upon the Leading Topics of the Day, Delivered at Pittsburgh, Pa." Philadelphia: Times and Keystone Job Office, 1847.

Douglas, Stephen A. *The Dividing Line between Federal and Local Authority*. New York: Harper & Brothers, 1859.

Hesseltine, William B., ed. *Three against Lincoln: Murat Halstead Reports the Caucuses of 1860*. Baton Rouge: Louisiana State University Press, 1960.

Howard, Benjamin, et al., eds. *Reports of Cases Argued and Adjudged in the Supreme Court of the United States*, 67 vols. Boston: Charles C. Little and James Brown and others, 1804–1861.

Inaugural Address of R. J. Walker, Governor of Kansas Territory. Lecompton, KS: Union Office, 1857.

Johnson, Charles W. *Proceedings of the First Three Republican Conventions of 1856, 1860, and 1864*. Minneapolis: n.p., 1893.

Journal of the Proceedings of the Convention Met to Form a Constitution and System of State Government for the People of Arkansas. . . Little Rock, AR: Albert Pike, 1836.

Journal of the Proceedings of a Convention of Delegates to Form a Constitution for the People of

Florida, Held at St. Joseph, December 1838. In Dorothy Dodd, ed., *Florida Becomes a State.* Tallahassee: Florida Centennial Commission, 1945.

Official Proceedings of the Democratic National Convention, Held in Cincinnati, June 2–6, 1856. Cincinnati: Enquirer Company, 1856.

Official Proceedings of the Democratic National Convention, Held in 1860 in Charleston and Baltimore. Cleveland: Plain Dealer Job Office, 1860.

Taylor, John. *Construction Construed, and Constitutions Vindicated.* Richmond: Shepherd & Pollard, 1820.

Yancey, W[illiam] L[owndes]. *An Address to the People of Alabama.* Montgomery, AL: Flag and Advertiser Job Office, 1848.

Secondary Sources

Books and Articles

Alexander, Thomas B. *Sectional Stress and Party Strength: A Study of Roll-Call Patterns in the United States House of Representatives, 1836–1860.* Nashville: Vanderbilt University Press, 1967.

Allen, Austin. *Origins of the Dred Scott Case: Jacksonian Jurisprudence and the Supreme Court, 1837–1857.* Athens: University of Georgia Press, 2006.

Bauer, K. Jack. *Zachary Taylor: Soldier, Planter, Statesman of the Old Southwest.* Baton Rouge: Louisiana State University Press, 1985.

Beeman, Richard, Stephen Botein, and Edward C. Carter II, eds. *Beyond Confederation: Origins of the Constitution and American National Identity.* Chapel Hill: University of North Carolina Press, 1987.

Belohlavek, John M. *George Mifflin Dallas: Jacksonian Patrician.* University Park: Pennsylvania State University Press, 1977.

Bemis, Samuel Flagg. *John Quincy Adams and the Foundations of American Foreign Policy.* New York: Alfred A. Knopf, 1949.

Benton, Thomas Hart. *Thirty Years' View; or A History of the Working of the American Government for Thirty Years, from 1820 to 1850,* 2 vols. New York: D. Appleton, 1854–1856.

Berkhofer, Robert, Jr. "The Northwest Ordinance and the Principles of Territorial Evolution," in John Porter Bloom, ed., *The American Territorial System.* Athens: Ohio University Press, 1973, 47–50.

Berwanger, Eugene H. *The Frontier against Slavery: Western Anti-Negro Prejudice and the Slavery Extension Controversy.* Urbana: University of Illinois Press, 1967.

Bestor, Arthur. "Constitutionalism and Settlement of the West: The Attainment of Consensus, 1754–1784," in John Porter Bloom, ed., *The American Territorial System.* Athens: Ohio University Press, 1973, 13–44.

———. "State Sovereignty and Slavery: A Reinterpretation of Proslavery Constitutional Doctrine, 1846–1860." *Journal of the Illinois State Historical Society* (Summer 1961): 117–180.

Borneman, Walter R. *Polk: The Man Who Transformed the Presidency and America.* New York: Random House, 2008.

Boyett, Gene Wells. "The Whigs in Arkansas, 1836–1856." Unpublished Ph.D. diss., Louisiana State University, 1972.

Brown, Everett Somerville. *The Constitutional History of the Louisiana Purchase, 1803–1812.* Berkeley: University of California Press, 1920.

Brown, Richard H. "The Missouri Crisis, Slavery, and the Politics of Jacksonianism." *South Atlantic Quarterly* 65 (Winter 1966): 60.

Brugger, Robert J. *Beverley Tucker: Heart over Head in the Old South*. Baltimore: Johns Hopkins University Press, 1978.

Carey, Anthony Gene. *Parties, Slavery, and the Union in Antebellum Georgia*. Athens: University of Georgia Press, 1997.

Carpenter, Jesse T. *The South as a Conscious Minority, 1789–1861*. Originally published, 1930; Columbia: University of South Carolina Press, 1990.

Cooper, William J., Jr. *Jefferson Davis, American*. New York: Alfred A. Knopf, 2002.

———. *Liberty and Slavery: Southern Politics to 1860*. New York: Alfred A. Knopf, 1982.

———. "'The Only Door': The Territorial Issue, the Preston Bill, and the Southern Whigs," in Cooper, William J., Jr., et al., eds., *A Master's Due: Essays in Honor of David Herbert Donald*. Baton Rouge: Louisiana State University Press, 1985.

———. *The South and the Politics of Slavery, 1828–1856*. Baton Rouge: Louisiana State University Press, 1978.

Craven, Avery O. *The Growth of Southern Nationalism, 1848–1861*. Baton Rouge: Louisiana State University Press, 1953.

Crofts, Daniel W. *Reluctant Confederates: Upper South Unionists in the Secession Crisis*. Chapel Hill: University of North Carolina Press, 1989.

Cunningham, Noble E. *The Presidency of James Monroe*. Lawrence: University Press of Kansas, 1996.

Dangerfield, George. *The Era of Good Feelings*. New York: Harcourt, Brace and Company, 1952.

Deyle, Steven. *Carry Me Back: The Domestic Slave Trade in American Life*. New York: Oxford University Press, 2005.

Dunn, Jacob Piatt. *Indiana: A Redemption from Slavery*, 2nd ed. Boston: Houghton Mifflin, 1905.

———, ed. *Slavery Petitions and Papers*. Indianapolis: Bowen-Merrill, 1893.

Earle, Jonathan H. *Jacksonian Antislavery and the Politics of Free Soil, 1824–1854*. Chapel Hill: University of North Carolina Press, 2004.

Etcheson, Nicole. *Bleeding Kansas: Contested Liberty in the Civil War Era*. Lawrence: University Press of Kansas, 2004.

———. *The Emerging Midwest: Upland Southerners and the Political Culture of the Old Northwest, 1787–1861*. Bloomington: Indiana University Press, 1996.

———. "Where Popular Sovereignty Worked: Nebraska Territory and the Kansas-Nebraska Act," in John R. Wunder and Joann M. Ross, eds., *The Nebraska-Kansas Act of 1854*. Lincoln: University of Nebraska Press, 2008: 159–182.

Eyal, Yonatan. *The Young America Movement and the Transformation of the Democratic Party, 1828–1861*. Cambridge: Cambridge University Press, 2007.

Farrand, Max. *The Legislation of Congress for the Government of the Organized Territories of the United States, 1789–1895*. Newark, NJ: Wm. A. Baker, Printer, 1896.

Fehrenbacher, Don E. *The Dred Scott Case: Its Significance in American Law and Politics*. New York: Oxford University Press, 1978.

———. *Prelude to Greatness: Lincoln in the 1850s*. Stanford, CA: Stanford University Press, 1962.

———. *Sectional Crisis and Southern Constitutionalism*. Baton Rouge: Louisiana State University Press, 1995.

———. *The Slaveholding Republic: An Account of the United States Government's Relations to Slavery.* Completed and edited by Ward M. McAfee. New York: Oxford University Press, 2001.

Filler, Louis. *The Crusade against Slavery, 1830–1860.* New York: Harper & Row, 1960.

Finkelman, Paul. *Slavery and the Founders: Race and Liberty in the Age of Jefferson,* 2nd ed. Armonk, NY: M. E. Sharpe, 2001.

Fischer, David Hackett. *The Revolution of American Conservatism: The Federalist Party in the Era of Jeffersonian Democracy.* New York: Harper & Row, 1965.

Foner, Eric. *Free Soil, Free Labor, Free Men: The Ideology of the Republican Party before the Civil War.* New York: Oxford University Press, 1970.

———. "The Wilmot Proviso Revisited." *Journal of American History* 56 (September 1969): 262–279.

Forbes, Robert Pierce. *The Missouri Compromise and Its Aftermath: Slavery and the Meaning of America.* Chapel Hill: University of North Carolina Press, 2007.

Ford, Lacy K. *Deliver Us from Evil: The Slavery Question in the Old South.* New York: Oxford University Press, 2009.

———. *The Origins of Southern Radicalism: South Carolina, 1800–1860.* New York: Oxford University Press, 1988.

Freehling, William W. *The Reintegration of American History: Slavery and the Civil War.* New York: Oxford University Press, 1994.

———. *The Road to Disunion: Secessionists at Bay, 1776–1854.* New York: Oxford University Press, 1990.

———. *The Road to Disunion: Secessionists Triumphant, 1854–1861.* New York: Oxford University Press, 2007.

Ganaway, Loomis Morton. *New Mexico and the Sectional Controversy.* Albuquerque: University of New Mexico Press, 1944.

Gellman, David N. *Emancipating New York: The Politics of Slavery and Freedom, 1777–1827.* Baton Rouge: Louisiana State University Press, 2007.

Gienapp, William E. *The Origins of the Republican Party, 1852–1856.* New York: Oxford University Press, 1987.

Gordon, Sarah Barringer. *The Mormon Question: Polygamy and Constitutional Conflict in Nineteenth-Century America.* Chapel Hill: University of North Carolina Press, 2001.

Hamilton, Holman. *Prologue to Conflict: The Crisis and Compromise of 1850.* Lexington: University of Kentucky Press, 1964.

———. *Zachary Taylor: Soldier in the White House.* Indianapolis: Bobbs-Merrill, 1951.

Hammond, John Craig. *Slavery, Freedom, and Expansion in the Early American West.* Charlottesville: University of Virginia Press, 2007.

Hammond, John Craig, and Matthew Mason, eds. *Contesting Slavery: The Politics of Bondage and Freedom in the New American Nation.* Charlottesville: University of Virginia Press, 2011.

Harris, William C. *Lincoln's Rise to the Presidency.* Lawrence: University Press of Kansas, 2007.

Hietala, Thomas R. *Manifest Design: Anxious Aggrandizement in Late Jacksonian America.* Ithaca, NY: Cornell University Press, 1985.

Holt, Michael F. *The Political Crisis of the 1850s.* New York: John Wiley & Sons, 1978.

———. *The Rise and Fall of the American Whig Party: Jacksonian Politics and the Onset of the Civil War.* New York: Oxford University Press, 1999.

Horsman, Reginald. *Race and Manifest Destiny*. Cambridge, MA: Harvard University Press, 1981.

Howe, Daniel Walker. *What Hath God Wrought: The Transformation of America, 1815–1848*. New York: Oxford University Press, 2007.

Hurt, R. Douglas. "Historians and the Northwest Ordinance." *Western Historical Quarterly* 20 (August 1989): 261–280.

Huston, James L. *Stephen A. Douglas and the Dilemmas of Democratic Equality*. Lanham, MD: Rowman and Littlefield, 2007.

Hyman, Harold M., and William M. Wiecek. *Equal Justice under Law: Constitutional Development, 1835–1875*. New York: Harper & Row, 1982.

Jennings, Thelma. *The Nashville Convention: Southern Movement for Unity, 1848–1851*. Memphis, TN: Memphis State University Press, 1980.

Johannsen, Robert W. *Frontier Politics on the Eve of the Civil War*. Seattle: University of Washington Press, 1955.

———. "Douglas, *Harper's Magazine*, and Popular Sovereignty," in *The Frontier, the Union, and Stephen A. Douglas*. Urbana: University of Illinois Press, 1989.

———. *Stephen A. Douglas*. New York: Oxford University Press, 1973.

Kastor, Peter J. *The Nation's Crucible: The Louisiana Purchase and the Creation of America*. New Haven, CT: Yale University Press, 2004.

Klein, Philip Shriver. *President James Buchanan: A Biography*. University Park: Pennsylvania State University Press, 1962.

Klunder, Willard Carl. *Lewis Cass and the Politics of Moderation*. Kent, OH: Kent State University Press, 1996.

Kukla, Jon. *A Wilderness So Immense: The Louisiana Purchase and the Destiny of America*. New York: Alfred A. Knopf, 2003.

Lamar, Howard Roberts. *The Far Southwest, 1846–1912*. New Haven, CT: Yale University Press, 1966.

Learned, Henry Barrett. "The Relation of Philip Phillips to the Repeal of the Missouri Compromise in 1854." *Mississippi Valley Historical Review* 8 (March 1922): 303–317.

Livermore, Shaw, Jr. *The Twilight of Federalism: The Disintegration of the Federalist Party, 1815–1830*. Princeton, NJ: Princeton University Press, 1962.

Lynd, Staughton. "The Compromise of 1787." *Political Science Quarterly* 81 (June 1966): 229–230.

MacLeod, Duncan. *Slavery, Race, and the American Revolution*. Cambridge: Cambridge University Press, 1974.

Malin, James C. *The Nebraska Question, 1852–1854*. Lawrence, KS: n.p., 1953.

Maltz, Earl M. *Dred Scott and the Politics of Slavery*. Lawrence: University Press of Kansas, 2007.

Martin, Sidney Walter. *Florida during the Territorial Days*. Athens: University of Georgia Press, 1944.

Mason, Matthew. *Slavery and Politics in the Early American Republic*. Chapel Hill: University of North Carolina Press, 2006.

May, Robert E. *The Southern Dream of a Caribbean Empire, 1854–1861*. Baton Rouge: Louisiana State University Press, 1973.

McClintock, Russell. *Lincoln and the Decision for War: The Northern Response to Secession*. Chapel Hill: University of North Carolina Press, 2008.

McCormac, Eugene Irving. *James K. Polk: A Political Biography*. Berkeley: University of California Press, 1922.

McCoy, Drew. "James Madison and Visions of American Nationality in the Confederation Period: A Regional Perspective," in Richard Beeman, Stephen Botein, and Edward C. Carter II, eds., *Beyond Confederation: Origins of the Constitution and American National Identity*. Chapel Hill: University of North Carolina Press, 1987, 226–258.

Merk, Frederick. *Slavery and the Annexation of Texas*. New York: Alfred A. Knopf, 1972.

Miles, Edwin A. "'Fifty-Four Forty or Fight'—An American Political Legend." *Mississippi Valley Historical Review* 44 (September 1957): 291–309.

Miller, William Lee. *Arguing about Slavery: The Great Battle in the United States Congress*. New York: Alfred A. Knopf, 1996.

Monroe, Dan. *The Republican Vision of John Tyler*. College Station: Texas A&M University Press, 2003.

Moore, Glover. *The Missouri Controversy, 1819–1821*. Lexington: University Press of Kentucky, 1953.

Morgan, Edmund S. *Inventing the People: The Rise of Popular Sovereignty in England and America*. New York: W. W. Norton, 1988.

Morris, Richard B. *The Forging of the Union, 1781–1789*. New York: Harper & Row, 1989.

Morrison, Chaplain W. *Democratic Politics and Sectionalism: The Wilmot Proviso Controversy*. Chapel Hill: University of North Carolina Press, 1967.

Morrison, Michael A. *Slavery and the American West: The Eclipse of Manifest Destiny and the Coming of the Civil War*. Chapel Hill: University of North Carolina Press, 1997.

Neely, Mark E., Jr., "The Kansas-Nebraska Act in American Political Culture: The Road to Bladensburg and the *Appeal of the Independent Democrats*," in John R. Wunder and Joann M. Ross, eds., *The Nebraska-Kansas Act of 1854*. Lincoln: University of Nebraska Press, 2008: 13–46.

———. *Lincoln and the Triumph of the Nation: Constitutional Conflict in the American Civil War*. Chapel Hill: University of North Carolina Press, 2011.

Nevins, Allan. *The Emergence of Lincoln*, 2 vols. New York: Charles Scribner's Sons, 1950.

———. *Fremont: Pathmarker of the West*. New York: D. Appleton-Century, 1939.

———. *The Ordeal of the Union*, 2 vols. New York: Charles Scribner's Sons, 1948.

Nichols, Roy F. *Blueprints for Leviathan: American Style*. New York: Atheneum, 1963.

———. *The Democratic Machine, 1850–1854*. New York: Columbia University Press, 1923.

———. *The Disruption of American Democracy*. New York: Macmillan, 1948.

———. *Franklin Pierce: Young Hickory of the Granite Hills*. Philadelphia: University of Pennsylvania Press, 1931.

———. "The Kansas-Nebraska Act: A Century of Historiography." *Mississippi Valley Historical Review* 43 (September 1956): 187–212.

———, ed. "The Mystery of the Dallas Papers (Part II)." *Pennsylvania Magazine of History and Biography* 73 (October 1949): 492–495.

Niven, John. *John C. Calhoun and the Price of Union*. Baton Rouge: Louisiana State University Press, 1988.

O'Brien, Michael. *Conjectures of Order: Intellectual Life and the American South, 1810–1860*. Chapel Hill: University of North Carolina Press, 2004.

Olsen, Christopher J. *Political Culture and Secession in Mississippi: Masculinity, Honor, and the Antiparty Tradition, 1830–1860*. New York: Oxford University Press, 2000.

Onuf, Peter S. *Jefferson's Empire: The Language of American Nationhood*. Charlottesville: University Press of Virginia, 2000.

———. *The Origins of the Federal Republic: Jurisdictional Controversies in the United States, 1775–1787*. Philadelphia: University of Pennsylvania Press, 1983.

———. *Statehood and Union: A History of the Northwest Ordinance*. Bloomington: Indiana University Press, 1987.

Overdyke, W. Darrell. *The Know-Nothing Party in the South*. Baton Rouge: Louisiana State University Press, 1950.

Parrish, William E. *David Rice Atchison: Border Politician*. Columbia: University of Missouri Press, 1961.

Peterson, Merrill D., ed. *Thomas Jefferson: Writings*. New York: Library of America, 1984.

Philbrick, Francis S., ed. *The Laws of Illinois Territory*. Springfield: Illinois State Historical Library, 1950.

Porter, Kirk H., and Donald Bruce Johnson, eds. *National Party Platforms, 1840–1960*, 2nd ed. Urbana: University of Illinois Press, 1961.

Potter, David M. *The Impending Crisis, 1848–1861*. Completed and edited by Don E. Fehrenbacher. New York: Harper & Row, 1976.

Quaife, Milo Milton. *The Doctrine of Non-Intervention with Slavery in the Territories*. Chicago: Mac C. Chamberlin, 1910.

Rable, George C. *The Confederate Republic: A Revolution against Politics*. Chapel Hill: University of North Carolina Press, 1994.

———. "Slavery, Politics, and the South: The Gag Rule as a Case Study." *Capitol Studies* 3 (Fall 1975): 69–85.

Rawley, James A. *Race and Politics: "Bleeding Kansas" and the Coming of the Civil War*. Philadelphia: J.B. Lippincott, 1969.

Ray, P. Orman. *The Repeal of the Missouri Compromise: Its Origin and Authorship*. Cleveland: Arthur C. Clark, 1909.

Rayback, Joseph G. *Free Soil: The Election of 1848*. Lexington: University Press of Kentucky, 1970.

Remini, Robert V. *Henry Clay: Statesman for the Union*. New York: W. W. Norton, 1991.

Richards, Leonard L. *The California Gold Rush and the Coming of the Civil War*. New York: Alfred A. Knopf, 2007.

———. *The Slave Power: The Free North and Southern Domination, 1780–1860*. Baton Rouge: Louisiana State University Press, 2000.

Riley, Padraig. "Slavery and the Problem of Democracy in Jeffersonian America," in John Craig Hammond and Matthew Mason, eds., *Contesting Slavery: The Politics of Bondage and Freedom in the New American Nation*. Charlottesville: University of Virginia Press, 2011, 227–246.

Risjord, Norman K. *The Old Republicans: Southern Conservatism in the Age of Jefferson*. New York: Columbia University Press, 1965.

Robinson, Donald L. *Slavery and the Structure of American Politics, 1765–1820*. New York: Harcourt Brace Jovanovich, 1971.

Rothman, Adam. *Slave Country: American Expansion and the Origins of the Deep South*. Cambridge, MA: Harvard University Press, 2005.

Russel, Robert R. "Congressional Issues over the Kansas-Nebraska Act." *Journal of Southern History* 39 (May 1963): 193.

———. "What Was the Compromise of 1850?" *Journal of Southern History* 22 (August 1956): 292–309.

Scroggs, Jack B. "Arkansas Statehood: A Study in State and National Political Schism." *Arkansas Historical Quarterly* 20 (Autumn 1961): 227–244.

Sellers, Charles. *James K. Polk: Continentalist, 1843–1846*. Princeton, NJ: Princeton University Press, 1966.

Sewell, Richard H. *Ballots for Freedom: Antislavery Politics in the United States, 1837–1860*. New York: Oxford University Press, 1976.

Shalhope, Robert E. *John Taylor of Caroline, Pastoral Republican*. Columbia: University of South Carolina Press, 1980.

Silbey, Joel H. *Party over Section: The Rough and Ready Presidential Election of 1848*. Lawrence: University Press of Kansas, 2009.

———. *Storm over Texas: The Annexation Controversy and the Road to Civil War*. New York: Oxford University Press, 2005.

Stampp, Kenneth M. *America in 1857: A Nation on the Brink*. New York: Oxford University Press, 1990.

Stegmaier, Mark J. *Texas, New Mexico, and the Compromise of 1850*. Kent, OH: Kent State University Press, 1996.

Sydnor, Charles S. *The Development of Southern Sectionalism, 1819–1848*. Baton Rouge: Louisiana State University Press, 1948.

Thomas, Emory M. *The Confederate States of America, 1861–1865*. New York: Harper & Row, 1979.

Thornton, J. Mills, III. *Politics and Power in a Slave Society: Alabama, 1800–1860*. Baton Rouge: Louisiana State University Press, 1978.

Transactions of the Kansas State Historical Society, 10 vols. Topeka, KS: 1875–1908.

Van Cleve, George William. "Founding a Slaveholders' Union, 1770–1797," in John Craig Hammond and Matthew Mason, eds., *Contesting Slavery: The Politics of Bondage and Freedom in the New American Nation*. Charlottesville: University of Virginia Press, 2011, 117–137.

———. *A Slaveholders' Union: Slavery, Politics, and the Constitution in the Early American Republic*. Chicago: University of Chicago Press, 2010.

Varon, Elizabeth R. *Disunion! The Coming of the American Civil War, 1789–1859*. Chapel Hill: University of North Carolina Press, 2008.

von Holst, Hermann. *The Constitutional History of the United States*, 8 vols. Chicago: Callaghan and Company, 1876–1904.

Walther, Eric H. *William Lowndes Yancey and the Coming of the Civil War*. Chapel Hill: University of North Carolina Press, 2006.

Walton, Brian G. "The Second Party System in Arkansas." *Arkansas Historical Quarterly* 28 (Summer 1969): 120–155.

White, Lonnie J. *Politics on the Southwestern Frontier: Arkansas Territory, 1819–1836*. Memphis, TN: Memphis State University Press, 1964.

White, Ronald C., Jr. *A. Lincoln: A Biography*. New York: Random House, 2009.

Wiecek, William M. *The Sources of Antislavery Constitutionalism, 1760–1848*. Ithaca, NY: Cornell University Press, 1977.

Wilentz, Sean. *The Rise of American Democracy: Jefferson to Lincoln*. New York: W. W. Norton, 2005.

Williamson, Chilton. *American Suffrage from Property to Democracy*. Princeton, NJ: Princeton University Press, 1960.

Wiltse, Charles M. *John C. Calhoun: Nullifier, 1829–1839*. Indianapolis: Bobbs-Merrill, 1949.
———. *John C. Calhoun: Sectionalist, 1840–1850*. Indianapolis: Bobbs-Merrill, 1951.
Wirls, Daniel. "'The Only Mode for Avoiding Everlasting Defeat': The Overlooked Senate Gag Rule for Antislavery Petitions." *Journal of the Early Republic* 27 (Spring 2007): 115–138.
Wood, Gordon S. *Empire of Liberty: A History of the Early Republic, 1789–1815*. New York: Oxford University Press, 2009.
Wunder, John R., and Joann M. Ross, eds. *The Nebraska-Kansas Act of 1854*. Lincoln: University of Nebraska Press, 2008.

Index